# FRONTIERS OF JIHÂD
### RADICAL ISLAM IN AFRICA

YINKA OLOMOJOBI

# FRONTIERS OF JIHÂD
**RADICAL ISLAM IN AFRICA**

Yinka Olomojobi

Safari Books Ltd
Ibadan

Published by
Safari Books Ltd
Ile Ori Detu
1, Shell Close
Onireke
Ibadan.
Email: safarinigeria@gmail.com
Website: www.safaribooksng.com

© 2015, Yinka Olomojobi

First Published 2015

All rights reserved. This book is copyright and so no part of it may be reproduced, stored in a retrieval system, or transmitted, in any form or by any means, electrical, mechanical, electrostatic, magnetic tape, photocopying, recording or otherwise, without the prior written permission of the author.

ISBN: 978-978-8431-83-1

"You can't go and kill innocent people and say 'Allah Akbar!' It is either you dont believe it or you dont know what you are saying.
So, it has nothing to do with religion; they are just terrorists and Nigeria will mobilise against all of them."

**President Muhammadu Buhari**
**Punch Newspaper,**
**Page 9, Thursday July 9, 2015**

# DEDICATION

For the innocents and the unspoken people who have died as a result of Islamist terror in Africa.

...And to the gallantmen/women who have lost their lives to acts of terror whilst serving their respective countries in Africa.

# Table of Contents

*Dedication*   *vii*
*Foreword*   *xiii*
*Preface*   *xvii*
*Acknowledgements*   *xxiii*
*List of Maps*   *xxv*
*List of Tables*   *xxvi*

## PART ONE: EXPLORING THE FRONTIERS OF JIHÂD

### THEORISING THE RADICALISATION OF ISLAM   1

- Introduction   1
- Explaining Radical Islam in Africa: A Critical Realist Approach   2
- The Use of Observation   4
- Criticism of the Critical Realist Approach   5
- The Use of Retroductive Reasoning   9
- Group Theory as a Model in Understanding Radical Islam   11
- Grievance as Model in Understanding Why Islamists Rebel   17
- Invented Tradition   22
- Cultural Theory: The Construction of Radical Groups   25
- Radicalisation of Islam in Africa   27
- Conclusion   39

### WHY RELIGION MATTERS?   49

- Introduction   49
- Classical Theories of Religion   51
- Functionalist Approach   51

- Sociological Approach　　　　　　　　　　　53
- Positivist Approach　　　　　　　　　　　　54
- Psychoanalyst Approach　　　　　　　　　　55
- Instrumentalist Approach　　　　　　　　　56
- Between Fundamentalism and Extremism　　57
- Between Religion and Globalisation　　　　62
- Conclusion　　　　　　　　　　　　　　　68

## JIHÂDISATION OF ISLAM　　　　　　　　73
- Introduction　　　　　　　　　　　　　　73
- Religion and Violence　　　　　　　　　　74
- Jihâd: The Double Edged Sword　　　　　　77
- Between Martyrdom and Jihâd　　　　　　　93
- Between the two Dars　　　　　　　　　　103
- Conclusion　　　　　　　　　　　　　　　106

## NEW FRONTIERS OF TERRORISM　　　　　113
- Introduction　　　　　　　　　　　　　　113
- The New Terrain of Global Jihâd in Africa　　115
- Complexities of Terrorism　　　　　　　　120
- Foundations of Islamic Terrorism in Africa　128
- Islamic Terrorist Networks　　　　　　　　133
- Does Islamist' Terrorism Work in Africa?　　138
- Conclusion　　　　　　　　　　　　　　　141

## PART TWO: RADICAL ISLAM IN AFRICA　　145

## RESURGENCE OF AL-QAEDA IN SOMALIA　147
- Introduction　　　　　　　　　　　　　　147
- Political Crises in Somali　　　　　　　　　148
- Primordial Attachment to Clans　　　　　　151
- The Rise of Al-Shabaab　　　　　　　　　　156
- Leadership and Power Struggles within Al-Shabaab　　　　　　　　　　　　　　161
- Factors Responsible for the Growth of Al-Shabaab　165

- Influence and support of al-Qaeda 165
- Foreign fighters and Social Networking 167
- Absence of a Central Government 169
- Proximity to the Middle East 170
- Funding 171
- Conclusion 172

**UNHOLY ALLIANCE IN THE MAGHREB** 179
- Introduction 179
- Seeds of Discontent 181
- Foundations of al-Qaeda in the Islamic Maghreb (AQIM) 185
- Conclusion 194

**TALIBANISM IN MALI** 199
- Introduction 199
- Political Imbalance 201
- Ansar Dine 203
- The Movement for Unity and Jihâd in West Africa (MUJWA) 208
- Religious Crisis in Mali 211
- Tuareg Quest for Self Determination and the National Tuareg Liberation Movement (MNLA) 213
- The Tuareg Rebellion 217
- Between Ansar Dine and MUJAO 219
- Intervention Intervention in Mali 224
- Conclusion 230

**OPENING THE PANDORA'S BOX OF BOKO HARAM** 235
- Introduction 235
- Ethnic and Religious Composition of Northern Nigeria 237
- Religious Rivalry in Northern Nigeria 238
- The Birth of Boko Haram Jihâd 239
- Political Paradox of Boko Haram 247
- Funding and Networking of Boko Haram 258

- Unholy blemish on Islam in Northern Nigeria 259
- Hoodwinked?—a Web of Conspiracy? 261
- The Fight against Terror 289
- Conclusion 291

## ANSARU: BROTHER IN ARMS WITH BOKO HARAM 297
- Introduction 297
- Ansaru's Grievance 298
- Leadership 299
- Jihâdist Activities 301
- Between Ansaru and Boko Haram 303
- Conclusion 306

## RADICAL ISLAM AND E-TERRORISM 309
- Introduction 309
- E-Terrorism: An Asymmetric Warfare? 310
- E-Terrorism and Free Speech 316
- Social Media and Radical Islam 321
- Twitter 322
- Facebook 323
- YouTube 324
- Bluetooth 325
- Funding of e-Terrorism 326
- Radical Groups and e-Terrorism 327
- Conclusion 330

# Epilogue 337

# Index 344

# FOREWORD

This is a work of incomparable importance as it focuses on the most contemporaneous central issue since the Cold War—the clash of the Western and Islamic civilisations. Although a significant research activity has developed on issues surrounding radical Islam since the tragic event of 9/11, this book provides a dispassionate, powerful and much needed exposition that explores the phenomenon of radical Islam and its ramifications across the world, but focusing on the frontiers of terrorism in Africa particularly. The author reveals quite convincingly the transnational and the global effect of the wave of radical Islamic thought and practice, flowing from the Middle East/North Africa to Asia, sub-saharan Africa to the West. Since September 2001, terms and names about events and *dramatis personae* that have captured the imagination of the international public regarding the phenomenon of radical Islam include such ones, as Osama Bin Laden and his al-Qaeda organisation, al-Qaeda in Yemen (al-Qaeda in the Arabian Peninsula), al-Shabaab, al-Qaeda in the Maghreb and now most recently, Boko Haram.

Certainly, one must agree with the writer's contention of the huge influence of Islamist ideology taking a centre stage in the world today. This debate is obvious in Charlie Hebdo, 2015 terror attack in France which has reawakened the world for the need to find a solution to the wave of death and destruction that is being channel across the world through radical Islam. But one must take cognisance of the most compelling issue about this book is that the author reveals that grievance emitting from poverty and deprivation is the foundation of radical Islam. I find this assertion to be true, as it explains the rift and sectarian violence being staged in many parts of the Arab world, the surge of the Arab Spring revolutions stemming from the Middle East and North Africa. And, particularly the sentiments of grievance occurring in Palestine over the deprivation of its land—these group emotions are the basis of radical Islam and its antecedent quest for jihad.

The book is a ten-chapter work. Each Chapter poses intriguing issues about the factors that promote radical Islam in Africa. To be more precise: is that this book, unlike any other, exposes a careful build-up of arguments and analysis. This could be seen in Chapter 1, where the author theorises about and carefully details most of the relevant intellectual ideas and insights that go into defining radical Islam as a phenomenon. Aside from using theories based on political science, the author adopts a philosophical approach to his work in order to understand the relationship between Islamists and their notions of jihad. Theoretical explanations of how religion takes the centre stage in the society and international relations as well as its instrumentalist uses are the focus of Chapter 2. Furthermore, in this Chapter, the writer demonstrates convincingly the new role that religion has found itself playing in the increasingly globalised world. Chapter 3 which carries the title of "Jihadisation of Islam" provides divergent expositions in Islam as a religion regarding jihad as an instrument for seeking redress to perceived grievances here on earth or/and as a means of spiritual connection with God. In Chapter 4 can be found a valuable analysis of terrorism, the complexities of defining the term, and its applications and contextualisation within and across Africa. The author aptly describes terrorism as an act that "generates a psychological notion of fear amongst the citizens of a state. It creates a situation of anxiety, therefore using propaganda to channel its grievance to the public, in order to be heard and taken seriously."

The keenness and forcefulness of the writer's thoughts and eloquent prose are illustrated in his expositions of radical

Islamist groups in Africa. In Chapter 5, the author takes us through the vicious activities of al-Shabaab. He informs us how the nature and character of Somalia's failed government has stimulated the formation of al-Shabaab. Most important, the author analyses how a failed state, such as Somalia has become symbolised by radical Islam. In Chapter 6, Dr. Olomojobi examines al-Qaeda in the Maghreb (AQIM). In order to understand AQIM, the author charts Algeria's violent past, the seeds of grievance, its bloody civil war and radical Islam exuding from the colonial and post-colonial history of Algeria. In Chapter 7, which the author titled: "Talibanism in Mali"—provides an exposition of the deeply divided society in Mali. The writer also explores the interconnectivity of the Tuareg struggle against marginalisation which later turned into a full blown pursuit for a breakaway state of their own, domestic terrorism and subsequent interface with foreign jihadi organisations.

Chapters 8 and 9 are devoted to case materials from Nigeria, where since 2009, the Boko Haram phenomenon had become a menace. In those two Chapters, author analyses the roots of the Boko Haram phenomenon, contradictions and inconsistencies in the policy of the Jonathan administration in fighting to stem the movement and the increasing attempts by Boko Haram leadership to seek common cause with other emergent terrorist groups both within and without. In profiling these radical groups, the author does not occupy the reader with contrived arguments, but he gives a display of facts that have not been compressed in a distinct study such as this book. The book ends with a discourse about the uses made by radical Islam in tapping into some of today's globalisations' benefits of mass consumerism and communications—social media and various platforms for propagating their ideology, its objectives, and recruiting adherence across the globe. Author also touches briefly in that last Chapter on e-terrorism, and how via globalisation the movement about radical Islam is able to raise funds and recycle proceeds from other syndicated business criminal activities via money laundering.

Dr. Olomojobi is a perceptive thinker and a profound political analyst who delivers his augments with facts, illustrating useful insights from other renowned scholars, whilst challenging the reader critically to think about the nature of a phenomenon—radical Islam—whose definition and analysis ordinarily evokes so much emotiveness. By and large, this is a dispassionate and objective work. The intellectual background from which the author comes, with his initial Law degree earned in Nigeria in 1990 and his Master's in International Law (Liverpool) in 1995 and PhD, Lancaster (International Relations) in 2010, both from England. Obviously, the author has more than adequate education and training to grapple with most of the issues thrown up by the subject of enquiry. Nor is Dr. Olomojobi new to this field of study. Two of his latest publications and actually single authored books are on *Human Rights: Gender, Sex and the Law in Nigeria*, published by a Nigerian Law publishing firm called Princeton Publishing Company, Lagos, 2013 and *Islam and Conflict in Northern Nigeria*, Malthouse Limited, Lagos, 2013, contain materials that are very germane to the present subject of study. *Frontiers of Jihad: Radical Islam in Africa*, is a carefully researched and ably written work, shorn of the usual jargons that tend to mark most social science related works, including those from Law. The implication is that the book is accessible to all and sundry, even while addressed principally to the intellectuals and policy makers at home and abroad.

I warmly recommend the book as a must-read.

**J 'Bayo Adekanye, PhD, FSSAN**
**Emeritus Professor of Political Science**
**Fellow of Social Science Academy of Nigeria**

# Preface

According to a 2009 report by Pew Research Center (PRC), the world consists of 1.57 billion Muslims, representing 23% of the world's population. This staggering amount of people reveals the importance of Islam in international politics. It also informs us that, although it is inconceivable that 1.57 billion people cannot be enshrined with radical ideology, however, their religion has been depicted as being a pacesetter for violence and terrorism in today's world. It certainly would be incorrect and absurd to agree with Rupert Murdoch when he twittered: "Maybe most Muslims are peaceful, but until they recognise and destroy their growing jihadist cancer, they must be held responsible."[1]

Nothwithstanding, violence emanating from Islam has been a significant debate in international politics since the atrocities of 9/11. In 2013, Islamic groups were at the top seven out of ten terrorists groups. Furthermore, seven Islamic states were at the top seven out of ten countries that were experiencing terrorism. An intriguing question is what has generated Islam to be positioned in this way? Is a minor percentage of Muslims accountable for extremism in Islam?

The questions above seek to explore whether Islam is a violent religion. This is for the reason that most atrocities emanating after the Cold War has been attributed to Islam.

---

[1] See 'Murdoch says Muslims must be held responsible for France terror attacks', accessed on the 15th of January at http://www.theguardian.com/world/2015/jan/10/rupert-murdoch-muslims-must-be-held-responsible-for-france-terror-attacks

Radical groups[2] such as al-Qaeda and the new extremist group—the Islamic State of Iraq and Syria (ISIS) have situated the world to be divided along ideological lines. Aside from the fact that Islam is practiced by the majority in the Middle East—Africa also has a vast number of Muslims—Islam is the religion of the majority in Africa. The vast number of Muslims in Africa further reveals that Africa cannot be left out in an analysis of Islam and conflict in global politics.

The 9/11 incident has generated the perception that radical Islam is a threat to Western ideologies. This episode also generated the augmentation of radical Islam in the world, which has simultaneously given birth to a new perspective of religion in international affairs. An overlooked observation by many scholars is that the world consists of many different civilisations and cultures. As a consequence, the ideals of democratisation, and liberalised religious beliefs and ways of life which are largely confined to Western societies are difficult to understand and appreciate in non-Western societies. The secularist views of the world as seen from the lens of Westernised societies can no longer deal with the diversities found in different cultures and societies. This difficulty has ushered in a new war of intolerance. This clash of ideologies indicates that religion in the world today is of extreme importance.

As Pentecostalism has become an eminent force in Christianity, especially in non-Western societies where reverse missions are taking place from non-Western missionaries to Western societies. Islam has taken prominent propulsion in non-Western societies where a perceived threat emanating from the West has provoked the drive towards radical Islam. An intriguing question to ask is whether the new role of one of the Abrahamic faiths has affected the other. Has the

---

2    The reader should note that 'Islamism' refers to political Islam which is the desire to have Islam as the centre of political structures in a state— it involves political theocratic determinism. It came into exiastence in the 20th Centuryby Sheikh Hassan Al-Banna (1906-1949) Militant Islam is when Muslims embark in an armed struggle in order to adopt Islam as a key component with political structures in a state. An Islamist is a radical Muslim who desires a Caliphate within a state or at the global level. All Islamists are Muslims, however, not all Muslims are Islamists. Radical Islam depicts an extremist interpretation of Islam —it is endorsed by Isamists/radical Muslims.

decline in religious affiliation in the West provoked a bloody rivalry between the faiths with the materialisation of radical Islam?

The clash of ideologies between Western and non-Western societies is largely based on differences in religion. A cornerstone of Westernised concept of human rights is freedom of religion. This freedom presupposes that different people from different cultures would have differences in ideologies. Equally, this differentiation implies that ideologies could be equated with religious beliefs. Aside from understanding the pivotal role religion has played in a vast number of non-Western societies, there is likely to be a distinct interpretation of how religion affects and forms the political culture of non-Western societies. Besides, religion may have different variables and connotations to different people. With this in mind, religion has the power to be a strong cultural and political force in some non-Western societies. The construction of this phenomenon reveals that the world and media focused on the atrocities of the Paris terror attacks which occurred on 9, January 2015, as opposed to the 7 January, 2015 butchery of 2,000 people in Baga, Borno State, in Northeast Nigeria, which was committed by Boko Haram. What generates a particular carnage to be more momentous than the other? Why do world leaders (including the former Nigerian President, Goodluck Jonathan) commensurate with President Francois Hollande of France whilst during that period they were reticent about the mass murders in Baga, north-eastern Nigeria? In many ways, religion has become a strong identity marker that is blended with ethnicity, nationalism and cultural values. This ideology may be seen to be consistent with the growing role of Islam in non-Western societies where Muslims are the majority — Religion in such societies acts as the conscience of its policies and its essence in international relations. Perhaps, it is then clear that liberal democracy cannot function in societies that have a strong primordial attachment to religion. Therefore, if these cultural differentials, theological ideas and a discourse on the religious dimension in international politics were easily detected fifteen years ago, perhaps the present state of the world, which is engrossed with the clash of ideologies, could have been averted.

The present surge of radical Islam started from the 9/11 atrocity. More to the point, this campaign against Westernisation has finally bearthed in Africa. Radical Islam's affinity with violence and its eagerness to use terror is difficult to analyse without an understanding of the essence of Islam in non-Western societies, such as the Middle East and Africa. A disparity within the sway of radical Islam, is that it is constructed differently in both Western and non-Western societies. This is revealed given the fact that Islamists are carrying out a crusade of death and destruction in parts of the Middle East (Syria and Iraq) and in Africa. Such deaths and destruction appears to be the ordinary course of living in such societies. However, the killing of twelve people on 7 January, 2015 in the Charlie Hebdo terror attacks in France ushered in the mantra of 'Je suis Charlie' and the march of a million people, who were joined by forty world leaders in solidarity against terrorism.

The burning of the Qur'an generates violence or provocation in some Western and non-Western societies. In 2005, the Danish cartoons controversies provoked and offended Danish Muslims. The Charlie Hebdo killing over satirical cartoons of Muhammad showcases the essence of Islam in Western societies. One is also reminded that a few centuries ago, burning the Bible in the Western world would induce dire consequences to the individual carrying out such an act. Simply put, religion has different meanings to different individuals. It could be argued that, since burlesque imitations of Prophet Muhammad is perceived to be derogatory by a majority of Muslims, it is then reasonable not to provoke people who have such sentiments, as it may generate violence. One must cautiously add that such provocation should translate to violence. However, it should be noted that different Muslims are subject to different constructions of reality.

An individual's social identity and social categorisation is positioned differently in Western and non-Western societies. A misconceived analysis by the media is that Islam is against Christianity and or the Jews. In understanding this religious factor, it should be a pointer for analysing international policies between Western states and non-Western states where Muslims are living. For instance, Islam which is the predominant religion in North Africa is considered to be the unifying factor. Also it is understood that Islam introduced a common language, common architecture and a common culture in the region (North Africa). It is then understood that globalisation has not removed religion from international politics—it has always been a part of history. Violence emanating from religion is not new. History tells us that religious violence started in the Middle Ages when Christian Crusades' attempted to conquer Jews, and Muslims. It seems that history has a way of repeating itself—however, it is only recently that policy makers and scholars deemed religion as part of international politics. The global war on terror cannot be used as a means to end radical Islam. In the same vein, the war on terror is not a war against Islam. This is for the reason that the critical issue that is somewhat overlooked is that radical groups are coalescing into a common franchise. Are Muslims becoming radicalized due to the economic failures of their respective states? The intent of this study is to explain 'how' and 'why' radical Islam finds a breeding ground in Africa. Before delving further, it is useful to note that radicalisation is the mental journey towards a belief system wherein an individual possesses extremist ideologies.

This book explores the sharing of ideas of how radical Islam is perpetuated by Islamists in the West, the Middle East and most important, Africa—which is crucial for combating terrorism. There is also the need to examine different dynamics of radical Islam in Africa. This treatise notes that no state in Africa can exclusively struggle against the rampage of radical Islam. If the war against terror is to be won, it is imperative to share intelligence within and outside the boarders of Africa. This study anticipates that policy makers in Africa would realise that there is a need for not only African solutions, but international solutions to eliminate the menace of the Islamist agenda in Africa and in the world in general.

# Acknowledgements

First and foremost, I would like to thank God for guiding me in writing this study. Indeed, God is the Greatest.

Executing this study required the help of many kind people. I wish to thank Mr. Jubril Shittu and Dr. Goodnews Osah who provided invaluable advice and assistance in writing this study. Special thanks goes to my former supervisor; Dr. Amalendu Misra who deserves memorable recognition for his scholarly support during my years as a PhD student.

My debt must also be acknowledged to Professor N.J. Udombana for very helpful critical suggestions and inputs into this study and for lending me his vast experience and knowledge in critical areas. My special thanks go to Emeritus Professor 'Bayo Adekanye for helping me rationalise and analyse complex issues in this study.

Most cordial thanks go to Emeritus Professor I.O. Agbede for mentoring me and providing me with invaluable advice, both as my former teacher and Dean at Babcock University, School of Law and Security Studies. I would also like to sincerely thank Chief Joop Berkhout, the doyen of publishing in Nigeria for exhibiting enthusiasm and confidence in this work and for ensuring its timely publication. In addition, I would like to show appreciation to Odetola Olalekan and Iwalola Adetunji for their useful and critical input in editing this study.

I could not have persevered without the encouragement of those who made me feel less forlorn in knitting this work together— Dr. Mike Eziakor, Mr. Seyi Apampa, Mrs Dorcas Odunaike, Mr. Ademola Taiwo and Mr. Tunde Adeyemi. A special word of gratitude goes to Mrs. Abiola Kalejaiye for her patience in editing this work. I sincerely appreciate Prof. John Illah for his useful suggestions in the course of his review of the manuscript.

My deep sense of gratitude goes to my wife and children for their unflinching support in the course of writing this book.

# List of Maps

- Map showing Nigeria's major ethnic groups
  and religious affiliation                                237
- Map showing Boko Haram strongholds and
  areas of attack                                          247
- Map of Somalia showing important cities and
  towns                                                    154
- Map showing the major cities/towns in Mali              219
- Map showing major cities/towns in Algeria.              181

# List of Tables/Graphs

- Table showing Jihadi stages of Islam   91
- Table showing Significant Incidents of Boko Haram: 1995-04/2014-04   267
- Graph showing leadership divisions in al-Shabaab   164
- Graph showing AQIM and its Regional Commanders   193

# PART ONE:
# EXPLORING THE FRONTIERS OF JIHÂD

# 1

# Theorising the Radicalisation of Islam

## Introduction

Radical Islam emerged in the 1990s after the Cold War as a new confrontation in international relations, particularly in the Middle East after the Cold War. It has been labelled as the 'clash of civilisations' (Huntington, 1996) and the 'war of ideas' (Phares, 2007). It is branded as 'radical' by its inclination to use aggression to govern institutions perceived to be anti-Islam. This ideology has been captured by other non-Western societies, especially in Africa. An intriguing question is how this form of radicalism finds a place and space to germinate in this region. Perhaps a more intriguing question is: How does one get to the root of the radicalisation of Islam in Africa?

To understand the significance of the problematic and analyses of this study, I need to anchor my arguments on critical realism, group theory, grievance (relative deprivation), invented tradition (imagined identities) and cultural theory. These theories are crucial in terms of understanding radical Islam in Africa. However, it must also be noted that radical Islam can be scrutinised in many ways aside from the above parameters just mentioned. Many other theoretical variables can be used to study assumptions of radical Islam in Africa. In a useful analysis by Botha (2008: 43), he perceptively notes that: "A fever is regarded as a symptom of an illness and is not treated in isolation. If it were, the body would find another way to manifest the illness." In other words, it would then be awkward to state that Islamists had "no country, no ideology; they're motivated by hate."[3] However, these theories should not be treated in isolation, but in conjunction with other theoretical strands to explain the essence of radical Islam in Africa.

## Explaining Radical Islam in Africa: A Critical Realist Approach

The understanding of radical Islam in Africa is shrouded with complexities. Nonetheless, this study seeks a practical explanation on the varied antagonisms of radical Islam in Africa. It will be argued that an understanding of the complexity of Islamists ideology in Africa requires a critical realist ontology. This being the case, this study attempts to answer intriguing questions such as: What are the causes of radical Islam in Africa?

This study employs an observatory approach to explain radical Islam from the perspective of critical realism. In the realist approach to social science, the methods of inquiry of natural sciences may be used in social sciences (Blaike, 1993). Scholars view the existence of radical Islam from one determining factor to another which produces sceptic solutions. Critical realism affirms that objects exist independently of being known or experienced by any person. What we see is real, what we touch has reality (Roark, 1982). The nature of the sciences is realist in its methods, as it endeavours to know how the world really is (Bricmont, 2001: 101-102).

---

3  See "President Rallies Troops at Travis Air Force Base," 17 October 2001 accessed on 21 March 2008 at: http://www.whitehouse.gov/news/releases/2001/10/20011017–20.html.

To the critical realist, scientific claims are true until they are falsified by a new observation. This observation could be scientific or anchored on social behaviour. Once a pattern of social behaviour has been observed by a method or methodology, it remains valid until faltered by a new method or methodology. To the critical realist, to claim that knowledge exists only to the extent of our awareness of that knowledge would constitute an 'epistemic fallacy' (Bhaskar, 1998: 27). In concise terms, as noted by Michael Williams:

> *If the world is an objective world, statements about how things appear must be logically unconnected with statements about how they are.... to realise our vulnerability to scepticism, we need only to recognise the simple logical point that our experience could be just what it is and all our beliefs about the world could be false* (Norris, 2003: 16).

In relating this to our inquiry into radical Islam in Africa, unforeseen variables that have not been identified by scholars would be sought after.

Although there is no sharp distinction between philosophy and social science (Bhaskar, 2003), the study of the social sciences requires a philosophical outlook on the way people construct their way of life in society. In determining the relationship between Islamists and their notions of jihâd, it is imperative to search for 'generative mechanisms' to explain this evolving phenomenon in Africa. The affinity to weave and consider every act of radical Islam as a result of religious undertones is tangential. There is the need to separate jihâdist ideology from Islam and investigate how they both are interrelated.

The lack of an ontological explanation has limited the practical solutions to radical Islam in Africa. It appears that the further profusion of theories on the subject, the more we are faced with mystification and misunderstandings about crucial issues. Therefore, this study is aimed at looking at the idiosyncrasies of radical Islam and jihâd within Africa. It does not aim to prevent radical Islam within the above purview, but to throw light on areas which have not been looked into by scholars in recent times.

In applying Bhaskarian thought, this study does not infer that radical Islam is a generating factor of jihâd. If it did, it would be a fallible statement. In short, this study seeks an explanation of how social dynamics procures the existence of radical Islam and its antecedent jihâd ideology—only an explanation based on observation can support such a statement. Critical realism searches for "What must be the case for science to be possible?" (Benton & Craib, 2001: 129).What must be the case for radical Islam to emerge? It is argued that observation would employ 'cause' analysis to answer the aforementioned questions.

## The Use of Observation

Observation compliments empirical study because it "may make us more confident about what we think exists" (Sayer, 2000: 12). Therefore, it is conveniently argued that the best method of studying society is by way of observation. Society which consists of varied social groups signifies that there are complex relationships, constituting different cultural, social, religious and economic attributes. However, individuals within a group may consider themselves as having a 'we' awareness of belonging (Smith, 1979:1). A group has various salient features which cannot be discovered solely by theoretical analysis. It is for this reason that the use of observation is a vital method in studying radical groups. The understanding of the organisational structure of a group is an important basis for explaining radical Islam in Africa.

Critical realism is a 'problem solver' in respect of seeking causal analysis of an event. Observations are used to obtain a valid analysis of a problem. A problem is regarded as an enquiry that needs an explanation. Thus, this study presents an enquiry that needs an explanation. It is therefore conceivable, that the best approach is preferred in analysing probable social predictions. 'Probable' because the best approach is susceptible to being fallible by other observations. In this respect, this study generates social predictions in attempting to explain radical Islamic groups in Africa. Lessons from the past can show not precise predictions, but trends about possible and likely futures (Patomäki, 2006). The lessons from jihâdist ideology in Africa, will provide a searchlight into possible trends that can give rise to radical Islam.

To the critical realist:

*Our knowledge of reality is a result of social conditioning and, thus, cannot be understood independently of the social actors involved in the knowledge derivation process. However, it takes issue with the belief that the reality itself is a product of this knowledge derivation process* (Dobson, 2002).

To the critical realist, a lot of causes interacting with each other, which include social agents often in very complex ways, produce several effects in different conditions (Archer, et al, 1999). For successful experiments, the world has to be 'structured, stratified and open' in order to explain social phenomenon.

## Criticism of the Critical Realist Approach

Fraassen (1980:202-203) a critic of critical realism and a constructive empiricist faults realism as a science. He argues that only that which is 'actual and observable' should be considered as science as opposed to what is not observable. Fraassen argues that science is knowledge only if all it states about observation is true. In addition, Fay (1990) has criticised critical realism, arguing that it proclaims into existence of a pre-ordered world with pre-existing structures'. He further states that critical realism affirms that it is the "job-and glory-of science" (Fay, 1990: 34) to uncover these structures to produce a true theory.

However, this study argues that not all claims are actual and observable by science, due to the reasoning that a part of knowledge is of things which are not produced by men (Bhaskhar, 1998: 16). By way of illustration, the law of gravity was in existence before Isaac Newton discovered it. Likewise, the penicillium was in existence before Sir Alexander Fleming noted by chance that the mould inhibited bacterial growth. The penicillium mould existed before it was discovered. Another illustration is that history has credited Christopher Columbus for discovering America. Without Columbus' voyage to America, wouldn't America still exist? America existed independent from Christopher Columbus' discovery. Did the River Niger (located in Nigeria) exist before being 'discovered' by the British explorer Mungo Park? These 'new' discoveries were already in existence, but were transferred into our 'world of construction.' It could be inferred that knowledge, although independent of our world, is not known to mankind in the real sense of the word, until embodied in a 'world of construction.' Thus, the analogy that: "We cannot see except by means of our eyes, so we can't see anything but our eyes," is unrealistic (Collier, 1999: 2). A realist acknowledges knowledge that has not been seen with his/her eyes. This ideology is the key concept of critical realism. The logical argument for this is that scientific facts or laws were true as they were discovered before they existed. To the critical realist: "Things do not happen by chance or without a reason. Behind events and courses of events, there are powers generating them" (Danermark, et al, 2002: 198). Thus, the aim of realist science is to explain observable events with construction and methods (Blaike, 1993). Social construction may be construed or interpreted by observation. As aptly noted by Sayer:

*A crucial role of social science must be to monitor and restructure the casual patterns of associations or sense-relations of unexamined knowledge, so that differences between necessary and contingent relations, and between warranted and unwarranted associations, are understood* (1984: 60).

In explaining radical Islam and the forces that promote jihâd in Africa, one must observe the peculiar construction of different states within the region. Each region has a peculiar construction of reality that enables radical Islam to exist. It would therefore be fallible to explain radical Islam within the same context in different states. As a result, it is pertinent to analyse different radical groups to understand their sense of jihâdist ideology. Critical realism's focal point is based on 'openness'; a theory must be subject to observed explanation. The use of observed explanation can justify epistemic gains which are useful in recognising new knowledge and exhibit a high standard of reliability and validity. In seeking a high reliability, this study does predict the occurrence of an event, but identifies and understands the phenomenon that is likely to produce an event. In understanding the relationship between jihâd and radical Islam, an explanatory analysis will provide a broad understanding of the real structures of the subject.

From a realist perspective, the explanation will not have a prognostic understanding of radical Islam and jihâd in the region, because this would concede to a consummation of the study. The explanation would only reveal 'tendencies' of how radical Islam has become part of the mysteries in Africa. Although, not all African states have the prevalence of radical Islam, what is certain is that the growth of Islamism affects the continent as a whole. Thus, this study would isolate other factors that limit or stimulate the growth of radical Islam. As aptly put by Bhaskar (1993:3):

> *Realism is not, nor does it license, either a set of substantive analyses or a set of practical policies. Rather, it provides a set of perspectives on society (and nature) and how to understand them.*

Critical realism takes the study of science beyond positivism, because positivism does not take account of observations. Furthermore, the social world is an open system and therefore cannot be subject only to scientific experimentation (Collier, 1994).

Knowledge is all embracing. Knowledge is discovered by observation, without observation there would be no knowledge. A feature of critical realism is that it is aware that change is the only permanent institution known to man. It is then clear that social science is fluid and subject to fallibilism. In addition, the world is an open system, hence social phenomenon is prone to change in the real world. Consequently, knowledge can only be transferred to our world of construction by observation. To the critical realist, the scientific world and the social world need a method or methodology of observation to explain a tendency. It is indeed complex using a method of observation, because predictions are fragile and variable in the social science. We argue that man is an imperfect being, knowledge is constructed by man, and therefore knowledge cannot be perfect, hence the predisposition to be fallibilism.

By using the critical realist approach, this study offers relevant analysis at a given point in time. The explanation of radical Islam in Africa is *intelligibilia*: That is, whatever is logical at a given point in time is the preferred explanation of an event, such as how and why some Muslims in Africa are drafted in the 'global battlefield.' Perhaps, at a future date a different understanding and explanation of radical Islam may emerge. This is the exquisiteness of critical realism. To illustrate my argument, some centuries ago scientists believed that the earth was flat. Now that science affirms that the world is round, the previous view is now deemed as fallible. Both explanations were germane for different times. Thus, it is erroneous to contend that there are absolute truths about scientific information (Sayer, 1984).

## The Use of Retroductive Reasoning

As stated earlier, critical realism offers the 'best' explanation in analysing social reality. What then is the 'best' explanation? Retroduction is an argument that "involves the postulation of social objects or mechanisms, with definable powers, whose existence or activation is thought to be making or to have made a significant causal contribution to a social phenomenon that a sociologist wants to explain." (Stones, 1996: 37). Similarly, "knowledge of this social reality can only be attained if we go beyond what is empirically observable by asking questions and developing concepts of the more fundamental, trans-factual conditions for the events and phenomena under study" (Danermark, et al, 2002: 96).

Critical realism is concerned with causation and causal analysis (Sayer, 1984). The critical realist is desirous of inquiring into what makes something happen. It seeks a "causal analysis' by "explaining why what happens actually does happen" (Danermark, et al, 2002: 52). This explains that Muslims are all placed in different social constructions, not only in Africa, but in the entire world. Thus, radical Muslims tend to construct the world from their own lens as they see it. In pursing this analysis, we would employ the use of counterfactual thinking by analysing what is considered 'present and absent' (Danermark, et al, 2002: 101). What is present in enabling radical Islam to exist in parts of Africa? What is absent from enabling radical Islam to exist in parts of Africa? In construing the former, radical Islam would not exist in parts of Africa if people did not have an overwhelming dependence on religion in their society.

However, a complication that occurs with retroductive reasoning is that it may be too embracive in analytical reasoning and therefore lacking comparative deductions when explaining an event. Again, critical realism solves this dilemma by acknowledging that any scientific law is subject to fallibility. Critical realism is concerned with analysing complex relationships. It acts as a searchlight into seeking an explanation of an event or a statement of fact. As perceptively pointed by Amit Ron (2002: 122):

> *What critical realists argue in addition is that empirical adequacy is also unnecessary. Since scientific laws are statements about the tendencies of structured entities, there is no logical necessity in specifying constant conjunctions of events as a condition for establishing a scientific law.*

In analysing the radicalisation of Islam in Africa, it is ideal to explain the 'conditions of possibility' for its existence. The 'conditions of possibility' or the 'generative mechanisms' (Danermark, et al, 2002: 21) are underlying social constructions which produce the social consequence or events in society.

Delving into the midsts of this, it is important to note that radical Islam in Africa goes beyond religious dictates. It has been viewed comprising other complex determinants such as historical, social, political and economic determinants. Thus, in understanding radical Islam, it is necessary to understand the Kantian transcendental argument into "what is, about why it came to be the way it is, and about how it ought to be" (Hammersley & Martyn, 2002: 35).

The application of the Kantian transcendental argument implies understanding ontological dualism (analytical dualism),[4] because the individual and society are separate social entities and neither can exist in seclusion from the other. Bob Carter (1998:66) in explaining analytical

---

[4] Analytical Dualism', is a term formed by Margaret Archer

dualism, referred to Lockwood's argument on the subject was distinguishing "how the parts of a social system gelled together (system integration) was analytically distinct from how agents and actors living within that system made sense of it (social integration)." Analytical dualism separates social structures (society) from culture and agency (the individual) (Porpora, 2001:265). In construing this, the 'system integration' in different African states, that is, its social construction, is different from the system of 'social interaction' of its people within the continent. Analytical dualism offers a method of viewing people, not only from a physical and materialist view, but also from natural and primordial forces.

## Group Theory as a Model in Understanding Radical Islam

This study examines group behaviour within a civilisation. It studies the causal links between radical Muslims and conflict behaviour. The group theory explicates the dynamics of human relations in society. It argues that, given the gregarious nature of man, his actions are better understood in the context of the group relations in which people are involved.

According to this perspective, what underscores every society is the organic interest that binds people together in groups and conditions the pressures, stress and dynamism of social life. Individuals within the group consider themselves as having a 'we' awareness of belonging (Smith, 1979:1). Society is a pluralist social configuration oriented towards the achievement of diverse interests. According to Macridis (1964:139), it is the organic interests amongst group membership that act as the binding element of group relationship and thus provides the power of a group as a deterministic social construct, either for good or evil. Clearly, an individual must be accepted in a social group before he/she is deemed a member. Notably, acceptance is about sharing in a common identity, such as religion.

One may safely suggest that radical Islamists as a mark of an individual's religious identity is formed by the construction of his/her group's identity. This being so, it may be clear that the acceptance of an individual as an Islamist implies sharing of a common religious identity and interests. This identification generates a sense of collectivisation and terrorist sympathies amongst radical Muslims. The reason an individual joins a radical Islamist group is due to the relationship they have with individuals already in the group (Munson, 2008). This acceptance of common interests and identity provides the sentiments of a 'we-group.' Inherent in the explication of the different group interests is the desire of groups to gain advantage over others and to institute their group hegemony in state affairs through the domination of political structures. This is often met with resistance and counter-resistant which usually engenders conflicts.

A group's sentiments of suffering in turn leads to a sense of frustration amongst the group and may be the causal link to hatred and violent conflict. Individuals learn how to consume hatred when they get involved with groups that have such prepositions. At this point, it is critical to the perceptive view of Govier's (2002: 35):

> *There may be an evolutionary explanation for rage and hatred...hatred of our enemies is a deeply natural thing, especially in a context where we have been attacked and believe our survival is in question.*

Perhaps, this theory is best suited to explain the argument that the prevalence of radical Islam in Africa is due to the dearth of socio-economic development in the continent. These groups advocate for change. They are faced with the longing of how their world would be if their imagined propositions were realisable. This unrealistic quest for change generates hate. This sentiment of hatred is showcased on May 22, 2013 in the hacking to death of a British soldier; Lee Rigby, by radicalised Nigerian born British citizens; Michael Adebolajo and Michael Adebowale. Their reason for committing this barbarity was due to grievance over the killing of Muslims living abroad by British soldiers. It is then not surprising that the offensive publication of Prophet Muhammad by Danish newspapers had a rebounding effect in other Islamist groups all over the world. Another illustration is the bombing of Planet Hollywood in Cape Town, South African in 1998 soon after America bombed Sudan. Another instance that reveals the dynamics of Islamists groups in response to grievance is found in northern Nigeria in the Kano riots (popularly called the Osama bin Laden riots) of 2001, where inter-religious riots were fuelled due to America's attack on Afghanistan. The dynamics of group identity provides for a psychological explanation on questions 'why' do radical Islamist groups behave the way they do? In understanding group dynamics about radical Islam, it should be understood that Muslims in non-Western societies have a strong identity mark towards their religion. This is exhibited in the manner pertaining to how Muslims are strongly united as a group in Western countries. Within this theory, individuals who belong to a social group, have sentiments of emotions towards group-related incidents that are associated or experienced by a seemingly similar social group (Smith, 1993). In line with this, Martha Crenshaw (1998: 251) asserts that:

> *The comfort of belonging to a community of like-minded may be the dominant psychological interdependencies, which should be identified and analysed.*

In analysing and identifying psychological orientation of radical Muslims, it is useful to note that Muslims are seemingly bonded to their history. This explains the rational behind why radical Muslims are desirous of repositioning themselves into their previous golden age of Islam (the Ottoman era). Islamists have come to the realisation that capitalism and socialism are westernised ideologies that have been too complex to implement in their societies. Another factor that gave rise to the awareness *(Sahwa)* of an Islamic identity among Muslims, especially in the Middle East, erupted after the collective embarrassment of Six-day war of 1967 between Israel and Syria, Egypt, and Jordan (representing Arab nationality). The defeat of Arab nationality/Nasserism snowballed the desire for the Arabs to search for an alternative identity—Islam. Hence, an option is seen as co-opting the merger of Islam with the state as the solution to its retarded socio-economic growth.

The essence of Islamic awakening and Islamic identity is found in the Shi'a's Iranian Islamic Revolution in 1979. The successful hostage taking of forty-nine Americans and the shift in power from a secular government to an Islamic state soared the modern beginning of radical Islam. However, more precise is the nine-year war between the Soviet Union and the Mujahedin of Afghanistan. This was the crucial ignition for Islamists and their agenda of a holy crusade. The significance of the Islamic revolution in Tehran and the Afghanistan war is captured by Gilles Kepel (2006: 136-137) when he notes perceptively that:

> *Thus, the Islamist question became part and parcel of the wider American-Soviet struggle, whose end—paradoxically—it would eventually hasten. In December 1979, the Soviet Union appeared to have everything going its way: the Red Army was in Kabul and the Americans were humiliated in Tehran. Yet within ten years the Soviet system had collapsed, and the Afghanist debacle had been a key contributor to its demise.*

Veritably, it is pertinent to note that in states where Muslims are a majority, the essence of *Dar-al-Islam* situates the dynamics of easy group formations of radical Islamists.

What is clear from the Soviet/Afghan conflict is that the war was considered to be a jihâd by many Muslims in the Middle East. After the demise of the war, in 1989, the victory of the Mujahedin created a sense of an imagined victory over one arm of the westernised military might. This perceived victory created an illusion that the other arm led by the alliance of America (referred to as the 'Great Satan' by Islamists) on the one part and Israel on the other could be defeated in order to establish a universal Caliphate (both America and Israel are considered to be cosmic enemies of radical Muslims). Al Zawahiri, then second in command to Osama bin Laden, noted distinctly that:

*The jihad battles in Afghanistan destroyed the myth of a superpower in the minds of the Muslim mujahidin young men. The USSR, a superpower with the largest land army in the world was destroyed and the remnants of its troops fled Afghanistan before the eyes of the Muslim youths and as a result of their action. That jihad was a training course of the utmost importance to prepare Muslim mujahidin to wage their awaited battle against the superpower that now has sole dominance over the globe, namely the U.S.* (Shannon and Dennis, 2007: 305-306).

Group dynamics reveals that individual identity is an important feature of Islamists. A striking question that arises in the context of group dynamics is: Where are the individuals that embrace these groups? In considering an answer to this—they are everywhere. A vast number of Muslims are desirous of establishing a system where their religious identity will be recognised, not only in their society, but in the entire world. However, this desire does not make such Muslims to be Islamists. Pipes (2001) observes that there is little or no disparity between a good Muslim in his/her day to day construction of reality and their desire to promote Islam as an ideal form of system as opposed to secular law. The truth here is that Islam is a way of life, hence to Muslims, secularisation in many ways conflicts with the intent and purpose of Allah's law. Perceptively, this is aligned with Juergensmeyer's (1993) argument, that secularism has failed Western society due to its incapacity to prevent the decay of Western society's hinge on decadence and immorality. This inability has ushered the birth of a 'new cold war.' This perhaps explains the quest of Islamic revival and militancy, especially after the crash of the Cold War, and its purported end of the history of the world with the triumph of democracy (Fukuyama, 1989).

Arthur Bentley (1908) laid the intellectual foundation for the group theory. As opposed to a collection of individuals, Bentley asserted that a group is a mass of activity (Varma, 2001:163). Thus, all groups must have an interest. He also affirmed, that "when the group is adequately stated, everything is stated" (Bentley, 1908:209). Therefore, groups have primacy in political analysis over and above institutions. Contrary to Bentley's obsession with procedures in his conceptualisation of groups, Truman (1951:37) notes that:

> *An interest group is a share-attitude group that makes certain claims upon other groups in society. If and when it makes its claims through or upon any of the institutions of government, it becomes a political interest group." This conceptualises groups to include those stable social groups, which do not necessarily have continuing policy goals, but can suddenly intervene in policy process* (Greenstone, 1975:265).

It is worth stressing at this point that a major critique of the group theory is its loose definition of groups, implying that the theory may not be a rigorous theory for social analysis. Group theory admits the possibilities of multiple group membership but it fails to inform us of the contextual implications of this criss-crossing group membership on the dynamics of social relations. A major shortcoming of the theory is its dissolution of individuals in the astringent current of group relations. This denies the reality that each member of a group is first and foremost a private individual and can exercise the freedom to exist in any group whenever they deem fit to do so.

In spite of the above limitations, one might argue that man's sociological make-up favours group existence. The importance of groups could be understood as the foundation of the formation of the personality and opinions of people. Thus, man/woman detached from group relations would be ill-at-ease and less efficacious. Within the context of this study and the political dynamics of Islam, religious loyalties are the primary defining elements of social existence of Islamists and, consequently, the root of religious and political violence.

## Grievance as Model in Understanding why Islamists Rebel

This study provides an asseveration that terror emanating from radical Islam is caused by collective grievance. Gurr (1970) argues that increased expectations when matched with increased frustrations, due to the failure in expectation realisations, are responsible for the instigation of social conflicts. Perhaps, this explains in context, all the perceived agitations between radical Muslims and Western civilisation. The condition of rising expectation and rising frustration is directly related to relative deprivation. Relative deprivation is used to explain the social and psychological generative mechanisms that lead to violence. Perhaps, an even more important aspect of Gurr's theory is that it attributes aggression to behaviourist constructions. It could be readily observed that the group dynamics plays an important role in understanding the phenomena in radical Islam. It seems that group dynamics could be used in recognising when Islamists would be under the perception of real and perceived injustices. If viewed from this perspective, it could be suggested that Islamists in Africa are aggrieved towards Western societies in terms of its prevalence of secularised model of governance and its antecedents of interventionist activities such as ushering non-Islamic practices in African societies. Thus, the ideal of using jihâd to attain an Islamic state could be viewed as a quest for liberty and to attain economic equity among Muslims. It is through these notions of grievance that Muslims are taught by extremists to hate westernised civilisation.

Wealth is concentrated in the Western world which has its foundation in Judeo-Christian culture. This sharp division is strikingly different from many societies where Muslims are living, especially in Africa. This backwash in terms of financial development has generated a yearning for societies that comprise mainly Muslims to aspire for economic development in order to enjoy living conditions enjoyed by Westerners. It has been empirically observed that terrorism is likely to emerge in states where there are economic deprivations in economic growth (Blomberg, Hess and Weerapana, 2004). Conversely, Pipes (2004) argues eloquently that poverty does not give rise to Islamism, but are based on questions of an individual's identity. It can of course be argued that one possible explanation for the existence of radical Islam is the interconnectivity of a religious identity (Islam) and poverty.

Perhaps, in many African societies, the yoke of grievance towards Westernised institutions is responsible for perceived agitations. It is possible, to speculate that the causal link of Islamists violence is due to perceptions of deprivation in terms of socio-economic, psychological needs and resource control. Individuals are therefore magnetised towards political violence when the state fails to implement vibrant socio-economic goals for its citizens (Howard, 2010). Nonetheless, the study and understanding of grievance is based on Gurr's (1970:13) definition of relative deprivation. Gurr defines relative deprivation as a "perceived discrepancy between value expectations and value capabilities." In other words, relative deprivation is connected with the individual or a group to perceived social injustices such as racism or discrimination. It can be seen in the disparity of what an individual needs and what he gets. These perceived social inequalities and injustices are the causal links to individuals or groups experiencing relative deprivation. It could be inferred from this that radical Islam sheds light into the economic realities of Muslims in Africa. This study would argue that economic depravities are a cause to show why Muslims rebel under the canopy of religion (Hafez, 2003). In using grievance as model in understanding why Islamists rebel in Africa, a pointer that cannot be overlooked is found in poverty, the plague of unemployment and its antecedent social problems contributes in no small measure to radical Islam. In order to illustrate what the source of grievance means, Stith (2010: 57) quotes Tanzanian President Jakaya Kikwete who posited that:[5]

> *Poverty seems to push people closer to their religions for protection, services, and material needs when the communities or government units in their areas cannot provide these amenities. This would be okay if it ended there. If this reaction is intensified, it may have disintegrative effects in the communities and then at the level of the nation. In other words, poverty tends to disintegrate people from the larger territorial community only to integrate them in their community of believers.*

---

[5] A speech at Boston University, on September 25, 2006.

Stith (2010: 640) in the same vein notes that: "If belief is the seed of radicalism, poverty is the fertilizer." The manacles of poverty and social tension are the prevailing ideology of why Islamists rebel in Africa. It is then not surprising that Islamists perceive that an apocalyptic caliphate is needed to provide unity and development for Muslims in Africa. In the eyes of the Islamist, radical Islam is the antidote for perceived grievances. Although economic deprivation is a useful premise in understanding the cause effect of radicalism in Islam in Africa, other variants are interwoven with this discourse. Deprivation inter-connected with demoralisation, ethnic animosities, political sectarianism, political subjugation and inter-religious animousities lead to apathy and conflict. In simpler terms, Misra (2008:8) explains that grievance is invoked when "the individual or group realises that it has been consistently and methodically kept underprivileged in relation to other constituent groups or communities." It is important to note that relative deprivation is connected to the individual or group as it is the causal link to frustration, which leads to collective violence (aggression). In essence, one may argue that aggression cannot exist without perceived group grievance. Therefore, "the frustration-aggression mechanism is in this sense analogous to the law of gravity: Men who are frustrated have an innate disposition to do violence to its source in proportion to the intensity of their frustration" (Gurr, 1970: 37).

It is pertinent to note that an important aspect of this study is that groups that possess strong identity markers are predisposed to recognising that their group's identity is threatened by or suffers from deprivation of socio-economic conditions. Socio-economic conditions such as the dearth of basic needs, resource distribution, economic wealth, social well-being and education are connected to the realisation of the suffering of an individual from the group. Therefore, in effect, economic grievance (in societies that have vast population of Muslims) is a fertilizer for radical Islam. An illustration of this argument is witnessed even in Western societies such as France, whom in many ways has fuelled radical Islam. On 27 October, 2005— 8 November, 2005 in the environs of Paris (274 towns throughout the Paris district), widespread insurgence by mostly Arab, North African, and Black African migrants were instigated due to socio-economic grievances. These grievances pertained to poor housing projects, social exclusion and racial discrimination amongst migrants who are mainly Muslim. Another case of social exclusion in France occurred in 2010 over the 'burqa ban', which became effective law in April 2011. It is therefore not surprising that on 9 January, 2015, terror attacks in Paris were perpetuated by radical Muslims trained by al-Qaeda in the Arab Peninsula.[6]

At this point, it must be emphasised that the problem with Africa seems similar to the description of the Arab world where:

> *The entire Arab sector, with all its oil wealth, is 'richer than it is developed.' Its economies are stagnant, illiteracy is widespread, political freedom is hardly to be found, and its inhabitants, especially its women, are denied the basic 'capabilities' and 'opportunities' of the modern world* (Fukuyama & Samin, 2002: 34).

Apart from the abundance of natural resources in Africa, another identical factor it shares with the Arab world is the growth of radical Islam and its twin cohort of violence. This violence could be essentially generated by popular dissatisfaction. Thus, it is right to take cognizance of the words of Diaa Rashwan that:

> *Radical Islamic groupings began to reorient their vision outwards, away from their societies, toward issues*

---

[6] There are 751 "no-go zones" which consist of squalid neighbourhoods which are governed by the Muslim community. These locales lack basic public infrastructures. The Muslims residing in these zones have found it a daunting task to find housing or economic opportunites in French cities.

*among which there is the widespread popular and official consensus in the Arab and Islamic worlds (...)* (Roussillon, 2002: 40).

It is argued that Gurr's seminal work is subject to limitations in analysing the psychological dimension to conflicts. His work rests on a single foundation: Frustration—aggression. Some of the ambiguity stems from the tenuous methods in measuring psychological variables in the context of conflicts and others are from the non-linear relationship between conflict and violence. Therefore, one may argue that frustration is not always the causal link to violence. Certainly, not all grievances lead to violence in order to engender a change in value capabilities and or value expectations (Gupta, 1990). One objection to the grievance theory in explaining the causal link of conflicts is the deterministic factors of financial potentials of instigating the conflict (Collier & Hoeffler, 2004). However, groups are very unlikely to admit economic factors or greed as the cause of conflict, as they usually attribute the causal link to sentiments of grievance (Collier, 2000:92). Notwithstanding its limitations, certainly Misra (2008:11) is precise when he suggests that grievance is a "useful framework to explain the dynamics of internal violence in some societies."

## Invented Tradition

For perspicuity, this study, draws on the concept of 'invented tradition' to explain Islamist nationalism. Hobsbawm strongly affirms that 'national cultures', especially in non-Western states, are recent inventions by its elites. Hobsbawm (1983) further argues that invented tradition is a set of practices normally governed by clearly accepted rules and of a custom or representative nature, which connects with continuity with the past.

Despite the above definition, the analytical significance of invented tradition theory within this study is drawn from Anderson's (1991) arguments in his acclaimed book: *'Imagined Communities.'* Nations, according to Anderson, are 'imagined communities.' Anderson's theory is based on a modernist perception, which suggests that the nation is a recent creation and, therefore, is a political invention constructed by print technologies with the emergence of modernity. To Anderson, nationalism invents nations where they have not previously existed. He further points out that people within a nation did not accede to be part of the nation, but only found themselves within the nation as a result of a metamorphosis of historical and political trajectories.

Significantly, Anderson's concept of nationhood may be suitable as an approach for explaining the history of a perceived Islamic nationhood and the formation of radical Islamic groups. The sentiments of brotherhood between Islamists help them to foment unity within and outside Africa. Perhaps, this explains the unity between al-Qaeda and its sub groups in Africa. Most important is that they imagine themselves to be part of a nation. The image of an Islamist identity as a corporate sentiment may be explained as a political project rather than an act of history. It could be argued that the quest for a globalised caliphate is a strong factor that formed transnational Islamist identities in Africa. Perhaps, this is largely the reason that there is a conceived perception of Islamists viewing one another as kith and kin and therefore belonging to a larger family and viewing outsiders as differentiated and separate (non-Muslims are commonly referred to as 'Kuffir'). It is therefore logical, that individuals have a preference for those with whom they share some variants of an identity (Hogg & Abrams, 1988). In this sense, radical Muslims imagine each other to belong to a nation.

Alternatively, Anderson's concept of nationhood helps to explain the dividing ideologies of Islam and the West. These divisions have created a flaccid coalition of groups, which are divided on geographic territories but have a hopeful reverie of creating a nation—a global caliphate. This political invention offers a satisfactory rationalisation of the problems associated with pre-colonial institutionalism, the myriad of individual groups, deep divisions among the people, people of multiple identities professing various faiths and individuals belonging to Islamists groups questing reformation of the world at large. The inherited and invented traditions of the colonialists, poses several problems. These problems are connected to the plethora of communities that have differentiating culture and national identities, which were fused as a result of a religious identity. A feature of Anderson's work that is relevant to this study is that radical Muslims from different states are fabricated into an imagined nation due to the prevalence of an Islamist identity. Hence, it could be argued that individuals are capable of imagining themselves as part of wider group (Anderson, 1991).

What this amounts to is that there is a strong understanding that there exist imagined identities, such radical Muslims, whom are bound together as an identity group due to a common religious identity. Therefore, our intention is to illustrate that the construction of these differences is imagined or, in other words, a mental impression, due to the fact that different people grew up in similar communities and partake in community activities together but are imagined differently due to an exclusive Islamist identity.

What seems depressing about Anderson's definition of nations is that it could be criticised for connoting that nations are not real. Assuming this, but not conceding that they are non-existent or are in a state of apparition, then, it may be argued that nations exist only in a state of utopianism and are mere illusory or are at best 'Alice in Wonderland' fairy tales. Anderson's socially constructed world may be seen as viewing nations not as they are, but how we want nations to be seen. However, Anderson's theory of invented traditions remains a useful guide in understanding the trajectories of radical Islamist groups.

## Cultural Theory: The Construction of Radical Groups

The world is constructed by various cultures. This sets an identity marker on every individual. The point, in short, is that there is need to stress the fact that individuals constitute the dynamics of group interaction. This being the case, culture can be understood as a social glue that unites individuals under an umbrella. In understanding culture, one has to demystify the ways and socialisation of a people. According to David Schneider, culture consists of " elements which are defined and differentiated in a particular society as representing reality—not simply social reality, but the total reality of life within which human beings live and die" (Andrade, 1984: 115). Individuals are therefore subject to strong pressures as a result of socialisation (Andrade, 1984: 97). Critical to the study of radical Islam in Africa, is that it is pivotal to note that groups are important in defining an individual's identity and may determine their outlook to life. In respect to this, there are cultural rules that define this construction. Against this perception is that "cultural rules are based on the individual's generalised desire to conform to whatever it is that other people are observed to do or whatever it is other people say one should do, rather than on what people really want to do"(Andrade, 1984:97). Individual identities are causally connected to the membership of the group the individual belongs to. Accordingly, the Islamist as an identity of an individual is formed by the construction of his group's identity.

More particularly, Islam as an identity marker is seen from the observation that religion is a cultural system (Geertz, 1973). This being so, it may be clear that the acceptance of an individual as a radical Muslim implies sharing of a common religious identity and interests. This acceptance of common interests and identity provides the sentiments of a 'we-group'. The construction of a 'we-group' connotes that complex issues such as political sentiments, sentiments of oppression and violent emotions are connected to every member of the group. Perhaps, it becomes clear 'how' and 'why' radical groups such as al-Qaeda can connect its complexity of oppression and aggression to other radical Islamic groups in Africa—there is a vicious circle. We are then informed that "cultural theory suggests that the views of any particular individual on matters are shaped by the nature of social groups of which they are a part, i.e., various organisations, peer group influences or other sources of authority, and by the degree to which individuals feel bonded to larger social groups" (Tansey & O'riordan, 1999:71). It then seems very much imaginable that in societies where radical Islam is prevalent, other moderate Muslims may be leered towards its ideology given the fact that as noted by Martin Luther King Jr: "...oppressed people cannot remain oppressed forever. The yearning for freedom eventually manifests itself..." (Washington: 1991: 297). This manifestation could germinate in different ways. For radical Muslims, violence and death may become a contrivance to become unchained from perceived oppression.

The main concern that arises from this is that to Marx, mans' consciousness is determined by his social being which is rooted in his society. This state of 'social being' relates to the phenomenon of everyday life in the individual. In this way, society is dependent on social relativity, as the distinctive character of society is that it is subject to change. Now, it is significant to note that the identity of an individual or a group is beyond his or their collective consciousness. Their experience and how they relate to society is consciously involuntary, as they do not choose the society where they find themselves. Individuals become products of their society without having a choice. Hence, they act and behave the way they do as a result of the reality of the society in which they were brought up in. It is significant to note that the identity of an individual or a group is beyond his or their collective consciousness. Their experience and how they relate to society is consciously involuntary, as they do not choose the society where they find themselves. Individuals become products of their society without having a choice.

## Radicalisation of Islam in Africa

At the centre of this study, as may already be clear is that, Islam, aside from being practiced by a majority of African people is also essentially a way of life to its followers. Islam then is part and parcel of politics and social-economic institutions to Muslims. This perhaps explains why some Muslims groups have integrated religion in their quest for political relevance and in combating the dregs of colonialism and the post-colonial institutionalised corruption and repressive governance in their states. At this juncture, it is pertinent to point out that radical Islamic ideology is not a cause-effect that generates terrorist activism. However, some significant factors tend to generate radical Islam.

One of such factors is a desire to preserve the *umma* against the intrusion of cultural interest and values, especially the influence of the western colonisation (Esposito, 1999). The main objective of these radical groups, however, is not an entire rejection of these values, it is an elimination of the sphere of influence of these supposed foreign influences and usurpation of governmental authority through the introduction of their own form of rule. It is not surprising that these groups are called 'self-styled jihadists,' as most use jihâd as a fog for nefarious activities. One distinct proof of this fact is that most jihâdist groups immediately declare a caliphate after conquering a territory. In addition, they also seek to implement basic social services such as the provision of water, health and welfare. This service, perhaps informs us that an essence of radical Islam is to eliminate perceived oppression.

Radical Islamists have a major grievance against the imposition of Western values on its religious ideologies (Esposito, 2002). The colonisation of Africa predominantly by France, England and other Western powers has magnified this grievance. Furthermore, perceived neo-colonialism of the Muslim community has given ground to the nursing of grievances. Amble (2012: 342) tells us that the "Key to al-Qaeda's chosen strategy to win the broader conflict with the West is the development of a shared sense of identity among the *umma*, the global Muslim community, encouraging the internalising of suffering endured by Muslims anywhere in the world." For instance, Osama Bin Laden's grievance was against the 'intrusion' by the West and their collaborators on the 'holy land'. Similarly, most known Egyptian terrorists today were radicalised during the reign of Anwar al-Sadat who was a pacifist to Western powers and an ally to Israel. A further possible perceived grievance is found in the National Liberation Front (FLN), the Group for Preaching and Combat (GSPC) and al-Qaeda in the Islamic Maghreb (AQIM). AQIM has openly sought to reduce French influence in the region through elimination of their 'puppets' and nationals. Thus, numerous *fatwas* have been pronounced by these radical Islamists calling for the perpetration of violent acts against westerners and their supposed 'puppets'.

It is quite tasking to articulate the position of Islam in African societies during colonial era because of the various types of Islam, directions of infiltration, varieties of local appropriation, and differing colonial, pragmatic policies driven by exigencies. However, the relationship has been described as a clash of two civilisations, one modern while the other locked in its distant past and cultural heritage. Among western powers, especially the French, Islam was viewed as a threat to their political objectives and goals. Various examples abound of the resistance of Islam to western values[7] — Some of the leaders involved in the struggle for Islamic liberation from western values include "Usman dan Fodio, Amir Abd al-Qadir, and Muhammad ibn Abdille Hasan" (Esposito, 1999:550). For them, their struggles represented something different. They were not only ready to struggle against Western imperialists, they also strived against their own people in their quest to preserve the values they deemed sacrosanct. Even today, in most African countries, the struggle of these jihâdists is still reflected, especially in societies characterised by the existence of a blend of socio-economic and religious cleavages. For instance, in Nigeria, there is a desire by Muslims to preserve their religious values in spite of the fact that Nigeria is a secular state. This desire is manifested in the existence of a Penal Code and also the institution of Sharia in most states in northern Nigeria. Smith (1920) points to the unchanging nature of the practical Islamic ideology when he remarked that the post-colonial struggles of Islamic groups have had the effect of making "state formation and its relation to colonial and pre-colonial eras complex and at times problematic."[8]

The second factor is the prevalence of poverty. Anthony O'Connor (1991:1) starts his book with a truism: "To think of Africa is to think of poverty." It is difficult to disagree with this extract. The reality about this statement describes the portrait of Africa to Western societies. However, O'Connor rightly points out that such imagery is absent from the mind

---

7   See Esposito, J. L. (Ed.), 1999. The Oxford History of Islam. Oxford University Press
8   See Nasr, S.V.R., 'European Colonialism and the Emergence of Modern Muslim States', in 'Oxford History of Islam', John L. Esposito (Ed) Oxford Islamic Studies Online, accessed on the 2nd of September 2014 at: http://www.oxfordislamicstudies.com/article/book/islam-9780195107999/islam-9780195107999-chapter-13>.

of the African for the reason that he/she cannot measure what poverty really is. Conversely, poverty is "a sense of helplessness, dependence and lack of opportunities, self-confidence and self-respect on the part of the poor" (Handley, et al, 2009:10). A causal variable that leads to radical Islam in Africa is the widespread indices of poverty. Due to years of exploitative colonial and post-colonial regimes, Africa has not been able to find a vibrant financial base for its economic development. Most Africa states are endowed with volatile economies and negative economic growth. Letiche (2010:164) shows: "That Africa lost half of its share in world trade to developing countries in Asia and Latin America. At the time of independence, most African countries were richer than those of Asia; now they are far behind." Economic grievance could then be traced to the fact that as at 2008, the United Nations pointed out that 47 percent of the people of sub-Saharan Africa lived on $1.25.[9] However, a scholar has argued that poverty is not the cause-effect of Islamic terrorism, by reason that the terrorists are usually from middle class families (Sageman, 2008). This perspective could be seen as being rather essentialist, as the profile of an Islamist terrorist is defined by different variables. However, what is clear is that the individual who chooses to become a terrorist imagines that his co-religionists are trapped within the confines of economic deprivation, impoverishment and deep-rooted beggary as a result of the ineptitude of the state. Perhaps, Paul Collier (2008: 5) notes this predicament when he asks Westerners the intriguing question:

> *Suppose your country is dirt poor, almost stagnant economically, and that few people are educated. You don't have to try that hard to imagine this condition—our ancestors lived this way. With hard work, thrift and intelligence, a society can gradually climb out of poverty, unless it gets trapped.*

---

[9] See 'Africa Hunger and Poverty Facts', accessed on the 23rd of February 2014 at: http://www.worldhunger.org/articles/Learn/africa_hunger_facts.htm.

A further possible explanation is that economic entrapment is indeed eminent when African states are ruled by gangster politicians, unintelligent dictators and 'animals in human skin' (using the aphorism of the late Fela Anikulapo-Kuti). These attributes tend to generate conflict either during or after such regimes. Radical groups appeal to the socio-economic conditions of their target population in attracting recruits. The values pursued by these radical groups include an opposition to oppression in all forms. They promote conservatism pointing out that exploitation is the cause-effect for the present predicament of individuals in their current state of impoverishment. The economic and social condition of a population is likely to generate grievance which is exploited by radical groups in gaining converts. On the part of the recruits, the economic benefits of membership and the idea of fighting for a worthy cause against 'oppression and inequality' are some of the factors which encourage them in joining radical groups. Thus, according to Hundley (2011:25):

> *Religious elites even argued that America used globalisation both in an attempt to spread its materialistic values and to offer freedoms and human rights as a bribe to steer Muslims away from their 'perfect' morality and faith. Additionally, these elites believed that secularisation—inherent to globalisation—is an attempt to institutionalise the removal of Islam from thought and action, so that Muslims become subservient to the West.*

It can plausibly be argued that, poverty alone is not responsible for the growth of radicals. Perhaps, the best and most articulate appreciation of the "rising poverty/rising conflict" model to explain the phenomenon of terrorism in global setting can be found in Adekanye (2007). Adekanye (2007:219) argues that there may exist other "structural background conditions" that generates terrorism in Africa.

He notes that factors such as differences between groups or individuals, customs, language, culture, religious and social identities are contributory dynamics of terrorism in Africa. Moreover, radicalism and even home grown terrorism will not exist in various developed countries in the Western world. Although, most pertinently, it is observed that the urban slums or ghettos of most European cities inhabited by families of poor, young, employed and maladjusted immigrants that radical Islam has come to find some of its most ardent supporters and recruits. The validity of this assertion is made succinct in consideration of probable factors which in conjunction with poverty may generate radicalism. Thus, factors such as oppression, prebendalism, deepening impoverishment of the masses and undue exploitation by a certain group in society may create a strong drive for radical growth. Therefore, the prolonged grievance exuding from the continued deprivation of basic essentialities may motivate groups to encourage radicalism. In citing an example of the economic variant of which one can point to the number of unemployed and uneducated youths in northern Nigeria, northern Mali and Algeria. For instance, one of the factors that aided the growth of Boko Haram in northern Nigeria was the high number of unemployed youths and *Almajiri*[10] who depended on either alms or rich benefactors for their daily sustenance. It is then not surprising that the *Almajiri* are prone to commit crimes. The construction of this reality was observed by Becker (1968), who perceptively argued that crimes emanating from the lack of economic resources are linked to poverty and lack of education. In an attempt to solve the associated problems attached to the *Almajiri,* Nigerian former President Goodluck Jonathan in 2012, initiated the Almajiri School Project, which is to provide educational and learning schemes to the downtrodden youths, especially in northeastern Nigeria, which is the centre of Boko Haram activities.

---

10     Unemployed young men/boys who are usually homeless.

A testable proposition is that there are economic incentives for participating in acts of terrorism and being a member of radical groups (Pham, 2011). Radical Muslims are offered a better hope and a better life in their societies and if they die—with the promise of an afterlife. Since conflict finds a place to germinate in such societies, it is then not surprising that Islamists have found a fertile land to wage war against perceived economic grievance. In societies where Muslims are majority, Islamist groups tend to organise individuals in believing that they have answers to these grievances (Barsalou, 2002). The use of religious sentiments to whip the passions of the individuals to formulate groups based on radicalism is to seek a process of eliminating grievances. Thus, it is readily observed that counterterrorist programs focused on de-radicalisation and stresses the need to promote some economic incentives in order to reduce the potential for these individuals to join the radical groups. One of such programmes was the Commander's Emergency Response Program (CERP) in Afghanistan and Pakistan.

The third rationale is where religion is a strong identity marker of Muslims. The arguments for religious primordialism are useful in understanding the historical determinism of Muslims mainly in non-Westernised societies (Olomojobi, 2013). For instance, Uthman dan Fodio's Jihâdist ideology and Arab activity are strong factors in explaining Islamisation and the primordialism of an Islamic identity amongst Muslims in some parts of Africa.

Equally important, is the fact that the strong identity marker of Islam promotes the quest for Islamic education. Islamic education has been given priority especially when one considers the various madrassas, mosques and institutions which are involved in the propagation of Islam. It is said that the propagation of Islam is also a duty of the ruling families in Saudi Arabia who have built various mosques, and invested heavily in promotion of their doctrine *(Wahhabism)*. However, some of these institutions of learning have been used to radicalise individuals thereby transforming them into cold blooded killers (Barkley, 2012). According to Farmer (2007): "The Saudi government and philanthropists have over the last thirty years on missionary activity and education to spread *Wahhabi* Islam. The results have been impressive as who's who of global jihâdist terrorism have arisen from the *Wahhabi* sect." *Wahhabis* in recent years have also proven to be part of the Takfiri, who are individuals who believe it is justified to kill Muslims who commit apostasy and collaborate with the enemy. [11]

What is equally, if not more important, is that it should be stressed that Africa has witnessed successive jihâds, starting from the time of King Muhammad Ture (1493–1528) of the Songhai Empire (founder of the Askiya Dynasty) who used a jihâd to reinforce his rule and revive the trans-Saharan trade. Diverse Islamists groups in Africa have embarked upon a seemingly interconnected jihâd due to grievances toward their socio-economic realities. The present problems of Africa are perceived to be as a result of colonialism — hence the West to the radical Muslim is regarded as the root of all evil. So it seems correct to infer that radical Islam is a precursor to terrorism. It is then safe to argue that Islam being a strong identity marker in most African societies generated the radicalisation of Islamic groups in the region. In a comparable manner which are also aggrieved towards perceived American hegemony.

It appears altogether not surprising that Islamists who possess a transnational connection perceive that the influence of colonisation and Western ideals of secularisation have influenced the socio-economic meltdown of their society. However, the question that remains unanswered is that

---

11   Farmer (2007) observed that fifteen of the nineteen 9/11 hijackers were from the sect. Furthermore, other notable members are Abu Al-Maddassi, mentor of al-Zarqawi, leader of Al Qaeda and Osama bin Laden.

if we strongly contend that Africa is in an abysmal state of meltdown in terms of socio-economic development due to colonialism—now that African states have gained independence—what have Africans and its leaders done to avert this appalling state of socio-economic disarray?

The fourth condition is the indefatigability of corrupt and prebendalistic regimes in Africa. It is useful to note that "...Africa is home to more failing states than any other region in the whole world" (Terdman, 2007:4). These features of Africa's predicament has been obvious as early as 1966 when Aristide Zolberg, an eminent political scientist commented of the state of Africa: "The most salient characteristic of political life is that it constitutes an almost institutionless arena with conflict and disorder as its most prominent features" (Joseph, 2003: 161). An even more abysmal depiction is provided by Mbembe (2001:3):

*Africa is portrayed as a vast dark cave where every benchmark and distinction come together in total confusion, and the rifts of tragic and unhappy human history stand revealed; a mixture of the half-created and the incomplete, strange signs, compulsive movements, in short a bottomless abyss where everything is noise, yawning gaps and primordial chaos.*

What seems dispiriting about this reality is that it is self-inflicted—created by African leaders who are thirsty of ripping the continent of its natural beauty and resources. The *vampidisation* of Africa has riddled the continent with crises and conflicts. This is illustrated in the regimes of Ghadaffi of Libya (tribal strife and the birth of local radical Islamic groups), Mubarak of Egypt (constant rebellion by the people and an unstable government) and Abacha in Nigeria (Niger Delta Militants and the augmentation of inter-religious conflicts). It is then not uncommon to agree that:

*This volatile mix of economic disparities and a democratic deficit has provided the ideal recipe for sustained conflict within African politics, laying the seeds of state failure or state collapse* (Solomon, 2013: 429).

Since conflict finds a place to germinate in such societies, it is then not surprising that Islamists have found a fertile land to wage war against perceived economic grievance. In societies where Muslims are majority, Islamist groups tend to organise individuals in believing that they have answers to these grievances. The use of religious sentiments to whip the passions of the people to formulate groups based on extremism.

In order to make sense of the image of Africa, one has to note the observation of Franklyne Ogbunwezeh:

> *The African continent is littered with failed states. Most of these states are economic backwaters, social apologies and political ruins. This landscape runs from the Casablanca to the Cape Town and from The Horn of Africa in the East to the Island of No Return in the West Atlantic. Most of these states true to type were the creatures of imperial convenience. To that end, they were meant to serve a purpose after which their ontological legitimacy or raison d' etre would then expire. At this expiration; the states, naturally not designed for self-propulsion; were condemned to tether on the brink, and finally implode upon the inglorious weight of their inherent contradictions. Colonialism designed and inspired the problems. But the decadence was then driven along by a horde of native pirates; trained in the fine art of piracy. These set of political actors were rogues personalities, weaned on selfishness. They were brilliant students of kleptocracy and political perversity. In about four decades they completely outclassed colonial perfidy and bested them in thievery. They did an inglorious job of mismanaging Africa, so much so that she is today the laughing stock of the world.* [12]

The above narrative, perhaps informs us 'why' and 'how' radical Islam finds a convenient hub in Africa. Africa is coloured

---

[12] Africa: The Ontology of Failed States', accessed on the 19th of March 2014 at: http://www.dawodu.com/ogbunwezeh1.htm.

by incessant conflicts, impoverishment of most of its citizens, the failure of an electoral system, the embedded custom of corruption and the malfunction of an economic system has co-opted radical Muslims to emerge in a quest to find solutions to destroy the decay erupting in their various states.

The fifth reason is based on networks and communication with other radical groups across the world. Through social media the propaganda of spreading hate messages is a crucial variable in formatting radical Islam. Clerics and Imams and heads of communities are capable of using religion as a fog for radical Islam. These have the power to convey messages of hope to underprivileged people in order to brew hatred towards the state. This is in cognisance of the fact that a 'hungry man is an angry man.' Aside from propagandising messages of hate, financing of warfare equipment by transnational networks is procured mainly through social networking. The perceived hatred of Westernised forms of socialisation such as drinking alcohol and its liberal sexual orientation are considered demonic by Islamists.

It is worth noting, at this point that we intend to establish later that the internet has been a useful tool by jihâdist groups.[13] The UN office on drugs and crime (UNODC) (2012:3) identified six categories through which the internet is used to carry out attacks: "propaganda (including recruitment, radicalisation and incitement to terrorism); financing; training; planning (including through secret communication and open-source information); execution; and cyber-attacks."[14] According to Ganor (2011):

> *The internet serves as a critical modern technology that in many cases connects various nodes of a terrorist network. Radical Islamic internet websites, blogs, forums, and chat rooms create virtual radical*

---

13  See Chapter 10.
14  See UNODC (2012) p.3 'Use of Internet for terrorist purposes. New York: United Nations', accessed on the 23rd of December at: http://www.unodc.org/documents/frontpage/Use_of_Internet_for_Terrorist_Purposes.pdf

> *Islamic communities, facilitating the spread of materials of incitement, supporting the radicalisation process and bridging geographic barriers. The internet allows such radical activists to circumvent censorship and prepare recruits to carry out attacks. Instead of the physical training facilities it lost in Afghanistan, al-Qaeda has begun using 'cyber replacements' in order to recruit and train terrorists. The internet provides the organisation direct access to a much larger pool of potential activists, all without the ability of government authorities to effectively monitor or thwart their activities* (Jessee, 2006:380 cited in Ganor, 2011:32).

The sixth aspect is the proliferation of arms and light weapons which has found their way across borders in Africa. According to the report by the Intergovernmental Action Group against money laundering in West Africa (GIABA), the amount generated by arms trade annually is in excess of $ 53 million (GIABA, 2013:3). There is a relationship between proliferation of arms and political instability. On the other hand, the collapse of a political systems or even a regime may have a drastic effect on the nature of proliferation of arms. For example, the end of the Cold War and collapse of the Soviet empire ushered in a new era of surplus arms which surfaced in conflict prone areas, especially in Africa and Asia. The existence of surplus arms may fuel conflict which may destabilise a country. Muammar Gadhafi, during his forty-two year reign as President of Libya was known to have sponsored, armed and trained the Tuareg, using them to carry out his political agenda in neighbouring countries such as Chad. Following Gadhafi's death during the Libyan civil war, the Tuareg returned to Mali with a surplus cache of arms from the Libyan conflict and waged an Islamist insurgency against the Malian government. According to a GIABA report, there were over 174,000 illicit firearms in Mali in 2012 alone.[15]

---

15 See GIABA (2013) 'The nexus between small arms and light weapons and money laundering and terrorist financing in West Africa', assessed on the 15th of September 2014 at: http://web.giaba.org/media/f/613_519_GIABA%20SALW%20Nexus-final.pdf

One of the factors which aided the movement of arms into Mali was the porous nature of the borders and the marginalisation of the Northern part of Mali from the South were the Central government was located. These arms fuelled conflict, especially in areas where government presence is weak or corrupt. The return of the Tuaregs to Mali with surplus arms was one of the factors which resulted in the formation of the National Tuareg Liberation Movement (MNLA) which took over Northern Mali. The already existing grievance against corruption in which funds earmarked for the provision of infrastructure and other basic services had been diverted made the Tuareg rebellion acceptable to the local population (Haysom 2014:2). The surplus arms and training the Tuareg rebels received in Libya made their insurgency against the Malian army a formidable one (see chapter 7).

## Conclusion

This chapter has endeavoured to highlight an approach of excogitating radical Islam in Africa. It has also charted the 'why' and 'how' radical Islam finds a place and space to operate on the continent. Perhaps most important, is that it reveals the importance of religion (Islam) in African political system.

# References

Adekanye, J. B. 2007. Linking Conflict Diagnosis, Conflict Prevention, and Conflict Management in Contemporary Africa: S elected essays. Ibadan: Ababa Press Ltd.

Ajaegbu, O. O., 2012. 'Rising Youth Unemployment and Violent Crime in Nigeria', American Journal of Social Issues and Humanities, 2(5).

Amit, Ron, 2002. 'Regression Analysis and the Philosophy of Social Science: A Critical Realist View', Journal of Critical Realism 1:1: 119-142.

Andrade, Roy, G.D., 1984. 'Cultural Meaning Systems', in Shweder, Richard, A., & Levine, Robert, A., (Ed.) Cultural Theory: Essays on Mind, Self and Emotion. Cambridge: Cambridge University Press: 88-122.

Archer, Margaret; Sharp, Rachel; Stones, Rob & Woodwiss, Tony (1999) 'Critical Realism and Research Methodology', (Opening remarks at the second plenary, CC Conference, Essex, 1998; Abridge), Journal of Critical Realism Alethia Vol 2 No.1, pp 12-16.

Barkley, L., 2012. Has Wahhabi Islam played a part in the rise of global terrorism? (Doctoral Dissertation, School of Theology, Religious Studies and Islamic Studies).

Barsalou, J. M., 2002. Islamic Extremists: How do they mobilize support?. US Institute of Peace.

Becker, G., 1968. 'Crime and Punishment: An Economic Approach', The Journal of Political Economy, 76, 169– 217.

Bentley, Arthur, 1994.The Process of Government: a Study of Social Pressures. New Brunswick, N.J.: Transaction

# References

Benton, T. & Craib, I., 2001. Philosophy of Social Science: The Philosophical Foundations of Social Thought. Basingstoke: Palgrave.

Bhaskar, R, 1993. Reclaiming Reality. London: Verso.

Bhaskar, R., 1998. 'Philosophy and Scientific Realism', in Archer, M., et al. ed., Critical Realism: Essential Readings, London: Routledge: 16-47.

Bhaskar, Roy, & Callinicos, Alex, 2003. 'Marxism and Critical Realism: A Debate', Journal of Critical Realism 1.2: 89-114.

Blaike, N., 1993. Approaches to Social Enquiry. Oxford: Polity Press.

Blomberg, S. Brock; Gregory D Hess & Akila Weerapana, 2004. 'Economic Conditions and Terrorism,' European Journal of Political Economy 20(2): 463–478.

Botha, Anneli, 2008. 'Challenges in Understanding Terrorism in Africa: A human Security Perspective', African Security Review 17:2, 28-41.

Bricmont Jean. 2001. 'Sociology and Epistemology', in Lopez, Jose & Potter, Garry (Eds.) 2001. After Postmodernism: An Introduction to Critical Realism. London: Athlone Press: 100-115.

Carter, Bob, 1998. "Dangerous Phrases: Realism," Race and Social Science, Journal of Critical Realism Alethia Vol 1 No.2: 5-8.

Collier, Andrew, 1994. Critical Realism: An Introduction to Roy Bhaskar's Philosophy. London: Verso.

Collier, Andrew, 1999. A'bout Aboutness', Journal of Critical Realism Alethia Vol. 2 No1: 2-5.

Collier, Paul, 2008. The Bottom Billion: Why the Poorest Countries are Failing and What Can Be Done About It. Oxford: Oxford University Press.

Crenshaw, Martha, 1998. 'Questions, Research, and Knowledge', in Reich, Walter. 1998. Origins of Terrorism; Psychologies, Ideologies, Theologies, States of Mind. Washington, D.C.: Woodrow Wilson Center Press: 247-260.

Dallas, M., 1982. 'Introduction to Philosophy', accessed on 11th July 2010 at: http://www.emporia.edu/socsci/philos/chp11.htm.

Danermark, Berth; Matts Ekstrom; Liselotte Jakobsen & Jan Ch. Karlsson, 2002. Explaining Society: Critical Realism in the Social Science. London & New York: Routledge.

Dobson, Philip J., 2002. 'Critical Realism and Information Systems Research: Why Bother With Philosophy?', Information Research, 7(2) [Available at http://InformationR.net/ir/7-2/paper124.html] Assessed on 10th March 2010.

Esposito, J. L., 1999. The Islamic threat: Myth or reality? Oxford University Press.

Esposito, J. L., 2002. Unholy war: Terror in the name of Islam. Oxford University Press.

Faksh, M. A. (1997). The Future of Islam in the Middle East: Fundamentalism in Egypt, Algeria, and Saudi Arabia. Greenwood Publishing Group.

Farmer, B. R., 2007. Understanding Radical Islam: Medieval Ideology in the Twenty-First Century. New York: Peter Lang.

Fay, Brian, 1990. 'Critical Realism?', Journal for the Theory of Social Behaviour, Vol. 20: 33-41.

Fraassen, Van, 1980. The Scientific Image. Oxford: Clarendon Press.

# References

Geertz, Clifford, 1973. The Interpretation of Culture: Selected Essays. London: Fontana Press.

Ganor, B., 2011. 'Trends in Modern International Terrorism', in Weisburd, David; Feucht, Thomas; Hakimi, Idit; Mock, Lois and Perry, Simon (Eds). 2011. To Protect and To Serve Policing in an Age of Terrorism. New York: Springer: 11-42.

Govier, Trudy, 2002. A Delicate Balance: What Philosophy Can Tell Us About Terrorism. Cambridge, Mass: Westview Press.

Hammersley, Martyn, (2002) 'Research as Emancipatory: The Case of Bhaskar's Critical Realism', Journal of Critical Realism 1: 33-48.

Handley, Geoff, Higgins, Kate and Sharma, Bhavna with Bird, Kate and Cammack, Diana, 2009. 'Poverty and Poverty Reductionin sub-Saharan Africa: An overview of the issues', Working Paper 299, Results of ODI research presented in preliminary form for discussion and critical comment.

Hogg, M. A., & Abrams, D. 1988. Collective Identity: Group Membership and Self-Conception. In M. B. Brewer & M. Hewstone (Eds.), 1988. Self and Social Identity. Malden, MA: Blackwell: 147–181.

Howard, Tiffiany, 2010. 'Failed States and the Spread of Terrorism in Sub-Saharan Africa', Studies in Conflict & Terrorism, 33:11, 960-988.

Hundley, L. (2011). Repeated Failures: Explaining the Rise and Tactics of the Current Wave of Radical Islamic Terrorism. The Monitor, 18-30.

Fukuyama, Francis, 1989. 'The End of History?', National Interest, 16.

Fukuyama, Francis & Samin, Nadav, 2002. Can Any Good Come of Radical Islam? Commentary, 34-38.

Hafez, Mohammed, 2003. Why Muslims Rebel: Repression and Resistance in the Islamic World. Boulder, Colo.: Lynne Rienner.

Haysom Simone, 2014. 'Security and Humanitarian Crisis in Mali. The Role of International Organisations', HPG Working Paper, assessed on the 27th of September, 2014 at: http://www.odi.org.uk/sites/odi.org.uk/files/odi-assets/publications-opinion-files/8829.pdf.

Huntington, Samuel P., 1996. The Clash of Civilizations and the Remaking of World Order. New York: Simon & Schuster Uk Ltd.

Joseph, A.Richard, 2003. 'Africa: States in Crisis', Journal of Democracy, Volume 14, Number 3: 159-170.

Juergensmeyer, Mark, 1993. The New Cold War? Religious Nationalism Confronts the Secular State. Berkeley: University of California Press.

Kepel, Gilles, 2006. Jihad: The Trail of Political Islam. London: I.B. Tauris & Co Ltd.

Lacher, W 2013. The Malian Crisis and the Challenge of Regional Cooperation. Stability: International Journal of Security and Development 2(2):18.

Letiche, M. John, 2010. 'Transforming sub-Saharan Africa', Journal of Policy Modeling 32: 163–175.

Mbembe, Achille, 2001.On the Postcolony. Berkeley: University of California Press.

Munson, Ziad, 2008. 'Terrorism', Contexts, 7: 78.

Norris, Christopher, 2003. 'Response-Dependence: What's in It for the Realist?' Journal of Critical Realism, 1.2: 61-88.

O'Connor, Anthony, 1991. Poverty in Africa: A Geographical Approach. London: Belhaven Press.

Okonkwo, H. I., & Alhaji, I. M., 2014. 'Contemporary Issues in Nomadic, Minority and Almajiri Education, Problems and Prospects', Journal of Education and Practice, 5 (24), 19-27.

Olomojobi, Yinka, 2013. Islam and Conflict in northern Nigeria. Lagos: Malthouse Press.

Patomäki, Heikki, 2006. 'Realist Ontology for Futures Studies', Journal of Critical Realism Volume 5, Number 1, pp. 1-31(31).

Pham, J. P. (2011). The dangerous "Pragmatism" of Al-Qaeda in the Islamic Maghreb. The Journal of the Middle East and Africa, 2 (1), 15-29.

Phares, Walid, 2007. Jihadism against Democracy: The War of Ideas. New York; Basingstoke: Palgrave MacMillan.

Pipes, Daniel, 2001. Commentary, November, 19-24.

Pipes, Daniel, 2004. 'God and Mammon: Does Poverty Cause Militant Islam?', in Martin, Gus. (ed.), The New Era of Terrorism: Selected Readings. Thousand Oaks: SAGE.

Porpora V. Douglas, 2001. 'Do Realists Run Regressions?' in Lopez, Jose & Potter, Garry (Eds.) 2001. After Postmodernism: An Introduction to Critical Realism. London: Athlone Press: 260-271.

Sayer, A., 1984. Method in Social Science: A Realist Approach. New York: Hutchinson Publishing Group.

Sayer, A., 2000. Realism and Social Science. London: Sage Publications.

Shannon, P. Vaughn and Dennis, Michael, 2007. 'Militant Islam and the Futile Fight for Reputation', Security Studies 16, no. 2: 287–317.

Smith, E. R., 1993. 'Social Identity and Social Emotions: Toward New Conceptualizations of Prejudice', in D. M. Mackie & D. L. Hamilton (Eds.), Affect, cognition, and stereotyping: Interactive processes in group perception. San Diego, CA: Academic Press: 297–315.

Smith, V. A. 1920. The Oxford History of India: From the Earliest Times to the End of 1911. Oxford: Clarendon Press.

Solomon, Hussein. 2013. The African state and the failure of US counterterrorism initiatives in Africa: The cases of Nigeria and Mali, South African Journal of International Affairs, 20:3, 427-445.

Smith, Charles W., 1979. A Critique of Sociological Reasoning. Oxford: Basil Blackwell.

Stith, R. Charles, 2010. 'Radical Islam in East Africa', The ANNALS of the American Academy of Political and Social Science, 632: 55.

Stones, Rob. 1996. Sociological Reasoning: Towards a Past-Modern Sociology. London; New York: Palgrave Macmillan Press.

Sugeman, Marc, 2008. Leaderless Jihâd: Terror Networks in the Twenty First Century. Philadelphia: University of Pennsylvania Press.

Tansey, James & O'riordan, Tim, 1999. 'Cultural Theory and Risk: A Review', Health, Risk & Society, Vol. 1, No. 1: 71-91.

Terdman, Moshe, 2007. 'Factors Facilitating the Rise of Radical Islamism and Terrorism in Sub-Saharan Africa',Global Research in International Affairs (Gloria) Center, The Project for the Research of Islamist Movements, African Occasional Papers, Volume 1, Number 1: 1-12.

Tausch, Nicole, 2011. 'Explaining Radical Group Behavior: Developing Emotion and Efficacy Routes to Normative and Nonnormative Collective Action', Journal of Personality and

# References

Social Psychology, American Psychological Association, Vol. 101, No. 1, 129–148.

Washington, James, M., 1991. The Essential Writings and Speeches of Martin Luther King Jr: A Testament of Hope. NewYork: Harper Collins Publishers.

Roussillon, Alain. 2002. 'Radical Islam after 11 September', The International Spectator: Italian Journal of International Affairs, 37:1, 35-45.

# 2

# Why Religion Matters

## Introduction

Any attempt to define religion would definitely have gaps with its interpretation. Different definitions have been formulated by historians, religious scholars, sociologists, anthropologists and political scientists. Yinger (Batson et al., 1993:6) rightly asserts that "any definition of religion is likely to be satisfactory only to its author" by reason of the fact that there are temples, churches, mosques, gods and spirits mediums. In this context, religion is as vast and broad as the cultures of the world. It is a phenomenon that means different things to different people. All notions of religion are centered on beliefs which are deeply rooted in the individual's sub-consciousness; hence, they are transcendental and metaphysical in context.

In an endeavor to provide an adequate definition of religion, Mcguire (1992) classified the meaning of religion into two definitions: substantive and functional. On the former, she attempts to define what religion really is. Mcguire adopts Spiro's definition of religion as "an institution consisting of culturally patterned interaction with culturally postulated superhuman beings" (Mcguire, 1992:11). It places emphasis on understanding human nature and its primordial origins of religion. On the latter, Mcguire adopts Geertz's celebrated and universally acclaimed definition, which emphasises religion's attachment to the individual and the social group. Geertz (1966:4) defines religion as "a system of symbols which acts to establish powerful, pervasive, and long-lasting moods and motivations in men by formulating conceptions of a general order of existence and clothing these conceptions with such an aura of factuality that the moods and motivations seem uniquely realistic." Here, it would appear that religion is defined by how it shapes our world and society.

Indeed, religion understood perceptively is therefore, a belief. This belief may be in the supernatural or natural phenomenon. However, religion entails a personal conviction; a conviction that induces a hope and an assurance of a transcendental intervention of infinite forces in the finite and mundane affairs of the believers. Perhaps with this in mind, Huntington (1996:27) defines religion as "the central force that motivates and mobilises people." This implies that religion defines what man is and defines his society. "Belief is a thought in your mind that causes the power of your subconscious to be distributed into all phases of your life according to your thinking habits" (Murphy, 1988:63). Clearly then, 'religion makes man' rather than 'man makes religion.' Therefore, it is acceptable that "all religions of the world represent forms of belief, and those beliefs are explained in many ways. The law of life is belief" (Murphy, 1988: 63). To a great extent in all societies, religion distinguishes what is good from what is bad. To its adherents, religious beliefs may be considered more important than life itself, as religion is used to explain the significance of life, the mysteries of life, an understanding of the universe, the environment and everything within it. It is important to note that religion lends a hand in explaining misfortune and prosperity to the individual.

No society has been known to exist without a religion. Religion determines the social conditions for societal identification. Furthermore, religion is at the core of the existence of man. Religion has provided the foundation for organic human existence, environmental health, jurisprudence, social harmony and family life. Man fashions religion for his own ends, which is usually the quest for happiness, power and wealth. Religion has been given different interpretations to suit political purposes, thus implying the possibility of religion to be humanly manipulated, corrupted, misrepresented and misinterpreted. This explains the foundation of the pervasive religious crisis regarded as the clash of ideologies. It was to this effect that Christianity, for instance, was a tool used in fostering ethno-nationalism in the Roman Empire, just as Islam presently is a tool of Arab ethno-nationalism and resistance to Westernisation and Americanisation of the Middle East.

## Classical theories of religion

The object of this section is to consider the early intellectual meanings of religion. These classical definitions have laid the foundation of overcoming the problematic definition of the subject. Although these classical definitions may be limited in scope, they provide robust insights into what religion is. Moreover, since religion is deeply rooted in all societies, it is useful to explore some definitions of what religion is.

## Functionalist approach

Marx's account on religion is the most popular study and critique of religious belief. He argues that *Die Religion ... ist das Opium des Volkes* – Religion is the opium of the people. To Marx, religion is an illusion that enables society to function. Religion helps to keep individual(s) complacent and enslaved by the suffocating and exploitative capitalist system. The Marxist ideology diminishes the socialisation of religion.

**To Marx:**

> *Religion is the general theory of this world, its encyclopedic compendium, its logic in popular form, its spiritual point d'honneur, its enthusiasm, its moral sanction, its solemn complement, and its universal basis of consolation and justification. It is the fantastic realisation of the human essence since the human essence has not acquired any true reality. The struggle against religion is, therefore, indirectly the struggle against that world whose spiritual aroma is religion* (Bruce, 1995:30).

All religious beliefs, Marx tells us, were made by man. Marx advocates for the abolition of religion so as to improvise the provision of 'real happiness' for people. Marx considers religion as a veil over people's eyes—a veil used as a mechanism to control people or to keep people in servitude.

Furthermore, Marx argues that the institution of religion is rooted in economics rather than divinity and the supernatural. Marx advocates dialectical materialism as a tool for the negation of the oppressive hold of religion on mass consciousness. And with dialecticism, the struggles of opposites would ensure the survival of superior forces, which consists of scientific empiricism. Thus to Marx, revolutionary postulation advocates the clash of the proletariats against their bourgeois oppressors for the redistribution of wealth and the eradication of religion, which is used as a weapon of control against the proletariat and as an obstacle to social and progressive change.

## Sociological approach

Weber in his treatise, *'The Social Psychology of the World Religions'*[16] identifies six religions: Confucianism, Hinduism, Buddhism, Christianity, Islam and Judaism. To Weber, religion is determined by economic and political factors within a geographical domain. Social, political and economic interests mould religious thought and ideology. In contradistinction to Marx, Weber argues that religion is not based solely on economic determinism but equally on social, political and economic practices. Weber argues that:

> *Not ideas, but material and ideal interests, directly govern men [and women's] conduct. Yet, very frequently the "world images" that have been created by "ideas" have, like switchmen, determined the tracks along which action has been pushed by the dynamics of interest. "From what" and "for what" one wished to be redeemed and, let us not forget, "could be" redeemed, depended upon one's image of the world* (Bruce, 1995:26).

Weber asserts that the primitive notion of suffering is explained by religion and, therefore, generates the psychological need for religion to exist. Religion provides the 'theodicy of good fortune' for those who are fortunate to encounter wealth and different forms of chastisement and abstinences are channels to attain phenomenal powers. Religion also promises salvation or the 'cure of the soul' which is comparable to the 'confession of sins.' For Weber, religion gives the individual the assurance of a saviour.

Weber in his treatise, attempts to define religion from a subjective view of experiences, notions, purposes and ideas of an individual. Weber articulates that man is attached to religion for oriented reasons, "That it may go well with you... and that you may prolong your days upon the earth."[17] Weber perceives

---

16   Weber's celebrated work on the study of religion is 'the protestant Ethic and the Spirit of Capitalism.' In this treatise, Weber seeks explanations on the protestant ethic or the doctrine of Calvinism and western capitalism wherein capitalism grew as a result of the protestant influence in encouraging people to form enterprise and the creation of wealth. See Bruce, 1995.
17   Deuteronomy 4:40.

God to be in the form of an 'enduring being.' This unique nature is the acceptance of a god as an enduring being and exists as a 'continuing activity' of a sect dedicated to God.

Among Weber's various concepts of God—is God as the 'God of Economy.' Here, Weber affirms that religion has been shaped by the 'economic situation' and the past of a people. Weber also notes that religion is not based purely on economic interests but is 'irrationalised' by other non-economic variables such as social and cultural determinants with economic factors at the background. Hence, all religions without exception are individually and communally conditioned. It can then be asserted that religion is often particularistic.

In evaluating both the Marxian and Weberian approach to religion, the basic similarity is that they both deny the existence of God and correspondingly argue that religion is a mechanism for social control. For Marx, the explanation for religion is located absolutely in economic motives. Weber added social, cultural and political factors in his explication of religion.

## Positivist approach

Durkheim in his treatise, *'The Elementary Forms of the Religious Life'* defines religion as "a unified system of beliefs and practices relative to sacred things…things set apart and forbidden—beliefs and practices which unite into one single moral community called a church, all those who adhere to them" (Bruce, 1995:44). Religion is the foundation of philosophy and science and that religion is within the ambits of social phenomenon. To Durkheim, religion provides a sense of social unity. He attributes that religious symbols are essential links to collective realities of a group and as such produce and preserve a collective awareness to these groups.

What is important to observe in the work of Durkheim is that all forms of thought and the structure of a social commonality falls in the existence of religion. Religious epistemological origins lie in time, space, class, force, personality and efficacy. Durkheim argues that 'God is society.' Durkheim views religion as the epitome of society, and that society is a symbol of civilisation. Durkheim considers totemism as the earliest form of religion. This is where symbols or a 'material expression' are considered as sentimental connotations to the individual.

## Psychoanalyst approach

In 1927, Freud wrote a manuscript titled, 'Civilisation and its Discontents.' Freud approaches religion from a psychoanalytical approach. Freud had an attraction to the occult sciences and to witchcraft. In his treatise, 'The Future of an Illusion,' Freud rationalised a religious belief to be within the concept of belief that is based on an 'infantile prototype.' This presupposes that beliefs are unchangeable and static once grounded in the individual as an infant. If religion is introduced to a child, it tends to have an enduring impact throughout the life of the individual.

To Freud, religion is innate in the individual due to 'man's helplessness and need for protection.' His argument for psychoanalysis is based on an individual's experience from childhood. According to Freud's psychoanalysis of religion and the individual, he notes that an individual:

> *is destined to remain a child forever, that he can never do without protection against strange superior powers, he lends those powers the features belonging to the figure of his father; he creates for himself the gods whom he dreads, whom he seeks for himself the gods whom he dreads, whom he seeks to propitiate, and whom he nevertheless entrusts with his own protection* (Bruce, 1995:204).

The child's longing for a father figure is a motive identical with his need for protection against the consequences of his human weakness. In these and similar discussions, Freud's analysis explains how deep religious karmic foundations are rooted in the individual.

Presently, there are attempts to re-Christianise Europe by Christian movements (Kepel, 1994:47). While claiming that there is a global religious revitalisation and de-secularisation of the world (Haynes, 2002:316), the ancient divine right of the monarchy over its subjects and its property has withered away in Western Europe at the onset of modernity. The withering of this 'divine right' has been instrumental to modernity and the establishment of 'secular nationalism.' Bearing this in mind, Juergensmeyer (1993:18) argues that secular nationalism is a kind of religion, as it answers the same needs for the individual identity.

## Instrumentalist approach

Religious instrumentalism posits the positivist ideology that religious belief cannot be authenticated empirically. The rationale of this argument is that religious objectifications such as God, angels, hell and/or heaven are not observable events/facts and therefore are non-deductible phenomena. Thus, the concept of truth to the religious instrumentalist is that it must have a verification mechanism. Chalmers (1999:4) helps us in understanding the verification process when he perceptively notes that, "a human observer has more or less direct access to knowledge of some facts about the world insofar as they are recorded in the brain in the act of seeing...two normal observers viewing the same object or scene from the same place will 'see' the same thing."

However, according to Braithwaite (1977), there are three main divisions of statement to validate truths: observation statements about empirical facts; scientific theorems and empirical facts and statements of mathematics and logical data. However, beyond the glory of science and its empiricist approach to observation, Braithwaite argues that although religious beliefs cannot be empirically verified, they have a functional role and a systematisation control over society and therefore cannot be wished away. In essence, religious instrumentalism does not probe truths or falsification about religion, but searches into the social construction of religion. In other words, religion is constructed through destruction and therefore, it is subject to reconstruction.

Religious instrumentalism probes into the idiosyncrasy of how religion shapes the individual and society. In interrogating the function of religion in predominantly African societies, religion is used to manage, mobilise, control and/or influence people for dominance and oppression. Since a majority of Africans display strong affinity in religion, it then has the propensity to be used as a vehicle to manipulate people for self interests of the elites. It is argued that the elites use religion as a political tool in order to amass patriotism from the masses for the reason that it is malleable to appeal to the sub-conscience of the common man/woman. One is tempted to enquire into Samuel Johnson's 1775 acclaimed statement: 'Is patriotism the last refuge of a scoundrel?'

## Between Fundamentalism and Extremism

The word 'fundamentalism'or 'fundamentalist' is a label that is altogether disconcerting and shrouded in complexity. During the Cold War, 'fundamentalism' was closely linked with communism by Western democracies. However, since the end of the Cold War, the label is frequently used as an insignia for fanatism. According to this perception, Euben (1999:44) argues that, "fundamentalism is a vehicle for reactionary, fanatical sentiment, which, given slightly different historical and political circumstances, might just as easily express itself in Marxism, or any other ideology similarly equipped to register the cry of the extremist." Religious fundamentalism is often referred to the early Christian crusades and in the rise of Protestant fundamentalism in America in the 19th Century. However, in the modern era, it has become fashionable to use the term to describe Islamic resurgence, especially after the Islamic revolution in Iran in 1979. Furthermore, after the 9/11 incident, it has been used as an identity marker for radical Muslims. In this context, if we extend this label towards religion, one may argue in a constricted manner that fundamentalism is a stereotypic adherence to a deviant and absurd form of a strict religious doctrine, which generates an extreme intolerance to other faiths, and is practiced in contrast to the orthodox and theological teachings of its sacred tradition. What is constructed here in a limited observation is that, "fundamentalism forms a strong mark in the individual's mind and has the tendency to commandeer the individual to fight and die for his religious belief and to embrace notions of justifiable homicide. This appeal is attached with some mystical reward in the afterlife" (Olomojobi, 2013:48). Religious fundamentalism separates an individual's religion from another. However, in respect of the explanation of an individual being labelled within the paradigm of religious 'fundamentalism'or 'fundamentalist', is that it may be argued that it is a positive aspect of an individual's religion. The argument here is that there are notions of confusion as to the definitions of religious fundamentalism and religious extremism. It is pertinent to point out that fundamentalism is often times confused with extremism. It then seems reasonable to enquire into an interesting dialogue:

> But the question about what is wrong in being fundamental remains unanswered. To abide by the laws of any profession or trade, an individual must abide by its fundamental doctrines, rules or guidelines. Thus, being fundamental about a religious belief may be insinuated to mean the correct doctrinal practices of that religion (Olomojobi, 2013:65).

Conversely, when the term extremism as opposed to fundamentalism is used, then it may be correct to define the former as:

> *the belief that there is only one correct set of religious teachings that clearly contains the fundamental, basic, intrinsic, essential, inerrant truth about humanity and the deity; that this essential truth is fundamentally opposed by forces of evil, which must be vigorously fought; that this truth must be followed today according to the fundamental, unchangeable practices of the past; and that those who believe and follow these fundamental teachings have a special relationship with the deity* (Altemeyer & Hunsberger, 1992: 118).

An extremist uses his/her religion as a forum for political militancy or advocacy. In this aspect, the divine command of the religion are coloured to generate an opinionated view of the essence of the dictates of one's religious obligations. These different colourations ultimately give rise to radical Islam. In understanding radical Islam, Calvert, (2004:40-41) notes that:

> *Radical Islamism is a fundamental, though disturbing, aspect of the modern experience of Muslims, anchored in the historical record of suppression by imperialist outsiders. Through recourse to the power of images drawn from the cultural memory of Muslims, radical Islamists have been able to craft a novel and uncompromising understanding of Islam, one whose core myth aims to inspire a movement of purifying, cathartic community rebirth. By demonising the political and cultural moorings of the Western 'other.'*

Within this interpretation, Wiktorowicz & Kaltenthaler (2006) using a rational choice argument note that radical Islamic groups use irrational modes of violence due to a spiritual incentive that lures Islamists into radical warfare. These spiritual incentives are most times in the form of religious indoctrination. This act is noticed with non-scriptural promises of salvation to martyrs and the assurance of being granted a prestigious life in heaven, such as being betrothed to seventy-seven beautiful virgins in the gardens of paradise. Irshad Manji (2004:57-58) attempts to capriciously explain the pointlessness of this, using the seventy-seven virgins by noting: "Allow me to decode this B-movie lingo for you...It's like a perpetual licence to ejaculate in exchange for a willingness to detonate..." Added to this, an intriguing question would be—what precious gifts are given to women martyrs? Would they be betrothed to handsome and muscular exotic 'chippindales' in paradise? These wild imaginations are confined to utopian ideologies. But the striking question is that how do these utopian illusions or religious fantasies find a place in the minds of radical Muslims? It seems that these individuals who are being shrouded with spiritual ignorance, have a desire to be bastions of death and destruction as they have been systematically scorned by the luxurious lives of individuals (usually politicians) who are intoxicated by ill-gotten wealth—it is then not surprising that the promise of wealth and a blissful life with beautiful damsels could be a motivating factor to enjoy in the afterlife after snivelling and suffering on planet earth. At this point, one is reminded of the popular lyrics of the late Fela Anikulapo-Kuti, 'Suffer suffer for world and enjoy in heaven'. The dearth of suffering perhaps explains the reason why the implementation of a caliphate is a persistent variable in the quest for Islamist groups. An imagined caliphate is perceived to be a final solution to the deprived existence of Muslims living in rentier states embodied by repressive development and ridden within a baseless economic management.

Generally speaking and in the strict sense of the word, the use of religious extremism is not unique to Islam alone. History tells us that Nazi Germany and the Third Reich used Christian extremism to cement its reign of terror on its European neighbours. The perceptions of radical Islam and the ideology of Nazism in Germany are strikingly similar, but they are coded with different phenomena. While Islamists view the world to be living in a state of *jahiliya* (paganism) and the need to eradicate apostates of Islam, Nazi Germany sought to implant the Aryan race as a superlative race to rule the world. More to the point, Hitler used religion (he termed this Positive Christianity), to augment this ideology. Using his words:

*My feelings as a Christian point me to my Lord and Savior as a fighter. It points me to the man who once in loneliness, surrounded by a few followers, recognised these Jews for what they were and summoned men to fight against them and who, God's truth was greatest not as a sufferer but as a fighter. In boundless love as a Christian and as a man, I read through the passage which tells us how the Lord at last rose in His might and seized the scourge to drive out of the temple the brood of vipers and adders. How terrific was His fight for the world against the Jewish poison. Today, after two thousand years, with deepest emotion, I recognise more profoundly than ever before the fact that it was for this that He had to shed His blood upon the Cross. As a Christian, I have no duty to allow myself to be cheated, but I have the duty to be a fighter for truth and justice… And if there is anything which could demonstrate that we are acting rightly, it is the distress that daily grows. For as a Christian, I have also a duty to my own people* (Baynes, 1942: 19-20).[18]

Perhaps a worthy observation between radical Islam and Nazi Germany is that they both were/are desirous of persecuting the Jews.[19] However, given the fact that Hitler was a Christian, it would appear absolutely incoherent if Christianity is blamed for the massacre of six million Jews.

---

18   Adolf Hitler, in a speech on 12 April 1922.
19   In line with this intent, Mahmoud Ahmadinejad, the former president of Iran in 2005 labelled Israel as a 'tumor' that should be wiped off the global map.

However, in another twist in the tale, one is inclined to portray that radical Islam and Nazism have a seemingly similar ideology—a desire to cause terror, death and destruction. History tells us that Haj Amin el-Husseini, the Mufti of Jerusalem in 1921 and the President of the Supreme Muslim Council (1922) attempted to use the position of his respective office to forge an unholy alliance with Hitler in an attempt to rid the world of Jews. In 1942, Haj Amin went on a state visit to Germany in order to create an alliance with Hitler. Haj Amin desired the state of an Arab Palestine. However, such an ambition was only realisable if Germany won the war.

## Between religion and globalisation

In contextualising globalisation, Adekanye (2007:228) argues perceptively that there are both positive and negative aspects of globalisation. In observing the affirmative aspects, he notes that globalisation has co-opted liberal democracy, global economic growth, state of the art communication technology, explosive new international markets and robust consumerism behaviour amongst developed and developing states. In charting the adverse aspects of globalisation, Adekanye notes the unconstructive events such as mass migration to Europe and America and its antecedent brain-drain on developing states, the spread of endemic diseases such as HIV/AIDS and the extension of transnational crime across continents. Furthermore, in showcasing the negative effects of globalisation, Adekanye (2007:229) tells us that: "Easy and fast means of international air travel and migration made possible by globalisation have meant that potential terrorists can jet into another country, perpetrate some acts of terrorist attacks against certain pre-selected targets, and then jet out, only to be found a few hours later mingling with other individuals or groups some continent away." This in some way informs us that globalisation has heightened radical Islam around the globe. Globalisation plays a central function in procuring terrorism. Connecting factors such as e-terrorism and the international flow of information are by-products of globalisation.

Within the context of a broader discourse, Mazrui (1999) has argued that the factors behind globalisation are religion, technology, economy and territorial domain. A key argument for the validity of Mazrui's observation in the context of religion is that religion and globalisation are interwoven into different conglomerations. As Western societies develop into complex systems, the emphasis on religion begins to wither away due to the evolvement of modern ways of implementing traditional knowledge.[20] One may then suggest that secularisation is equated with modernisation. In this model, tradition is confronted with mordernity. The ideals of secularisation are confined to Western societies and have not been adopted by societies where Islam, Buddhism and Hinduism are predominant, even when such societies are modernised (Der Veer 1999:17). In some quarters, extremism in Islam is a religious response to modernity (Tibi, 1993). This seems probable, in light of the prevailing economic decline and the inability to compete with technological development of Western societies. Yet it is important to emphasise that religious primordialism is prevalent in societies where Islam, Buddhism and Hinduism are predominant. The integrative dilemma of post colonialism in most non-Western societies[21] and the absence of a gradual social mobilisation of people (Deutsch, 1963) are factors that engender primordialism in non-Western states. Similarly, Geertz (1963) tells us that primordial ties exist mainly in the 'new states' of Africa and Asia. Likewise, Horowitz (1985) argues that political parties

---

20  Even ideologies based on westernisation may be argued to be withering away. The recent crash of the American financial system can in some ways be seen as the demise of Anglo-Saxon laissez-faire capitalism and a challenge to Fukuyama's (1992) theory on the accomplishment of the westernised society-liberalised capitalism.

21  Western literature has classified non-Western societies with many tags, such as the 'land of the savage people'; the 'uncivilised' world; the 'underdeveloped world'; the 'Third World'; and more recently, the 'Developing States'. However, the phrase; non-Western societies suitably distinguishes and delineates the two civilisations.

tend to be organised along ethnic lines in plural societies such as in Africa, Asia and the West Indies.

It seems glaringly obvious that religious primordialism thrives in non-Western societies due to its persistent decline in the development of economic and educational institutions. Western societies have been able to generate wealth and reduce conflicts, whilst in a vast number of non-Western societies have generated conflict and reduced their potential of creating wealth. It may be argued that when Western societies are threatened with a decline in the development of economic growth, people may seek consolation in religion. The Daily Telegraph (United Kingdom) reported that since December 2008, thousands of individuals in the United Kingdom have been turning to religion due to its economic downturn.[22] Now, it certainly goes too far to equate Western societies with non-Western societies. Yet, in other non-Western societies, which are modern societies, with educational and economic growth, their descriptive make up may not be within the ambits of modernity or secularity. In such systems, tradition and modernity are in collision. Where the state attempts to impose secularisation, the cultural identity of the people may reject such imposition.

For instance, the destruction of the ancient Babri Mosque in India on December 6, 1992 by 200,000 Hindus amounted to a rejection of secularisation of the state.[23] A similar rejection of secularisation of the state is noted in some states in northern Nigeria, where there has been a resurgence of Sharia law. Moreover, there has also been a *jeremidisation* of Christianity in African states and an escalating wave of missionaries from non-Western societies berthing in the Western world. In a broader perspective, the resurgence

---

22    See 'People turning to religion for economic advice', accessed on the 10th of September 2009 at: http://www.telegraph.co.uk/news/newstopics/religion/5146664/People-turning-to-religion-for-economic-advice.html

23    This was due to the Indian Supreme Court ruling prohibiting the building of a Hindu temple that would replace the Mosque as a result 3,000 people lost their lives due to the subsequent carnage.

of religion in both Western and non-Western societies has ushered in a resurgence of Islamist ideology. This is noted by the fact that the advancement in economic and scientific discovery by the West has positioned Muslim societies, especially in Africa to be inclined to poverty and political prebendalism. An explanation of this depiction is that unlike Western states, most African states did not experience social communication (Deutsch, 1953), which generated nation-states. This social transformation was absent in nation-states that evolved through the process of colonialisation. In cognisance of this realisation, Lawrence (1998: 48) argues empathetically that:

> *While most Europeans and Americans have lived within "secure" national borders for several generations and see themselves as beneficiaries of the tradition of nation-state loyalty, many Third World citizens, and Afro-Asian Muslims in particular, do not share either their experience or their trust. For most Muslims, it is hard to applaud the arbitrary, top-down process, imposed from outside, by which almost all Afro-Asians came to assume their present form.*

To emphasise and underline different religious cultures in different states, Lincoln (2003) identifies two cultures: The Maximalist and the Minimalist culture. The former refers to the period wherein religion is the central sphere of the community. This culture was practiced in Europe before the enlightenment era. Today, the Maximalist culture is dominant in non-Western societies, such as the Middle East and in African states. Benjamin Barber (2005:157) identifies the Maximalist culture as the 'Jihâd'—"a throwback to premodern times; an attempt to recapture a world that existed prior to cosmopolitan capitalism and was defined by religious mysteries, hierarchal communities, spellbinding traditions, and historical torpor." The Minimalist culture, on the other hand, is signified by secularised culture. Religion is positioned to the private sphere of the individual and greater emphasis is placed on capitalism. This is prevalent in Western societies. Barber (2005:157) continues with describing this culture as the 'McWorld'—"....Westernisation—that has gone on since the Renaissance birth of modern science and its accompanying paradigm of knowledge constructed as power." Perhaps this delineation is what defines whether the individual has a strong primordial attachment to religion or not. However, one of the incongruities in this analysis is that some Western states, such as the United Kingdom have established a state church—the Church of England, yet, it is still termed as a secular state.

It is purposeful to keep the above characteristics in mind when interconnecting religion and globalisation. As Madan (Der Veer 1999:17) rightly observes—the West has a distinctive characteristic of being secular whilst the East is characterised by religious traditions. Green (2006:12) concurring with Lewis (2002:96) suggests that the concept of secularism has its foundations in Christianity. He illustrates where the founder of the faith, Jesus, admonishes, to "give to Caesar what is Caesar's and to God what is God's"—thus, separating religion from politics. Historically, the quest for secularism came into existence due to the ideological struggle with the Roman Catholic Church, reformation taking place in Europe and the inception of Western enlightenment (Crippen, 1988:318). But the issue here is that secularism is not prevalent in Islamic societies due to the unity of religion and sharia. As pertinently noted by Lewis (2002:100): "The absence of a native secularism in Islam, and the widespread Muslim rejection of an imported secularism exemplified by Christianity, may be caused by certain profound differences of belief and experience in these two religious cultures."[24] The preceding argument may

---

[24] However, the non secularisation of religion practiced in the Middle East is similar with that practiced in African societies, even in societies where Christianity is dominantly practiced. This is in view of the fact that religion has different perceptions by different people in different societies. Another important distinctiveness of both religions is that in Islamic states, especially in the Middle East, an individual's basic identity is in religion as opposed to the Western world where the individual's identity is based on the nation-state (Lewis, 2002: 102).

showcase the seeming clash of Islam and the West. Yates (2007:133) is precise when he notes that:

> *The crux of jihad's hostility, indeed, the basis for the resentment of the jihadists, is that the modern world appears to be made in the image of this godless 'occidentic'; it is the secularising technologies and ideologies of foreign infidels that have shaped the world and which have undermined the authority of traditional Muslim institutions within the umma itself. It is the hegemony of Western ideas in every area of life that appear to seduce and, in turn, degrade Muslim societies; it is the attraction of its globalised popular culture that tempts Muslims to spurn their cultural heritage, customs, and faith in order to ape the decadent and pornographic lifestyles of the West.*

It seems obvious that the individual in a Western society is nurtured on the ideals of classical liberalism, which includes the freedom of thought and religion. This thought eliminates an overwhelming dependence on religion in the Western world. In this current age of globalisation, otherwise referred to as 'McDonaldisation', there persists greater economic activity, new consumer cultures and communicative networks between nations. The concept, globalisation, has always existed but its dynamics has changed to make economic activity between states expedient by technology (Juergensmeyer, 2005:26).

The point, however, is that in modern times, in Western societies, there is a shift from national identity to an individual identity. The individual identity is placed on the growth of capitalism, democracy and education. The shift towards individualism is based on the concepts of a modern economy. The modern economy is based on globalisation, needs and choices and the principles of laissez faire (Frank & Meyer, 2002). These ideals are not pre-eminent in non-Western societies. The ideals of laissez faire and liberal democracy were concepts that took hundreds of years to develop to its present state. Furthermore, it is considered as a threat to some Islamic cultures which are theocratic in nature. Perhaps this explains the reason that led to the downfall of the Shah of Iran in 1979 due to the separation of religion and politics. It is important to reiterate that the ideology of democracy was developed over time due to the social mobilisation experienced by nations (Deutsch, 1953). More to the point, Easterly (2006:105) notes that, "Alas, democracy is not a quick fix for poor countries, just as free markets are not a quick fix."

## Conclusion

Quite clearly, Western societies are distinguishable from non-Western societies by their ability to create profusion and reduce conflict. Democracy as a form of governance is still in its infancy stage in a vast number of non-Western societies. But in some sense, both Western societies and non-Western societies need each other to thrive towards post-modernity. Barber (1995: 155) is cognisant of this relationship, when he notes that, "McWorld cannot then do without jihâd: it needs cultural parochialism to feed its endless appetites. Yet neither can jihâd do without McWorld: for where would culture be without the commercial producers who market it and the information and communication systems that make it known?"

# References

Adekanye, J. B., 2007. Linking Conflict Diagnosis, Conflict Prevention, and Conflict Management in Contemporary Africa: Selected Essays. Ababa Press Ltd.

Altemeyer, B., & Hunsberger, B. 1992. Authoritarianism, Religious Fundamentalism, Quest, and Prejudice. International Journal for the Psychology of Religion, 2, 113–133.

Barber, R. Benjamin, 2005. Jihad vs McWorld. New York: Ballantine Books.

Batson, Daniel C.; Schoenrade, Patricia & Ventis, Larry W., 1993. Religion and the Individual: A Social-Psychological Perspective. New York: Oxford University Press.

Baynes, H. Norman (ed.), 1942. The Speeches of Adolf Hitler, April 1922-August 1939, Vol. 1 of 2, pp. 19-20, Oxford University Press.

Braithwaite, R.B. 1971. An Empiricists View of the Nature of Religious Belief. Philadelphia: R. West.

Bruce, Steve, 1995. The Sociology of Religion. (1) An Elgar Reference Collection, Aldershot.

Calvert, John, 2004. 'The American Encounter with Islam: The Mythic Foundations of Radical Islam', Orbis, 29-41.

Chalmers, A. F. 2009. What is This Thing Called Science?. Third Edition. New York: Open University Press.

Crippen, Timothy, 1988. 'Old and New gods in the Modern World: Toward a Theory of Religious Transformation', Social Forces 67 (2):316.

Deutsch, W. Karl, 1953. Nationalism and Social Communication: An Inquiry into the Foundations of Nationality. Cambridge, Mass. M.I.T. Press.

Easterly, William, 2006. The White Man's Burden: Why the West's Efforts to Aid the Rest Have Done so Much Ill and So Little Good. Oxford University Press.

Euben, Roxanne. L., 1999. Enemy in the Mirror: Islamic Fundamentalism and the Limits of Modern Rationalism. A Work of Comparative Political Theory. Princeton; New Jersey.

Frank, David John & Meyer, W. John, 2002. 'The Profusion of Individual Roles and Identities in the Postwar Period', Sociological Theory 20 (1): 86-105.

Freud, Sigmund; Gay, Peter & Strachey, James, 1989. Civilization and Its Discontents. New York: W. W. Norton & Company.

Fukuyama, Francis, 1992. The End of History and the Last Man. New York: The Free Press.

Geertz, Clifford, ed., 1963. The Integrative Revolution: Primordial Sentiments and Civil Politics in the New States, Old Societies and New State. New York, Free Press: 105-157.

Geertz, Clifford, 1966. 'Religion as a Cultural System', in Banton, ed., Anthropological Approaches to the Study of Religion. London: Althone: 1-46.

Green, W. Scott, 2006. 'What Do We Mean by "Religion" and "Western Civilisation"?' in Jacob Neusner, Religious Foundations of Western Civilisation: Judaism Christianity and Islam. Nashville: Abingdon Press: 3-26.

Haynes, Jeffrey, 2002. 'Religion and Politics', in Linda Woodheadl Paul Fletcher, Hiroko Kawanami & David Smith, Religions in the Modern World. London & New York: Rutledge: 316-331.

Horowitz, Donald L., 1985. Ethnic Groups in Conflict. Berkeley: University of California Press.

Huntington, Samuel P., 1996. The Clash of Civilisations and the Remaking of World Order. New York: Simon & Schuster Uk Ltd.

Juergensmeyer, Mark, 1993. The New Cold War? Religious Nationalism Confronts the Secular State. Berkeley: University of California Press.

Juergensmeyer, Mark, ed., 2005. Religion in Global Civil Society. Oxford; New York: Oxford University Press.

Kepel, Gilles, 1994. The Revenge of God: the Resurgence of Islam, Christianity and Judaism in the Modern World. Cambridge: Polity Press.

Lawrence. Bruce, B., 1998. Islam Beyond Violence: Shattering the Myth. New Jersey: Princeton University Press.

Lewis, Bernard, 2002. What Went Wrong? The Clash between Islam and Modernity in the Middle East. London: Weidenfeld & Nicolson.

Lincoln, Bruce, 2003. Holy Terrors: Thinking about Religion After September 11, Chicago, Ill.: University of Chicago Press.

Manji, Irshad, 2004.The Trouble with Islam: A Wake-Up Call For Honesty and Change. Edinburgh & London: Mainstream Publishing.

Mazrui, Ali, 1999. 'Globalisation and Cross-Cultural Values: The Politics of Identity and Judgement', Arab Studies Quarterly 21, no 3: 97-110.

McGuire, B. Meredith, 1992. Religion: The Social Context. 3rd Edition. Belmont, California: Wandsworth Publishing Company.

Murphy, Joseph, 1988. The Power of Your Subconscious Mind. London: Simon & Schuster Inc.

Olomojobi, Yinka, 2013. Islam and Conflict in Northern Nigeria. Lagos: Malthouse Press.

Tibi, Bassam, 1993. 'The Worldview of Sunni Arab Fundamentalists: Attitudes toward Modern Science and Technology' in Marty, E. Martin E. & Appleby, R. Scott, Fundamentalisms and Society: Reclaiming the Sciences, the Family, and Education. Chicago & London: The University of Chicago Press: 73-102.

Van Der Veer, Peter, 1999. 'The Moral State State: Religion, Nation, and Empire in Victorian Britain and British India', in Peter Van Der Veer & Lehmann, Hartmut, ed., Nation and Religion: Perspectives on Europe and Asia. Princeton University Press: 15-43.

Wiktorowicz, Quintan & Kaltenthaler, Karl. 2006. The Rationality of Radical Islam, 'Political Science Quarterly, Vol. 121, No. 2 pp. 295-319.

# 3

# Jihâdisation of Islam

## Introduction

It is best to begin by noting that Islam emanates from salâm, meaning 'peace.'[25] The intriguing question then is if the given name of Islam is peace, then what is inferred by 'jihâd.' The term 'jihâd' has been overbeaten by different Muslim jurists. The usage of this term is interwoven with historical trajectories of a complex nature. Perhaps, the most misconstrued interpretation of jihâd is that it is imputed to mean terrorism. However, the ways in which jihâd is understood and interpreted have deep suggestions for Islamic political discourse in African states. It seems correct to underscore that Jihâd is divided between a modernists and a traditionalists' interpretation. This conceptualisation has ushered in the materialisation of Islamist self-proclaimed jihâds which are disturbing developments in Africa. A pointer to these conceptualisations is that Islamic culture is not monolithic. It has varied interpretations to different cultures. In understanding jihâd, one has to underscore that Islam is heterogeneous. It is suggested that scholars should

---
[25] The Qur'an (59:23) refers to God as exuding peace: "He is God; there is no God but He. He is King, Holy, Peace, Faithful, Preserver, Mighty, Compeller, Sublime. Glory to be God above everything they associate with Him. He is God, the Creator, the Maker, the Form-giver. To Him, belong the Names Most Beautiful. All that is in the heavens and the earth glorifies Him. He is Mighty, Wise."

explore the varied meanings of jihâd in different cultures. As correctly noted by Yates (2007: 141):

> *Islam is presently undergoing a struggle to define its place in the global modern world — a struggle not likely to be resolved conclusively or uniformly, precisely because Islam, like Christianity — indeed, like the West — is not monolithic. Islam speaks with many voices — better yet, many voices speak through Islam.*

The traditionalists or the orthodox consensus hold the view that jihâd in the Islamic world is an imperative for the eradication of infidels. If this is conceivable, then it could be argued that the desire of jihâd is longer a plausible cause since Islam is the prevalent religion in Islamic societies.

The conventional connotation of the word 'jahada' (abstract noun, juhd) otherwise known as 'jihâd' is not confined to the concept of a 'holy war' but 'struggling in the way of God.' It also means 'striving'; that is, striving with God. It should be noted that the term 'holy war' in the context of Islam was coined by Orientalists when they started enquiring about the religion of Islam. It is important to note that the term 'holy war' is non-existent in the holy Qur'an. Jihâd then is perceived as an effort to submit one's self (jihâd al-nafs) with the will of Allah, otherwise known as the greater Jihâd (al-jihā̄d al-akbar). It is described as a personal obligation (fard 'ayn). In line with this interpretation, Esposito (1998: 12) notes that: "In its most general sense and application in Muslim life, jihâd refers to the vocation of Muslims to strive or struggle to realise God's will, to lead a virtuous life. This includes the Muslims' universal mission and obligation to spread God's will and rule."

## Religion and violence

It is worthy to note that Muslim militants pursue political goals in a state, whilst radical Muslims have a global religious ideology. At cursory glance, jihâd or a violent strand of religion is not only prevalent in Islam. One of the greatest paradoxes of religion is that they all have connotations of violence. Appleby & Martin (2002:16) have philosophised that:

> *For all the current focus on fiery Islamic extremists, religious fundamentalism are not confined to any particular faith or country, nor to the poor and educated. Instead, they are likely to spring up anywhere people perceive the need to fight a godless, secular culture- even if they have to depart from the orthodoxy of their traditions to do it. In fact, what fundamentalists everywhere have in common is the ability to craft their messages to fit the times.*

In reality, it will readily be observed that most religions have annotations about war and peace or to state in another order — good and evil. It is argued that the exegesis of good and bad are not exclusive to any religion. This reality was noted by President Barak Obama when he cautioned that:

> *How do we, as people of faith, reconcile these realities — the profound good, the strength, the tenacity, the compassion and love that can flow from all of our faiths, operating alongside those who seek to hijack religions for their own murderous ends? And lest we get on our high horse and think this is unique to some other place, remember that during the crusades and the inquisition, people committed terrible deeds in the name of Christ. In our home country, slavery and Jim Crow all too often was justified in the name of Christ.*[26]

If this is understood, one would readily note that in Hinduism, the Rajputs were symbols of the sword of Hindustan, protecting the ethos of Hinduism. In Buddhism,

---

26  See 'Who's Worried About Americans Being 'On a High Horse'?', accessed on the 6th of February 2015 at http://www.nationalreview.com/campaign-spot/397995/whos-worried-about-americans-being-high-horse-jim-geraghty

in the *Mhayana Mahaparinirvana Sutra*, Buddha is claimed to have killed Brahmin dissidents in his previous life in order to protect Bhuddhism. In Judaism, the Children of Israel used military might to capture land that was perceived to be flowing with 'milk' and 'honey'. In Christianity, Revelation 19:15, in referring to the second coming of Christ, states that, "out of His mouth comes a sharp sword with which to strike down the nations. He will rule them with an iron scepter..." Moreover, Jesus Christ warned that, "the kingdom of heaven suffers violence, and violent men take it by force" (Matthew 11:12, KJV). Also, in Islam, the concept of jihâd is used to wage a holy war to preserve the *umma*. Notwithstanding these sacred texts which may appear to be militant in nature, from a broader perspective, they advocate the protection of their religious identities from perceived threats to its sacrosanct order. Khadduri (2006:56) makes the point clear by explaining, "...the jihâd is often expressed in terms of strife, and there is no doubt that in certain verses, the conception of jihâd is synonymous with the words war and fighting." This explains the essence that submission to the will of God of an individual's faith is one of religion's sacred duty. Also, killing for one's religion is an absolutely devout act that is a variant to show total surrender of an individual's faith and provides a moral reason for violence in the protection of one's faith (Bandura, 1998). These observations do not imply that religions are violent in nature, but it reveals that religion prevails in all aspects of life. Religion cannot be wished away, as it has social implications.

In Abrahamic mythology, the cosmic war in heaven where the archangel (Lucifer/Ibis) led a third of the angels to war with God, wherein the loyal angels of God fought and drove Lucifer/Ibis from heaven may be regarded as the first jihâd. The call for religious violence is not a new phenomenon. During the Christian crusades, violence was used to acquire economic expansionism. Moreover, "the crusaders aimed to free Europe of the economic hegemony of Islam" (Napoleoni, 2003:57). The golden era of Islam was depicted by economic growth and robust trading relations within its enclave. However, the incessant crusades eventually destroyed Islamic hegemony. Coupled with the negative effects of the petrol dollar economies largely depicted in the Middle East, its people have been tainted with economic inequities. Thus, "as the crusades had presented the starving population of Europe with a chance for a better life, today, the modern jihâd offers people a way to feed their families and hope for the future" (Napoleoni, 2003:60). Perhaps more crucial, is that Muslims are desirous of attempting to recapture the golden era of their hegemonic power during the Ottoman Empire (1299–1923).

## Jihâd: The double edged sword

It is vital to note that the essence of striving to be aligned with Allah implies that a believer has to contend with intense demands for him/her to strive to be holy in line with God's commandments. This creed is found in Qur'an, 22:78:

> And strive (jahidu) for Allah as you ought to strive (haqq jihadihu). He elected you and did not impose upon you any hardship in religion—the faith of your father Abraham. He called you Muslims before and in this (the Qur'an) that the Apostle may bear witness against you and you may be witnesses against mankind. So, perform the prayer, give the alms and hold fast to Allah. He is your Master; and what a blessed Master and a blessed Supporter!

The above capitulation does not accede to the use of violence. However, jihâd in terms of self perseverance commonly known by Sufi Muslims as lesser jihâd *(al-jihāˉd al-asghar)* or Jihâd of the sword *(Jihâd bin saif)* is an obligation to preserve the *umma* when it is under threat by non-Muslims. This is a collective obligation *(fard kifaya)*. However, as would be noted later, radical Islamist thought, considers jihâd to be an individual duty *(fard 'ayn)*. It has been argued that, jihâd is not within the realm of an individual duty, since it is outside the five pillars of Islam (confession of faith; prayer, fasting, alms-giving and pilgrimage (Roy, 2002: 41). Before delving further, one must be reminded that Islam, like its other Abrahamic related faith - Christianity, is an imported religion to Africa. Christianity came predominantly by way of the gun and trade, whilst Islam came mainly by way of the sword.

In a similar sense, in its co-Abrahamic faith, the obligation to strive to be holy is found in the admonition of Jesus Christ when he said, "Strive to enter in at the strait gate: for many, I say unto you, will seek to enter in, and shall not be able." (Luke 13:24, KJV). What is presumed here is that striving to be holy is not exclusive to Islam. A similar command is reinstated in Hebrew 12:4, where Paul admonishes that, "Ye have not yet resisted unto blood, striving against sin." It seems that the perception of jihâd as a spiritual obligation to attain righteousness is unique to the Abrahamic faiths.

The use of religion as a defense mechanism is not only exclusive to Islam, but also in Christianity. The Bible in Leviticus 24:20: "Breach, for breach, eye for eye, tooth for tooth: as he hath caused a blemish in a man, so shall it be done to him again." A seemingly similar decree is found in the Qur'an 5:45: "We ordained therein for them: Life for life, eye for eye, nose or nose, ear for ear, tooth for tooth, and wounds equal for equal. But if any one remits the retaliation by way of charity, it is an act of atonement for himself. And if any fail to judge by (the light of) what Allah hath revealed, they are (no better than) wrong-doers." Crucially, the concept of jihâd as a defensive mechanism is clear from the scriptures of the Qur'an:

> *To those against whom war is made, permission is given (to fight), because they are wronged;- and verily, Allah is most powerful for their aid;- (They are) those who have been expelled from their homes in defiance of right,- (for no cause) except that they say, "our Lord is Allah.. Did not Allah check one set of people by means of another, there would surely have been pulled down monasteries, churches, synagogues, and mosques, in which the name of Allah is commemorated in abundant measure. Allah will certainly aid those who aid his (cause);- for verily Allah is full of Strength, Exalted in Might, (able to enforce His Will). (They are) those who, if We establish them in the land, establish regular prayer and give regular charity, enjoin the right and forbid wrong: with Allah rests the end (and decision) of (all) affairs* (Qur'an, 22:39-41).

It could very well be that the language here presupposes that a Muslim is obliged to fight a just war, as instructed by the Qur'an (17:33): "Do not kill the soul that God has made sacred, except for a just cause." Here, Islam may be perceived to be synonymous with violence so far one is perceived to be fighting a just cause. The concept of a just war is not exclusive to Islam. In the ancient Roman Empire, the doctrine of *bellum justum* was used in sanctioning war when necessary or the justification of war for retaliatory purposes. It is upon the above perception of jihâd of the sword that Islam has been militarised by Islamists. This discernment has been made popular by 'al-Qaeda and other Islamist Movements' (AQOIM).

Perhaps one may argue that from AQOIM's perception that jihâd against the West is based on a retaliatory response emanating from the Western European Christian crusades between 1095 and 1291 into the Middle East in order to occupy the 'Holy Land' from Muslims and to suppress the growth of Islam. In many ways, the crusades could be conceived as an attempt to colonialise land that was perceived to be the essence of Islamic civilisation. Moreover, the Christian crusades coupled with the colonialisation of Islamic states by Western Europe could be deemed to be a reprisal campaign by AQOIM through the ideology of global jihâd. Moreover, political interference in states such as Afghanistan and Iraq has triggered radical Islamists[27] to conceive that there is a need for change in the universal order. They are desirous for Islam to occupy a pivotal role not only in international politics, but also as a hegemonic role in the world. A tendency that may exacerbate the jihâdisation of Islam is the current *jeremidisation* of Christianity taking place in the world. Jihâd may then be perceived as contending with a perceived modern Christian crusade. It seems this explains the reason why churches cannot be established in many Middle Eastern states such as Saudi Arabia and Iran, as it is perceived as a form of Western intrusion.

Crucially, it seems that the jihâdists are using a preemptive defensive mechanism against Western powers, especially within notions of grievance that America continues to oppress their Muslim brothers in Israeli occupied regions of Palestine such as Gaza and the West Bank. Another crucial issue instigating jihâd ideology is reprisals for dehumanising a number of Muslim prisoners in Guantánamo Bay. If radical Islam in the Middle East is largely due to Israeli occupation of Palestine, a striking question would be to consider why an ostensibly similar radical ideology is being brewed in Africa. Perhaps, sentiments of being oppressed and suppressed by Western forms of institutions generate a place for radical Islam to grow in the continent. In this context, it is significant to suggest that the perceived invented tradition of colonialists, such as the notion that Western economic policies are

---

27  Radical Islam is not the same ideology as militant Islam. Militant Islam is the desire of Muslims to attain political status such as establishing an Islamist government in a state. Palestinian Hamas, the Algerian Islamic Salvation Front (FIS) and the Lebanese Hezbollah are militant Islamic groups desirous of nationalist and political liberation.

exploiting Islamic societies and the supposed injustice attributed to Western military in Afghanistan and Iraq is a justified retaliation for Islamists for the death of innocent lives procured by bombers in New York's 9/11 and in London's 7 July, 2005 bombings. It could be argued that the attacks on the Western world have been wilfully selected on American and its military allies. One begins to ponder why jihâdists' attacks are not prevalent in Sweden or in Switzerland. It then seems that it is not the entirety of the Western world that is at odds with Islamists.

Furthermore, Assaf Moghadam (2008/09: 55-56) also recognises clearly that: "al-Qaeda's understanding of occupation is much broader. It includes a long history of injustices manifested today in the military, religious, political, economic, and cultural humiliation of the larger Muslim world by the "Crusader-Zionist alliance." In attempting to hit the nail on the head, Byman (2003:145) notes the witty expression of Peter L. Bergen:

> Bin Laden "does not rail against the pernicious effects of Hollywood movies, or against Madonna's midriff, or against the pornography protected by the U.S Constitution. Nor does he inveigh against the drug and alcohol culture of the West or its tolerance for homosexuals. He leaves that kind of material to the American Christian fundamentalist Jerry Falwell... Bin Laden's grievances are focused on power—who possesses it, why it is used, and (in his judgment) how it is abused.

In this sense, Gunaratna (2002:84) is certainly correct when he notes that: "The principal aims of jihad are to remove oppression and injustice; to establish justice, wellbeing and prosperity; to eliminate barriers to the spread of truth." It must be hastily added that, the essence of jihâd is the desire to fight perceived oppression. Perhaps, this perception is noted by Osama bin Laden's utterance: "as for the question why are we fighting and opposing you, the answer is very simple: because you attacked us and continue to attack us."[28] Another seemingly similar rhetoric is noted by Egerton (2011: 12) where he notes that, "For militant Salafists, 'the suffering and humiliation of Muslims around the world are not unconnected episodes, but a chain in a series of transgressions by the 'Crusader-Zionist' alliance against Islam and Muslims." In another sense, it answers President George Bush's lamentation:

> *Americans are asking, 'Why do they hate us?' They hate what they see right here in this chamber: a democratically elected government. Their leaders are self-appointed. They hate our freedoms: our freedom of religion, our freedom of speech, our freedom to vote and assemble and disagree with each other.*[29]

Jihâdist ideology towards USA is all about hating its foreign policies and not about hating 'our freedoms and liberty'. Simply put, if the USA moderates its policies towards the Middle East in terms of the Palestinian/Israel conflict, exhibits a non-interference position towards the politics of oil in the Middle East and moves away from regime change in Africa (such as ousting Kwame Nkrumah in February 1966), then the imminent of jihâdist threats would cease to exist towards the West. Furthermore, the augmentation of *Dar al Islam* is showcased by Western intervention in Islamic states such as Iraq and Afghanistan. It seems that amongst Muslims, radical Islam finds a place and space to operate where oppression is prevalent within Islamic societies.

In a broader perspective, when societies consist of vast populations of Muslims who are shrouded with relative deprivation, such societies are prone to have the emergence

---

28  Letter to the Americans, 6 October 2002, in Lawrence, (2005:162).
29  See 'President Bush's address to a joint session of Congress and the nation 20th September, 2001', accessed on the 20th of July 2012 at: http://www.washingtonpost.com/wpsrv/nation/specials/attacked/transcripts/bushaddress_092001.html

of radical Islam. Grievance is channelled through religion. It will be observed that states such as the United Arab Emirates do not experience radical Islam for the reason that the state has co-opted confidence in public infrastructures and economic growth. In another dimension, where states with poor economic growth have evenly distributed its allocation to the populace, wherein there is a sense of bridging the economic divide amongst its citizens, such states are not likely to experience radical Islam. This sentiment is illustrated to a limited degree in a Western society—America. A vast number of African-Americans in the 1960s were lured to Islam by black supremacist teachings due to a perception of rejection, oppression, fear and anxiety generated by racism and seeking honour and equality for their race. This apparent reaction is growing in many parts of Africa, where oppressive regimes have produced sentiments of grievance in the minds of its citizens. This in many ways further elucidates us on Boko Haram's philosophical connotation that 'westernised education is a sin'.

An illustration of the above narrative is observed in the horn of Africa—Somalia where the United States led by the Unified Task Force (UNITAF) occupied its territory on humanitarian grounds from August 1992 to March 1994. This event may have been considered as an occupation of Africa by al-Qaeda (Daniel. 2003: 145). However, it was eventually considered as a triumphant victory by *Dar al Islam* when the UNITAF was withdrawn by President Clinton as a result of the deaths of eighteen members of the task force in the Battle of Mogadishu in 1993. Furthermore, the increased pressure from the West in respect of human rights abuse by the Islamist regime and totalitarian rule of General Omar al-Bashir of Sudan (who is the first sitting leader of a state to be charged for international crimes by the International Criminal Court) is also another source of Western interference.[30] However, this purported amplification of *Dar al Islam* conflicts the Qur'anic sura that there should be no compulsion in religion (Qur'an 2:256). This holy text is made clearer by the notion that God indeed desires multitude of customs and religions:

> *If it had been your Lord's will, all of the people on Earth would have believed. Would you then compel the people so to have them believe?* (Quran 10:99).

Perhaps on a deeper level, it is not surprising that Islam is in a way connected to the complexities of struggle. Bernard Lewis showcases this intricate part of Islam when he noted perceptively that "... the advent of Islam itself was a revolution. ... The Prophet Muhammad began his career in Mecca as an opposition leader, and was for some time engaged in a struggle against authority as established among his people and in his birthplace" (Khashan, 1997:7).

The key point is that jihâd as conceived by Islamists places more emphasis on the military activity than spiritual activity. Perhaps this perception is borrowed from Prophet Muhammad's hijra (migration to Medina) in 622CE due to the Prophet being persecuted by the Meccans. Prophet Muhammad had to embark on military expeditions to sustain the *umma* by raiding caravans from Mecca between 622CE and 623CE. Furthermore, the incessant conflict with the Meccans between 623CE and early 624CE ensured that there was much activity emanating from the lesser jihâd. A notorious conflict at this time was the Battle of Badr in 624 CE. In this battle, which the Muslim army decisively won—with a standing army of 313 with 2 horses and 70 camels. On the contrary, the Badr army had a stronghold of 950 infantry with 100 horses and 170 camels. Similarly, in the Battle of Hunayn in 630CE, which the Muslim army won, the army consisted of 12,000 men whilst Hawazin army consisted of 20,000 men. Most of these expeditions in many ways were

---

30   See 'Warrant issued for Sudan's Bashir', BBC News. 4 March 2009, accessed on the 3rd of July 2013 at: http://news.bbc.co.uk/2/hi/africa/7922727.stm

suicidal in the sense that the Muslim army were sometimes at a disadvantage due to their undersized army. Ultimately, Mecca and its Quraish tribe were conquered by Prophet Muhammad and the Muslim army in 630 CE. These events reveal that Prophet Muhammad was a brilliant commander and an excellent tactician at warfare. Perhaps, one may argue that in a sense, the expeditions of Prophet Muhammad have been inherited by modern Islamists who desire to protect their world as *Dar al Islam*. This entails where a perceived adversary attempts to obstruct Muslims from striving to attain holiness according to the will of God. This imperative is in accordance with the Suwarian tradition,[31] where Muslims are compelled to live in harmony with non-Muslims.

It has been argued by Islamic jurists that jihâd entails a 'revolution' against unbelievers in order to convert them to become Muslims (Bonner, 2006). In this context, jihâd has become synonymous with the word 'sword'. In this sense, jihâd is transformed into a political agenda. It is observed that the term 'jihâd' is based on how Muslims interpret the Qur'an. Thus, the notion of jihâd is based on a double edged sword. It could be inferred by moderate Muslims as a quest to align their faith with the will of God. To the Islamist, it is based on warfare. It is important to reiterate that all religions have some iota of violence by the 'sword.' Again, it is important to note that this perception is found in Christianity, where Saul was commanded by God to:

> *Now go and smite Amalek, and utterly destroy all that they have, and spare them not; but slay both man and woman, infant and suckling, ox and sheep, camel and ass.* (1st Samuel, 15:3)

If this argument is tenable, then it is not surprising that Islam in the eyes of a few is conceived as destroying the *kuffir*.

---

31  Al-Hajj Salim Suwari, a late fifteenth-century Soninke Islamic scholar, provided a guide for Muslims in a non-Muslim society. His tradition, known as the Suwarian tradition, this tradition was against converting people to Islam, Suwari believed that people would convert to Islam under the guidance of God.

It is easy to see why the 'al-Qaeda and other Islamist Movements' (AQOIM) target Muslims living within *Dar al Islam*. Thus, such attacks may be conceived to be outside the scope of a jihâd. But, it is argued yet again, that the construction of Islam is not static, it is conceivably dynamic. It is therefore not altogether surprising that in the concept of jihâd by Islamists means war against the *kuffir* (infidels). In this context, jihâd could connote a political or economic ideology. In other parlance, jihâd is defined by the desire to take over the reins of power in a state for economic reasons. The question of jihâd becomes problematic for the reason that a jihâd can be used as an umbrella to overthrow a state that had a puritan Islamic culture. One must remember the influence of Khomeini in Iran. The Islamist revolt in 1979 gave way to a new picture of Islam in international relations — Islam thereafter was taken as a serious political debate.

It is important, however, to note that the theory of fighting a just war may be subject to scrutiny — as a just war may in fact be unjust. This assertion is found in the ancient Kanem-Bornu Empire. The 'Kanem-Bornu axis', the 'oldest continuous Islamic state in Africa' are a seemingly similar cultural group with the Hausa-Fulani by being rooted in Islam and charia long before the advent of the British colonialists. The Kanuri people, known by the Hausa as Beriberi, have adopted the Hausa language and culture. Despite this, it is interesting to note that the Fulani army led by Uthman dan Fodio in 1808 and 1810 attempted to conquer the former Kanem-Bornu Empire. Although, the Empire practiced a puritan form of Islam, the attack may be seen as illegitimate, since there was an absence of lax Muslims. However, in another dimension the attack was due to the fact that the Kanem-Bornu Empire assisted in defending the Hausa kings, who were considered as unbelievers *(Kuffir bil Takhlit)* by the Fulani army. The Capital of Bornu, Gazargamu, was captured by the Fulani and its military leader, Gwoni Mukhtar. The Bornu ruler, Mai Ahmed, suffered defeat but called upon the scholar Sheikh

Muhammad Al-Amin-Al-Kanem (a Muslim scholar and non-Sayfawa commander) in 1808, who resisted the Fulani attack. The political construction of the jihâd is noted by the fact that the Fulani jihâdists ventured to wage a military attack on the Bornu Empire despite the puritan form of Islamic practice in the Empire. In this case, the jihâd on Kanem-Borno could be termed as an unjust war — a war against Muslims. As captured by Joseph Kenny (2001):[32]

*The jihâd which 'Uthmân Dan Fodiye launched in 1804 to conquer large tracts of northern Nigeria had the religious motivation of purifying the ruling society from its casual attitude towards Islamic practice and its continued patronage of traditional religious practices. It can be accepted that this was 'Uthmân Dan Fodiye's motive for the jihâd. Nevertheless, this does not exclude economic or social motivations, but rather presupposes them, since Islam purports to be not only the right way to God but also the right formula for economic and social success. The all-inclusiveness of Islam makes Muslims expect that its establishment will bring a better and more prosperous society and a greater enjoyment of the goods of this life as well as those of the next.*

Moreso, it is worthy to note Shenton's (1986:4) succinct observation that the aim of the jihâd was to constitute a nation of Muslim commoners, whose leaders would be responsible for maintaining policies of war, taxation and governance. Shenton tells us that the jihâd was concerned with providing a balance of power to the literate scholars *(malami, sing, malami)*, who were a strong force in the success of the jihâd and who had in the past been excluded from the mantle of leadership in their communities due to their status from birth.

---

[32] 'The Spread of Islam in Nigeria: A Historical Survey', Paper given at Conference on Sharî`a in Nigeria Spiritan Institute of Theology, Enugu, 22-24 March 2001, accessed on the 2nd of May 2008 at; http://www.diafrica.org/kenny/Sist.htm

However, another glimpse behind the curtain shows that the perception of jihâd as a revolutionary ideology is revoked by the sacred letters of the Qur'an (2:256): "Let there be no compulsion (or coercion) in the religion (Islam)." In line with the precepts of the Qur'an, Ghulam Ahmad,[33] in his critical acclaimed book 'Noor-ul-Haq' (The light of truth,)[34] notes that:

> *The Holy Qur'an only allows fighting with those who stop God's people from believing in Him, entering in His faith, carrying out His commandments, and worshipping Him. It commands us to fight against those who fight against Muslims without any reason...*

Despite the usage of suicidal killings perpetuated by Islamists radicals, these acts are considered as sacred aberration to moderate Muslims. In showcasing this religious anomaly, David Cook (2004:140) concisely notes that:

> *For many contemporary Muslims, the radicals are an embarrassment, a group that drags them back to a primitive and stark view of the world (and especially of non-Muslims) with which they are not comfortable. It is of crucial importance, therefore, for the radical Muslims to sacrifice their more moderate brethren, which they regularly do through the process of declaring them to be non-Muslims (takfir), and to discredit their spirituality (by placing an inordinate emphasis upon fighting the jihâd as a salvific action) in order to redraw the boundaries.*

From another perspective—to the Western media, the concept of jihâd has a different meaning. It simply means 'war'. This meaning has been popularised by Western media since the aftermath of 911— thanks to the Islamists who have justified such concepts. This reminds us of the Buddhist emperor Ashoka's advice (in the 3rd Century B.C.E.) that, 'by

---

33  Self acclaimed 'promised Messiah and the founder of the Ahmadiyya reformist movement. The movement was founded on 23 March 1889
34  Part 2, page 45

belittling another person's religion, a person belittles his/her own.' Despite this conception of jihâd by Western media, it seems that Western scholars have a different view of jihâd. They argue that jihâd is devoid of violence. In its literal meaning, they seem to prefer to emphasise that jihâd is a spiritual inclination for Muslims, whilst using jihâd for violent ideology is unholy war amongst Muslims (Esposito, 2003). In fact, for Bonner (2004: 399), "Jihâd is a multi-faceted phenomenon both in theory and practice. There is no single, all-embracing concept that has been applied within the long, complex and sometimes even tortuous, course of Islamic history." When the context of jihâd is perceived as a religious mandate to end socio-economic oppression, jihâd takes the form of the unsheathed sword. This obligation is conceived by the Qur'an 9:5 and 9:29:

*But when the forbidden months are past, then fight and slay the pagans wherever ye find them, and seize them, beleaguer them, and lie in wait for them in every stratagem (of war); but if they repent, and establish regular prayers and practise regular charity, then open the way for them: for Allah is Oft-forgiving, Most Merciful.*

*Fight those who believe not in Allah nor the Last Day, nor hold that forbidden which hath been forbidden by Allah and His Messenger, nor acknowledge the religion of Truth, (even if they are) of the People of the Book, until they pay the Jizya with willing submission, and feel themselves subdued.*

This tradition custom is supported by the counsel of Abu Bakr, the father-in-law of Prophet Muhammad:

*I have been ordered to fight the people until they profess that there is no god but God and that Mohammed is the messenger of God, perform the salah and pay the zakah. If they do so, their lives and property are inviolable to me, unless [when] the [law of] Islam permits them [to be taken].*[35]

---
35   Quoted in Rudolph, (2005: 127)

The powerful dynamics of Islamic culture and its heterogeneous nature should be appreciated, "only then can the variety of contemporary Muslim views—including jihâd as self-defence, jihâd as terrorism, and jihâd as moral improvement—be appreciated as alternative expressions of a broad, multi-stranded religious tradition" (Van der Krogt, 2010: 128). It is then clear, that one would agree that Islam is broadly anti-essentialist. It is conceived as spiritual obligation or a quest for economic dominion, whilst to others it is deemed as violence against westernised institutions otherwise termed as terrorism.

Given this discussion, Muslims' interpretation of jihâd would depend on their construction of society where they find themselves. Many people find themselves participating in different cultural and intuitive religious beliefs even though they have not critically evaluated the cultural facts behind these consructions. Muslims are diversified—from different ethnic groups and cultures—they do possess different constructions of Islam. This condition is interwoven with socio-political development in the state where Muslims live. To showcase this argument, where Muslims live a state that consists of socio-economic development, it seems that jihâd would be interpreted as a spiritual imperative for Muslims to seek God's will. However, where Muslims are living in a state that lacks a socio-economic base for its citizens, disgruntlement and grievance may situate Muslims to conceive jihâd as a vehicle to end prebendalism and a quest for achieving socialisation of wealth amongst its citizens.

## Table showing Jihadi Stages of Islam
*Courtesy: Hazim, & Bunker, 2006: 436-437.*

| Stages | Name | Attributes |
|---|---|---|
| Stage 1 | Prophethood | **570 to 632:** The birth and rise of Muhammad in Arabia and the new religion of Islam. |
| Stage 2 | Caliphate according to Sunnis and the beginning of the Imamate through Al according to Shiites | **632 to 661:** The four successors of Muhammad or the Rightly Guided Caliphs ruled during this time period, and the Sunnis hold that this period was known as a righteous period that guided all of the believers appropriately. Shiites hold that Ali alone was rightly guided and the other caliphs were usurpers. |
| Stage 3a | A Lesser Apostasy commences Islamic Empires Begin | **661 to mid-1800s:** This period was characterised by apostasy and a general turning away of the faith. There were still periods of growth, revival, and stunning military accomplishments but Islamic piety did not approach the previous periods of Muhammad and the Rightly Guided Caliphs. The last caliphate fell in 1924 and this was merely symbolic; jihadists refer to this frequently in their writings. |

| | | |
|---|---|---|
| Stage 3b | Complete subjugation of Muslim lands and ensuing rebellions from time to time.<br><br>The most significant was led by a self-appointed Mahdi in Sudan. Resistance begins with a Mahdi figure. | **1880–1899:** A member of the sufi sect, the Mahdi, Muhammad Ahmad Abdallah and his followers waged successful military campaigns against the Turks and British, effectively uniting Sudan under his leadership until defeated by the British in 1899 at the Battle of Omdurman. |
| Stage 4a | The birth of Israel, Pan Arabism & Islamism and jihads in Afghanistan, Lebanon, the Iranian Revolution and Khomeiniism, Palestine and unrest in Chechnya and Bosnia as well | **1979**: Russia invades Aghabistan Abdullah Azzam and others called for supranational campaigns against apostates, oppressors and foreign millitary bases in Islamic lands.<br><br>**1967:** Six Day War Israel defeats the Arab Alliance of Egypt, Syria and Jordan and the Sahwa, Islamic Awakening begins. The intellectual underpinnings were started by Sayyid Qutb.<br><br>**1948:** Israel became a nation as well.<br>**1932:** The unification of Saudi Arabia.<br>**1924:** Fall of the Ottoman Empire and last recognisable caliphate. |
| Stage 4b | Al Qaeda and other terrorist groups become active on a global level | **1988 to the present:** The beginning of global upsurge in supranational propaganda and campaigns |

|  |  | designed to bring about emirates. Provinces and territories such as Afghanistan have sharia as the foundation of law. |
| --- | --- | --- |
| **Stage 5a (Future projections)** | New Caliphate | **Yet to be fulfilled:** The caliphate is the womb from which the Mahdi will emerge. It is also the only true foundation of a just Islamic nation other than Muhammad's prophetic ministry. |
| **Stage 5b (Future projections)** | Mahdi | **Yet to be fulfilled:** The end of the world draws near with his emergence. |

## Between Martyrdom and Jihâd

The act of self-sacrifice is not a new ideology. The seeds of self-sacrifice could be traced to the order of Ismailis (the assassins) in modern Iran and Syria in the 11th and 13th century. Bernard Lewis (1967: 48) tells us that the Ismailis "were a secret society, with a system of oaths and initiations and a guarded hierarchy of rank and knowledge. Their secrets were well kept, and information about them is fragmentary and confused." However, what is known is that members of this order were willing to die for Ismaili Islam and for their religious leader — the Hasan ibn Sabah (1034-1124, otherwise known as the da'i'). The Ismailis was a branch of Shi'ism, but differed with its constitution of seven imans as opposed to twelve imans of Shi'tes. The da'i convinced his followers to commit acts of self sacrifice in killing notable people he so chose — that if they died during the act they would have a free passage to paradise. However, martyrdom is not a new conception in mainstream Islam. Muslims, predominantly the Shi'ites celebrate the martyrdom of saints who died in an attempt to save the *umma*. This is observed in the celebration of the death of Husain (he fought and died whilst rebelling against Yazid, the 3rd Shi'te *Imam*, who practiced an adulterated form of Islam). Perhaps, the depiction of Husain in some ways makes him a 'symbol of simulation' by Shi'tes. Nonetheless, in modern times, according to a recent Pew Research Center poll, majority of Muslims oppose violence in the name of Islam.

A vast majority of Muslims who participated in a research[36] opined that suicide bombings that usually target civilians are not tolerable. The opinions were indicated by Pakistan (89%), Indonesia (81%), Nigeria (78%) and Tunisia (77%), and 62%—majority of Palestinian Muslims. What this presupposes is that the Islamists who have used suicide bombings as a tool for military strategy for socio-political agendas have perverted the message of the Qur'an. However, before delving further, it is important to note that to the radical Islamist, suicidal missions are acts of martyrdom. The slim line of distinction between the two is that, "intention of the martyr is emphasised as entirely distinct from the intention of the suicider. Whereas suicide is motivated by desperation and despair, martyrdom is driven by self-sacrifice for a higher cause" (Brahimi, 2010: 100). The influential texts of the Egyptian radical—Sheikh Youssef al-Qaradawi, a revered Islamic scholar who commands about 60 million worldwide audiences in his popular al Jazeera phone-in programme 'al-Sharī'a wa al-Hayāh' is noted for his arguments for the use of suicide operations against Israel. He justifies this act by perceptively noting that:

> *But a clear distinction has to be made here between martyrdom and suicide. Suicide is an act or instance of killing oneself intentionally out of despair, and finding no outlet except putting an end to one's life. On the*

---

36  See 'Muslim Publics Share Concerns about Extremist Groups Much Diminished Support for Suicide Bombing', accessed on the 3rd of November, 2013 at: http://www.pewglobal.org/2013/09/10/muslim-publics-share-concerns-about-extremist-groups/

> *other hand, martyrdom is a heroic act of choosing to suffer death in the Cause of Allah, and that's why it's considered by most Muslim scholars as one of the greatest forms of jihad.*[37]

The intriguing question then is why are suicidal missions a popular tactic of warfare among Islamists? Perhaps, an answer is found by a "Council of Scholars from the Arabian Peninsula" for the Chechens where Cook, (2005:142) perceptively notes, "Martyrdom or self-sacrifice operations are those performed by one or more people, against enemies far outstripping them in numbers and equipment, with prior knowledge that the operations will almost inevitably lead to death." Therefore, the main ideology behind suicide killing is that it "is frightening because its perpetrators behave like robots who seem to be devoid of that very instinct that normally unites all human beings: the survival instinct" (Küntzel, 2008:227).

Another striking question is what influences radical Muslims to undertake martyrdom or self-sacrifice operations. In other words, what is the causal explanation for the manipulation of Muslims? An insight is found from the proponents of jihâdism—in the utterance of elites such as imams, mullahs (Muslim preachers), Islamic clerics and perhaps most crucial, the early teachings of Islamic radicals.

Notwithstanding, the fact that the Qur'an prohibits suicide as a form of military strategy, radical Islamists take cognisance of verse 4:74 of the Qur'an as a prerequisite for suicidal warfare. Using the proverbial adage that 'diamonds cut diamonds', it seems that the Qur'an is used as the knife to co-opt and justify radical Islamic thought by Islamists. The source of texts is useful in understanding the ideology of radical Islam: "Let those (believers) who sell the life of this world for the hereafter fighting in the cause of Allah and

---

37  See 'The Qaradawi Fatwas', accessed on the 23rd of November 2014 at: http://www.meforum.org/646/the-qaradawi-fatwas.

whoso fights in the cause of Allah—and is slain or gets victory, We shall bestow on him a great reward." Notwithstanding these texts, Islamists attempt to find a complimentary sanction from the Qur'an in 2:216:

> *Fighting is prescribed for you, and ye dislike it. But it is possible that ye dislike a thing which is good for you, and that ye love a thing which is bad for you. But Allah knoweth, and ye know not.*

Within a broader debate, another verse used by Islamists to justify suicide killing is:

> *And some people sell themselves for the sake of Allah's favor. Allah is kind to His servants* (Qur'an 2:207).

The interpretation of these verses to Islamists is that voluntary suicide is a necessary evil, when a purported threat to *Dar al Islam* is eminent. Such a death is deemed necessary in order to prevent an incursion to sanctimony of the *umma* and to uphold one's duty in honouring God—by killing innocent people for a just cause such as being dispossessed of the *Dar-al Islam*. However, ploughing through the Qur'an, it is evident that death by suicide is wrongful deed. Cognisance should be taken to Qur'an 5:32:

> *If any one slew a person - unless it be for murder or for spreading mischief in the land - it would be as if he slew the whole people: and if any one saved a life, it would be as if he saved the life of the whole people.*[38]

Again, the Qur'an 2:194 accentuates that: "Whoever transgresses against you, respond in kind." This extract in many ways shows that suicide bombing of innocents cannot be seen as a comparable military strategy with conventional warfare.

---

38     A striking question from examining the sources of these texts is that they are somewhat contradictory. One text depicts that there should be no compulsion in religion whilst the other seems militant in nature. At this point, one must mention that the Qur'an was written in 2 phases by the Prophet Muhammad. The first phase was written in Mecca between the year 622 and 623CE. During this period, the umma (Community of Islam) was in a relatively peaceful state—Islam was seen as a new movement. It seems that during this point in time the need to sheath the sword was not necessary. The second period was when the umma left Mecca and settled in Medina in 623 AD. In Medina, the Umma—was under threat by its tribal neighbours.

Another vital strategy of the use of suicidal killings is to instil fear into the enemy—the fear factor. This tactic is used by Boko Haram in Northern Nigeria situating the eastern part of the region into a dreaded zone. Even where a Muslim is affected by death in such circumstances, they are perceived to be involuntary martyrs, who would receive the same rewards as the voluntary martyrs in the afterlife (Rogan, 2010: 480). In line with this, Hassan (2009) notes that:

> *Suicide bombings have high symbolic value because the willingness of the perpetrators to die signals high resolve and dedication to their cause. They serve as symbols of a just struggle, galvanise popular support, generate financial support for the organisation and become a source of new recruits for future suicide missions.*[39]

However, the idea of suicide attacks has been argued as unjustifiable according to some Islamic scholars. Muhammad Munir (2008) in an article written in the international review of the Red Cross, argues that suicide is rigorously prohibited in Islam. Munir notes that:

> *The Prophet (PBUH) is reported to have said, 'none amongst you should make a request for death, and do not call for it before it comes, for when any of you dies, he ceases [to do good] deeds and the life of the believer is not prolonged but for goodness.'... Any person carrying out a suicide attack should not forget that Allah has entrusted him with life and that it is not his personal possession to destroy as he pleases.*[40]

The use of suicide bombing has also been linked to its ability to be utilised to maximising impact against targets. The attack can be carried out at a particular time and place. Suicide attacks are an avenue for projecting a group's activities and attracting more recruits and funding from

---

[39] Hassan, R. 2009. What Motivates the Suicide Bombers? YaleGlobal Online, A Publication of MacMillan Center Assessed on the 26th of October, 2014 at: http://yaleglobal.yale.edu/content/what-motivates-suicide-bombers-0.

[40] Munir, M. 2008. Suicide Attacks and Islamic Law. International Review of the Red Cross, 90 (869), 71-89, assessed on the 26th of October at: http://www.academia.edu/221071/Suicide_Attacks_and_Islamic_Law.

interested parties to support their cause. For example, more than $100 million was raised for the al-Quds group in Saudi Arabia following their success in executing suicide attacks against Israeli targets.[41]

It should be stressed again that terrorists also engage in suicide attacks to motivate members of their group. Among members of a terrorist network, a high degree of respect is usually accorded individuals who lay down their lives for the sake of the cause. An individual taking his own life is very different from engaging the enemy on the battlefield and getting killed. This may be why suicide probably represents the highest form of dedication to a cause as an ultimate form of sacrifice based on an unwavering conviction about the importance of a political struggle. Martyrs who engage in suicidal acts usually undergo a lot of planning and tactical walk-throughs in the execution of targets to which they have been assigned especially those relating to the handling of the suicide vests and explosives.

As the above suggests, there is a form of group psychology to martyrdom through suicide bombing. Individuals within jihâdist groups either volunteer to join the ultimate sacrifice or are picked to carry out the task. They undergo a thorough form of conditioning or indoctrination to prepare their minds for the task of martyrdom or to be more realistic—suicide. This is especially important as the suicide bomber is made to believe he is serving a higher spiritual obligation. This is also one of the reasons why suicide bombers either pre-record videos or take photographs informing the 'world' about the reasons for their attacks. Through their training, they are encouraged and admired by their fellow colleagues who are inspired by their bravery in what has been described by Madsen (2004:3) as the "culture of martyrdom." The idea of being remembered as a hero in addition to the benefits to be gained in the afterlife is one of the factors that increases the motivation of these groups.

---

41  See 'Saudi Arabia: Terrorist Financing Issues', assessed on the 26th of October, 2014 at: http://www.congressionalresearch.com/RL32499/document.php

The origins of radical Islam started with the ideology of Ibn Taymiyyah (1263 – 1328). Taymiyyah was desirous of positioning Islam within the interpretation of the Qur'an and the Sunnah (practices and injunctions of Prophet Muhammad), jihâd, *umma* and *Jahiliyya* (the state of ignorance from the guidance of Allah). This ideology was followed by Muhammad Ibn-Abd-al-Wahhab (1703-91). Wahhab started the sect commonly known as Wahhabi which is also translated to mean *salafi,* or ancestors. Wahhab advocated the practice of Islam in its purest form. He further urged that Islam should be practiced as it was in the time of Prophet Muhammad. Most crucial is that Wahhab advocated jihâd against lax Muslims. Along these lines, another radical thinker; Rashid Rida (1866-1935), an Egyptian scholar, who emphasised that only a salafiyah model of Islam should be practiced. He also strongly advocated against the 'westoxication' (Piscatori, 1986) of Islam. These thoughts were further exemplified by Sayyid Qutb (1906-1966) who expounded Islamic revivalism and revolutionary Islam, based on his social *laissez-faire* criticism of the United States. He strongly maintained that jihad is an important pillar of Islam. Qutb maintained that, "The foremost duty of Islam in this world is to depose Jahiliyah from the leadership of man, and to take the leadership into its own hands and enforce the particular way of life which is its permanent feature" (Springer et al, 2009:78).

Qutb was largely influenced by Sayyid Abu'l Ala Maududi (1903-1979), an Islamist from India and founder of Jamaat-i-Islami (Islamic Party). Maududi sought to revive Islam by advocating that Islam is not just a religion but a way of life. Furthermore, Maududi identified that Muslims must avoid living in a state of *jahiliyya* (living in a state of ignorance) as "deviations of self-proclaimed Muslims, the influence of imperialist powers, and the use of non-Islamic laws were akin to this earlier period of ignorance" (Wiktorowicz, 2005: 78). Another prominent individual who pushed forward the need for Islam to take a radical position in the world is Sheikh

Hassan Al-Banna (1906-1949). Al-Banna founded Al-Ikhwan al- Muslimeem (the Muslim Brotherhood). He was particularly desirous in separating Western culture from Islam through political networks created by the Muslim Brotherhood. These foundations have given the fertiliser for radical Islam to be implanted into Islamist groups.

It is important to note that Qutb questioned the moral decay of Islam in Egypt and thought to blame secularisation for Islam's failure to carve out a niche for Islam in the modern world. Qutb's ideology has influenced Islamist groups such as the Islamic Political Organisation; the Muslim Brotherhood (which was founded by al-Banna) and the foremost Islamic terror group, al-Qaeda. Contemporary radicals that have been influenced by al-Banna are Hamoud al Aqla al Shuebi, a Saudi Arabian prominent cleric who supported attacks on the World Trade Center towers and the Pentagon on the 9th of November, 2011.

A contemporary propagator of radical Islam is Dr. Ayman al-Zawahiri, the leader of al-Qaeda, who has been a source of radicalising other Islamist movements. Al-Zawahiri is notoriously known for his fatwa written in conjunction with Osama bin Laden called, 'Jihâd against Jews and Crusaders'[42] and his infamous book, *'Knights Under the Prophet's Banner'*.[43] These manuscripts advocate war against the West. Along the lines of this way of thinking, Sheikh Youssef al-Qaradawi notes that, "Allah Almighty is just; through his infinite wisdom he has given the weak a weapon the strong do not have and that is their ability to turn their bodies into bombs as Palestinians do."[44] Again, Qaradawi makes clear that: "He who carries out a martyrdom operation ... sells himself to Allah in order to buy paradise in exchange."[45] Perhaps, Qaradawi has distorted the meaning and intent of Qur'an (3:169): "Never think that those

---

42    World Islamic Front Statement', The Washington Post, 23 February 1998.
43    See 'Knights Under the Prophet's Banner', accessed on the 3rd of November at: http://azelin.files.wordpress.com/2010/11/ayman-al-zawahiri-knights-under-the-prophets-banner-second-edition.pdf
44    See 'Controversial preacher with 'star status', accessed on the 7th of July 2013 at:http://news.bbc.co.uk/2/hi/uk_news/3874893.stm
45    MEMRI Special Dispatch Series, no. 542, July 24, 2003.

who are killed in the way of God are dead. They are alive with their Lord, well provided for."⁴⁶ These radical mindsets have generated many Muslims to view suicide bombing not only as a religious creed, but as prestigious act. Thus, there is a communal prestige for relatives, wives and mothers whose relative, husband or son has died a martyr. A notable individual is Mariam Farahat (Umm Nidal), a Palestinian who endorsed, encouraged and sacrificed her three sons for *Fidaai* (martyrdom). Umm Nidal, commenting on one of her son's death said:

> *The depths of my heart that Allah would cause the success of his operation. I asked Allah to give me ten [Israelis] for Muhammad, and Allah granted my request and Muhammad made his dream come true, killing ten Israeli settlers and soldiers. Our God honoured him even more, in that there were many Israelis wounded.*
>
> *When the operation was over, the media broadcast the news. Then, Muhammad's brother came to me and informed me of his martyrdom. I began to cry, 'Allah is the greatest,' and prayed and thanked Allah for the success of the operation. I began to utter cries of joy and we declared that we were happy. The young people began to fire into the air out of joy over the success of the operation, as this is what we had hoped for him.*
>
> *After the martyrdom [operation], my heart was peaceful about Muhammad. I encouraged all my sons to die a martyr's death, and I wish this even for myself. After all this, I prepared myself to receive the body of my son, the pure shahid, in order to look upon him one last time and accept the well-wishers who [came] to us in large numbers and participated in our joy over Muhammad's martyrdom...* ⁴⁷

---

46   The verse here is imputed for those who have died defending the Umma.
47   See 'Mother of terrorist Bomber talks...', accessed on te 20th of December 2014 at: http://landofthejews.tripod.com/israel/id8.html

Most crucial is that this extract tells us that by the sacrifice of their lives— death in itself is regarded as a lethal weapon (Baudrillard, 2002: 20). In other words, the radical Muslims deem that a few innocent lives must be sacrificed to save the greater number of people.

Equally important is the role of the mosques. It is beyond doubt that some mosques provoke radical teachings to moderate Muslims. A mosque of notoriety was the North Central London Mosque, in Finsbury Park. This mosque became associated with al-Qaeda. Moderate Muslims such as Richard Reid (the shoe lace bomber) became radicalised as a result of his radical Imam—Abu-Hamza al-Mazri. In northern Nigeria, the radical group—Boko Haram started its radical beliefs in a mosque in Maiduguri, Borno State, where it professed its ideology of 'Western education is a sin.'

It seems that suicide attacks generate sentiments of just dominance over their enemy, which generates a perception that it will eventually prevail over their adversaries (Dolnik, 2003). Moreover, terrorist groups presume that violence is the preeminent strategy to promote and achieve their political goals (Crenshaw, 1985). The effectiveness of suicidal missions has shown dividends in 1983/84 where America withdrew her soldiers from Beirut, Palestine due to the prevalence of suicide bombings by Hizbullah. Most important, it is noted that the utterances of these influential mindsets informs us what can be done with religion—it can be used to stoke terrorism. On the other hand, it could be used as a socio-economic transformative weapon for people—it was used in this sense by Bishop Desmond Tutu, Reverend (Dr) Martin Luther King Jr and Malcom X.

It seems that Islamists reverberate the counsel of Emiliano Zapata whose ideology was that: 'It is better to die on your feet than to live on your knees.' What this portends is that the Islamists perceive that he/she is fighting to stay alive. Putting it more bluntly, Khosrokhavar (2005: 64-65) states that, "…

martyrs themselves speak of a dissymmetry themselves and their enemies. They are not afraid of dying, but their enemies are terribly afraid of it. Even in death, the martyrs feel that they are involved in a confrontation, defying the other and demonstrating their own superiority."

Ultimately as Pape (2005) argues in a useful analysis that the use of suicide killing by Islamists is a form of weapon against foreign occupation of territories. This strategy is used against a perceived infiltration and domination of *Dar al Islam* by non-believers (*kuffir*). In line with this, Martha Crenshaw (1985) suggests that terrorist organisations deem that violence is a mechanism to achieve their political goals. Thus, Islamists aspire for the world to be under the umbrella of a caliphate. This perceived clarion call is observed in northern Nigeria where Boko Haram has been crusading for an Islamic State for Nigeria.

## Between the two Dars

After observing that the utterances and texts of Islamic clerics and scholars are the cause-effect of jihâdist tendencies, one must focus on how they justify their claims. In seeking an answer, it is useful to note that jihâd of the sword has two strands: the defensive and the offensive jihâds (Wiktorowicz, 2005). There is a clear distinction between the jihâd of defense and jihâd of attack. Defensive jihâd pertains to a holy war against the *Kuffir* (non-believers) that have interfered or politically occupied with the *umma* which comprises the *Dar al Islam*. An illustration of *Dar al Islam* is the struggle to reacquire land from non-Muslim rule in places such as Afghanistan, Chechnya, Kashmir, and Palestine. Jihâd is also a term that is used when Muslims are in an offensive position with non-Muslims. In this depiction, Muslims have occupied non-Muslim territories *(Dar al Harb)*. They perceive such territories to be living in an ungodly atmosphere, thus the need to convert such communities/states by the sword. Such societies are regarded as "a territory outside the pale of Muslim law" (Khadduri, 2006: 170). Most important, is that Muslims living in *Dar al Harb* are under no obligation to observe its laws. It is therefore not surprising that Muslims encounter opposition as "the Prophet Muhammad began his career in Mecca as an opposition leader, and was for some time engaged in a struggle against authority as established among his people and in his birthplace" (Lewis, 1987: 25)

In many ways, the ideology of *Dar al Harb* illustrates that Muslims seem not to integrate with other religious groups when they are in the minority, in societies in Western Europe. It is suggested that the non-integration of a vast majority of Muslims in such societies has generated Islamophobia, as it appears to be an intricate task in understanding Islam. Before delving further, it is important to note that Islamophobia is beyond the scope of this chapter, the context and concept of the term has generated intense debates by the academia and media. This is hardly surprising as non-Muslims are considered *kuffir* by Islamists. Needless to say, this makes it very difficult to enquire into the subject matter. However, a precise definition of Islamophobia is provided by Gottschalk & Greenberg (2008:5): "A social anxiety toward Islam and Muslim cultures that is largely unexamined…This anxiety relies on a sense of otherness, despite many common sources of thought." This signifies the raison d'être that *Dar al Harb* is an altogether complex and perhaps a difficult concept to understand, as more than half the world is *Dar al Harb*. However, on a deeper level, the modern world is made up of too many 'phobias', such as anti-Semitism and Westernophobia. These 'phobias' are usually fables and based on biased information presented by others who are petrified about understanding another's culture. On a critical focus, Burki (2011: 586) informs us that:

> *Dar al Harb might demographically be the land of the infidels and non-believers (kuffir) but, ultimately, the entire world is Dar al Islam according to Allah. This strategy of broadly defining Dar al Islam in order to thereby characterise their "war" as being a defensive jihâd is based on a historical reality: the boundaries of Dar al Islam remain unclear. Many Muslims believe that the legitimate boundaries of Dar al Islam include all territory that has been reclaimed by the "crusaders" and others such as Spain, much of Eastern Europe, the Caucasus, the Indian sub-continent, etc.*

The above extract reveals that Islam permits Muslims to be in a central position in the world. Since most part of the Muslim world has not achieved this leading position, the quest for asserting dominion is part of their desire. There is nothing wrong to have this desire. Nevertheless, Islamists, in trying to achieve such an ambition have resorted to redefining the boarders of *Dar al Islam*. They have resorted to the violent quest for a caliphate. One can conveniently trace this quest in the mindset of al Zawahiri, then second in command to Osama bin Laden when he ardently argues that:

> *The jihad movement must adopt its plan on the basis of controlling a piece of land in the heart of the Islamic world on which it could establish and protect the state of Islam and launch its battle to restore the rational caliphate based on the traditions of the prophet.... Armies achieve victory only when the infantry takes hold of land. Likewise, the Mujahid Islamic movement will not triumph against the world coalition unless it possesses a fundamentalist base in the heart of the Islamic world* (Springer et al, 2009:45-46).

## Conclusion

On refelction, the caliphate, otherwise known as the *Amir al-Mu'minin* (commander of the faithful) ruled over terrain known as *Dar al Islam*. The caliphate was established after Prophet Muhammad's death. By Abu Bakr (to Sunni Muslims) and became known as the Rashidun. To the Shi'tes, Ali is regarded as the first caliph. Under the Ottoman Empire, the caliphate was used to describe the Middle East, North Africa and vast parts of Europe. This caliphate ended in 1924. There is a strong desire by Islamists to create a new caliphate ordained by God to dominate the world against modern democracies. Research by Phares (2007; xv) demonstrates that, "All in all, the history of the twentieth century boiled down to a series of struggles between two major camps: the fortresses of authoritarianism and the houses of democracy." More plausibly, this explains the rationale behind the perceived clash of civilisations between Islam and the West (Huntington, 1996); and the new frontiers of jihâd in Africa. What this portends is that Islam has a unifying force within its adherents. On a deeper level, Clark (1990) rightly points out the bonding potentials of Islam, especially the capacity of Islam to create solidarity among groups. Clark notes that people desire to belong to social structures and are opposed to conflict. Clark (1990) argues that in this regard:

> *The major religions of the world, of course, come first to mind. It is no accident that they arose in parallel with the earliest civilisations, largely to ameliorate some of their worst excesses, and even today, they represent important sources of sacred social meaning for tens of millions of people. Islam is perhaps the chief contemporary example* (Clark, 1990:51).

In an attempt to gain an understanding of this extract, Abbas (2011:40) posits that: "The concept of *umma* has become the designation of a collective identity since it can unite Muslims from many different backgrounds." One begins to wonder where lies the justification for warring with the people of the *Dar al Harb* and the institution of the world as *Dar al Islam*. It is argued that such misinterpretation is similar to the issue of *istishhad* (martyrdom) in Islam. Again, in this regard, the Qur'an makes it clear that:

*You shall spend in the cause of God; do not throw yourselves with your own hands into destruction* (Quran 2:195).

The concept of martyrdom in Islam was popularised by Islamists' jihâd against Israeli occupation in Palestine in the 1980s. This was necessitated from the fact that Israel was viewed as a strong enemy who could not be fought on the battle field. Jihâd has now evolved as a tactic and strategic offensive against powerful enemies who possess superior military might. Thus, jihâd embarked by radical groups use terrorism as a military strategy. In other words, terrorism as a military strategy is concerned with maximum risk for minimum gain as a tool for militancy — you win small, you lose big.

# References

Abbas, Tahir, 2011. Islamic radicalism and Multicultiral Politics: The British Experience. London & New York: Routledge.

Ahmad, Ghulam. 1889. 'Noor-ul-Haq', (Part 2) accessed on the 1st of March 2014 at: http://aaiil.org/urdu/books/mirzaghulamahmad/noorulhaq/noorulhaq2.pdf

Appleby, R. Scott & Marty E. Martin, 2002. 'Fundamentalism,' Foreign Policy 128, ProQuest Business Publication: 16-22.

Atran, Scott, 2006. 'The Moral Logic and Growth of Suicide Terrorism',The Washington Quarterly, Volume 29, Number 2.

Bandura, A., 1998,'Mechanisms of Moral Disengagement'. In W. Reich (Ed.), Origins of Terrorism. Washington, DC: Woodrow Wilson Center Press: 161-191.

Baudrillard, Jean, 2002. The Spirit of Terrorism. London; New York: Verso.

Booney, Richard, 2004. Jihād: From Qur'ān to bin Laden. New York: Palgrave Macmillan.

Bonner, Michael, 2006. Jihâd in Islamic History: Doctrines and Practice. Princeton, NJ: Princeton University Press.

Brahimi, Alia, 2010. Crushed in the Shadows: Why Al Qaeda Will Lose the War of Ideas Studies in Conflict & Terrorism, 33:93–110.

Burki, Shireen Khan, 2011. 'Haram or Halal? Islamists' Use of Suicide Attacks as "Jihâd", Terrorism and Political Violence, 23:4, 582-601.

# References

Byman, Daniel, 2003. Al-Qaeda as an Adversary: Do We Understand Our Enemy? World Politics, Volume 56, Number 1, 139-163.

Clark, E. Mary, 1990. 'Meaningful Social Bonding as a Universal Human Need', in Burton, John. Ed., 1990. Conflict: Human Needs Theoery. New York: St Martins Press: 34-59.

Cook, David, 2005. Understanding Jihad, Berkeley; Los Angeles: University of California Press.

Crenshaw, Martha, 1985. 'Theories of Terrorism: Instrumental and Organisational Approaches,' in Rapoport, David C., 1985. (ed)., Inside Terrorist Organisations. London: Frank Cass.

Dolnik, Adam, 2003. /Die and Let Die: Exploring Links between Suicide Terrorism and Terrorist Use of Chemical, Biological, Radiological, and Nuclear Weapons', Studies in Conflict and Terrorism, Vol. 26, No. 1, 17–35.

Egerton, Frazer. 2011. Jihad in the West: The Rise of Militant Salafism. Cambridge: Cambridge University Press.

Esposito, John, L., 1998. Islam and Politics. Fourth Edition. New York: Syracuse University Press.

Esposito, John L., 2003. Unholy war: Terror in the Name of Islam. New York: Oxford University Press.

Gottschalk, Peter and Greenberg, Gabriel, 2008. Islamophobia. Lanham: Rowman & Littlefield Publishers

Gunaratna, Rotan, 2002. Inside Al Qaeda: Global Network of Terror. London: Hurst & Company.

Hassan, R. 2009. What Motivates the Suicide Bombers? Yale Global Online, a Publication of MacMillan Center assessed on the 26th of October, 2014 at: http://yaleglobal.yale.edu/content/what-motivates-suicide-bombers-0

Hazim, Hakim & Bunker, Robert J., 2006. 'Perpetual Jihad: Striving for a Caliphate', Global Crime Vol. 7:3-4,436-445,

Huntington, Samuel P., 1996. The Clash of Civilizations and the Remaking of World Order. New York: Simon & Schuster Uk Ltd.

Kenny, Joseph, 2001. 'The Spread of Islam in Nigeria: A Historical Survey', Paper given at Conference on Sharî`a in Nigeria Spiritan Institute of Theology, Enugu, 22-24 March 2001. Accessed on the 2nd of May 2008 at http://www.diafrica.org/kenny/Sist.htm

Khadduri, Majid, 2006. War and Peace in the law of Islam. Baltimore: The John Hopkins Press.

Khashan, Hilal, 1997. 'The New World Order and the Tempo of Militant Islam', British Journal of Middle Eastern Studies, Vol. 24, No. 1; 5-24.

Khosrokhavar, Farhad, 2005. Suicide Bombers: Allah's New Martyrs. London: Pluto Press.

Küntzel, Matthias, 2008. 'Suicide Terrorism and Islam', American Foreign Policy Interests: The Journal of the National Committee on American Foreign Policy, 30:4, 227-232

Lawrence, Bruce, 2005 Messages to the World: The Statements of Osama Bin Laden. London; New York: Verso.

Lewis, Bernard, 1967. The Assassins. London: Weidenfeld & Nicolson.

Madsen, J. 2004. Suicide Terrorism: Rationalising the irrational. Strategic Insights, 3(8), 1-6.

Moghadam, Assaf , 2008/09. 'Motives for Martyrdom: Al-Qaida, Salafi Jihad, and the Spreadof Suicide Attacks', International Security, Volume 33, Number 3, Winter, 46-78.

Munir, M. 2008. Suicide Attacks and Islamic Law. International Review of the Red Cross, 90 (869), 71-89, assessed on the 26th of October at: http://www.academia.edu/221071/Suicide_Attacks_and_Islamic_Law

Napoleoni, Loretta, 2003. 'Modern Jihad: The Islamist Crusade', SAIS Review, Volume 23, Number 2, 53-69.

Pape, Robert A., 2005. Dying to Win: The Strategic Logic of Suicide Terrorism. New York: Random House.

Phares, Walid, 2007. Jihadism Against Democracy: The War of Ideas. New York: Basingstoke: Palgrave MacMillan.

Piscatori, James P., 1986. Islam in a World of Nation-States, New York: Cambridge University Press.

Rogan, Randall G., 2010. 'Jihad Against Infidels and Democracy: A Frame Analysis of Jihadist Ideology and Jurisprudence for Martyrdom and Violent Jihad', Communication Monographs, 77:3, 393-413.

Roy, Olivier, 2002. Globalised Islam: The Search for a new Ummah. London: Hurst & Company.

Rudolph, Peters, 2005. Jihad in Classical and Modern Islam. 2nd Edition. Princeton: Markus Wiener Publishers.

Shenton, W. Robert, 1986. The Development of Capitalism in Northern Nigeria. Toronto: University of Toronto Press.

Springer, Devin, R., Regens, James, L., & Edger, David, N., 2009. Islamic Radicalism and Global Jihad. Washington, D.C.: Georgetown University Press.

Stith, R. Charles, 2010. 'Radical Islam in East Africa', The ANNALS of the American Academy of Political and Social Science; 632: 55.

Van der Krogt & Christopher J., 2010. 'Jihād without apologetics', Islam and Christian–Muslim Relations, 21:2, 127-142.

Wiktorowicz, Quintan, 2005. 'A Genealogy of Radical Islam', Studies in Conflict & Terrorism, 28:2, 75-97.

Yates, Joshua, 2007. 'The Resurgence of Jihad & The Specter of Religious Populism', SAIS Review, Volume 27, Number 1:127-144.

# 4

# New Frontiers of Terrorism

## Introduction

Islam first arrived in Africa by jihâd of the Muslim Rashidun army of the Rashidun Caliphate (632–661). From this point, Islam gradually assimilated into North Africa through trade with Arabs through trading routes. Egypt was under the control of the Islamic Caliphate until 1171. Islam later became the dominant religion in North Africa and was an influential political tool in the Mali Empire (c. 1230 to c. 1600), the Songhai Empire (c.1464–1591). Other expansionist efforts came through the Usman dan Fodio jihâd of 1804 which ushered in the Sokoto Caliphate. Islam has been growing at a fast rate amongst Africans for the reason that its values are commensurate with traditional African ways of life. Islamic culture as well as many traditional African societies accepts communal living and social customs such as polygamy. However, the rapid growth of Islam in Africa has witnessed a parallel growth in radical Islam.

Within the new frontiers of global jihâd berthing in Africa, it is readily observed that the individuals at the forefront are of African heritage. Ayman az-Zawahiri, the leader of al-Qaeda, after the demise of Osama bin Ladin and Saif al-Adel, the military head of al-Qaeda, are both associates of the Egyptian Islamic Jihâd (EIJ). Moreover, another African named Abu Yahya al-Libi, a Libyan from the Libyan Fighting Group (LIFG) is a prominent leader of al-Qaeda. It appears that there has been a paradigm shift from radical Islamists leadership from the Middle East to Africa. We are then bound to ask ourselves why terrorism is particularly rampant in Africa? The aura of complexity and diversity in Africa reveals the difficulty in explaining radical Islam in Africa. An attestation of this proclivity of Africa as the new frontier of radical Islam is noted by Krech (2011: 132):

> ...in the period between 2009 and 2011, al-Qaeda activities have been registered in nineteen African nations or regions: Algeria, Burkina Faso, Djibouti, Egypt, Eritrea, Ethiopia, Ghana, Kenya, Libya, Mauritania, Morocco, Niger, Nigeria, Puntland, Somalia, Somaliland, South Africa, Sudan and Uganda. Al-Qaeda appears to be advancing more and more from the north and east to central and southern Africa. Even in South Africa there are now al-Shabab support groups.

The often quoted dictum — 'African solutions to African problems', is pivotal in understanding and seeking solutions to radical Islam on the continent. It would readily be recalled that Osama Bin Laden resided in the Sudan in 1991, after he was stripped of his Saudi nationality in 1994. Bin Laden viewed Africa as the new frontier for creating networks for his new organisation—al-Qaeda. At this point in time, when Osama had been expelled by Saudi Arabia, many states in the Middle East were weary of his brand of ideology. However, in Sudan, Osama who was later joined with his friend; Zawahiri, was given political succour and security by Hassan al-Turabi under his Islamist government, which had taken the reins of power in 1989.

## The New Terrain of Global Jihâd in Africa

The new terrain from which the global jihâd is being waged is in Africa. While radical Islam is known to have existed on the African continent in various forms over the years, a new trend appears to have emerged which has overshadowed existing perceptions of radicalism. Several incidents of terrorism which have been carried out in the past, such as the 1998 embassy bombings in Nairobi, Kenya, and the Tanzania bombings cannot in any way be compared to events such as the hostage taking of over 416 workers at a gas plant in Algeria; the Westgate shopping mall attacks in Nairobi, Kenya, or the establishment of Islamic caliphates in some parts of northern Mali and in northern Nigeria (Agbiboa, 2013).[48] Unlike attacks which took place in the past, some of which were masterminded by Arabs who found their way on African soil, these new campaigns have been spearheaded by Africans, and have been described as overt, brutal campaigns, a display of the growing power and boldness of these terrorist groups in showing a firm resolve to their cause.

It is important to stress that jihâdist incursion has always been a part of African history and a crucial aspect of the growth and expansion of Islam in Africa. Islam came into Africa in the early 7th century, especially during the great persecution. The great persecution is described as a period in the early history of the growth of Islam when a lot of followers of the Islamic religion emigrated from Saudi Arabia, the birth place of the religion to other parts of the globe following stiff opposition from the authorities. According to Levtzion and Pouwells (2000:1):

> *Islam reached Africa through two gateways, from the east and from the north. From both directions the carriers of Islam navigated across vast empty spaces,*

---

48   Agbiboa, D. E., 2013. 'Al-Shabab, the Global Jihad, and Terrorism without Borders', accessed on the 27th of October, 2014 at: Al-Shabab, the Global Jihad, and Terrorism without Borders.

*the waters of the Indian Ocean and the sands of the Sahara desert. Both ocean and desert, which so often are considered to be barriers, could be crossed with appropriate means of transportation and navigational skills, and they were, in fact, excellent transmitters of religious and cultural influences. Densely populated lands, on the other hand, functioned as filters, their numerous layers slowing down the infiltration of religious and cultural influences.*

In reality, Islam became the dominant religion in North Africa in the Twelfth century C.E. The spread of Islam in North Africa came in conjunction with Arab rule. The great persecution was responsible for the growth and spread of Islam, particularly in northern Africa. The settling of Arabs resulted in the replacing of the traditional cultures of these areas with Islam. This is perhaps the reason why there is a Muslim majority in the population of North African countries of Egypt, Tunisia, Algeria and Libya. The substitution of traditional beliefs with Islam occurred gradually and had some degree of cultural influence derived from customs of the society where it was introduced.[49] The intertwining of Islam with local cultures featured quite evidently in West Africa and could be attributed to the role of both missionaries and traders in spreading the religion. Some of the cultural influences on the practice of Islam include the role of education and also the existence of Brotherhoods.[50] The role of education has been summarised on the 'Exploring Africa Matrix' of the Michigan State University (ND)[51] as Follows:

*From its beginning, Islam taught the importance of education. Everywhere in the world Islam has spread, it has fostered education. Early in its expansion in Africa,*

---

49 See Hil, 2009.
50 Examples of such brotherhoods include the Tijjani order, Muridiyya Brotherhood, Layenne Brotherhood, Qadiriyya Brotherhood, and the Salihiyya Brotherhood. Furthermore, Ikwan-al Muslimi which emanated from Egypt and had a large following.
51 Michigan State University (ND) Religion in Africa: Islam in Africa, accessed on the 3rd of September 2015 at: http://exploringafrica.matrix.msu.edu/students/curriculum/m14/activity3.php

> *Muslim scholars built libraries, and opened schools and libraries. Cairo, with a number of Islamic universities, became a center of learning and scholarship. In West Africa, Muslim scholars developed an impressive library and university at Timbuktu in Mali. These distinct features have always played a huge role in the growth and spread of Jihâdist campaigns in Africa.*

As the influence of the traders and missionaries grew, so did Islam. However, it was not until the 13th Century that Islam became adopted as the official religion of these West African empires by the rulers after they undertook pilgrimage to the holy city of Mecca. One of such leaders who made such trips was Mansa Musa of Mali, who during his reign built notable edifices monuments in the cities of Timbuktu and Djenne.

The infusion of traditional customs in the practice of Islam did not sit well with some of the scholars and religious teachers who believed in a sacred adherence to the tenets of Islam. These scholars sought to bring about a change in the way things were done and thus formed groups which they propagated their ideologies to their followers. However, in certain instances, they were seen as intrusive and unduly extreme by the authorities who sought to suppress their movements either with threats, detention or actual force. Subsequently, these groups responded to these threats with an insurgency against the state. For instance Uthman dan Fodio owned a *Madrassa* where he propagated his beliefs before organising an insurgency. In a similar twist, the Boko Haram sect until 2009 was more or less a peaceful sect confined to the propagating their beliefs in the expanse of land granted them by the Bornu state government, while some of the insurgencies such as that of Askia and Uthman dan Fodio were successful, others were not.

The nature of Jihâd in early African history will help us understand the motive behind radical Islamic groups which currently exist. Islam in Africa is mostly interconnected with the Sunni Brotherhood, with a blend of traditional values. Rosander & Westerlund (1997) have referred to this phenomenon as 'African Islam'. This refers to Islam which is accommodative of African culture. Most Jihâd campaigns point to a similar cause, that is, pervasion of values and doctrine of Islamic teachings and oppression of a group by the other, and exploitation of the majority at the hands of the minority. In addition, the Jihâdists campaign involve invocation of a moral authority emanating from the heart of Islam itself, thus representing a campaign for promotion and preservation of moral values from the holy land. For instance, the Fulani conquest by Uthman dan Fodio was legitimised with the assistance of Abd al-Qadir al-Jilani, founder of the Qadiriyya brotherhood. In was through the struggles of Uthman dan Fodio that the concept of *Kuffir* (the declaration of a Muslim as an infidel) was introduced.[52] In Somalia, Sayyid Muhammad Abdallah Hassan began a jihâd in 1898 to purify the country from the Ethiopian and European 'unbelievers.' The Sayyid belonged to the Salihiyya Brotherhood, an offshoot of a *tariqa* founded by a disciple of Ahmad ibn Idris. Jihâds in the past were also characterised through exploitation of grievances of a population in order to achieve the Jihâdist goals. Uthman dan Fodio was able to succeed using the grievance of the local Fulani herdsmen. These feats have been reproduced in recent times in Iraq, Mali, the Islamic State in Iraq and Syria (ISIS), AQIM and the Movement for Unity and Jihâd in West Africa (MUJAO) who all have some form of connection to the Global jihâdist group, al-Qaeda. But first, it is important to examine the features of this global jihâd in Africa in which has planted its base from it plans to inflict deadly blows on Western civilisation.

---

52   See Gwandu A. A. (2010) 'The Nature and Character of Shaykh Abd Allah Foduye the Nature and Character of Shaykh Abd Allah b. Foduye', Usmanu Dan Fodiyo University, Sokoto online, accessed on the 1st of December 2014 at: https://madanitimbukti.wordpress.com/tag/shaykh-uthman-dan-fodio/

A few African states have recently been experiencing a new wave of terrorist activity due to the upsurge in Islamic extremism. Islamists terrorism which was largely confined to the Middle East has made an overwhelming intrusion into Africa. States such as Nigeria, Somalia, Sudan, Kenya and Tanzania have now experienced Islamist jihâdist group formation—thanks to the regions failed state policies that are blended with prebendalistic craft and rentier systems of governance. With the disorganisation of al-Qaeda in the Middle East due to the fallout of the Taliban and the constant drone attacks on terrorist cells in Yemen and Pakistan, radical Islamists seem to have found a comfort zone in Africa, either as a safe haven for radical Islamists or as zones that breed Islamist groups—it has now become the new frontier for Islamic terrorism—again, thanks to obituary of communism and the vegetative state of capitalism. The reason for this quick intrusion is for the reason that Africa has not been a center of debate by the international community on the ground that it is perceived that the continent has nothing to offer. In the same manner, it would be recalled that the Taliban in Afghanistan was not considered as threat by the West prior to 9/11. Moreover, America never thought that there would be another Islamist attack on the World Trade Center after the February 26, 1993 bombing.

With the large influx of Taliban - styled transnational cells emanating in many parts of Africa, it is fair to predict that another incident as chaotic as 9/11 may arise in the future. In this development with the global threat of radical Islam, African problems are best resolved, not only by Africans, but by the international community. It is speculated that the grand plan of al-Qaeda and ISIS is to launch a colossal attack on the West, using African as the launching pad. In such a situation, the searchlight as to who is responsible would become a challenge—would it be the state or the terrorist group?

## Complexities of Terrorism

The term 'terrorism' has its foundations during the French revolution of 1789-1799. At this point in time, the French monarchy committed atrocities and burdened its people. In the light of this, the people of France considered it a delight to use violence towards the agents of the Monarchy—this legitimate enchantment at committing violence against agents of the state led to the French revolution. The expression represented the drastic change from a monarchy to a new dispensation of democracy. On the global level, terrorism took international recognition in 1934, when the French Foreign Minister and King Alexander 1 of Yugoslavia were assassinated in France. In modern times, acts of terrorism were also perpetuated by the Irish Republican Army against the United Kingdom in their quest for self-determination.

In the modern world, the term 'terrorism' is perhaps the most used political idiom since the Cold War. Whittaker (2007:2) correctly notes that there are more than a hundred printed versions of terrorism. Consequently, the phrase 'terrorism' has a wide and complex meaning. In 1980, the Central Intelligence Agency of United States of America defined terrorism as:

> *The threat or use of violence for political purposes by individuals or groups, whether acting for or in opposition to established governmental authority, when such actions are intended to shock, stun or intimidate victims. Terrorism, has involved groups seeking to overthrow specific regimes, to rectify perceived national or group grievances, or to undermine international order as an end in itself.*[53]

This definition seems all embracive as it includes groups. In a similar language, Article 2(1) (b) of the United Nations Convention on the Suppression of the Financing of Terrorism (1999) defines terrorism as:

---

53  See https://www.cia.gov/news-information/cia-the-war-on-terrorism/terrorismfaqs.html.

> ...any other act intended to cause death or serious bodily injury to a civilian, or to any person not taking an active part in the hostilities in a situation of armed conflict, when the purpose of such act by its nature or context is to intimidate a population or to compel a government or an international organisation to do or to abstain from doing any act.

The language above notes that terrorism is confined to the intimidation of innocents or coercing a state to act by commission or omission during war. In a broader expression, the United Nations Security Council Resolution 1566 (2004) defines terrorism as:

> ...criminal acts, including against civilians, committed with the intent to cause death or serious bodily injury, or taking of hostages, with the purpose to provoke a state of terror in the general public or in a group of persons or particular persons, intimidate a population or compel a government or an international organisation to do or to abstain from doing any act, which constitute offences within the scope of and as defined in the international conventions and protocols relating to terrorism, are under no circumstances justifiable by considerations of a political, philosophical, ideological, racial, ethnic, religious or other similar nature...

The language here defines terrorism within the realm of criminal acts that promote terror to individuals under broad categories. Perhaps, a concise definition is:

> *The use of violence by non-state actors against noncombatants designed to influence an audience in order to achieve a political outcome* (Freeman, 2008:54).

However, from this extract, is there a difference between acts of terrorism committed by non-state actors and the state? This definition does not cover acts of terrorism that are committed by the state. Perhaps, a broader definition is provided by African Union:

> *Any act which is a violation of the criminal laws of a State Party and which may endanger the life, physical integrity or freedom of, or cause serious injury or death to any person, any number or group of persons or causes or may cause damage to public or private property, natural resources, environmental or cultural heritage.*[54]

From a particular perspective, this definition would embrace states/regimes who are committing gross human rights abuse on their own citizens. It could be argued that the Arab Spring uprising consisted of deeds of terrorism by states such as Libya and Egypt whilst trying to cling on to power. Moreover, the preceding stratocratic regimes across the continent could be deemed to have committed acts of terrorism to its citizens given the fact that these regimes were flagrant abusers of human rights. The definition of terrorism by the African Union (AU) does not provide that perpetrators of terrorism should have any objective for their acts, nor does it define who a terrorist is. The act of attacking people and or property suffices to be an indicator on who is the terrorist. Again, one notices a gap in the definition provided by the AU for the reason that non-violent acts may constitute terrorism. For instance, a threat to a state government that there is an explosive device in its parliamentary building would constitute a terrorist act as its intent is to procure fear.

On another point, a state may be regarded as a terrorist if it commits/sponsors acts of terrorism on another state. Afghanistan under Taliban regime is confined to this categorisation when it supported al-Qaeda in the 9/11 attacks on America. Again, on another dimension, a state

---

[54] OAU Convention on the Prevention and Combating of Terrorism (the Algiers Convention) by the 35th Ordinary Session of Heads of State and Government held in Algiers, Algeria, in July 1999.

may indirectly be responsible for terrorist acts in another country. This is illustrated by the Russian support of Donetsk pro-Russian rebels in Ukraine in 2014. It must be noted that terrorism is a complex discourse, as in many situations, a terrorist may be regarded as a freedom fighter by other groups. As the often quote notes that 'one person's terrorist is another person's freedom fighter.' For instance, Nelson Mandela was officially labelled as a 'terrorist' by Western powers such as the USA and Britain whilst in prison, but to many he was regarded as a liberator. One readily recalls Margaret Thatcher labelling Mandela and his African National Congress (ANC) as: "The ANC is a typical terrorist organisation ... Anyone who thinks it is going to run the government in South Africa is living in cloud-cuckoo land."[55] Paradoxically, Mandela was removed from the terrorist brand when he became President of South Africa in 1994. During the fight against colonialism, opposition fighters such as the Mao Mau in Kenya were labelled 'terrorists' by the British in the 1950s. In the same sense, a terrorist in the modern world depends on who is making the observation/allegation. For instance, the Islamist fighters (Mujahedin) in the 1980s who later became the Taliban were regarded as freedom fighters by America (America formed the Mujahedin, but not the Taliban) were in later years labelled as terrorists by the West. On the other hand, Islamists consider the West (America) the terrorist. It then appears that to the imagination of Islamists, that they are now terrorising the terrorist. As seen from the above, the definition of terrorism has generated different meanings both from the academia and from the media.

We should bear in mind that the aim of the Islamist terrorist is that they envisage that their acts/threats of killing the innocents would create sentiments of fear in

---

55  See 'Mandela: from "terrorist" to world statesman', accessed on the 1st of November 2013 at: http://www.euronews.com/2013/12/05/nelson-mandela-a-man-who-will-remain-in-our-collective-consciousness-long-after/

the minds of civilians or non-combatants, thereby gaining attention by civilian population. Islamists have the absolute conviction that they are doing the right thing, but they do not realise that they have taken the wrong path—the road to death and destruction. Terrorism aims at overwhelming and demoralising society in order to induce the state to yield to its demands. It seems appropriate that the politics of fear is confined to Richardson's (2006) three Rs analogy— revenge, renown and reaction—she argues that terrorists are rational individuals who are seeking 'revenge' towards an aggressor—a desire to become 'renowned' (publicity and glory) and—the power to 'react' (confrontation and ability to resist) to the enemy. This notion enables the 'world' to understand their political/religious ambitions so that their political/religious desires would be conceded to (McCormick, 2003). In another dimension, terrorists aim at disrupting economic activities in order to paralyse the government. If terrorism is defined in terms of seeking political ends or disrupting the economy of a state—would it be adequate to suggest that it is different from war—since war seeks to achieve these ends. In seeking to answer this enquiry, an act of war seeks to destroy the military forces of another state. Terrorism, as noted above, seeks to destroy non-combatants. Conversely, in Africa it is readily observed that radical Islamic groups target non-combatants and stage guerrilla tactics aimed at weakening/destroying the states military forces. In a broader insight, wars are conducted between states and they are subject to the law of armed conflict (the Hague Conventions).

As we have seen, delving into these varied meanings and dimensions may engender complex and divergent views. What is clear is that the terrorist operates in the shadows—their individual identities are unknown—they are everywhere. This awareness instils fear. It then seems correct to define terrorism as the act of inducing fear. If terrorism is viewed as such, then would a provocative phone call that falsely informs individual(s) that there is a bomb in their vicinity be regarded as a terrorist act? A question that may be striking is if the intended audience of the terrorist act is not prone to fear—could such an act be confined as terrorist? A retort to this is that any act that can induce fear to a reasonable person under a given circumstance is within the ambits of terrorism. In consonance with our definition, terrorism in simple terms as noted by Radu (2002: 276) is all about "attacks against largely or exclusively civilian targets in order to inspire fear." Terrorism generates a psychological notion of fear amongst the citizens of a state. It creates a situation of anxiety therefore using propaganda to channel its grievance to the public, in order to be heard and taken seriously. Ruthven (2012:45) illustrates the impact of fear by correctly observing that:

> *The 'propaganda of the deed' showing people jumping from skyscrapers or bodies pulled from the London underground creates an atmosphere of panic, a mood that empowers the terrorists by creating the impression that, militarily speaking, they dispose of forces beyond their numbers or the size of any constituency for which they may speak.*

But why is fear essential in propagating terrorism? Fear is a progandising tool that has been used for centuries. It was used by the Third Reich to instill obedience to Hitler during the Second World War and by bandit elements such as the Sicilian Mafia in Italy. In todays' world, it is used by dictators, especially in Africa, to co-opt the state's citizenry to obedience and servitude. In simple terms, Altheide (2006: 17) notes that: "...the politics of fear is set in motion by appealing to audiences' emotions and stereotype."

He further perceptively writes that: "Fear does not just happen; it is socially constructed and managed by political actors to promote their own goals" (Altheide, 2006: 18).

It is sensed that Islamists in Africa have understood the social construction of how the notion 'fear' has been used by nepotic leaders. They have learnt that a strand of the leadership system of many African states is the use of fear to harass, exploit, deceive and manipulate their people.

In making sense of 'terrorism'—terrorists' acts are usually defined by law or the dictionary such as the killing innocent citizens. The issue here could then connote that the killing of innocents during war is within the definition of terrorism. If this is agreeable, then it could be argued that the bombing of innocents in Hiroshima and Nagasaki was an act of terrorism by the United States in the Second World War. In another instance, it could be asserted that the mass bombing of the Palestines by Israel on July 2014, which witnessed the deaths of many children and women, were deeds of terrorism by Israel.

Another inquisitive thought is whether the air strikes on Iraq and Afghanistan in the early 2000s by America which killed thousands of innocents could be termed as terrorist attacks—since its key objective was political in nature— desiring a change of regime. These acts may have ushered the increasing efforts of terrorist activities against America and its allies. Perhaps, the French philosopher, Baudrillard (2002: 4-5) speaks the mind of the terrorist, when he noted perceptively that: "For it is that superpower which, by its unbearable power, has fomented all this violence which is endemic throughout the world, and hence that (unwittingly) terroristic imagination which dwells in all of us."

However, this is only an aspect of the issue. It is crucial to defend peace against terrorists' attacks, not only in Africa, but in the entire world. The essence of defence are within the realms of providing education, dismantling corruption, empowering grassroot people, economic transparency and bridging the gap between the rich and the poor.

It is important to recognise that Islamist based terrorism is in the realm of international concern in the world today. This anxiety is seen in the parlance: 'Muslims are not terrorists but all terrorists are Muslims.' Terrorism is not exclusive to Islam alone. It is practiced all over the world when groups are desirous in obtaining political change through violence. Even in Western societies, organisations such as the Irish Republican Army (IRA) and the Basques separatist group unleashed wave of terrorists' attacks. The intriguing question then is what generates Islam to be positioned in such a manner? One answer to this question is found in the perceived sentiments of injustice. In order to understand the issues surrounding Islam and terrorism, it is crucial to understand the nature and content of what constitutes grievance to the Islamist as terrorism does not spring out from a void vacuum.

Aside from the notion that terrorism could take the form of political grievance by revolutionary groups, it is now popularised by the perceived 'clash of ideologies— Westernisation and Islamisation. As pointed by Gus (2003:28) that: "Behind each incident of terrorist violence is some type of deeply held belief system that has motivated the perpetrators. These belief systems are, at their core, extremist systems characterised by intolerance."

From our discussion above, it is observed that terrorism is difficult to combat as there are different meanings of the term. In the context of this study, terrorism is defined as a strategy of fighting Westernised institutions by Islamists, due to the intolerance of Judeo-Christian ideologies. At this point, it is suggested that evangelical Christianity vastly spreading across Africa is conterminous with the rise of Islamist terrorists groups in the region. The proselytising of Christian missionaries may have instigated moderate Muslims to have perceived threats to their identities. Global jihâdisation is procured by the 'evangelism' of Islamists who have sentiments of subjugation. From these incidents it may be convincing to infer that economic inequalities are rooted in terrorism (Abadie, 2006; Piazza, 2006).

The tolerance of another individual's religion is an intolerable act amongst religious extremists. What extremists say in plain terminology is that 'my way is the path of righteousness—your way is the path of hell.' It is revealed that an individual's faith is superior and glorious to another individual's faith—these sentiments of a just war in the context of a jihâd on the infidels. This insight has engendered an apocalyptic age that expounds a clash between good and evil which has generated the modern day terrorism. The paradox about the terrorist is that he/she is considered as 'evil' in the eyes of those who are threatened by the terrorist group—the terrorist group also considers its target as being an embodiment of 'evil'—hence the terminology of America as the "Great Satan" by the late Ayatollah Khomeini of Iran— This explains why the terrorist does not have any empathy towards its targets—they believe that they are engaged in a cosmic war between good and evil—Hate leads to the desire to cause conflict, death and destruction.

## Foundations of Islamic Terrorism in Africa

Here we have arrived at the crux of the matter. It is important to reiterate that Islam is the religion of the majority in Africa. The Middle East—North Africa axis has the highest amount of Muslims of any region of the world (93% of its estimated 341 million inhabitants are Muslims). In sub-Saharan Africa—Muslims constitute 30% of the population and 24% in the Asia-Pacific region.[56] This situates Africa as a veritable ground for the growth of Islamic radicalism due to the influence of Islam in its ancient empires.

Furthermore, the sway of Islam was co-opted in cultural, political and commercial life styles in ancient kingdoms, which could be seen as the seed of Islam as a popular force

---

56  See http://www.themuslimtimes.org/2013/06/africa/worlds-muslim-population-more-widespread-than-you-might-think, accessed on the 11th of July 2014.

in Africa. Examples of such Kingdoms were the Ghana Empire (before c. 830 until c. 1235); the Mali Empire (c. 1230 to c. 1600); the Songhai Empire (1464–1591); and the Kanem-Bornu Empire (ca. 700 - 1376) which is the oldest Islamic civilisation in Africa; the Sokoto Caliphate (1804-1903). In addition, the influence of the Muhammad Ahmad bin Abd Allah in 1881, the Sudan co-opted the nation into an Islamic kingdom. These early foundations have enabled Islam to be closely connected with African traditional religion, in the sense that Islam is seemingly similar in respect of regulating and embracing ways of life. Perhaps most important is that it was brought to Africa through commercialisation and not through the barrel of a gun. Aside from the trans-Saharan Trade, Islam was planted in sub-Saharan Africa by the use of jihâd. One of such militant conquests was conducted by Uthman dan Fodio (1804-1810). However, it is pertinent to point out that Islam before the Jihâd in sub-Saharan Africa was chiefly a religion of the elites/ruling class. Uthman dan Fodio aimed to establish, not only a puritan form of Islam, but also a caliphate amongst different towns and city states in modern day Nigeria.

Equally significant is that Africans have participated as crusaders of the Islamic faith. After the 5th crusades (1249-1250) the Mongol Empire suffered a series of defeats by the Sanni Mamluk Empire in Egypt in 1259. The Sanni Mamluk Empire was able to resist the crusaders and the raging Mongolian Empire by the use of slaves mainly acquired from Africa. These slaves were called the mamluk. The mamluk became a standing army for the Muslim world. In the modern world, in some ways, Africans, through the influence of Islam have been used as a vehicle for standing armies, as seen in the Libyan Civil war (2011) where the Tuaregs of Mali and Chadians were used as Gaddafi's private army. Another interesting development is that Africans are now the main flux of foreign fighters in states where they are not citizens. There is seen in the exchange of Islamists in groups such as Ansar Dine and Boko Haram.

The inspiring events in Tehran, Iran in 1979 where the perceived apostate Shah, Mohammed Reza Pahlavi, was deposed by the Shia branch of Islam, informed radical Muslims that dictatorial and despotic regimes could be toppled and replaced with an Islamic government. This revolution has been centrally placed in the minds of Islamists in Africa. It is important to remember that, as stressed earlier, the social and economy of many African states procured a desire for change. Needless to say, most terrorists in Africa started their 'bloody careers' as Islamic fighters in Afghanistan during the Afghan/Soviet war in the late 80s. The turnover of radical Islamists was in high numbers. Ahmad Rashid (1999) perceptively notes that forty Islamic countries contributed to the Mujahedin. Moreover, he notes that the Afghanistan war had a profound influence on 1,000,000 Islamists. After the Mujahedin won the war in 1989, which "deflated the myth of the invincible Soviet Army" (Bluth, 1995: 38) and created a strong spirit of morale among the Mujahedin. The fighters disillusioned by their victory imagined that the conquest confirmed the supremacy of jihâd therefore was a rallying point for propaganding across the globe in the bid to influence Muslims to join in a universal jihâd—one of their strong holds was in Africa.

In contextualising terrorism in terms of Islamist groups in Africa, the collective quest for a global caliphate becomes apparent in the minds of radical muslims in order to achieve justice from a broken down, demoralised secularised world. More to the point, Mamdani (2002:771) rightly tells us that "Islamic global war was not a brainchild of bin Laden; the CIA and Pakistan's Inter Services Intelligence (ISI) hoped to transform the Afghan jihâd into a global war waged by Muslim states against the Soviet Union." This act has laid the foundation of Islamophobia in the West, as these Islamic fighters aggrandised the emergence of al-Qaeda, which has proven to be America's biggest nightmare since the Cold War. Al-Qaeda has been the base for other transnational radical Islamists groups from the Middle East to the Maghreb and berthing in Africa. In Africa, this unholy birth has undeniably started with the bombing of the US embassies in Tanzania and Kenya in 1998 and the bombing of the twin towers in New York on the 11th of September 2001. This allegorises that the ideology of Islamist groups is one and the same with all other radicalised Islamist groups. However, most important is that it reveals that radical Islam in Africa does not only depend on internal dynamics of a state, but also essentially on the international factors.

It may remain debatable that a defining feature of Muslims in Africa lies in their religious identity. It is important to note that the people of Africa are more religious than other individuals around the world. This identity acts as a mark of mobilisation, as it creates sentiments of solidarity. In some ways, the consolidation of this identity is as a result of the competitiveness with individuals of other faiths, such as Christianity. This creates intensity in Islamic activism, therefore, the Muslim has a desire to integrate religion with the way the state in governed. The visible problem notably in African states such as Nigeria is that religious leaders are not only competing on the basis of inter-religious competition. but also with politicians and traditional rulers. This is readily seen especially amongst Christian leaders where the desire to acquire private jets seems to be fashionable. These trends have ignited a seemingly similar awakening amongst radical Muslims who do not want to be left out in the quest to be relevant. This appeal has ushered the desire for Sharia law in sub-Saharan Africa. In this sense, radical Islam in the region connects to transnational grievances. Radical Islam has the propensity to position itself as a voice of resistance against exiguity and oppressive governments.

In its most extreme form, this oppression is evident from the fact that individual's in sub-Saharan Africa are at the bottom billion (living below poverty level) in the world (Collier, 2008). Since most states in the region have lost confidence bestowed upon it by its citizens, individuals tend to search for an alternative institution to embed their faith upon. It is then not surprising that to Muslims, the attraction to radical Islam becomes desirable as an alternative solution to poverty. This fatal attraction generates the radical Muslim to embrace terrorism. An observation connecting this argument is noted by Robert Taber in 1965, which is pertinently quoted by Robert M. Cassidy (2008:1):

*Tomorrow's guerrilla armies, in Africa, ....will be drawn from the ranks of the world's have–nots, the hungry peasants and the urban slum dwellers who meet the first requirement of the guerrilla, having nothing to lose but their lives.*

Of course, it is hard to exaggerate how 9/11 has pre-empted the rise of transnational Islamist groups around the world, especially in Africa. These groups are interwoven with organisational networks—networks such as training camps, sharing logistics and most important, financial assistance are used to expand terrorist networks in the region. Islamist groups in Africa have now joined the campaign to confront Judeo-Christianity and its westernised establishment. Al-Qaeda has used viable networks to co-opt Africa in its global jihâd. The seemingly similar objective of radical Islamists groups across Africa is that they perceived grievance towards America/Israel as indicated by the 1980 bombing of an Israeli hotel in Nairobi; the US embassies in Tanzania and Kenya in 1998 (mentioned above) and the bombing of Planet Hollywood in Cape Town, South African in 1998. A striking question emanating from the above is how is radical Islam propagandised to moderate Muslims? It is suggested that propagation of propaganda that was used by the Nazis' that sold Nazism to the Germans, who deemed it usual to slay six million Jews is similar to the approach that Islamists use propaganda to moderate Muslims. History tells us that before the 2nd World War, the German people had sentiments of grievance—economic anti-semitism towards the Jews for reason that the Jews largely controlled the German economy. Again, history tells us that the front page of the London Daily Express on 24 March, 1933 made the headlines: *'Judea Declares War on Germany: Jews of All the World Unite in Action'*. The news read:

> *The Israelite people of the world declare an economic war on Germany. It is not sufficient that we should buy no goods made in Germany. We must refuse to deal with any shopkeeper who sells any German-made goods. What we are proposing is to bring the German people to their senses by destroying their export trade on which their very existence depends.*[57]

This extract reveals that the selling point of effective propaganda lies in searching wherein lies an individual(s) grievances—it is found mainly in economic grievance.

## Islamic Terrorist Networks

Africa has been the home to a superfluity of armed conflicts. However, what is striking is that despite the overabundance of armed struggle on the continent, there has been an absence of transnational conflict. It should be stressed that Western involvement came in form of selling weapons to either guerrilla fighters, such as the UNITA rebel movement in Angola or assisting the sovereignty of state-nations such as Nigeria during the Nigerian Civil War (1967-71). Conversely, this depiction has now changed—

---

57  See Rescuing Israel: The Holocaust – The Motive', accessed on the 2nd of December 2014 at: http://12bytes.org/articles/history/rescuing-israel-the-holocaust-index/rescuing-israel-the-holocaust-the-motive

thanks to Islamist-based terrorist networks. Radical Islam has brought in a new kind of war within the continent—transnational terrorism —which is a brand terrorism. Most Jihâdist networks in Africa are transnational in operation. It would seem that the easy presence of Islamist terrorism in Africa is mainly due to the porous borders along the region. This has generated the easy flow of smuggling of arms and inter-connecting violent jihâdists from the Maghreb into Africa. In some instances, these desires are conceded to by state governments who are weary of the effect of mass killings would have on civilians (Pape, 2003; 2005).

The rise of terrorism amongst Islamist groups in Africa is due to the rise of transnational Islamic groups emanating from the Middle East. The underlying issue here is that Middle Eastern states such as Saudi Arabia, Pakistan, have in many ways contributed to the revivalism of Islam in Africa. The quest for Saudi wealth is a significant factor that influences many Muslims in the region. Moreover, the Arab world is considered by many Muslims all over the world to be the founders of their faith. It is considered a sacred honour for Muslims to undergo a pilgrimage to Mecca, Saudi Arabia for their Hajj. Moreover, the sacred language of the Qur'an is written in Arabic. To many African Muslims, it is perceived that, had it not been for the Arabs, Islam would not have existed. These influences have enabled Islamists to bring its 'gospel' of radical Islam to Africa.

The role of new media cannot be wished away. In a deeply networked world, technology such as mobile-technology and the internet are used in conveying radical messages that are easily assimilated by moderate Muslims. The ideology of radicalisation of Islam is spreading fast among moderate Muslims Africa. This mission of proselytising Islam is co-opted through religious entrepreneurs and its message of radical Islam.[58]

---

58   See chapter 10.

The hope of a better life is the desire of many moderate Muslims. To frustrated moderate Muslims, Islamists offer a gateway to the ideals of a good life as enjoyed in Western societies. Coupled with the increase in socio-economic uncertainty in many African states has ushered Islamists groups to reposition their quest for Islamic extremism as a suitable option from *prebendalism* and the politics of personal acquisition. More to the point, the perceived threat to Islamic culture and global Islamic identity generates transnational Islamists groups to engage in terrorist activities. A vast majority of Muslims in Africa have a strong commitment to Islamic ideals—it is a distinguishing mark of their identity.

The reader will easily intuit that al-Qaeda realised that the grievances of Muslims in Africa were a suitable and fertile ground for implanting radical Islam. Al-Qaeda embarked on a radicalisation process not only in the Middle East, but all around the globe, especially Africa that has a vast population of Muslims. The strategy used by al-Qaeda was the establishment of family networks (cells) through the process of decentralisation of networks. These cells act as centres for recruitment of Muslims who have become propagandised and radicalised. Muslims joining these groups imagine that they belong to a global Islamic family sharing an identical emotive appeal in creating a globalised caliphate. Benjamin & Simon (2002: 397) in making sense of the common appeal of radical Muslims, as reiterated earlier cites an excerpt:

> *How can [a Muslim] possibly accept humiliation and inferiority when he knows that his nation was created to stand at the center of leadership, at the center of hegemony and rule, at the center of ability and sacrifice? How can he possibly accept humiliation and inferiority when he knows that the divine rule is that the entire earth must be subject to the religion of Allah—not to the East, nor to the West—to no ideology and to no path except for the path of Allah?*

In showcasing how humiliation and inferiority appeal to the power of group dynamics, Muslims—in September 2012, many Muslims in Indonesia, Egypt, Thailand and Tunisia went on a violent rampage, burning American flags at embassies when YouTube aired the 'blasphemous' internet movie depicting Prophet Muhammad as a con, womaniser and paedophile. More to the point, al-Qaeda in the Maghreb (AQIM) called for aggression on American diplomats all over the world. It seems that a threat to the sanctimonious order of Islam awakens the spirit of Muslims to become radicalised.

Al-Qaeda's first port of entry into Africa in terms of membership and recruitment is in Eygpt through the Eyptian Islamic Group (EIG) and Algeria, through the Algerian-based Salafist Group for Preaching and Combat (GSPC). Another crucial observation is that al-Qaeda is slowly being assimilated as sub-groups in various Islamist/ Salafists groups in Africa. This is evident by the merger of the Libyan Islamic Fighting Group (LIFG) and the union of the Egyptian Islamic Jihâd with al-Qaeda. Other states that have acquired the al-Qaeda franchise are; al-Qaeda in Mauritania, al-Qaeda in Mali, al-Qaeda in Sudan and al-Qaeda in Morocco. On January 2014, AQIM announced the merger between Ansar al Sharia Tunisia and the Okba Ibn Nafaa Brigade.[59] Droukdel, the leader of the Salafist Group for Preaching and Combat (GSPC) appointed Khaled Chaieb, an explosives expert (aka Lokman Abou Sakhr) as leader. This union created al-Qaeda in Tunisia. What this portends is that al-Qaeda's area of operation in Africa is larger than the region where it was founded—the Middle East. In addition, there would be a likely increase in abduction of Westerners and the creation of a vibrant empire of drug smuggling/trafficking in order to fund jihâdist operations. It seems that there are strong indications that al-Qaeda in

---

59 See 'Terrorism in the Sahel and the sub-Saharan Africa: More than a Regional Threat', assessed on the 26th of July 2014 at: http://eurasia.ro/?p=53951

Nigeria may soon evolve. Boko Haram may be delighted in having acquiring the al-Qaeda franchise as the former is desirous of purging western education from the region and creating an Islamist empire.

Not surprisingly, one must note that most terrorist attacks in Africa are partly guerrilla campaigns due to the fact that these Islamists groups attack military posts or confront military personnel. This tactic has been employed by Boko Haram in northern Nigeria. The thrust of terrorism portrayed by Islamists appears to be uncontrollable, largely due to the mechanism of its operations and ideologies of murder. For instance, al Qaeda's motto—"You love life; we love death," has proven to be a driving force for terrorists. Indeed, Osama bin Laden re-echoes this slogan when he pledges that: "What Westerners don't understand is that we love death as much as they cling to life. My greatest regret is that I have yet to die a martyr, because this life is corrupt" (Ouellet et al, 2014: 658). This proclamation is used as propaganda to procure asymmetric warfare.[60] Asymmetric warfare by Islamists has its profound effects on civilians. On the 12th October, 2002, bombings of Bali Island, in Indonesia, killed 202 people. The 2004 Madrid, Spain bombing killed 192 people. The 2005 London bombings killed 56 people. Most horrific is the 9/11 attacks n New York and Washington, DC, where 3,017 people were killed. The catastrophic events perpetuated in the West by Islamists has reduced considerably since the death of its henchman; Osama bin Laden in May, 2011.

A new dawn area of Islamists terrorism is occurring in Africa. The death of Osama bin Laden did not put an end to radical Islam. This epitomises that radical Islam is not about individuals. It is about the imagined perception of fighting for oppressed individuals for the preservation of their faith. However, despite the new wave of terrorism in Africa, a

---

60 "Asymmetric warfare implies that singularly weaker forces are capable of imposing devastating costs on a massively stronger enemy" (Rathbone & Rowley, 2002:15).

striking question given the myriad of Islamists groups across the region is whether their campaigns are successful. In a recent study by Abrahms (2012), it was observed that out of 125 campaigns waged by various groups, 30% of such campaigns were successful in coercing the target state to address their political demands. A similar observation is found in the Niger Delta region of Nigeria where militants were able, to some extent, coerce the Nigerian government to make concessions about their socio-economic grievances.

## Does Islamist' Terrorism Work in Africa?

Recent studies have indicated that terrorism is an effective strategy in the sense that states' are sometimes coerced in yielding to the demands of terrorists (Dershowitz, 2002; Pape, 2005). Particularly, Dershowitz (2002) argues empirically that terrorism in Palestine has been a positive force to the Palestian cause as it has changed the behaviour of international politics towards the region (the United Nations granted an observer status to the Palestine Liberation Organisation). Conversely, if it is argued that terrorism can be successful, are the ultimate desired goals achievable? If the terrorists' desired goal remains unfulfilled, then it is safe to argue that terrorism may be effective but not successful (Crenshaw, 1995: 475). If we contextualise terrorism within the context of radical Islam—their desired goals are usually not conceded to by state governments. Terrorism based on Islamism could be referred to as maximalist goals (Abrahms, 2006). Abrahms (2006) further informs us that terrorists with maximalist goals can achieve their objectives when they attack military targets other than civilian targets. This indeed may be correct. However, it is suggested that where a radical Islamist group attacks military units, it changed its operatives into guerrilla warfare. The characterisation of terrorism is within the confines of targeting non-combatants. These refer to "demands over beliefs, values, and ideology..." (Abrahms, 2006:53). Abrahms (2006:59) in an empirical analysis asserts that states' do not grant concessions to terrorists groups demanding maximalists' ideology.

The intriguing question then is: Why do radical Islamist groups in Africa persist on terrorist activities when they have little or no chance in obtaining their concessions? Does the basis of radical Islam in Africa centre on religious utopianism? At a cursory look, one must note that on peculiar circumstances, terrorist attacks could have a desired outcome. One of such events is the Madrid train bombings which took place on the 11th of March, 2004. This event took place three days before the general elections in Spain. The grievance of the Islamists (al-Qaeda) was pointed at the role played by Spain in its support to America in respect of its attack in Iraq. Most important, is the fact that it is perceived that the bombings were devised to sway the course of the election to replace the Partido Popular (PP) government that supported Spain's involvement with the war in Iraq with the Spanish Socialist Workers Party (PSOE) who were opposed to the war. As a result of the bombings, the PSOE won the election and immediately withdrew Spain as an American ally in the war in Iraq.

Ostensibly, Islamic radicals in furtherance of their terrorists' activities use the following methods; hijacking, bombing, sabotage of civilian aircrafts, kidnapping, sporadic killing of people (by gunmen) and the most notorious of them; suicide attacks. Despite the plethora of these techniques, the objectives of radical Muslims are most times not conceded to by their governments. It is argued that the objectives of Islamists are usually incomprehensive and altogether impracticable. Methods and strategies of radical Islamist groups may differ, but it appears that they all have the same objective of finding relevance in their society and most important, the creation of an Islamic state. For instance, Boko

Haram in Nigeria is desirous of situating a caliphate in Nigeria. The striking question is where will other Nigerians, who are non-Muslims and moderate Muslims relocate to? Besides their ideology: 'Western education is a sin', seems more confusing as the group uses state of the art military equipment and possess sophisticated cars—mostly manufactured by western-based technology.

It is worth noting, in this connection, the unfeasible objective of al-Qaeda is to establish a global caliphate and the desire to exterminate Israel from the face of the earth. These ideals seem entirely ridiculous and unattractive, as the world consists of many civilisations. It is suggested that Islamists groups do understand that their goals are unrealisable as they are contrary to the sovereignty of most states. It is suggested that even though radical Islamists know that their ideologies are merely imaginative, they are connected by their underlying desire to be recognised as a product (Brachman, 2009). This quest for recognition cumulated in the 9/11 attack on the World Trade Centres in New York.

The latent plan of the 9/11 attack was to usher an Islamic response to applaud the assault and then mobilise jihâdists groups, with al-Qaeda as the hub of the multinational of terrorist networks to pursue a holy war with America and its free market liberalism. This plan was unsuccessful as many Muslims all over the globe vehemently condemned al-Qaeda. It is suggested that the inability to compete with westernised institutions and the reluctance of being seen relegated to the background is what propels radical Muslims to embrace terrorism. Perhaps, equally important is the notion that they understand that they cannot win a war with a superior army may also procure Islamist terrorists to used asymmetrical warfare. Above all these arguments is the salient factor of grievance due to economic marginalisation which is based on a 'universal revolutionary creed' (Stern, 2003) which is centred on anti-westernisation and anti-semitism—the perceived infidels.

## Conclusion

It is worth noting that, radical Islamists have a poor organisational structure. With the destruction of many Islamists cells in Afghanistan and Yemen in 2001, the restructuring of transnational networks has been difficult in the Middle East as disparate to Africa. It is suggested that although Islamist terrorist groups understand that their goals are usually unachievable, they are bonded by the psychological will as a group to resist imagined threats to their identity with the purview of attaining an Islamic empire. On a crucial note, Islamic terrorism cannot be wished away in Africa, until its leaders are ready to usher in economic development and equitable distribution of wealth. A point that is worthy of mention, is that it must be understood that the only time law-abiding individuals or members of a group become terrorists is when they are under threat by another individual(s) or perceived aggressive group. Terrorism does not exist as a result of frivolities—it exists due to threat perception—the politics of survival is: confronting perceived terror with terror.

# References

Abadie, A., 2006. 'Poverty, Political Freedom, and the Roots of Terrorism', *The American Economic Review* 96 (2), 50–56.

Abrahms, Max, 2006. 'Why Terrorism Does Not Work', *International Security'* Vol. 31, No. 2, 42-78.

Abrahms, Max, 2012. 'The Political Effectiveness of Terrorism Revisited', *Comparative Political Studies*, 45: 366.

Agbiboa, D. E., 2013. 'Al-Shabab, the Global Jihad, and Terrorism without Borders', assessed on the 27th of October, 2014 at: Al-Shabab, the Global Jihad, and Terrorism without Borders.

Altheide, David, L., 2006. *Terrorism and the Politics of Fear.* Oxford: AltaMira Press.

Baudrillard, Jean, 2002. *The Spirit of Terrorism.* London; New York: Verso.

Benjamin, Daniel & Simon, Steven, 2002. *The Age of Sacred Terror: Radical Islam's War Against America.* New York: Random House Trade Paperbacks.

Bluth, Christoph, 1995. *The Collapse of Soviet Military Power.* Aldershot: Daetmouth Publishing Company.

Brachman, M. &Jarret M., 2009. *Global Jihadism: Theory and Practice.* London: Routledge.

Cassidy, Robert, M., 2008. *Counterinsurgency and the Global War on Terror: Military Culture and the Regular War.* Stanford: Stanford University Press.

Collier, Paul, 2008. *The Bottom Billion: Why the Poorest Countries are Failing and What Can Be Done About It.* Oxford: Oxford University Press.

Crenshaw, Martha. 1995. 'Terrorism in the Algerian War', in Crenshaw Martha (ed)., 1995. *Terrorism in Context.* Pennsylvania: Pennsylvania State University Press: 473-513

Dershowitz, Alan, 2002. *Why Terrorism Works: Understanding the Threat, Responding to the Challenge.* New Haven, Conn.: Yale University Press.

Freeman, Michael, 2008. Democracy, Al Qaeda, and the Causes of Terrorism: A Strategic Analysis of U.S. Policy', *Studies in Conflict & Terrorism,* 31:1, 40-59.

Gus, Martin, 2003. *Understanding Terrorism: Challenges, Perspectives and Issues.* Thousand Oakes: London; New Delhi: Sage Publications

Hill, Margari, 2009. 'The Spread of Islam in West Africa: Containment, Mixing, and Reform from the Eighth to the Twentieth Century', Freeman Spolgi Institute Stanford University, accessed on the 1st of October 2014 at: http://spice.fsi.stanford.edu/docs/the_spread_of_islam_in_west_africa_containment_mixing_and_reform_from_the_eighth_to_the_twentieth_century

Krech, Hans, 2011. 'The Growing Influence of Al-Qaeda on the African Continent', *Africa Spectrum* 46:2, 125-137

Lewis, Bernard, 1987. 'The Shi'a in Islamic History', in Shi'ism', Martin Kramer (ed.), *Resistance, and Revolution.* Boulder, CO: Westview Press).

Levtzion, Nehemia & Pouwels, Randall, Lee, 2000. The *History of Islam in Africa.* Ohio University Press.

Mamdani, Mahmood, 2002. 'Good Muslim, Bad Muslim: A Political Perspective on Culture and Terrorism', *American Anthropologist, New Series,* Vol. 104, 3, 766-775

McCormick, G. H., 2003. 'Terrorist Decision-Making', *Annual Review of Political Science,* 6, 473-507.

Ouellet, Eric, Lacroix-Leclair, Jérôme & Pahlavi, Pierre, 2014. 'The Institutionalization of Al-Qaeda in the Islamic Maghreb (AQMI)', *Terrorism and Political Violence* Vol. 26, issue 4: 650-665.

Pape, R. A., 2003. 'The Strategic Logic of Suicide Terrorism', *American Political Science Review*, 97, No 3: 1-19.

Pape, R. A., 2005. *Dying to Win: The Strategic Logic of Suicide Terrorism*. New York, NY: Random House.

Piazza, J.A., 2006. 'Rooted in poverty? Terrorism, poor economic development, and social cleavages', *Terrorism and Political Violence* 18(1) 159–177.

Stern, Jessica. 2003. 'The Protean Enemy,' *Foreign Affairs* 92, no. 4: 38.

Rathbone, Anne & Rowley, K. Charles, 2002. 'Terrorism', *Public Choice*, Vol. 111, No. ½: 9-18.

Radu, Michael, 2002. 'Terrorism after the Cold War: Trends and Challenges', *Orbis*, vol. 46, no. 2, 275-287.

Rashid, Ahmad, 1999. 'The Taliban Exporting Extremism', *Foreign Affairs* Vol.78(6),22-35

Richardson, Louise, 2006. *What Terrorists Want: Understanding the Terrorist Threat*. London: John Murray.

Rosander, E., & Westerlund, D., 1997. *African Islam and Islam in Africa: Encounters between Sufis and Islamists*. Athens, Ohio: Ohio University Press.

Ruthven, Malise, 2012. *Encounters with Islam on Religion, Politics and Modernity*. London; New York: I.B. Tauris.

Whittaker, D.J., 2007 'Definition of Terrorism', In Whitaker, D.J. (ed). *The Terrorism Reader* (3rd Edition). London: Routledge: pp: 3 – 11.

# PART TWO:
# RADICAL ISLAM IN AFRICA

# 5

# Resurgence of al-Qaeda in Somalia

## Introduction

The world consists of diverse ethnic groups. There are about 6,000 different ethnic groups in the world and 130 different nationalities. Very few states are homogeneous, such as Norway, Portugal, Greece, Malta, Iceland and Somalia in Africa. Ethnic diversity is a cause of most conflicts (Azar, 1984). Thus, it would be inferred that a homogenous state is less likely to witness conflicts. However, this is not the story for Somalia. The daunting task of having a united Somalian nation despite its seeming similar cultural composition and homogeneity has become impossible. It was increasingly difficult to achieve a common nation for the reason that these groups represented different clans and regions within Somalia. Most crucial is the antecedents of radical Islam in Somali. Consequently, if a state such as Somali is sustained by an invented tradition of unity, (Anderson, 1991), what are the factors hampering the nation-building efforts?

In this chapter, the discussion will focus on the nature of the (dis)unity of the Somali people. We propose to do it in the following manner: Gurr's (1970) relative deprivation thesis (Grievance) to highlight the separatism between clans; we underscore Benedict Anderson's (1991) argument's on invented tradition to pitch our arguments on the division between people belonging to different clans; we also explore Paul Collier's and Hoeffler's (2004) arguments on the perceptions of greed to explain the crises within the leadership in al- Shabaab. The greed theoretical model is useful in explaining the causal link of civil wars in states that are non-developed or developing states, which are characterised by poverty, economic exploitation, uneven distribution of resources and lack of provision of basic needs. Finally, we underscore Almond, Appleby and Sivan's (2003) arguments on the perceptions of justifiable homicide in the eyes of religious extremists.

## Political Crises in Somali

To begin with, in 1960, British Somaliland and Italian Somalia gained independence. These two nations decided to become stitched and formed the Republic of Somalia. However, in 1969 its young democracy was cut short by a coup d'état led by Major General Muhammed Siad Barre (also known as Jaalle Siyaad) which ousted Abdirashid Ali Shermarke. Barre's tenure of decadence ended in 1990. Thereafter, Somalia became a state, ruled by warlordism. The genesis of this state of fragility started during the reign of Muhammed Siad Barre in the late 1980s. The reason behind the uprising of the warlords could be attributed to the experimental unique ideology, but non-profitable political adventurism into Marxism, nationalism which was blended with Islamic ideology.

After General Mohamed Siad Barre took over the reins of power in 1969, the capitalist oriented states gave lucrative financial handouts to Somalia. This assistance was done, not on humanitarian grounds, but to prevent the Soviets from influencing Somalia to shift its political ideology towards socialism. This political but toxic mixture which Barre dubbed as 'scientific socialism' delved the state into a blind political and economic direction. This absurdity was further complicated when Somalia shifted loyalty towards the Soviet Union. However, the political love affair with the Soviets was short-lived. In 1977, the Soviet Union recognised the regime of Mengistu Haile Mariam of Ethiopia (a socialist regime). In addition, the Ethiopian-Somali War 1977-1978 (Ogaden War)[61] created an environment whereby Ethiopia pitched tents with the Soviets whilst Somalia became an American ally.

Now, Ethiopia had been a rival to Somalia mainly due to the fact that they differ mainly on religious grounds. Subsequently, Barre expelled Soviet diplomats, and thereafter become pro-America. Somalia utterly lost the war with 25,000 troops killed in battle. In a shortwhile, Barre lost confidence amongst the people of Somalia—its people remembered their primordial attachment to their clans. In order to shorten a seemingly long debate, Barre attempted to bury the Somalian people's imagined sense of their loyalty to their primordial identities. The mistake of Barre's political adventurism is noted by Luling (1997: 289) when he perceptively noted Abdalle Omar Mansur's observation:

> *The most serious problem in Somalia today is that our cultural traditions are not compatible with the construct of a modern state. We Somalis are prisoners of a culture that we had created in the past and one which we refuse to re-examine…we must reinvent ourselves and in the process launch the construction of a new, viable state.*

---

61  General Barre desired to expand Somalia land by annexing Ogaden by attacking Ethiopia.

The Barre regime was coloured with gross human rights abuse[62] with a blend of brinkmanship as is the case with most regimes in Africa at the time. The result which inevitably led to a civil war between the Somali Armed Forces and varied militant groups, most notable are the Somali Armed Forces Democratic Front, the Somali National Movement, the Somali Patriotic Movement, Somali Democratic Movement, the Somali Democratic Alliance, the Somali Manifesto Group and the United Somali Congress. The collective front of these militant and political groups eventually led to the ousting of Siad Barre in 1991.

After the demise of Barre, the country still in a porous state with the absence of a political and economic base, the militant and political factions that ousted Barre forthwith contested for supremacy. The contest was not only between different groups, but also based on intra-group conflicts especially witnessed by United Somali Congress where its leaders; General Muhammed Farah Aidid and General Ali Mahdi Muhammed, in 1991 conflicted with each other in order to gain control of Somalia.[63] Moreover, General Aidid decided to wage war against the Unified Task Force (UNITAF) for reasons of being sidelined by the humanitarian effort of the coalition forces led by America (Adams, 2008). However, Aidid's foremost contention was that he wanted to rule a united Somali.

In 1993, the foreign intervention, by the UNITAF, under the banner; 'Operation Restore Hope', led by United States and the second phase intervention by the United Nations Operation in Somalia II (UNOSOM II) became a failure.[64] This intervention led to the unsuccessful US intervention in the battle of Mogadishu (Black Hawk Down incident), in 1993, where eighteen US soldiers were killed. Moreover,

---

62   The Barre regime had the worst record of Human rights abuse. See UNDP, 2001. Human Development Report 2001—Somalia. UNDP, New York

63   The 1991 Djibouti talks appointed General Ali Mahdi Mohamed as interim-president. This appointment was rejected by Aidid.

64   The United Nations passed a resolution 794 for the purpose of upgrading the peacekeeping mission of the task force to a peace enforcement mission.

rival warlords and competing clans situated Somalia into abysmal state. In addition, before the downfall of Barre, Somaliland, situated in the northeast became unstitched on 18 May, 1991, rom Somalia whilst Puntland became semi-autonomous in the east in 1998.

## Primordial Attachment to Clans

Clans are a significant marker of an individual's identity in Somalia. Clans are seemingly similar with ethnicity in many ways. An ethnic group as a "a type of cultural collectivity, one that emphasises the role of myths of descent and historical memories and that is recognised by one or more cultural difference like religion, customs, language or institutions" (Smith, 1991:21). However, clans are different in the sense that they are primogeniture in nature. They are kin-groups consisting of cousinly networks resident in a particular neighbourhood. Both ethnicity and clanism are primordial markers of an individual. But the issue here is that ethnicity is not prevalent in Somali. In explaining how clan and religion interrelate, clanism in Somali acts as a double-edged sword—it promotes social harmony among its members and at the same time, it is divisive with non-clan members even though they are members of the same faith (Islam). The underlying observation here is that, in the absence of the unifying umbrella of ethnicity, individuals tend to have strong sentiments about their clans which act as a social glue to individual identities sharing the same faith (Islam).

Clanism in Somalia signifies the essence of an individual's origin and sense of loyalty. Clanism is a strong force for competing for resources which are invariably scarce or even nonexistent in Somalia. Another important feature of clans in Somali is that they have unique customary laws which preside over their commune. Hesse (2010:249) perceptively takes cognisance of the isolating effect of clans in Somalia:

*Somalis further classify themselves into sub-clans, or even sub-sub-clans and beyond. For example, in the Isaaq clan, which falls under the umbrella 'Samaale' clan structure, there are no less than three (some scholars say as many as eight) sub-clans: the Habar Awal, Habar Jaalo, and the Harhajis. The Habar Awal are then divided into at least two sub-sub-clans: the Sa'ad Muse and the Lise Muse . . . and so on. Classification can even extend right down to the household level: if a man has more than one wife, for example, some in the household might stress the clans, sub-clans or sub-sub-clans associated with one maternal line over another. What is more, not all Somalis agree to which lineage lines other Somalis belong. Somali genealogy presents individuals with a seemingly infinite number of ways to affiliate with, or disassociate from, fellow Somalis which may be the point.*

It is important to note that there are six major clans in Somalia. The first four are grouped as the Darod, Dir, Hawiye and Isaaq, communally known as 'Samaale'. The Samaale are made up 75% of the population. Second group, the Digil and Rahanweyn of southern Somalia, are grouped as the Digil-Mirifle, they comprise 20% of the Somalian population. Arabs constitute 5% of the population. It should also be noted that these clans are further divided into sub-clans. In addition, sub-clans are also sub-divided into sub-sub-clans. These divisions allowed politicians and various warlords to successfully invent a 'we' against 'them' in order to generate conflict and division within Somali. It could readily be noted that to the Somalis, that the loyalty to one's clan takes precedence over and above sentiments of nationality. Amongst the people of Somalia, clanism permits people to imagine that they share an identity which is different from other individuals despite similarities in religion, language and culture. Seth Kaplan (2010:82) captures the paradox of this imagined identity by perceptively noting that:

> *Somalia embodies one of postcolonial Africa's worst mismatches between conventional state structures and indigenous customs and institutions. The fact that Somalis share a common ethnicity, culture, language, and religion might seem to be an excellent basis for a cohesive polity, but in reality the Somali people are divided by clan affiliations, the most important component of their identity.*

The inability to have a common voice singing from the same hymn led to a gross human rights abuse, a totalitarian regime, mass pauperisation of the people, the absence of state structures, famine and the mass exodus of one million Somalians abroad. From 1991-2004, the scramble for Somali was swinging from one warlord to another.

Despite attempts by international agencies to foment a peace process, much remained to be achieved in terms of establishing an effective government. Reconciliatory efforts such as the 1993 conference on National Reconciliation in Addis Ababa; The 1997, National Salvation Council; the December 1997 Cairo Peace Conference; The 2000 Somalia National Peace Conference; The 2001 National Commission for Reconciliation and Property Settlement, and the 2002 Somali Reconciliation Conference, had little or no effect. However, after reconciliatory efforts in 2004, a Transitional Federal Government (TGF) backed by Ethiopia and based in Baidoa, the south-central Bay region of Somalia, was established to bring the state out of its state of anarchy. The TGF became internationally known as the government in Somali. However, in the real sense of the word, this was difficult to achieve *sticto sensu* due to the fact that any form of secular government was seen as connoting oppression—thanks to the dictatorship of Mohamed Siad Barre.

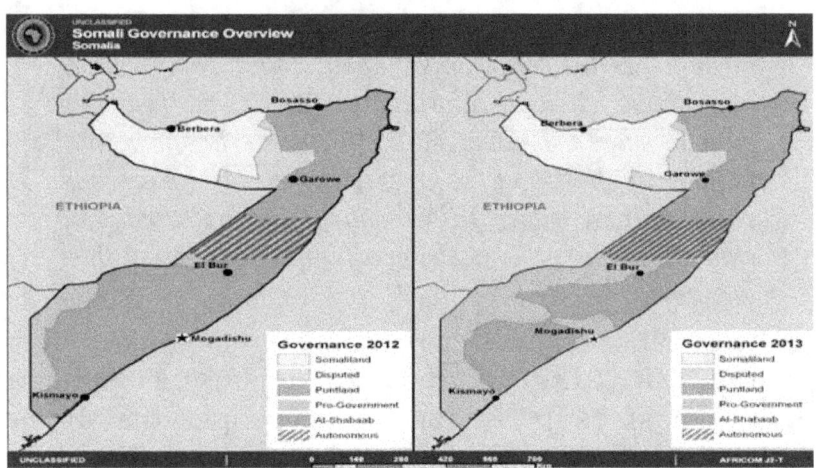

**Map of Somalia showing important towns and cities, courtesy United States Africa Command**

The lack of government and infrastructure reveals that Somalia became reminiscence of the primitive age—there was an absence of a judicial system and the antecedent non-existence of the rule of law. People began to look for solutions to their meagre and stymied style of living. Now it can readily be observed that the state of poverty in Somalia was a key factor that created an atmosphere for radical Islam to be accepted by Sunni Muslims. In describing the corruption and poverty in Somalia, James Fergusson (2013) correctly captures Somalia as the 'world's most dangerous place,' in the befitting title of his book: *'The World's Most Dangerous Place: Inside the Outlaw State of Somalia'*. The book unveils that sentiments of grievance were attached to the breakdown of all state infrastructures and the depth of insecurity in the now anarchic state. An answer to resolve this devastation of the horn of Africa was found in religion—Islam. Religion is a strong identity of the Somali people. Most of its citizens are Sunni Muslims but belong to the Sufi brotherhood. Muslims found solutions to these problems—the application of Sharia law. In 2004, most of the Sharia courts were administered in some parts of the state by Islamic Courts Union (ICU). The ICU sought to usher in a degree of sanity and to quell the ravaging warlords.

This initiative was applauded by many Somalis, as the warlords operated with credible norms of social justice. However, the ICU attempted to usher a strict form of interpretation of the Qur'an through the Sharia courts. The ICU sought to usher in a degree of sanity and to quell the ravaging warlords. Thus, the ICU shut down movie theaters, viewing centers for soccer matches and co-ed events such as sports. Cigarettes, alcohol and *khat*, the popular leafy narcotic chewed by Somalis, were banned. Opposed to external interference in the affairs of the Somali, the ICU conquered vast portions of territory controlled by the TFG backed by the Ethiopian army. After seizing Mogadishu, they inflated their control in central and southern Somalia. In many ways, this ushered in some degree of sanity and peace in the regions controlled by the ICU. However, in some regions within the control of the ICU, Salafist modes of interpreting the Qur'an were applied by other extremist groups affiliated to the ICU. In this sense, radical Islam found a place and space to operate and compete for power in Somali. The cloak of nationalism changed into Islamic radicalism. The attempt to introduce Sharia as the only source of government was opposed by Somalia's TFG.

Furthermore, the moral and physical support which the ICU received from radical groups such as al-Qaeda became an increasing concern to Ethiopia (a Christian state) and to major Western powers that were anxious of the implications of the Islamisaton of the State. However, the support to the ICU emanating from radical groups waxed stronger. Roggio (2007) summarises it in the following way:

> *Osama bin Laden, Ayman al-Zawahiri and other senior al-Qaeda leaders praised the 'Somali Jihad' in video*

*and audiotapes. Al-Qaeda media outlets produced propaganda in Somali and Arabic, with video of Arab and Somali jihadis training and fighting side by side. Hundreds of millions of dollars were funneled into the Islamic Courts coffers by backers on the Arabian Peninsula. Foreign fighters flooded into Somalia, some estimates put the number at over 3,000. Iran provided arms, while Hezbollah provided training for Somali Islamists.*

Eventually, armed confrontation between the Islamic Courts and the TFG and Ethiopian forces broke out towards the end of December 2007, following a fatwa issued by leaders of the Islamic Courts against Ethiopia. After intense fighting, with hundreds of casualties on both sides, Ethiopian armoured columns, backed by air and artillery support, punched through and took Mogadishu, breaking the deadlock and defeating the ICU forces.

## The Rise of Al-Shabaab

The rise of al-Shabaab as seen above is as a result of the presence of a failed state. Somali is largely seen as "the world's most utterly failed state"[65] that has given rise to insecurity, not only within the Horn of Africa, but to the world at large. The insecurity within the state has heralded piracy, famine[66] and perhaps, most destructive incident of Islamic terrorism. Al-Shabaab started as a youth militia unit of an Islamic organisation known as al-Itihaad al Islamiya (AIAI). The AIAI was a group of elitist Somali Wahhabis who were desirous of overthrowing the Barre regime and planting an Islamic state. Eventually, in the later years of the civil war, the organisation consisted mainly of young militants. David Shinn (2011) eloquently captures the genesis formative years of al-Shabaab:

---

[65] Economist, September 4, 2008.
[66] Famine in Somalia (2010-2012), killed 260,000 people. See: http://www.businessinsider.com/somalia-is-the-most-failed-state-on-earth-2013-7?op=1#ixzz30B5bZPwX, accessed on the 22nd of April, 2014.

> *Small numbers of Somalis studied the Salafi views of the Muslim Brothers in Egypt and Wahhabi teachings in Saudi Arabia beginning even before Somali independence in 1960. As they returned to Somalia, the followers of these schools of Islamic thought had little initial success in propagating their views among Somalis who overwhelmingly followed Sufi Islamic beliefs. In the 1970s, some of the Wahhabi believers created The Unity of Islamic Youth (Wahdat al Shabaab al Islamiyya) and The Islamic Group (al Jama'a al Islamiyya). These two organisations merged in 1982 and changed their names to The Islamic Union (al Ittihad al Islamiyya or AIAI). All of the adherents were Somali, although they imported Islamic fundamentalist concepts from Salafism and Wahhabism* (2011: 204).

Al-Shabaab became prominent in 2006 after the invasion of Ethiopia (Ethiopian occupation lasted from 2006 to January 2009). Ethiopia's reason for invading Somalia was to halt the spread and significance of the ICU. More to the point, radical elements within the ICU called for a jihâd against its Kuffir neighbour. The invasion of Ethiopia witnessed the demise of the ICU. The ICU became fractionalised between the liberalists who were followers of Sheikh Sharif Sheikh Ahmed and other Islamist groups (Sheikh Ahmed later became President of the TFG in 2009) such as Hizbul Islam; Ahlu Sunna Waljama'a and the Alliance for the Re-liberation of Somalia (ARS). The prominent splinter group from the ICU that desired to ensure that the strict code of salafist Islam is properly enforced and administered in Somali is known as al-Shabaab (also known as Harakat al-Shabaab al-Mujahideen/party of the youth).

Essentially, the organisation established Sharia law in its occupied territories and in many ways, these efforts secured the trust of the people. However, despite the popularity of al-Shabaab amongst the locales of the southern part of Somali,

Ethiopia was unsuccessful in destroying the organisation. Eventually in 2009, Ethiopia withdrew its armed forces from Somalia. The African Union Mission to Somalia (AMISOM) which largely consisting of 8,000 Ethiopian, Uganda and Burundi troops thereafter took the mantle as a peacekeeping force in the region. Since the departure of the Ethiopian forces, al-Shabaab has controlled much of the southcentral Somalia as well as parts of Mogadishu. It is important to bear in mind that on August, 2014, the Somalian government offered amnesty for members of the group. This programme witnessed over 700 Islamists accepting the conditions of the amnesty.[67] Further applaud to the Somalian government came on October 5, 2014, when Somalia's National Army and the AMISOM in Somalia claimed strong hold territories belonging to al-Shabaab (Six towns including the important municipality of Barawe) were captured by AMISOM. On October 27, 2014, President Hassan Sheikh Mohamud announced that al-Shabaab had lost all its terrain. However, the group continues to target the undermanned AMISOM and the TFG.

Al-Shabaab became resilient to the intervening forces of Ethiopia and vigorously attempted to resist the Ethiopian forces. After the invasion, the group took on a new cloak, as Islamist guerrilla fighters. This activity was successful as al-Shabaab was able to appeal to Somalians using sentiments of nationalism. Yet again, in 2009 the group had a significant rebirth—it became linked with al-Qaeda. Al-Shabaab made *bayah* (allegiance) with al-Qaeda. Al-Shabaab's new foe became the West—launching global jihâd. Godane, the leader of al-Shabaab eulogised and swore loyalty to Osama bin Laden and his global ideology of jihâd (Shinn, 2011). In response, the US Government designated al-Shabaab as a terrorist organisation under Section 219 of the Immigration and Nationality Act (as amended). Al Shabaab was easy to assimilate and unite with al-Qaeda, given the fact that they had similar styles

---

67  Al Shabaab Cut Down To A More Manageable Size', accessed on the 5th of November 2014 at: http://www.strategypage.com/qnd/somalia/articles/20141029.aspx

of asymmetrical warfare, usually in the form of suicide bombings. From September 2006 until December 2009, thirteen martyr attacks took place in Somali (Ibrahim, 2010: 286). Bryden (2014:15) perceptively argues that "aligning al-Shabaab more closely with al-Qaeda, Godane has tried to boost his group's international profile and linkages, hoping to create opportunities for his fighters to train abroad and gain battle field experience in foreign conflicts."

On a deeper level, one observes that in 2006, America funded the Alliance for Restoration of Peace and Counterterrorism, a group of anti-Islamic warlords against the ICU. Although the ICU eventually defeated this group, it is suggested that this may be a panacea that silently gave birth to the abhorrence of the West by the ICU.

The renaissance of al-Shabaab witnessed the reorganisation of the group. The group then witnessed an incursion from al-Qaeda fighters from Afghanistan and foreign fighters from all parts of the world. In order to showcase its affiliation with al-Qaeda with its desire to wage jihâd against the West, on the 11th of July 2010, al-Shabaab as a protégé of al-Qaeda executed its first jihâdist attack. The group coordinated a suicide bomb attack in Kampala Uganda (a restaurant and rugby club). The bomb killed 74 people who had gathered to watch the Soccer World Cup. Meanwhile, it would be recalled that the al-Qaeda bombings of 1998, devastating the U.S. embassies in Nairobi, Kenya, and Dar es Salaam, Tanzania, killing 223 and injuring over 4,000 people (Thomas, 2013) had links to the AIAI, as the perpetrators (Abu Talha al-Sudani, Saleh Ali Saleh Nabhan and Fazul Abdullah Mohamed) were linked with al-Qaeda and used Somalia as a safe haven.

Most significantly, al-Shabaab's main aim is to eradicate AMISOM and then plant an Islamist regime. It applies guerrilla tactics and asymmetrical warfare towards an inadequate but better trained force. However, an underlying agenda is to join force in a global jihâd. In order to achieve this desire, the group has built viable networks and training grounds by taxing people of the south central region of the country.

Although al-Shabaab has lost control of a vast portion of southern and central Somalia, evidence suggests that it has an organisation that is still resilient and potent. This is clearly portrayed when al-Shabaab came into international attention on 21st September, 2013. Al-Shabaab murdered sixty-seven people by using arms and grenades in the Westgate Mall, Westlands, Nairobi, Kenya. This attack is perceived as a rebranding of the organisation under the leadership of Godane (Bryden 2014). The attack was also a reprisal for foreign intervention in Somali nation. An al-Shabaab spokesman, Ali Mohamud Rage, as far back as in October 2011, had threatened Kenya with retaliation if it did not get its soldiers off Somali soil. He said: "We, the Mujahideen, say to the Kenyan government: have you thought of the repercussions of the war against us? We are far more experienced in combat than you."[68] In February 2015, al-Shabaab in a propaganda video called for attacks on shopping malls in Canada, the UK and the United States. In pursuit of al-Shabaab's ideology of terror, death and destruction, on April, 2, 2015, the group attacked Garissa University College in Kenya and killed 147 innocent people whilst injuring many other individuals.The target of the group were non-Muslims.[69]

Perhaps, it is not necessary to list and comment on the vast number of attacks carried out by al-Shabaab, conversely, Miller (2013) informs us that since 2007, al-Shabaab has carried out almost 550 terrorist attacks, which has killed more than 1,600 people and injuring more than 2,100 people. Moreover,

---

68  See http://www.euronews.com/2013/09/25/behind-al-shabaab-s-war-with-kenya-terrorist-group-may-have-even-surprised-/ Assessed on the 27th of September 2014.

69  See 'Al Shabab gunmen attack Garissa University College in Kenya, as many as 147 dead in shoot-out', accessed on the 4th of April 2015 at: http://www.nydailynews.com/news/world/gunmen-attack-kenya-university-fierce-shootout-article-1.2170720.

Miller also notes that the number of violence accredited to al-Shabaab has been augmented rapidly from less than ten in 2007 to more than two hundred in 2012. AMISOM has increasingly found it difficult to totally eliminate al-Shabaab, for the reason that, that AMISOM has inadequate military resources which are needed for surveillance and logistics. Al-Shabaab uses improvised explosive devices (IEDs) and suicide missions in its attempt to resist AMISOM.

## Leadership and Power Struggles within Al-Shabaab

The leader of al-Shabaab is titled 'Amir.' The 'Amir' is supported by a ten-member council (shura majlis). This council is the highest decision body of al-Shabaab. Under this council, there is an advisory council or the general *shura majlis* who oversees the operations of the activities of groups in complying with the ideology of the sect. An important group under *shura majlis* is the military branch. The military branch is divided into the *Jaysh Al-'Usr* (the army of hardship and suffering) and the *Jaysh al-Hisbah* (Shariah Enforcer). The machinery of implementing jihâdist warfare is organised through its military operations. Al-Shabaab has a functional and structured organisation. It is important to note at this point, that al-Shabaab's connection with al-Qaeda has conveyed a strong structural organisation of the group. Al-Qaeda plays the role as a parent organisation towards the group. It certainly seems probable that all military actions undertaken by al-Shabaab are sanctioned and co-ordinated by al-Qaeda.

The early beginnings of al-Shabaab started under the leadership of Sheikh Hassan Dahir Aweys. Aweys was the leader of the AIAI. Under his leadership, the AIAI was transformed into al-Shabaab and thereafter became ICU's youth militia. However, Sheikh Aweys became an important chieftain within the ICU and transferred the mantle of leadership to Aden Hashi Ayro. Ayro who had no formal education received his military training in Afghanistan in the 1990s. After his training, he returned to Somalis in 2003, thereafter he became a member of the ICU. Ayro died on May 1, 2008, after a US strike in Dhusamareb, the capital of the central Galguduud region of Somali.

After the death of Ayro, Sheikh Mukhtar Robow became the leader of the organisation. Robow was a veteran of the Soviet/Afghanistan war. He was also a Deputy Commander in the ICU. However, his tenure as leader of the organisation ended in May 2009. He then became a spokesman for the group. Shuriye (2012:277) quoting a source noted that Robow is alleged to have boasted that:

> *We will take our orders from Sheikh Osama bin Laden because we are his students ... Most of our leaders were trained in Al-Qaeda camps. We get our tactics and guidelines from them. Many have spent time with Osama bin Ladin.*

However, Robow was removed as spokesman of the group, for reasons that he was alleged to be negotiating with the TFG.[70] He is well educated, having received his education in Qur'anic schools and studying law at the University of Khartoum in Sudan in the 1990. Robow is thought to be an efficient strategist. Robow is known to have endorsed the enlistment of foreign fighters in the organisation.[71] Sheikh Moktar Ali Zubeyr, also known as Muktar Abdirahman Godane, succeeded Sheikh Mukhtar Robow.

At first sight, it should be noted that the coup of Godane and his rise to power in 2009, was due to the bone of contention between the two warlords (Godane and Robow), given the fact that Robow protected TFG politicians who belonged to his clan. Godane was a veteran of the Soviet/Afghanistan

---

70   See 'Somalia's Divided Islamists," International Crisis Group', accessed on the 11th of November, 2010 at: http://www.crisisgroup.org/~/media/Files/africa/horn-of africa/somalia/B74%20Somalias%20 Divided%20Islamists.ashx

71   See more detailed history- 'Profile: Sheikh Mukhtar Robow (Abu Mansur)', accessed on the 29th of April at: http://www.criticalthreats.org/somalia/al-shabaab-leadership/sheikh-mukhtar-robow-abu-mansur-november-14-2011.

war. Godane is from the separate state of Somaliland. Godane was the first second-in-command of al-Shabaab. Another important leader of the organisation was Ibrahim Haji Jama Mee'aad, also known as Ibrahim al-Afghani. Afghani was also an influential member of the group. Afghani contested the leadership of the group with Godane on accusations that Godane had become dictatorial. However, Afghani was killed in 2013 in the town of Baraawe by members of al-Shabaab on Godane's orders, due to leadership rivalry. In September 2014, the U.S. military confirmed it killed Godane in a targeted airstrike on an al-Shabaab encampment in Somalia. However, al-Shabaab remains strengthened in its resolve and there have been retaliatory attacks in line with the vows of the group to revenge Godane's death. After the death of Godane, an unknown Islamist, Ahmed Omar, became the leader of the group.

This rivalry has significantly reduced members of the organisation. The rivalry in the organisation has splintered the group in two factions. The faction against the former leadership of Godane is mainly the muhajiriin (foreign fighters) and the other part is the supporters of Hassan Dahir Aweys. The main grievance of Aweys towards Godane pertained to the disagreement of al-Shabaab's merger with al-Qaeda. Nonetheless, in 2010, Aweys merged his faction, Hizbul Islam with al-Shabaab.

A personage worthy of note is Omar Hammami (Abu Mansour al Amrik), an American muhajiriin, who in October 2012 expressed that there was a friction between muhajiriin (foreign fighters) and al-Shabaab. On the 5th of September, 2013, Hammami declared that he had broken away from al-Shabaab due to the disorientation of the group in terms of leadership. However, on the 12th of September, 2013, Hammami was killed on the orders of al-Shabaab's intelligence service (the Amniyatt Mukhabarat). Perhaps, the most important observation here is that the diverse loyalty to clans amongst members of al-Shabaab generates conflict amongst leaders and members of the group. In line with this argument, Thomas (2013:418) is correct when he notes that:

*While al-Shabaab's militant Islamist ideology theoretically transcends the Somali clans by using religion to unite the Mujahideen, the realities on the ground suggest 'clannism' remains a permanent issue of contention within the group.*

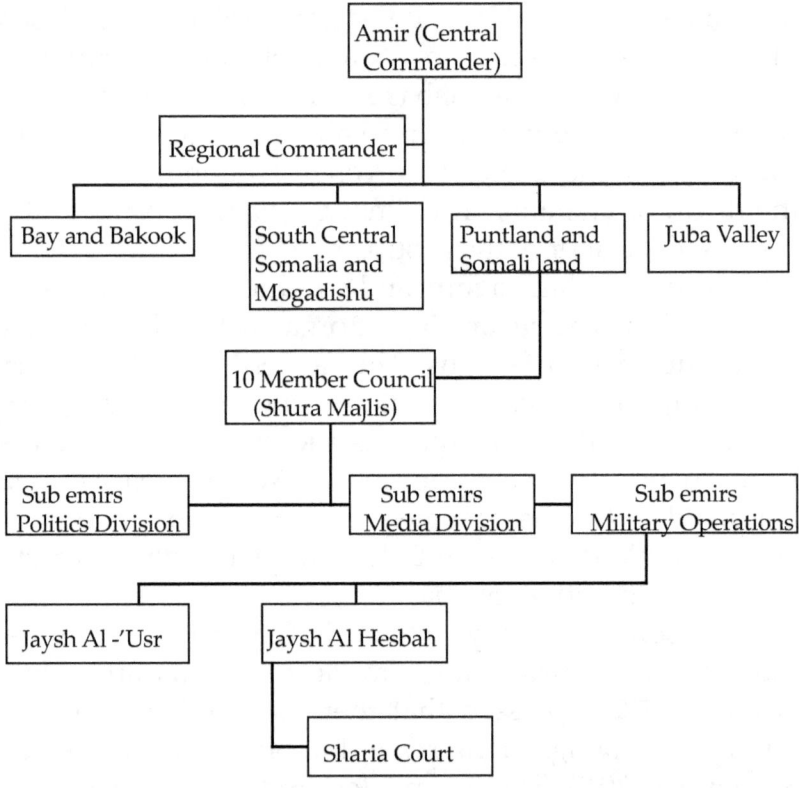

**Leadership divisions in Al-Shabaab, Source: Shuriye (2012:277)**

## Factors Responsible for the Growth of Al-Shabaab

Al-Shabaab has outlived its purpose in Somali. It is losing key towns and foreign fighters. Perhaps most crucially, it is fast becoming a dysfunctional group with disorganised orientation and leadership. Despite these factors, an intriguing question to ask is why the group has not withered away.

The offensive led by the TFG has forced al-Shabaab away from the suburbs and this led to a change in the groups' tactics. The clampdown on the activities of the group led them to resort to more desperate measures, particularly the use of suicide bombings and assasinations carried out by its infamous Amniyat network. The Amniyat network is one of the groups' deadly networks and it is also reported to have suffered a huge setback during the 2013 internal rift which led to the killing of about two hundred of its members. However, the group still remained deadly in its attack. According to Sheehan & Porter (2014:5):

*The clandestine Amniyat network remains the most intact and feared part of the organisation. Some of Amniyat's operatives pose as secularised Somalis and assume roles across the full spectrum of Somali society, including in positions in the SFG and foreign missions. It serves as both an effective intelligence network and an operational arm of al-Shabab, with units specialising in assassinations, explosives, and hit-and-run attacks.*

## Influence and Support of al-Qaeda

A strong influence in interlinking al-Shabaab with al-Qaeda is Abu Hafs al Masri. Masri was loyalist to Osama bin Laden. In 1992, whilst bin Laden was residing in Sudan, on several occasions sent Masri to Somalia. Masri's mission was to meet with Somalian Islamists and sell the concept of jihâd from a radical perspective. Masri also coordinated the provision of training facilities to Islamists. After forming al-Qaeda in

1988, Osama was banished from Saudi Arabia in 1992, thereafter he shifted his base to Khartoum, Sudan, until US pressurised Sudan to oust bin Laden in 1996. Osama had observed that the state of affairs in Somalia would be a safe haven for al-Qaeda in the near future. More to the point, Osama perceived that his stay in Sudan would be shortlived. In 1996, Osama bin Laden moved back to Jalalabad, Afghanistan. Interestingly enough, al-Qaeda supported the Islamic militants in the 1993 battle of Mogadishu.[72] This started an early foundation of a friendship between al-Shabaab and al-Qaeda. A crucial angle to these developments is that al-Qaeda's association with al-Shabaab is an opportunity to create a safe haven for its disorganised cells operating in the Middle East.

The merger of al-Shabaab with al-Qaeda was purported to continue the attack on Western societies and establishments. The objective of striking at Western societies was taken seriously when a note uncovered in a dead body of Fazul Abdullah Mohammed, an al-Shabaab fighter and leader of al-Qaeda, who in East Africa in 1998 participated in the US Embassies Bombings in Kenya and Tanzania. The note read:

> *Our objectives are to strike London with low-cost operations that would cause a heavy blow amongst the hierarchy and Jewish communities, using attacks similar to the tactics used by our brothers in Mumbai.*[73]

Aside from merging with al-Qaeda, al-Shabaab has links with other groups that are linked with radical Islam. To say the least, there are some questionable logical assumptions to support al-Shabaab's allegiance with Boko Haram. Hansen (2013) observed that al-Shabaab and Boko Haram have strong connections. He tells us that a vast number of members of Boko Haram sect were trained in Somalia by al-Shabaab. Hansen further showcases that ongoing cases in American courts

---

[72] 'Al Shabaab's Threat to Kenya', accessed on the 12th of May 2014 at: http://www.stratfor.com/weekly/al-shabaabs-threat-kenya

[73] 'Evidence suggests that Al-Shabaab is shifting focus to 'soft' targets', accessed on the 12th of May 2014 at: http://edition.cnn.com/2013/09/26/world/london-bombing-plot-qaeda/index.html

illustrate that Somalis were bringing bombing materials to Nigeria. An important issue here is that the inter-relationship of group dynamics tends to enhance the objective of a common desire. The interconnectivity of al-Shabaab with other radical Islamist groups such as al- Qaeda and Boko Haram procures a unique sense of purpose, broadens its sphere of authority and most crucially augments the power of groups to build influence and achieve goals.

## Foreign fighters and Social Networking

Foreign fighters are the backbone of al-Shabaab. America's largest population of Somali-Americans is in the state of Minneapolis, (the North Star state). Thomas Hegghammer (2010: 57-58) defines a foreign fighter as an agent who (1) has joined, and operates within the confines of an insurgency, (2) lacks citizenship of the conflict state or kinship links to its warring factions, (3) lacks affiliation to an official military organisation, and (4) is unpaid. However, a cursory observation of foreign fighters in Somali reveals that most of the fighters have links with al-Shabaab. Large numbers of American citizens of Somali descent are recruited from Minneapolis. Al-Shabaab mainly recruits by adverts on the internet, twitter feeds and through radical messages in the Mosque. Recruitment adverts on the internet luring disaffected Somali youths to join "the real Disneyland of African jihad"[74] are used as propaganda. Another advert poetically calling for foreign fighters goes:

> *This is a message to the youth in the West; a caring brother sends you a friend request, tossing a few clothes in a backpack and joining their jihâd is the smart call, just like the brothers in the Westgate Mall.*[75]

---

[74] 'Al-Shabaab's American recruitment drive: 'Betray the US and join "the real Disneyland" of African jihad', accessed on the 11th of May 2014 at: http://www.telegraph.co.uk/news/worldnews/africaandindianocean/kenya/10335139/Al-Shabaabs-American-recruitment-drive-Betray-the-US-and-join-the-real-Disneyland-of-African-jihad.html

[75] 'Al-Shabaab sends request to intending US Jihadists', accessed on the 20th of May 2014 at: http://www.punchng.com/news/world/al-shabaab-sends-request-to-intending-us-jihadists/

Usually these fighters are children of Somali immigrants and Somalis in diaspora. These fighters are usually torn between two cultures—they are not assimiliated into their western homes nor are they fully inculcated into Somalian culture. This interbreeding provokes a lack of identity and the quest to explore an imagined meaningful existence of their essence of being. Foreign recruits from other countries include Britain, Australia, Sweden and Canada. These states possess vast numbers of Somali migrants. The face of al-Shabaab was at a point in time in 2009, that of a foreign fighter—Omar Hammami. Hammami advertised for the enlistment of foreign fighters in videos and on the internet, urging Somalis to fight in the name of Islam. More to the point, a vast number of American and Somali citizens from Western societies who have spent time in Somali thereafter returned to America with ideas of radical Islam. Thus, Leuprecht & Hall (2013: 288) tell us that:

> *Expatriates from Maryland to California have reportedly travelled to Somalia to join AS (Al-Shabaab), but most hail from the 'Twin Cities' region of Minnesota, home to America's largest Somali diaspora, whose concentration of 25,000 members represents about one-third of the total Somali diaspora in the United States.*

Crucially, the intrusion of foreign fighters in al-Shabaab is observed when five men planned an attack on Holsworthy army barracks, near Sydney in Australia.[76] The men who were Australian citizens of Somali descent sought to initiate a *fatwa* in Australia under the notion that Islam was being attacked by the West. At the end of a twelve-week trial, three of the men were found guilty.[77] It is believed that the perpetrators of the violence in Westgate Malls in Kenya were foreign fighters from Minneapolis, USA.[78]

---

76 'Australia Lists Somali Al-Shabab as Terrorist Group', accessed on the 5th of May, 2014 http://somaliswisstv.com/2009/08/21/australia-lists-somali-al-shabab-as-terrorist-group/

77 'Three men guilty of planning terror attack on Holsworthy Army Barracks', accessed on the 17th of May 2014 at: http://www.dailytelegraph.com.au/news/nsw/three-melbourne-men-guilty-of-planning-terror-attack-on-nsw-army-base/story-e6freuzi-1225975368101

78 'Minn. imams condemn terrorist attack at Nairobi mall, al-Shabaab', accessed on the 11th of May 2014 at: http://www.myfoxtwincities.com/story/23509422/minn-imams-condemn-terrorist-attack-at-nairobi-mall#ixzz31QYHvwwZ

More crucially, al-Shabaab possesses a vast amount of sleeper cells, especially in Kenya, and most likely in America. One should be reminded that a vast number of Somalis live in Kenya and the perhaps more significant is the influence of al-Qaeda in radicalising young Somalis who live in neighbouring Somali (Phillips, 2002). It therefore comes not as a surprise that Islamic terrorism is rampant in Kenya. Furthermore, al-Shabaab is aggrieved at Kenya's military intervention in Somali via AMISOM. It is crucial to note that these cells are dormant, but can be activated at any time. The implication of these cells is that they may strike at any time in any part of the Western world. A vast number of Somalis have migrated to a vast number of Western societies since their nation became engulfed with war. A vast majority of these individuals are strongly attached to their clans and essentially to their religious beliefs—Islam. This creates an enabling determinant for Muslims to become radicalised. Moreover, in most Western societies, Somalis are closely knit together unlike other people from other African states. This tells us that they have the propensity to be radicalised and criminalised by al-Shabaab, clearly presenting a significant threat to Western societies and particularly African states. The primordial bond of being attached to Somali is in some ways stronger than the new found home in America and other western societies.

## Absence of a Central Government

It should be emphasised that a state of anarchy sits on a double-edged sword. It could be seen as progressive in the sense that it gives the individual(s) absolute freedom and it could be restrictive and altogether destructive as it gives individual(s) the freedom to do as they desire to other individual(s). It is the former situation that generates human rights abuses, absence of the rule of law and the presence of rule by the sword in such societies. Thus, it is rightly noted that "If the Failed States Index were a championship, then Somalia would be the undisputed four-time champion."[79]

Although the TFG has gradually gained control of key areas in Somalia, the pace of economic growth remains slow by security threats emanating from al-Shabaab and other militia groups. The United Nations finds it absolutely impossible to account for revenues towards Somalia. Given the condition of ineptitude in social structures, the state is confronted with widespread corruption wherein the demarcation between the public and private sectors are difficult to distinguish.[80] In addition, there is a dysfunctional judicial system in the state. With these variants in place, al-Shabaab administers Sharia law and a blend of traditional law (Menkhaus, 2000) with harsh punishments of flogging for minor offences and amputations for stealing. This then situates Somali to be tantamount with the perception of a failed state. As noted above, the violence emanating from warlords and the politics of clanism has been a strong determinant in the absence of a functional state in Somalia.

## Proximity to the Middle East

According to the Jonathan Masters (2014) of the Council of Foreign Relations, many al-Shabaab fighters, especially the commanders of the group, travelled to and fought in Afghanistan in the late 1990s after being pushed out by the Ethiopian army and its Somali supporters. The experience gained from the Afghan war galvanised and transformed al-Shabaab into the most powerful Somali guerrilla group, well-funded with thousands of foot soldiers. The group also had members in Western countries that have carried out attacks. The first al-Shabaab trained suicide bomber, Shirwa Ahmed, was a Somali-American from Minnesota. His act of suicide led to the death of twenty-four persons

---

79   Messner, J. J. 2011. 'Somalia Tops the Failed States Index for the Fourth Year Running', accessed on the 12th of May 2014 at: http://library.fundforpeace.org/fsi11-overview
80   Transparency International locates Somalia at the bottom list of 175th position out of 175 states.

in Hargeisa (Masters, 2014). Thus, in the words of Rob Wise (2011:5), a counterterrorism expert at the Center for Strategic and International Studies, "The Ethiopian invasion was responsible for transforming the group from a small, relatively unimportant part of a more moderate Islamic movement, into the most powerful and radical armed faction in the country." In areas under al-Shabaab control, there is draconian adaptation and application of sharia law, prohibition of various types of recreation, such as cinema and, the buying and selling/sale of *khat* (a narcotic plant often chewed), smoking, the shaving of beards, and many other 'un-Islamic' activities (Wise 2011:3). According to a Committee on Foreign Affairs report of the United States House of Representatives (2014:2), stonings and amputations have also been meted out as punishment on adulterers and thieves.[81]

## Funding

Al–Shabaab is known to have a pervasive financial network which stretches from various countries located in the Middle East and Africa to the Western World. The group relies mostly on funding from various state sponsors and Somali people in diaspora.[82] Saudi Arabia, Yemen, Syria, Iran, Qatar, and Eritrea have been cited as prominent state backers. According to Kambere (2012):[83]

> *A number of observers have asserted that Eritrea sponsors al-Shabaab in an attempt to counter the regional power, Ethiopia, Eritrea's long-time enemy. Eritrea has consistently denied the allegations. Eritrea reportedly supplies weapons, military training, and even troops to fight alongside al-Shabaab's militants.*

---

81  Committee on Foreign Affairs Report (2014). "Al-Shabab, How great a Threat?"House of Reps. 113th congress, First Session. Washington: U.S. GOVERNMENT PRINTING OFFICE
82  See Kambere G. (2012) CTX Vol. 2 No. 3, August 2012https://globalecco.org/financing-al-shabaab-the-vital-port-of-kismayo#5
83  'Financing al Shabaab: The Vital Port of Kismayo', CTX Vol. 3, accessed on the 15 opf December 2014 at: https://globalecco.org/financing-al-shabaab-the-vital-port-of-kismayo

*In addition, a United Nations report claims that Eritrea has sent $80,000 per month to some members of al-Shabaab through the Eritrean Embassy in Nairobi for almost a decade.*

According to Byman (2005:22) the use of non-state actors is consistent with a state's desire to covertly put a check on the power of a state deemed too powerful, while maintaining a 'degree of deniability.' Al-Shabaab's ties with other radical groups, especially al-Qaeda has not only benefited the group financially, but also technically, through the reception of financial assistance. In order to clamp down on al-Shabaab's funding, sanctions have been imposed on either states or persons known to be sponsoring the group. This has had the opportunity of crippling the group's activities although to a minimal extent, as the group has devised means of generating revenue through the sale of contraband such as narcotics, charcoal and ivory, or even kidnapping. According to Doshi V (2014:1)[84] Andrea Crosta, executive director of the Elephant Action League (EAL), was quoted as saying that "The amount of ivory smuggled by al-Shabaab was up to three tons monthly."[85] The funds generated by al-Shabab are used in the purchase of sophisticated arms, recruitment and training of fighters, and even bribery of officials for the purpose of gathering intelligence about security operations and vulnerabilities.

## Conclusion

As we have seen, it seems that our arguments based on economic grievance and prebendalistic nature of Somalis government has inspired a radical Islamic group to further

---

[84] See 'Elephant Campaign: How Africa's 'white gold' funds the al-Shabaab militants: Ivory smuggling has become an attractive and profitable enterprise for terrorist groups', accessed on the 1st of December 2014 at: http://www.independent.co.uk/voices/campaigns/elephant-campaign/elephant-campaign-how-africas-white-gold-funds-the-alshabaab-militants-9102862.html

[85] See Doshi V. (2014) Elephant Campaign: How Africa's 'white gold' funds the al-Shabaab militants http://www.independent.co.uk/voices/campaigns/elephant-campaign/elephant-campaign-how-africas-white-gold-funds-the-alshabaab-militants-9102862.html

destabilise the state. However, from our discourse, it is latent observed that the group has become disoriented. In order to cut a long discourse short, Ibrahim (2010:292) best sums it up:

> *Unless al-Shabaab develops pragmatism that could drive it to transform itself into a political party, change its current leadership and revert to the earlier ideology of the Union of the Islamic Courts, it risks implosion due to its inability to capture durable popular support, govern effectively, or to bring about improved conditions for the general population. In other words, al-Shabaab will likely face an unholy end.*

The lack of unity amongst the ICU emanated from the fact that they are clan or sub-can based (Marchal, 2012:263). Auspiciously, ideological terrorists groups do not have a long life span (Fettweis, 2009). Al-Shabaab is fast losing its grip in terms of occupied territories in Somalia. There has been a turbulent inter-play of politics and clanism between leaders of the group. Foreign fighters who were the backbone of the group are rapidly shifting away from the corrupted ideological sense of purpose. The group is also losing popular support by the Somali people. The group has mislaid its ideological and nationalistic principles. It is then safe to predict that the group would finally disintegrate in less than five years, but it may metamorphose into another Islamist organisation as — 'Jihâd only ends upon the demise of the *Kuffir*.' This reasoning perhaps informs Fettweis (2009: 288) to rightly suggest that a fragile ideological group tends to fade away by noting that:

> *In the penultimate stage, remnants of ideological groups fight on, in a weakened, decentralised form, robbed of their inspirational and tactical leadership. At the point when the banner of the group is being carried on by disconnected individuals ("lone wolves") rather than from a coherent center, the final stage—group death—is not far off.*

In the recent past, al-Shabaab has lost important towns such as Baidao, Hudur, Wajid—these towns were strategic locations for the group. In another dimension, foreign fighters have started to abscond from al-Shabaab, for the reason that they are taking precautionary measures in protecting their lives. These fighters are now staying at a refugee camp in Hagadhere. Perhaps, the main negative perspective of al-Shabaab is that it lacks moral support by Somalis. This is given by the fact that the group has been at the spearhead of killing and maiming Somalis since it lost its nationalist goals, as reiterated above. Nor Barud, the Vice Chairman of the Somali Religious Union stated that:

*Al-Shabaab are claiming to be religious, but killing innocent people in sacred places like mosques show they are not true Muslims.*[86]

---

[86] 'SOMALIA:Somalia launches ideology war against Al-Shabaab'. Assessed on the 12th of May 2014 at: http://www.midnimo.com/2014/03/17/somaliasomalia-launches-ideology-war-al-shabaab/

# References

Adam, H., 2008. *From Tyranny to Anarchy: The Somali Experience.* Trenton, NJ: Red Sea Press.

Almond, A., Gabriel, Appleby R. Scott & Sivan, Emmanuel, 2003. *Strong Religion: The rise of fundamentalisms around the world.* Chicago,Ill.; London: University of Chicago Press.

Anderson, B., 1991. *Imagined Communities: Reflections on the Origin and Spread of Nationalism,* London: New York: Verso.

Azar, Edward E., 1984. 'The Theory of Protracted Social Conflict and the Challenge of Transforming Conflict Situations', in Dina A. Zinnes, ed., *Conflict Processes and the Breakdown of International Systems:* Merriam Seminar Series on Research Frontiers, Vol. 20, Book 2, University of Denver: 81-99.

Bryden, Matt., 2014. The Reinvention of Al-Shabaab: A Strategy of Choice or Necessity? *A Report of the CSIS Africa Program.* Accessed on the 9th of May 2014 at: http://csis.org/files/publication/140221_Bryden_Reinvention Of Al - Shabaab_Web.pdf.

Byman, D., 2005. *Deadly connections: States that Sponsor Terrorism.* New York.

Collier, P. and Hoefffler, A., 2004. *Greed and Grievance in Civil War (Civil Wars between 1960 and 1999),* Washington DC: World Bank 78.

Doshi V., 2014. Elephant Campaign: How Africa's 'White Gold' Funds the al-Shabaab militants: Ivory smuggling has become an attractive and profitable enterprise for terrorist groups', accessed on the 1st of December 2014 at: http://www.independent.co.uk/voices/campaigns/elephant-campaign/elephant-campaign-how-africas-white-gold-funds-the-alshabaab-militants-9102862.html

Fergusson, James. 2013. *The World's Most Dangerous Place: Inside the Outlaw State of Somalia*. London: Bantam Press.

Fettweis, J.Christopher, 2009. 'Freedom Fighters and Zealots: Al Qaeda in Historical Perspective', *Political Science Quarterly* Volume 124 Number 2: 269-296.

Gurr, Robert T., 1970. *Why Men Rebel*, Princeton, N.J., Published for the Center of International Studies, Princeton: University Princeton University Press.

Hansen, S. Jarle., 2013. *Al-Shabaab in Somalia: The History and Ideology of a Militant Islamist Group, 2005-2012*. London; Hurst Publishers.

Hegghammer, *Thomas. 2010.*, 'The Rise of MuslimForeign Fighters: Islam and the Globalization of Jihad', International Security, volume 35, issue 3, 53-94.

Hesse, J. Brian. 2010. 'Introduction: The myth of 'Somalia', *Journal of Contemporary African Studies*, 28:3, 247-259

Ibrahim, Mohamed, 2010. 'Somalia and global terrorism: A Growing Connection?', Journal of Contemporary African Studies Vol. 28, No. 3, July 2010, 283-295.

Kambere G., 2012. 'Financing al Shabaab: The Vital Port of Kismayo', CTX Vol. 3, accessed on the 15 opf December 2014 at: https://globalecco.org/financing-al-shabaab-the-vital-port-of-kismayo

Kaplan, Seth, 2010. 'Rethinking State-building in a Failed State', *Center for Strategic and International StudiesThe Washington Quarterly* Vol. 33:1; 81-97.

Leuprecht, Christian & Hall, Kenneth, 2013. Networks as strategic repertoires: Functional differentiation among Al-Shabaab terror cells, Global Crime, 14:2-3, 287-310

Luling, Virginia, 1997. 'Come back Somalia? Questioning a collapsed state', *Third World Quarterly*, 18:2, 287-302.

Masters. J., 2014. 'Al-Shabab', assessed on the 10 of September at: http://www.cfr.org/somalia/al-shabab/p18650

Marchal, Roland. 2012. 'Joining Al-Shabaab in Somalia', in Deol, Jeevan & Kazmi, Zaheer (ed.) *Contextualising Jihadi Thought*. London: Hurst & Company: 259-274.

Miller, Erin, 2013. 'Al-Shabaab Attack on Westgate Mall in Kenya', 'National Consortium for the Study of Terrorism and Responses to Terrorism', Accessed on the 10th of May 2014 at: http://www.start.umd.edu/sites/default/files/publications/local_attachments/STARTBackgroundReport_alShabaabKenya_Sept2013.pdf.

Menkhaus, K., 2000. 'Traditional conflict management in contemporary Somalia', in I. W. Zartman (ed.) *Traditional Cures for Modern Conflicts: African Conflict 'Medicine'*. London: Lynne Rienner, pp. 183–99.

Messner, J. J., 2011. 'Somalia Tops the Failed States Index for the Fourth Year Running', accessed on the 12th of May 2014 at: http://library.fundforpeace.org/fsi11-overview.

Phillips, J., 2002. 'Somalia and al-Qaeda: Implications for the War on Terrorism, Backgrounder #1526, Heritage Foundation, Washington. Assessed on the 10th of May 2014 at:http://www.heritage.org/research/reports/2002/04/somalia-and-al-qaeda-implications-for-the-war-on-terrorism.

Sheehan, M. A., & Porter, G. D., 2014. 'The Future Role of US Counterterrorism Operations in Africa'. Assessed on the 14 of September at: http://mercury.ethz.ch/serviceengine/Files/ISN/177356/ipublicationdocument_singledocument/64683e49-2b24-41d0-afc4-582626706cd6/en/CTCSentinel-Vol7Iss2.pdf

Shinn, David, 2011. 'Al Shabaab's Foreign Threat to Somalia', *Orbis* Vol. 55, Issue 2: 203-215.

Shuriye, O. Abdi, 2012. 'Al-Shabaab's Leadership Hierarchy and its Ideology', Academic Research International Vol. 2: 274-285.

Smith, Anthony, D., 1991. *National Identity*. London: Penguin.

Roggio, Bill. 2007. 'The Rise & Fall of Somalia's Islamic Courts: An Online History', accessed on the 5th of October at: http://www.longwarjournal.org/archives/2007/01/the_rise_fall_of_som.php

Thomas, J. Matthew. 2013. 'Exposing and Exploiting Weaknesses in the Merger of Al-Qaeda and Al-Shabaab', *Small Wars & Insurgencies*, Vol. 24, Issue 3: 413-435.

Wise, Rob, 2011. 'Al Shabaab', Center for Strategic and International Studies (CSIS) and the Homeland Security & Counterterrorism Program Transnational Threats Project, accessed on the 9th of September 2014 at: http://csis.org/files/publication/110715_Wise_AlShabaab_AQAM%20Futures%20Case%20Study_WEB.pdf

# 6

# Unholy Alliance in the Maghreb

## Introduction

Islamic Maghreb consists of Arabic-speaking North African states; Algeria, Libya, Mauritania, Morocco and Tunisia. Of particular interest for the purposes of our study is the state of Algeria. Algeria is one of the longest colonised states in the world (Levine, 2005). It was colonised by the Ottomans in the 16th Century and later by France after its invasion in 1830. The French introduced the politics of illiberality — which allowed the French to dispossess the Algerians from their land and property. These demarcations set the pace for localised grievance towards the French.

Subsequently through the years, Algeria had a large colony of Europeans settling and exploiting the economy. Despite the French ideology of assimilation, in reality, there was a wide divide between the Muslims of Algeria and the French. Colonial rule monopolised Algeria's wealth. There was a significant practice of apartheid by the French on Muslim populations. The seeds of radical Islam were sown during anti-colonial movement of the people of Algeria who were desirous of gaining independence from France.

As a result of the contentious history of Algeria, the fertilisation of grievance became conterminous with political discourse of the state. This state affair gave rise to angry and alienated Muslims. The backbone behind the political struggle of Algerians was the National Liberation Front (FLN), whom in 1954 started to engage the French army. The FLN was fundamentally established to circumvent the French colonialists and essentially to obverse the atrocities of France. The FLN at this point in time was led by Larbi Ben M'Hidi and Ramdane Abane. An important aspect of their leadership is that they considered that the colonialisation of Algeria by the French had adulterated the practice of Islam in their country. In order to gain recognition with the people of Algeria, the FLN used religion as a rallying point for Algerian nationalism. However, the essence of Algerian nationalism started in 1931, by the Algerian Association of Ulama who coined the aphorism: 'Islam is my religion; Arabic is my language; Algeria is my Fatherland.' The mobilisation of Islam became an effective tool in fighting French imperialism. In order to effectively confront the French government, the FLN employed underground tactics. Perhaps, the roots of jihâd in Algeria started during the struggle for independence when the FLN named its subversive tabloid as the *'El-Moudjahid'* (the Jihâd-Fighter) in 1956 (Filiu, 2009: 214). The FLN was a powerful mobilising tool, not only for Algerians, but also for other aspiring national liberating groups. Crenshaw's (1995: 474) astute observation informs us that:

> *The FLN became a powerful model for later national liberation organisations, such as the Palestine Liberation Organisation. It inspired groups as diverse and distant as the Front de Libération du Québec in Canada and the Argentine urban guerrilla movement, as well as Palestinian nationalists.*

In 1956, the FLN established the Zone Autonomed'Alger (ZAA) to resist the colonialism of France. However, the French government, under the military tactics of General

Jacques Massu, disbanded both the FLN and the ZAA from Algeria. However, despite the ban placed on these groups, Islam provided a strong sense of unity amongst the nation perhaps arguably igniting a 'jihâd' against the French. Perhaps more crucially, the solidarity provided by Islam events led to the battle of Algiers which eventually led to the independence of Algeria in 1962. It is important to note that the seeds of jihâd had been sown into the heart of the Algerian people when its masses were plagued with localised grievance, injustice and the exploitation of colonialisation.

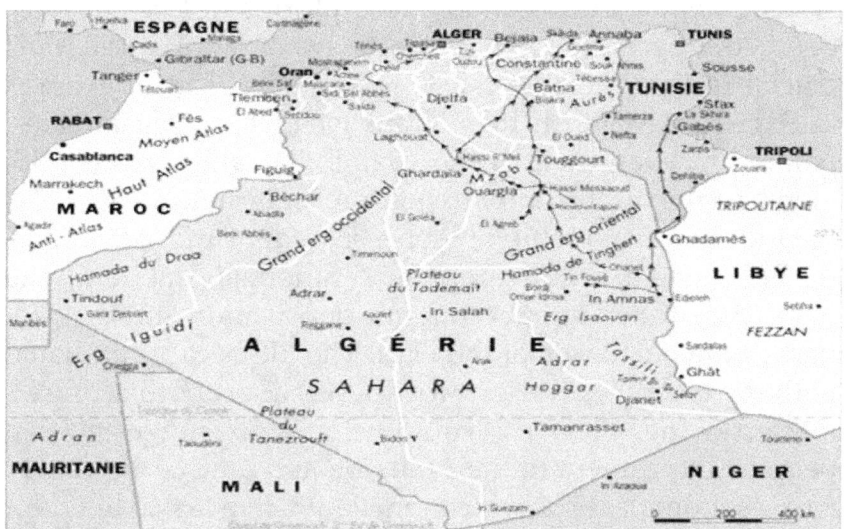

Map showing major town and cities in Algeria. Courtesy:http://www.brahim123.sitew.com/#Algerie.A

## Seeds of Discontent

The crucial defining point in the politics of Algeria arose during the reign of Houari Boumediene (19 June, 1965 – 10 December, 1978). Boumediene enforced a single-party state under the National Liberation Front (FLN). The autocratic rule of Boumediene shut opposition and multi-party politics. After the death of Boumediene in

1976, discordant voices began to rise. Notably, in 1985, the *Mouvement islamique alge´rien* (MIA) began protesting the single party regime of the FLN during the reign of Chadli Bendjedid (9 February, 1979 – 11 January, 1992). Bendjedid did not have the political will to balance the interests of the FLN and improve on the vibrant economic base created by Boumediene. The cumulating effect of this episode led to public grievance and mass dissent. Protests led to the 1988 October riots, where Algerian youths began violently protesting economic grievances and the lack of democratic reforms by the Bendjedid regime. Due to a heated political system, Bendjedid began to make reforms in 1989. In 1989, Bendjedid permitted a multi-party system in Algeria. Most crucial is that these impulsive riots based on grievances in Algiers gave birth to militant Islamist organisations— political parties such as the Islamic Salvation Front (FIS) then had the opportunity to become legitimate.

Under the leadership of 'Abbassi Madani and 'Ali Benhaj, the FIS began to acquire popularity amongst Algerians who were disgruntled about economic deprivation and the one-party state party rule of the FLN. The FIS became affiliated with the Islamic Salvation Army (AIS) in order to acquire a military wing. Clearly, it could be strongly suggested that people's attachment to their religion at a time of discontent and economic austerity channelled Islam as a liberator to Algerians. Islam as a social institution which could be considered as a strong identity among the Algerians found a place as a unifying element for the disgruntled masses. Moreover, Algerians desired to go back to their history and culture as it was before their nation became colonialised by France. This depiction is best summed up in the words of Smith (2009: 58): "A disenchanted population would look for answers to daily problems and a revised and recharged version of Islam was on the way." It is argued that the essence of radical Islam became a popular phenomenon amongst the masses in Algeria. It seems that where a state comprises a large majority of Muslims who are bourgeoned with grievance towards the state, sentiments towards Islamist ideology tends to emerge.

The Islamists took advantage of this depiction and began to implement and implant Islamists ideology in many parts of Algeria. They forbade Westernised social concepts such as alcohol, western music and cinemas. In 1991, when Algeria had its first multi-party parliamentary elections, it was not surprising that the FIS came out victorious. Its victory had its roots in the FIS' provision of social amenities and welfare packages to the underprivileged and most important, its message of Islamic revivalism to Algerians who were already aggrieved by weak political/economic base of the Bendjedid regime. This victory illustrated that the Algerian people have a strong identity marker in Islam. However, this victory was short-lived as the military intervened on the notion that the FIS would transform Algeria into an Islamist state. The military placed Mohammed Boudiaf, as an interim Head of State. However, Boudiaf was assassinated in June 1992. The aftermath of the military coup was an eleven year (26 December, 1991 – February 2002) protracted civil war between the Algerian government and diverse Islamists groups—the dawn of Islamist terrorism and the birth of the Algerian jihâd. This period labelled as the 'black decade,' witnessed a vast number of Algerians being slaughtered.

Ensuingly, the events leading to the cancelation of the election won by the FIS, the birth of two Islamists groups came into existence. The first was the Armed Islamic Movement (MIA) which functioned in the countryside and the Armed Islamic Group (GIA) which was based in the municipal part of Algeria. Essentially, the GIA became the most notorious. It unleashed a reign of terror in Algeria by attacking Westerners and government officials. Principally, under the leadership of Jamal Zitouni and Antar Zouabri, the GIA was desirous of establishing a caliphate in Algeria. It should be noted that a vast number of the GIA militia were veterans of the Afghanistan/Soviet war in the 1980s. Hence, it is not surprising that the GIA used Salafist ideology derived from the al-Qaeda's orientation. This explains the brutal creed of the GIA.

Under the leadership of Zitouni and Zouabri, a holy war was commenced with France. This holy war took effect in 1994 (Christmas Eve) with the abduction of an Air France Airbus. In addition, the onslaught continued with the killing of the Trappist monks of Tibehirine in 1995. The objective of the holy war also witnessed a vast number of bombings and sporadic killings of civilians in both the municipal and townships of Algeria. One source of this violence was GIA's desire to achieve "collective excommunication of Muslims," otherwise known as *takfir al-Mujtama* (Pham, 2011: 242), which is an Islamic practice used when Muslims are not following the precepts of Islam.

Another source of this violence was linked to the affiliation of the FIS and the AIS, who were not in support of a caliphate in Algeria. AIS abstained from attacking foreigners in Algeria and refrained from conducting aggression outside the borders of Algeria. The GIA carried out its campaign of terror outside the borders of Algeria—on November 1995, the GIA in Paris carried out the assassination of Abd al-Baqi Sahrawi, a prominent member of the FIS.

This clash of ideologies brought about an armed struggle between the GIA and the FIS/AIS. The strategy of the GIA is seemingly similar to the tactics of Boko Haram who crave for an Islamist state in Nigeria and voice their grievance by killing innocent civilians. However, another Islamist group called the Salafist Group for Preaching and Combat (GSPC), sprung up in 1998. The GSPC had a similar objective of establishing a caliphate, but did not consider the community of Muslims living in Algeria as its enemy as was the case of the GIA. The GSPC main targets were Algerian public actors, such as the armed forces and public offices. These targets were a response to GIA aggression against the people of Algeria carried out in the 1990s (Marret, 2008).

The Algerian government had the daunting task of fighting the terrorists and preventing people from being radicalised by Islamists. Again, it is worth mentioning that the victory of the Mujahedin over the Soviet Union in the 1989 was a wakeup call that awakened the religious sensibilities of the common Algerian. The atrocities committed by the GIA pre-empted the birth of an organisation known as the Salafist Group for Preaching and Combat (GSPC). The GSPC was perceived by the aggrieved Algerians to end the incessant killing of civilians perpetuated by the GIA. The GSPC has a strong perception that an Islamic caliphate would rid Algeria from corrupt governance and promote better standards of living for its citizens.

## Foundations of al-Qaeda in the Islamic Maghreb (AQIM)

The leader and founder of the GSPC, Hassan Hattab, sought to inspire Islamist and nationalist sentiments amongst Algerians. Hassan Hattab was born in 1967 in Rouiba, Algeria. He joined the paratroops in the Algerian military. He deserted the Algerian armed forces and joined the GIA. In 1994, Hattab became a chieftain in the GIA. He functioned as the commander in Boumerd`es in the Kabylia Mountains region in North East Algeria. At some point, Hattab became disgruntled with the GIA for their sporadic killing of innocent civilians. Hattab's main focus was to attack the armed forces and government targets of Algeria in order to establish a caliphate. However, a dilemma that faced the leadership of Hattab's control and objectives of the GSPC was the limited financial resources to continue the escapade of bombing and guerrilla tactics against the Algerian armed forces.

Hassan Hattab needed to find a quick solution by raising capital by unconventional methods. A solution to this problem came by the smuggler and renown kidnapper in the personage of Mokhtar Belmokhtar (also known as Khalid Abu Al-Abbas a.k.a. Laaˆouar (one-eyed). Belmokhtar was born in Algeria in 1972 and was a veteran of Afghanistan/ Soviet Union. In 1999, Belmokhtar founded the *Shahada Katibat* (Martyrs' Battalion) in Ghardaïa, Algeria, and thereafter integrated the Martyrs' Battalion with the GIA.

However, Belmokhtar as Hattab became disillusioned with the GIA and shifted towards the ideology of Hattab's GSPC in July 2000. More to point, Belmokhtar was in charge of procuring weapons by raising funds through smuggling of cigarettes and weapons from Libya, Mauritania, Niger and Chad through the help of the Tuaregs. He was able to acquire the loyalty of the Tuaregs, given the fact that he married the daughter of a high ranking chief (Smith, 2009). Given his vast experience in the Afghanistan war, Belmokhtar created strong links with al-Qaeda Islamists. He became the main link between the GSPS and al-Qaeda. During this period, an infamous act was committed by Amari Saifi, a.k.a. Abderrazzak El Para, (a field commander in southern Algeria formerly called Zone 9) and Belmokhtar in 2003.This was the abduction of thirty-two European tourists. The government of Germany eventually paid five million euros for their release.[87] Again, Belmokhtar actively participated in the abduction of United Nations employees; in 2008 his men kidnapped the Canadian diplomats Robert Fowler and Louis Guay. In the same year, he also participated in negotiations for the release of two Austrian abductees. Other terrorist atrocities that were committed outside Algeria (before the northern Mali crises) occurred

---

87  See 'Cash-strapped al-Qaeda turns to kidnappings in Algeria', accessed on the 11th of July 2014 at: http://magharebia.com/en_GB/articles/awi/reportage/2008/10/17/reportage-01

on 25 November, 2011 when AQIM kidnapped four tourists in Timbuktu, Mali. Again on 30 September, 2011, AQIM carried out the bombing of a car in Timbuktu that killed two persons. As previously noted, AQIM has a strong base in northern Mali.

After it was apparent that the GSPC were adamant in committing gross atrocities on the Algerian people, it became an unpopular group. The operations of the GSPC became confined outside Algiers, especially in the southern part of Algeria. The network of the organisation grew outside the boarders of Algeria. Other countries in the Maghreb such as Libya, Mauritania and Tunisia became targets of the GSPC.

In this atmosphere, the ungoverned spaces around the borders of these various countries provided safe havens to the terrorist group. According to Byman (2005:222), one of the most important forms of assistance a state can offer a terrorist group is a safe haven. The existence of safe havens allow for easy recruitment, proselytisation, indoctrination and recruitment of radicals. In comparison with Guerrilla groups, Byman notes that terrorist organisations become as potent as guerrillas when granted a safe haven in which they are free to operate. The existence of a sanctuary in Somalia provided for by the Islamic courts union led to the boldness of the group when it became more militarised to launch open assault campaign against the Transitional Federal Government. Quite similarly, Sunni support in Iraq and the inability of the Syrian government to quell the rebel insurgency provided a sanctuary to radical Islamist groups such as ISIS and the Al-Khorasan group, known to be two of the most brutal groups that ever existed. The Taliban in Afghanistan also provided a sanctuary to al-Qaeda in Iraq, and the large ungoverned space of northern Mali and Southern Algeria also provided a safe haven to AQIM.

The aftermath of 911 conveyed the negative conspiracy theory of Islamophobia in Western societies. The GSPC was confronted with pressure to change its radical stance in the nationalisation of Islam. However, to the surprise of many, the GSPC viewed the crime committed by al-Qaeda as worthy of emulation. The journey from a national jihâdist group to an international jihâdist organisation was not without twists and turns. The reason for Hattab's rejection by the chieftains of the GSPC was for the reason that Hattab rejected turning the GSPC into a group based on the ideology of global jihâd. Hattab viewed such a project as unrealistic based on the viewpoint that jihâd was an ideal that a caliphate was attainable only in countries where Islam is the religion of the majority. He argued that in such a state, Islam is more of a public matter and not a private matter. Nabil Sahraoui and Abdelmalek Droukdel were strongly opposed to the rationale of Hattab.

A turning point in the mission of the GSPC occurred in 2003, when Hassan Hattab was removed as its leader and replaced with Nabil Sahraoui (killed in a shootout with Algerian forces in June 2004). Belmokhtar became aggrieved about the removal of his friend and confidant. More crucial he was aggrieved that he was not granted leadership of the GSPC after the death of Sahraoui. When Abu Musab Abdel Wadoud, aka Abdelmalek Droukdel became the new leader of the GSPC, his views became totally aligned with the ideology of al-Qaeda. In January 2007, this connection procured the GSPS to be reoriented in terms of their jihâdist objectives. These radical objectives had sown in a vast number of GSPC fighters through their sojourn as fighters in Afghan crusade against the Soviets. Droukdel became particularly influenced by the ideology of al-Qaeda through internet, especially through the jihâdi Internet community (Filiu, 2009: 221). This demonstrates that "...the views of any particular individual on matters are shaped by the nature of the social groups of which they are a part" (Tansey & O'riordan, 1999:71). The new view of Droukdel became fixated with global jihâd. Droukdel affirmed his loyalty to Osama bin Laden, saying empathically that: "Only Allah knows how much we miss you, and how hard it is for us to be far from you... We are eagerly awaiting your instructions and orders regarding the next phase."[88] A reply to this jihâdi request came on September 11, 2006 when Zawahiri proclaimed: "This blessed union will be a thorn in the throat of the American and French crusaders" (Filiu, 2009: 223). On 11 December, 2006, in order to commit itself to its new found ideology, the GSPC launched its potential new image by attacking a bus conveying workers of a foreign company linked with Halliburton consortium.

The GSPS changed its ideology as well as a rebranding of the organisation to al-Qaeda in the Islamic Maghreb (AQIM) in January 2007. The rebranding of the group gave it a 'globalised' image. Soon thereafter, Droukdel disconnected Belmokhtar from AQIM for 'fractious behaviour.'[89] On March 3, 2007, AQIM commenced its association with al-Qaeda by targeting a Russian contractor in order to show its spirit of camaraderie with the Chechnya Muslims being suppressed by Russia (Filiu, 2009:223). On the 11th of April, 2007, the new labelled group, AQIM, demonstrated its affiliation with globalised jihâd by the bombing of three cars near the Prime Ministers in Algiers which killed over thirty people with one hundred and fifty people injured. This deed was celebrated as the 'Badr of Maghrib', by al-Qaeda (Filiu, 2009: 213). The significance of this unholy amalgamation implies that AQIM now has a broader base to inflict terrorist activities. It includes Algerian civilians as well as Westerners and their institutions. The alliance ushered contention with both the near enemy; the Algerian

---

88   Soriano (2011:279).
89   See 'Mr Marlboro' lands a seismic blow, assessed on the 11th of |July 2014 at: http://www.independent.co.uk/voices/comment/mr-marlboro-lands-a-seismic-blow-8458855.html

state and the far enemy; the United States (Steinberg & Werenfels, 2007). AQIM is a well-funded organisation, which engages in kidnapping, hostage taking, ransom demands, smuggling of cigarettes, humans and weapons, and also an extensive network of drug smuggling. However, AQIM's main strategy is the use of abduction and kidnapping of citizens of Western states. It is speculated that AQIM has raised more than $50 million in ten years.[90] It is perhaps unclear why an Islamic nationalist group changed its goals to become an international jihâdist organisation. When an enquiry is raised as such, an answer may be provided with the observation of Steinberg and Werenfels (2007:410):

> ...because they allow the American military to operate on Algerian soil, and the USA becomes the target of resentment because, despite its rhetoric of democratisation, it continues to cooperate closely with an authoritarian regime. This might have prompted the GSPC to seek closer contact with anti-American terrorists in Iraq...

American interference seems to be a reoccurring variable that pre-empts Islamic radical groups to snowball into international terrorism. As noted earlier in chapter 4, American interference in states such as Afghanistan and Iraq has conveyed a destabilisation in these states and most crucial, it has provoked Islamic terrorism in the region such as the jihâdist group; the Islamic State of Iraq and Syria (ISIS). AQIM still continues with its incessant attacks on the Algerian military. This objective is made clear by Droukdel when he uttered that:

> We would like to make it clear that the war in Iraq today is not a war between Arabs and non Arabs, and it is a war between Muslims and the enemies of Islam, the war between America and the Crusade of the Gods and an alliance with all other races (Soriano, 2011:286).

---

[90] See 'al Qaeda in the Lands of the Islamic Maghreb (AQIM) - (Salafist Group for Preaching and Fighting', accessed on the 11th of July, 2014 at: http://www.trackingterrorism.org/group/al-qaeda-lands-islamic-maghreb-aqim-salafist-group-preaching-and-fighting-see-separate-entry.

Conversely, despite AQIM's global jihâdist objectives, the group still has strong links with criminal elements in Algeria and Mali. It embarks upon smuggling of narcotics and illicit drugs in the guise of making money. AQIM has become strong influence in salafi-jihâdist ideology in West Africa.

According to Thornberry and Levy (2011), AQIM has worked to reinforce social development in the Sahel by inter-marrying into local ethnic groups, engendering profits for poor neighbourhoods and also providing basic ammenities such as water, foodstuffs, and medicine. This has improved the legitimacy of government among the groups they exert their influence, especially in the Sahelian region where government is somewhat far from the people.

AQIM's growing presence and power represents a threat to Western countries. In an address to parliament, Prime Minister David Cameron said there was a need to intervene in order to prevent future terrorist occurrences on the home soil of European countries. Thus, he said that the UK must be ready to help regimes destabilised by terrorist activities. Thus, according to Prime Minister Cameron:

> *The crisis in Iraq must not be dismissed as having nothing to do with us as the same Islamic jihadists are also planning to attack the UK…I'd disagree with those people who think this is nothing to do with us and if they want to have some form of extreme regime in the middle Iraq that won't affect us, it will…the people in that regime, as well as trying to take territory are also planning to attack us at home in the United Kingdom. So the right answer is to be long term hard-headed, patient and intelligent interventions that we make and the most important intervention of all is to make sure that these governments are fully representative of the people who live in their countries that they close down the ungoverned space and they remove the support of the extremists.*[91]

---
91  See David Cameron: Isis is planning to attack UK', accessed on the 10th of September 2014 at: http://www.worldaffairsjournal.org/content/david-cameron-isis-planning-attack-uk

AQIM has influenced the political upheaval in Mali through its brethren in arms—Ansar Dine Movement for Unity and Jihâd in West Africa (MUJWA, a.k.a. MUJAO).[92] Most crucial is that AQIM has a substantial influence in the Sahel, which is the boundary between the Arabs of north African and the dark-skinned sub-Saharan Africa. This border has a strong historical symbol to both sides as it was a vibrant trading link between both civilisations. It was also the channel through which Islam became the religion of majority in Africa. The link between these two geographical expressions is borderless. This has permitted the ease of terrorist activities within the regions. Pham (2011:18) tells us that:

> ...the borders of the region are virtually unguarded, permitting ease of movement as well as access to populations that, if not exactly clamoring for AQIM's message, are at least somewhat receptive to it due to both their social, economic, and political marginalisation and historical memories of jihad out of the desert.

The porous borders have been a useful passage for smuggling network from the Sahel to Europe and for the implementation of other nefarious activities such as human trafficking. These networks have helped in bolstering financial accruement for procuring terrorist activism for AQIM. The group also aims to achieve its former objective of embarking on guerrilla tactics and committing terrorist acts towards the Algerian government as embarked upon before the GSPC/AQIM alliance. In furtherance of its terrorist activities, in April 2014, in a mountainous part of the eastern region of Algiers, the group launched an ambush, killing fourteen Algerian soldiers. The gross activities of these terrorists reveal that the GSPC/al- Qaeda alliance has augmented the frontiers of jihâd in the Magreb; the Sahel, through its links with Ansar Dine and in Sub-Saharan Africa

---

[92] See Chapter 8

by sharing intelligence with Boko Haram and al-Shabaab (joined al-Qaeda in 2010). A clearer perspective, illustrating the dynamism of the alliance, is provided by Marret (2008: 549) where he notes that:

> GSPC/al-Qaeda in Islamic Maghreb now claims to be a pragmatic (and self-proclaimed) umbrella organisation on both sides of the Mediterranean Sea, providing resources and, possibly, an identity to smaller groups, a better pool of expertise, shared know-how, 'economies of scale,' and an increased sense of support. The label 'al-Qaeda' itself can also potentially induce an increased 'public' awareness. The GSPC has progressively and openly adopted broader goals, from 'regionalisation' to solidarity and cooperation with transnational jihadi networks.

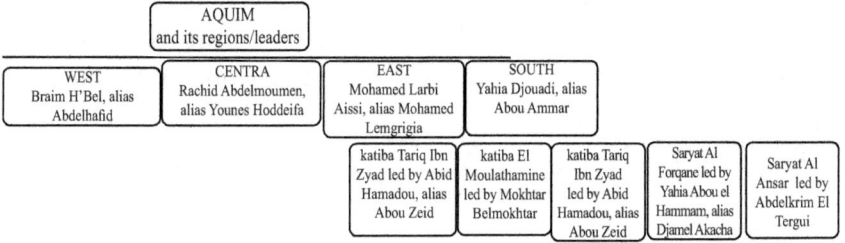

**AQIM and its Regional Commanders**

Al-Qaeda's control and network seems to be getting colossal and creating new terrorist hub/cells in Africa. Islamism has moved beyond the Middle East and has now gained a significant outreach in Africa. Perhaps, it is now clear that Islamism in Africa operates in multi-dimensional approach. It acts with a double-edged sword. It attacks its citizens, security forces and public sector infrastructures and at the same time sets out to attack citizens of western states and its institutions. With this objective, it seems highly probable that an event similar to 911 or the 7th July, 2005, bomb attacks in London may occur in the future in a western society. However, it should be noted that it appears that AQIM finds it almost impossible to perpetrate it acts of terror outside Algeria. In line with this, Filiu, (2009B: 10):

> *The security paradox posed by AQIM is that its inability to project its 'global' terror beyond Africa intensifies the pressures from al-Qaeda central to achieve such a breakthrough and to force the Algerian jihadi leadership to live up to this commitment. This jihadi challenge must therefore be taken very seriously because AQIM is longing to reconcile its violent record with its global agenda. But jihadi propaganda must be systematically deflated by stressing the fact that AQIM basically kills Algerian Muslims, most of them civilians.*

Despite the probability of AQIM committing terrorist activities in the West, *Ouellet et al (2014),* using an institutional analysis admirably argues that AQIM lacks a domestic organisation structure which threatens its continued existence. However, one cannot overlook the traditions and political agenda of al-Qaeda and its overarching desire to achieve a unified caliphate.

## Conclusion

The depiction of human savagery conducted by AQIM portends that the group is losing popular support form Algerians and other Muslims in the Sahel. In many respects, the group has been alienated by Algerians. In other words, the group has broken the hearts of the people. In many ways it has not only put an indelible stain in the Umma (community of Muslims), but also tarnished the spiritual essence of Islam to Algerians. Many Algerians have lost their lives or their loved ones to the GSPC/al-Qaeda alliance. Amongst the mayhem of violence, the GSPC/al-Qaeda has actually achieved nothing in terms of political and religious gains. Even the former GSPC founder, Hattab, has repeatedly called on AQIM to lay down its arms. It seems that the intent and objective of the group has been overturned by greed and nepotism, the perceived 'virtues' which the group was once considered to abhor. Conversely, using the words and ideology of al-Qaeda's founder, Osama Bin Laden: "We do not anathematise people in general, nor do we permit the shedding of Muslim blood."[93]

The hypocrisy attached to this statement is momentous, as it showcases the gross misinformation attached behind radical Islam.

Nevertheless, it appears that the 'globalisation'[94] of the group purports to uphold the history of violence emanating from Algeria before its independence to its turbulent history of violence as an independent state. Moreover, flowing from the above, it is clearly observed that the group has now moved beyond a salafi-jihâdist group to a criminalised mafia group, specialising in the smuggling of narcotics, abduction for ransom and bombing Algerian establishments. This deadly cocktail of blood and savagery indicates that the group lacks a radical ideology, but at best the organisation could be described as a highly effective, well organised defamed criminal gang.

---

93    Statement of 16 December 2004, in Lawrence, (2005: 262).
94    Glocalization is a term popularized by Robertson (1992). In the context of this chapter it was also used by Marret ( 2008)

# References

Byman, D., 2005. *Deadly Connections: States that Sponsor Terrorism.* New York.

Crenshaw, Martha. 1995. 'Terrorism in the Algerian War', in Crenshaw Martha (ed)., 1995. *Terrorism in Context.* Pennsylvania: Pennsylvania State University Press: 473-513.

Filiu, Jean-Pierre, 2009. *'The Local and Global Jihad of al-Qa'ida in the Islamic Maghrib', The Middle East Journal* Volume 63, 2: 213-226.

Filiu, Jean-Pierre, 2009B. Al-Qaeda in the Islamic Maghreb: Algerian Challenge or Global Threat? Carnegie Papers, Carnegie Endowment for International Peace.

Guido Steinberg & Isabelle Werenfels, 2007. 'Between the 'Near' and the 'Far' Enemy: Al-Qaeda in the Islamic Maghreb', *Mediterranean Politics,* 12:3, 407-413.

Lawrence, Bruce, 2005. *Messages to the World: The Statements of Osama Bin Laden.* London; New York: Verso.

Levine, Mark, 2005. Why They Don't Hate Us: Lifting the Veil on the Axis of Evil. Oxford: Oneworld Publications Limited.

Marret, Jean-Luc, 2008. 'Al-Qaeda in Islamic Maghreb: A "Glocal" Organization', *Studies in Conflict & Terrorism,* 31:541–552.

Ouellet, Eric , Lacroix-Leclair, Jérôme & Pahlavi, Pierre. 2014. 'The Institutionalization of Al-Qaeda in the Islamic Maghreb (AQMI)', *Terrorism and Political Violence* Vol. 26, issue 4: 650-665.

Pham, J. Peter, 2011. 'The Dangerous "Pragmatism" of Al-Qaeda in the Islamic Maghreb', *Journal of the Middle East and Africa,* 2:15–29.

Pham, J. Peter, 2011. 'Foreign Influences and Shifting Horizons: The Ongoing Evolution of al Qaeda in the Islamic Maghreb', *Orbis,* Spring: 240-254.

Smith, Gregory A., 2009. Al-Qaeda in the Lands of the Islamic Maghreb. *Journal of Strategic Security,* 2 (2): 53-72.

Robertson, Roland., 1992. *Globalization: Social Theory and Global Culture,* London: Sage.

Soriano, Manuel R., Torres. 2011. 'The Evolution of the Discourse of al-Qaeda in the Islamic Maghreb: Themes, Countries and Individuals', *Mediterranean Politics,* Vol. 16, No. 2, 279–298.

Thornberry W & Levy J., 2011. 'Al-Qaeda in the Islamic Mahgreb', Washington DC: CSIS, assessed on the 3nd of September 2014 at: http://csis.org/files/publication/110901_Thornberry_AQIM_WEB.pdf

# 7

# Talibanism in Mali

## Introduction

Insights into the awakening of Islamists terrorism in Mali remain complex and intriguing. It is interwoven with several intricate elements that have a strong connectivity with the historical determinism in Mali. Before setting ahead, it is useful to note that Mali was once considered as a pillar of democracy before 2012. However, the democracy could only be described as fragile, characterised by the exclusion of various groups from political participation and ethnic domination of a group by the other, a notable characteristic of political societies in the West African sub-region. Yet—it could safely be branded as the land of the Taliban in Africa.

In order to chart how Mali became a tense, unsettled and competitive political system, let us take a cursory look at the nature of political conflicts, particularly in West Africa. Political conflicts involve the struggle between groups for the allocation of values. Despite the fact that the nature of man is inherently conflictual, political conflicts do not necessarily manifest themselves unless there has been some perceived actual grievance which has either not been addressed at all or to a reasonable satisfaction. The nature of radical Islam is itself political as it represents a desire by certain groups to change the way things are done within a particular society. This is why radical groups publicise their manifesto and ideology. In doing this, they articulate their grievances and the objectives they desire to achieve, no matter how unreasonable such demands may seem. Prolonged grievance may result in an excarcebation of the precipitating conditions of conflict. However, such conditions may continue to exist without conflict actually erupting. For example, the marginalisation of a political group or conditions of poverty may exist without those affected resorting to violence. However, prolonged grievance coupled with insensitivity on the part of the authorities responsible for improving the prevailing conditions of either poverty or social inequality has the potential to generate such groups to resort to violence in achieving their goals.

Superficially, political conflicts in West Africa reflect prolonged grievance within societies divided across various lines. The nature and causes of the division may not be limited to the allocation of resources, wealth, power, or even the process of governance. Resource control shapes behaviour and social processes for all actors within the state, ranging from the individual to specific groups often manifested in cleavages such as race, gender, class, or religion. These definintely have the potential to maximise conflict potentialities.

These dynamics explained in the above paragraph are clearly reflected in the formation of Ansar Dine. Ansar Dine, otherwise known as 'defenders of the faith,' is an Islamist group that is enjoined with the Movement for Unity and Jihâd in West Africa (MUJWA, a.k.a. MUJAO). The MUJWA is desirous of promoting al-Qaeda's ideology of global jihâd into West Africa. The MUJWA which was formed in December 2011 operates within Gao. MUJWA is led by Hamada Ould

Mohamed Kheirou, a Mauritanian. Kheirou was a former fighter for al-Qaeda in Iraq in 2003.

## Political Imbalance

In order to chart the rise of radical Islam in Mali and to connect these complex issues, it is imperative to understand the events that generate the existence of the political imbalance in Mali. We intend to do this by underscoring the turbulent political history of the Tuareg and the Malian government and thereafter we will showcase the rise of Islamism in northern Mali in particular.

After Mali gained independence from France on 22 September, 1960, its President, Modibo Kéïta, created a one party state based on the ideology of socialism. At this point in time, Mali became an ally of the Soviet Union. However, the reign of Kéïta was short-lived (by African standards at the time) as he was ousted in a coup in 1968 by Moussa Traoré, who held office for twenty-three years. During Moussa Traoré's reign, he banned all political parties and in 1978 established a one party system via the Union Démocratique du Peuple Malien. This party embarked on a trail of corruption and prebendalism as its ideal of governance which left Mali without a viable economic base. In 1991, Traoré was overthrown in a military coup by Amadou Toumani Touré, who then established a democratic government on 12 January, 1992, ushering Alpha Oumar Konaré to power via the Alliance pour la Démocratie en Mali (ADEMA). After two terms of office, Konaré stepped down, thereafter Amadou Toumani Touré, then known as the 'soldier of democracy,' came into power via democratic elections in 2002.

Amadou Toumani Touré practised a consensus government which comprised a system of an all inclusive government. Touré's consensus government produced stability, secularisation and viable democratic governance in the region. However, this form of government had its failures and weaknesses as it was not able to embrace the divergent voices in Mali. A crucial element to Mali's destabilisation was the fact that Touré institutionalised the military as a machinery of corruption. Perhaps most crucial, was the fact the Touré's regime suppressed and discriminated against the Tuareg. Touré's self-formed consensus government became a huge failure due to the escalation of corruption and nepotism among government officials and the failure of a decentralised government which situated 64 percent of the Malian population to be under the poverty line (Dante, et al, 2003: 170). In explaining the concept of relative deprivation, Cristiani and Fabiani (2013: 81) note that:

> *The weakness of the Malian economy; the poverty, its landlocked location and the poor infrastructure and communications have isolated the country from global markets while adding to the difficulty of controlling the national territory.*

Furthermore, the Tuareg were enshrined with grievance pertaining to the attempt of Touré to prolong his regime. This scenario is best described by the Lecocq, et al. (2013: 5):

> *By the time of the coup, Toure' had lost nearly all legitimacy in the eyes of everyday Malians. Toure''s 'rule by consensus' had become a mere euphemism for absolute rule with checks and balances existing only on paper while journalists and others were afraid to challenge the president's agenda. Meanwhile, the perception in Bamako was widespread that Toure''s aversion to conflict extended to all areas of politics, rendering him unwilling to enforce the rule of law or to punish venality among those close to him. He had kept a tenuous peace in the north by buying off northern leaders, but failed to deliver on promises to bring development. He took millions of dollars of US military assistance intended to help drive out AQIM, but never went after the group on*

*Malian territory. The gangrene of corruption had long infected the army, where nepotism and profiteering ran amok.*

At the same time, the Tuaregs had to compete for scarce resources in a country that was already plagued by extreme poverty. Aside from the systematic abuse and dominion over the Tuareg by the Malian government, the regime was at this time regarded as a club of largesse for the military. Solomon (2013:14) noted perceptively that:

*Corruption under the Touré government became increasingly institutionalised. One facet of this corruption relates to the military. Over this period, recruitment into the armed forces required being fortunate enough to have a relative at the level of a colonel or a general, and skill sets hardly seemed to matter. Under the circumstances, the fact that the Malian armed forces crumbled so spectacularly in 2012 in the face of the Tuareg insurgency could hardly have come as a surprise.*

## Ansar Dine

This is a jihâdist group in northern Mali. Ansar Dine was formed in 2012 as a result of a blend of Islamic nationalism and al-Qaeda networking emanating from Algeria. Ansar Dine operates within Timbuktu and Kidal. The group is led by Iyad Ag Ghaly, a former Tuareg insurgent leader and Malian diplomat in Saudi Arabia from 2008–2010 who became the leader of Ansar Dine.[95] Iyad was a prominent figure in the *Mouvement National de Libération Touareg* — National Tuareg Liberation Movement (MNLA). It is important to note that the MNLA is desirous for an independent state. The MNLA was led by Mohamed Ag Najem, a fighter who had participated in the Arab spring uprising in Libya. However, Iyad rejected the aspiration of national objectives for the Tuareg and inculcated Islam into

---

95    United States and the United Nations listed Iyad ag Ghali, as a global terrorist

politics. Iyad had previously led two insurgencies against the Malian state in the 1990's and in 2006.

Ansar Dine comprises of the Tuaregs and fighters from Nigeria, Pakistan, Somalia and Algeria.[96] The Kel Adagh, that is, the Tuareg confederation are the legitimate representatives of the cause of Tuaregs in Mali. Al Ghaly wanted to lead this confederation but was denied the position. It was shortly after this that Al Ghaly formed Ansar al-Dine. The full name of Ansar Dine is Harakat Ansar al-Dine, which means 'defenders of the faith.' The objectives of Ansar Dine is to wage a holy war against those who do not adhere to the strict interpretation of Islamic rules and establishment of a sharia based Islamic order in the areas under their control. This reason is particularly why the group immediately imposed sharia rule once they have a city under its control.

The tactics of the Ansar al-Dine include kidnapping/ hostage taking, torture, murdering and beheadings. In a narrative summary about Ansar al-Dine released by the United Nations Security Council (UNSC) on 20 March, 2013, pursuant to resolution 2083 (2012) which designated the group as a foreign terrorist organisation,[97] Ansar Dine was listed as being affiliated with al-Qaeda. In October 2011, AQIM leader, Abdel Malek Droukdel wanted to use an organisation to expand al-Qaeda's influence in the Sahelian region and increase the groups' presence and control over northern Mali (Thornberry & Levy, 2011). It was intended that the group mask its original identity through adoption of a name which had no apparent link to al-Qaeda or AQIM. Droukdel therefore approached Al Ghaly to form Ansar Dine. Beyond the desire of AQIM to have a local presence in Mali, Castelli (2014) tells us that the region was suitable for AQIM given the fact that the region's peculiar landscape sheltered

---

[96] Another group called the Signatories in Blood-in-Blood Battalion, a splinter group form AQIM which is led by the Algerian Mokhtar Belmokhtar. It was formed in 2012. Its operations are mainly based in Algeria. Its operations have not been significant in Mali partly due to the intervention of France in Mali in January 2013.

[97] See http://www.un.org/en/ga/search/view_doc.asp?symbol=S/RES/2083(2012)

it against military intrusion; the Malian state consisted of fragile economy; AQIM had coalition of local tribes; and they had access to illicit finances in the state. Commenting on the irregular landscape, Cline, (2013: 618) notes that:

> *Mali is rather ill-formed in terms of its borders. Its border with Mauritania essentially appears drawn by a cartographer's pen rather than through any particular logic.*

These factors enumerated above were a good playing ground for the assimilation of AQIM into Mali.

It is important to note that Ansar Dine's membership is made up of mostly Tuaregs. The group has also received military recruits and veteran fighters from AQIM with numerous members joining their ranks, thus increasing the group's number to between 500 and 2500 fighters. In addition to the manpower donation from sympathetic terrorist affiliations, Ansar Dine incorporated various fighters from indigenous population of the Bella and Songhai ethnic groups. The motivation for the groups joining Ansar Dine's rank owed to their grievance against the Tuaregs whom they felt was only representing only Tuareg interests, thus marginalising the group as a result of the peace deal signed between the Mali government and Tuaregs. A report online in The Hindu,[98] compiled by Sethi Aman noted that there was grievance owing to preferential treatment given to Tuaregs based on the fact that Tuaregs occupied major positions in the government and in the army despite their low level of education. This grievance was exploited by Islamists in recruiting the Songhai people in joining rebel ranks.

It is vital to note that AQIM's influence on the group is quite evident. Ansar Dine has received huge military, logistical and financial support from AQIM. In 2013, Iyad

---

98   See 'Battle reveals Islamists riding over ethnic faultlines', accessed on the 20th of January 2014 at: http://www.thehindu.com/todays-paper/tp-international/battle-reveals-islamists-riding-over-ethnic-faultlines/article4305856.ece

Ghali received a payment of 400,000 euros from Tariq ibn Zyad brigade of the al-Qaeda Sahelian outfit. Ansar Dine is also believed to have financial backing from Qatar.[99] Byman (2005:21) perceptively notes that:

> Yet, despite being such unsavory and unpromising partners for states, many terrorist groups regularly receive state support. This support is forthcoming because the terrorist group can serve the strategic interests of foreign states, gain their leaders' sympathy for ideological reasons, or play a role in bolstering leaders' domestic positions.

In line with this, Boghard (2014) notes that:

> Qatar and Kuwait have been singled out as terrorist financing trouble spots. The State Department's latest annual Country Reports on Terrorism, covering 2013, refers to 'increased reports' of Kuwait-based individuals funding extremists in Syria, and to the 'significant terrorist financing risk' of Qatar-based fundraisers.[100]

Ansar Dine since its formation till 2014 has conducted about seventy operations in the Sahelian region. Its influence has mainly been in northwest Mali in areas including Timbuktu, where it destroyed a world heritage site after capturing the city. Ansar Dine has been engaged in widespread destruction of lives and property since the beginnnning of its campaign in Mali against government and security forces. The group engaged extensively in the widespread destruction of lives and property, using arms from both neighbouring Libya and also the looted armouries of various military bases it attacked in northern Mali. The group is known to have some presence in the northern cities of Tessalit, Gao, Kidal, Oglhok, and Timbuktu. The ability of Ansar Dine to successfully execute their attacks is based on the extensive experience and discipline of its fighters.

---

99   See http://www.un.org/sc/committees/1267/NSQI31613E.shtml
100  See Boghardt, Lori Plotkin, 2014. 'The Terrorist Funding Disconnect with Qatar and Kuwait', The Washington Institute Policy, Watch 2247, accessed on the 27th of December 2014 at: http://www.washingtoninstitute.org/policy-analysis/view/the-terrorist-funding-disconnect-with-qatar-and-kuwait See also Byman, D. (2005). Deadly connections. States that Sponsor Terrorism. New York.

In March 2012, Ansar Dine claimed control of Tinzaouten, Tessalit and Aguelhok, three towns in northern Mali approaching to the Algerian border. On April 3, 2012, the group was reported to have started implementing sharia in the areas under their control. In Timbuktu, they engaged in the destruction of ancient Sufi shrines. Following the military coup on 22 March, 2012, which ushered Captain Amadou Sanogo into power and the subsequent collapse of the Malian army, Iyad Ghali's Jihâdist allies began operations to subjugate areas in northern Mali under their control. Thus, the Jihâd and Tawhid movements took control of major Azawad cities. The various groups in their conquest of Malian cities exploited the grievances of the existing populations. Ansar Dine also used tribal dimensions and the lack of a formal government authority to consolidate their rule. Thus, according to Al-Ma'ali & Mahmoud, (2012: 6-7):

> *Ghali's group took it upon itself to besiege and storm the city of Kidal, exploiting the tribal dimension of the city, inhabited mostly by people from the al-Afoghas tribe to which most of Ghali's fighters also belonged. As for the historic city of Timbuktu, Iyad Ghali took advantage of the negotiations that were taking place between the National Movement for the Liberation of Azwad and fighters belonging to the militias of the city's Arab tribes to carry out a surprise attack with a large military force led by a legion from al-Qaeda in the Islamic Maghreb. That, in turn, was led by the Emir of the al-Furqan squadron, Yahy Abu al-Hammam...*
>
> *It was this coordination to which Iyad Ghali referred in his first speech to the people of Timbuktu on 4 April, 2012, after his forces took control of the city. In that speech he stated that:*
>
> *... your brothers from the Mujahideen and the Ansar al-Dine organisation have come together and vowed to*

*uphold what is right, to implement the religion, to lift injustice off of the oppressed, to reunify the Muslims...*

In January 2013, another movement named the Islamic movement of Azawad, a splinter group from Ansar Dine, came into existence. The issue of grievance is no less the same in the case of the MUJWA. The MNLA pointed to AQIM's deviation from the fundamental principles and the promotion of personal interests by the leaders rather than group interests as the reason for the formation of the group.[101] Thus, the groups aimed at propagating salafist jihâd ideologies in West Africa. The group is made up of largely Mauritanians, Arabs and few Egyptians, Saudis, Nigerians and foreigners from western countries. There are also a few recruits from the local population. The issue of Western recruits is a growing concern among western countries. This is largely based on the ability of such individuals to return home and radicalise home grown terrorists or even launch attacks on the homeland.

## The Movement for Unity and Jihâd in West Africa (MUJWA)

The activities of the MUJWA are not limited to kidnapping and ransom demands, conducting attacks against foreign targets and imposition of sharia in areas under their control. It also includes propaganda carried out through social media platforms such as Facebook, twitter and jihâdi forums and YouTube. It is important to also note that MUJWA, in carrying out their crusade, rely on spiritual authority from their affiliation with the global jihâdi group, al-Qaeda. In order to propagate their jihâd in the western part of the Sahel region, they also claim to be descendants of or have affinity with ancient Jihâdi figures such as Uthman dan Fodio, El Hadj Umar, and Cheikou Amadou.

---

101  One of such reasons was the refusal the undue favouritism given to members of the group of Algerian origin.

The group's influence in Mali was clearly evident during the Malian crisis in their seizure of the towns of Gao, Douzeita and Kidal in 2014. The MUJWA also clashed with MLNA for control of these towns and minor ethnic groups such as the Songhai Ifogha. In October 2013, three aid workers in a camp in Algeria were kidnapped. On February 7th, 2014, the MUJWA was responsible for the killing of thirty-one Tuareg in an attack in Tamkoutat in northern Mali. The attacks signalled a change of tactics from attacking strictly military targets to attacks directed at civilian population. However, the group suffered huge blows of defeat when two of its top commanders were killed in a French airstrike in the region.

Predictably, MUJWA was described by a foreign and commonwealth office report[102] as one of the most integrated within the drug trade and narcotic smuggling network (2013:7). The report also listed most of the group's members as known smugglers. Islam as a religion kicks against the use of drugs. However, there is to some extent a justification which the smugglers use to their advantage — they cite historical accounts of the adaptation of faith with trade in order to achieve their desired goals and raise funds for the group's activities. Thus, they use the ends to justify the means. According to a 2013 UN office on drugs and crime (UNODC) report on transnational organised crime in West Africa,[103] drug smuggling is a very lucrative business practised by narco-rings in the Sahel region. It is an elaborate network, involving even government officials in the region. The UNODC (2013:11) in their report also stated that these drugs come from Latin America, and pass through West Africa on their way to their final destination in Europe. According to the UNODC, the amount of money made on the sale of these drugs exceeds even the defence

---

102  Foreign and Commonwealth Office (2013)Traffickers and Terrorists: drugs and violent jihad in Mali and the wider Sahelhttps://www.gov.uk/government/uploads/system/uploads/attachment_data/file/256619/Oct_2013_Traffickers_and_Terrorists.pdf

103  See UNODC (2013). Transnational organised crime in West Africa: a threat assessment. Vienna: UN office on drugs and crime

budgets of these West African countries (UNODC 2013:3). This has made the environment in which terrorists seek safe haven as not one of ungoverned spaces allowing terrorists to act freely, but a different style of governance in which the governments of the nations affected turn a blind eye to terrorist activities. Most government officials are on the payroll of these terrorist organisations. In addition, the vast Sahara makes the tracking of the activities of these groups a heinous task. In addition to the sale of narcotics, MUJWA raises funds through kidnapping of expatriates and government officials. MUJWA demands ransom for release of prisoners and have been engaged in dastardly acts of kidnapping, especially in the last year. The group is also financed by al-Qaeda.

Under these circumstances, it is not surprising that the two groups (Ansar Dine and MUJWA) have links with al-Qaeda in the Islamic Maghreb (AQIM), which has a strong presence in Algeria, Mali, Niger, and Mauritania. AQIM considered Ansar Dine as a useful tool in helping to promote its agenda for a universal jihad. Ansar Dine was assured by AQIM that collaborating with their group would help in imposing a strict interpretation of Islamic law in northern Mali. In 2011, AQIM embarked on kidnappings and violence towards citizens of western states in Mali. With the collaborative partnership with Ansar Dine and MUJWA, AQIM has been able to counter Mali's military counter attacks.

Emanating from these sporadic kidnappings, the MUJWA emerged in late 2011 as a splinter group of AQIM. The MUJWA was able to emerge from AQIM for the reason that Mali had been a safe haven, recruitment centre and training ground. Perhaps the sum total of MUJWA's mission is to act as tool for targeting western interests, especially abducting French citizens for huge ransoms, attacking foreign interests and Algerian gendarmerie bases. The main financial base of the group is the illicit trade in cocaine. The key in understanding the trajectories of radical Islam in Mali as useful guide lies in the cocktail of the MNLA, Ansar Dine and the MUJWA, which provides us with an intriguing blend of a complex and dangerous mix of ideologies springing from politics, nationalism and religion through the barrel of different guns with a complex mix of diverse fighters—terrorists and rebels.

## Religious Crisis in Mali

Islam is the predominant religion in Mali. Islam was significantly practiced as an elitist religion during the time of the Songhai Empire (mid-15th to the late 16th century). It is practiced according to the dictate of Sufism. However, Sufism gradually became unpopular with the influence of Wahabism and Jihâdi–Salafi in the late 1990s. Radical Islam, found a comfort zone in northern Mali for the reason that its people were pauperised by the practitioners of Sufism (those at the helm of affairs in Mali). The level of poverty in northern Mali is not surprising as Mali is one of the poorest countries in the World.[104] The influence of these strict interpretations of the Qur'an generated radical Islam, particularly in northern Mali. More to the point, the creed of Wahabism and salafi-Jihâdi created a space for the ideology of al- Qaeda to spread in mosques and amongst the youth who were disoriented about being marginalised by the central government in Bamako. Salafist groups such as Algerian-based Salafist Group for Preaching and Combat (GSPC), had the opportunity to radicalise the deprived citizens of northern Mali. In due course, GSPC was transformed into AQIM during the late 1990s. It also continued its message of radical Islam. Aside from its message of radicalisation, the GSPC and AQIM ushered in economic opportunities for the impoverished men in form of smuggling of cocaine and illicit goods in and out of Mali.

---

104  ranked 175th on the Human Development Index

During Sanogo's brief reign, the military lost the important cities of Kidal, Gao, and Timbuktu to the MNLA in conjunction with Ansar Dine. The MNLA and Ansar Dine complimented each other in the conquest of North east Mali. The role played by the two groups is that, whilst the MNLA was responsible for military aggression, upon occupation of the territories, Ansar Dine implemented strict sharia law, which included public executions, amputations and floggings whilst despising Sufism. Aside from these atrocities in the name of Islam, the two Islamists groups went on a rampage of looting and raping defenceless women. Beyond their pact of brotherhood, the MNLA were desirous of establishing an independent secular state of Azawad, whilst Ansar Dine was eager of imposing Sharia across the entire state of Mali. The MUJWA on the other hand supported Ansar Dine financially. The MUJWA was able to render such support as they engage in drug trafficking in the Sahel and southern Algeria. Moreover, they perceived that the confused state of Mali with the MNLA and Ansar Dine would act as an advantage in the pursuit of a universal jihâd. In addition, on 23 October, 2011, MUJWA abducted three humanitarian workers from Tindouf, Algeria. On 5 April, 2012, they also kidnapped seven Algerian diplomats, in Gao, Mali. On 23 March, they attacked Gendarmerie Nationale base in Tamanrasset, Algeria. Furthermore, on 29 June, 2012, they attacked the Gendarmerie Nationale, base in Ouargla, Algeria.

At this point, it should be noted that the Tuaregs in Mali are fractionalised. They are divided by clans and ancestral lineages. Although these divisions are not strong indicators of diversity among the Tuareg, they represent an affiliation to social prestige. The Ifogas clan is known for its royalty and have maintained a position of rulership over other Tuareg clans. The Amenokal who is an Ifogas is known as the traditional ruler of the Tuareg in Mali. Interestingly, most of the Tuareg revolts have been coordinated by the Ifogas from Kidal under the banner of the Movement for the Azawad (MPA) which was then led by Iyad ag Ghali. Another clan called the Taghat Melet which is based in Kidal operates under the front of the Revolutionary Army for the Liberation of the Azawad (ARLA). Another clan known as the Idnane clan is closely linked to the Taghat Melet through the ARLA. The region of Gao and Menaka is divided into factions of the Idnane, the Iwellemmeden, the Kel Essouk and the Chaman-Amas. Timbuktu is categorised by main two clans: the Kel Instar and the Iwellemmeden. These clans mentioned above are also divided in sub-clans. It is suggested as would be noted later, that the varied factions within the Tuareg acted as a platform for criss-crossing group membership within the MNLA, Ansar Dine and the MUJWA. It is also important to note that members of these clans are present in the Islamists groups and in the MNLA. It is suggested that these divisions in clan membership is a determining factor in the group constitution of the MNLA and the Islamists groups.

## Tuareg Quest for Self-Determination and the National Tuareg Liberation Movement (MNLA)

Now, the Tuareg are a semi-nomadic people who dwell in parts of Mali, Niger, Burkina Faso, Algeria, and Libya. They are 'a people without a state' (Smith, 2009: 60). Their division is similar to the partition of the Kurdish people, who are divided and marginalised between Iraq, Iran and Turkey. However, the realisation for a separate state for the Turaeg as is the case for the Kurdish people seems impossible for the reason that such divisions would threaten the sovereignty of states. The constitutional understanding of most states does not recognise the right of self-determination. It is quite important to add here that the doctrine of *uti possidetis'* is one which African countries adopted in order to preserve the integrity of colonial boundaries and promote peace. However, as seen in the example of Sudan, the doctrine has allowed various ethnic dominated governments to oppress minority groups. In December 1893, the Tuaregs were dispossessed of their land (Timbuktu, a center of Islamic culture) by the French army. After a long and bloodied resistance by the Tuareg, they eventually yielded to French rule in 1917. In the 1960's, after Mali gained independence, the Tuareg rebelled in the Adrar N'Fughas mountains against the new independent state. However, the rebellion was crushed by the Malian government.

Another nationalist rebellion occurred in May 1990-1996 and 2006 between Tuareg tribesmen and Malian soldiers. These conflicts were prompted by the demands of the Tuareg for a separate homeland in the Azawad and Kidal regions of Mali. The aspiration of nationalism by the Tuareg is not uncommon in deeply divided societies as Horowitz (1985: 187) eloquently puts it: "The quest for power for an ethnic group is sought to confirm status and avert threats and ethnic domination from other ethnic groups."

It is important to note that the conflict arising from the Turaeg does not lie within ethnic animosity with other ethnic groups in Mali, but lies with the quest for self-determination. This is evident in the Tuareg quest for autonomy in other states such as Niger who are desirous of achieving self-rule. Clearly, this grievance explains the aspiration for Tuareg nationalism in the realisation that the Tuareg imagined that their national identity was under threat. In simple terms, nationalism may erupt when "its fear and hatred of others" (Anderson, 1991:141) emerge. After the 2006 conflict, a peace accord was signed in Algiers between the two factions.

According to Adekanye (2007), peaceful transition is one of the ways of resolving political conflicts. Adekanye argues that power sharing may serve to stem the potentiality of conflict through the integration of persons who have been involved in the transition struggle, mostly the key figures of such struggle, it does not entirely eliminate the conditions which served to project the grievance which generated the grievance in the first instance. As socio-economic conditions worsen, the grievance becomes more openly manifested in what is described by Adekanye (2007) as the two (faces) phases of transition. In this situation, the aggrieved population demand to see the actual representation of their struggles reflected in the power sharing arrangement than a mere figurehead benefiting from the process and becoming part of the problem. Therefore, Adekanye (2007) posits that power-sharing arrangements last for only four to five years. The reason for this is that most of the basic problems associated with power-sharing relate to the exclusionary nature of representation. Thus, there are growing demands by the excluded people for a more inclusive nature of representation. Demands of this nature include trans-ethnic issues such as the growing gap between the rich and poor, emerging elites and mass population and the rural and urban areas. This results in a magnification of grievance.

In another respect, the cultural difference between the Tuareg and other Malians also promoted disparity among Malians, as the Arab Tuareg regarded themselves as superior to black people who otherwise referred to as the 'Zingiya.' The Tuaregs imagined themselves to be Arab (Seely, 2001: 506). In this sense, the Tuareg perceived other Malians to be lesser Muslims. The cultural imperative of prayer and worship being conducted in Arabic is used as a fog for differentiation. Furthermore, this cultural division was also extended among the Tuareg community. This was particularly illustrated in the implementation of sharia law amongst the people of Gao. Huckabey (2013: 147) notes the ethnic animosity between the black sub-Saharan Tuaregs and the Berber/Arabic Tuaregs:

*Moreover, western news stories told of a seemingly race-based, selective application of the harsh Islamic law by MUJAO, according to Gao residents, the victims of sharia punishments were from Mali's black African ethnic groups, while the jihadis were mostly lighter-skinned Arabs—both Malian and foreign—and Tuaregs.*

Thanks to political tensions emanating from Tuareg nationalism and AQIM's subtle intrusion in northern Mali, Touré's consensus government was not able to resolve the peace agreements (1992 and 1995) between the Tuareg and Malian government. Moreover, to make matters worse, the Tuareg were conspicuously omitted from government infrastructures and economic empowerment. Sequel to these grievances, on 16 January, 2012, a vast number of Tuareg separatist groups began demanding for greater political autonomy for northern Mali. In March 2012, due to the system of consensus, it was difficult to have a consensus candidate for the April elections. Given the fact of the inability to achieve a consensus candidate, tensions arose in northern Mali (historically called Azawad) for reason that Touré was inclined to prolong his tenure in power.

However, despite attempts at resolving conflict between the Tuareg and Malian army, internal strife was brewing within the Tuareg fighters. Tuareg fighters from the Kidal region otherwise known as the Mali-Niger Tuareg Alliance (MNTA), led by Ibrahim Bahanga and soldiers of Tuareg heritage from imghad, led by Colonel Elhaj Gamou clashed in 2006. This conflict witnessed the defeat of the Bahanga-led militias and their eventual withdrawal to Libya. The future repercussion cumulated to the 2012 revolt. It is then not surprising that the Tuareg quest for nationalism was sitting on a 'keg of gun powder.' It was then not unanticipated that the Tuareg started to violently opposing the Malian government in 2012 through the channel of the MNLA.

## The Tuareg Rebellion

A crucial dimension to the violent conflict by the Tuareg through the MNLA is that many of the rebels were mercenaries from Libya—they had supported the regime of Muamur Ghadafi in the Arab spring uprising in 2011. The Libyan government under Ghadafi had been a staunch supporter of the Tuareg. Ghadafi established an independent Tuareg army in Libya known as the "Islamic Legion" (also known as the Islamic Pan-African Legion) which was created in 1972. The Islamic Legion actively participated in the Chadian–Libyan conflict (1978-1987) and the Libyans under Muamur Ghadafi funded the Tuareg with military weapons and logistic support in its fight against the Malian government in the 1990s. Flowing from this conflict, a vast influx of arms was imported into Mali by Tuareg tribesmen. The stock pile of illicit weapons consisted of assault rifles, logistical equipments, vehicle-mounted heavy machine guns, rocket launchers, ammunition and explosives.[105]

These returnees formed the MNLA Islamic-based opposition to the government of Mali. The story behind Islamic extremism as reiterated above started after the Libyan civil war (February–March 2011). In October 2011, the Tuaregs engaged the Malian military in conflict in January 2012. Another twist to the conflict occurred on 21 March, 2012, wherein Ansar Dine, along with MNLA militarily, occupied the northeast region of Mali. The MNLA formed a new Republic on 6 April, 2012, which they christened— Azawad.[106] On 22 March, 2012, disgruntled junior officers, taking advantage of the uprising in northeast Mali, organised a military coup d'etat led by Captain Amadou Sanogo. The coup was widely accepted by Malians as a result of Mali's democratic failure. Sanogo was in power from 22 March, 2012 – 12 April 2012. Under a deal presented under the support of

---

105 (2013) Chapter Nine: Sub-Saharan Africa, The Military Balance, 113:1, 477-542,
106 Land of Transhumance' (the nomadic movement of peoples to sustain grazing herds).

Economic Community for West African States (ECOWAS), by Burkina Faso President Blaise Compaoré, on 6 April, 2012, Captain Sanogo relinquished power to Dioncounda Traoré to act as interim president of Mali. Sanogo also appointed Prime Minister Cheick Modibo Diarra, a former NASA astrophysicist as interim Prime Minister. However, in December 2012, Diarra was forced to resign as Mali's interim president, Dioncounda Traoré,[107] appointed Django Sissoko as interim Prime Minister.

In November 2012, about 3,300 troops from ECOWAS were endorsed by the African Union (AU) to support the Malian government in its bid to oust the AQIM and Ansar Dine due to the notion that African and western unsecured interests were at stake. The UN Security Council Resolution 2085 of 20 December, 2012 co-opted Mali's old colonial master 'France' to intervene. Although ECOWAS were mandated by UN resolution to intervene, the organisation was not ready to confront the insurgents immediately due to logistics. France intervention has been viewed as neo-colonialist interference on Mali''s sovereignty. However, on a deeper level, France intervened due to the probable threat of the insurgents besieging the capital, Bamako, where citizens of France were at a risk of being killed/abducted.

The French intervention as noted above, and the ECOWAS under the (MISMA) in Mali (Operation Serval) commenced on 11 January 2013. In a few weeks after the intervention, the strategic cities of Timbuktu, Kidal and Gao were recaptured by the 4,000 French-led forces in the early part of February 2013. Subsequently, Ansar Dine and MUJWA, with support from AQIM, have been raging insurgency attacks on the French and its allied forces. In March 2013, the United States and the United Nations designated Ansar Dine and the MUJWA as terrorist organisations. After democratic elections (July–August 2013 presidential election) on 4 September, 2013, Ibrahim Boubacar Keïta was elected as President of Mali.

---

107   Dioncounda Traoré suffered a humiliating attack at his presidential residence on 21 May 2012 by protesters.

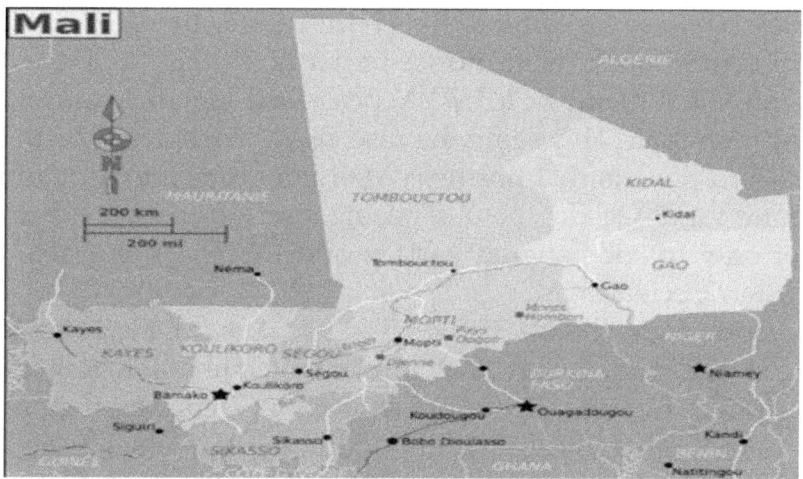
Map showing the major cities/towns in Mali. Courtesy of en. Wikipedia.org

## Between Ansar Dine and MUJWA

These divisions enumerated above make the Tuareg a complex and intricate people. It is then not surprising that the MNLA slit with Ansar Dine and its brother in arms, MUJWA, over ideological differences. In June 2012, due to the differences in political ideology, the seed of discord was sown between MNLA and Ansar Dine. On 26–27 June 2012, the discord emanated into the battle of Gao between MNLA on the one part and Ansar Dine and MUJWA on the other part. The main crux of the battle was that the MNLA were aggrieved about the harsh Islamic law being implemented by the Islamists.

The battle witnessed the defeat of the MNLA, other regions such as Timbuktu, Ansongo, Tessalit and Aguelhok came under the control of the Islamists. With the assistance of AQIM, the MNLA lost the battle and their "strained marriage of convenience" (Solomon, 2013: 16) with Ansar Dine seized to exist. The Islamists celebrated their victory with the mass destruction of mausoleums and Sufi shrines; destroying the UNESCO world heritage city of Timbuktu, which consisted of Islamic culture and history—the Islamists believed that such artefacts were idolatrous. By 17 July, 2012, the MNLA had lost control of all its territories in northern Mali. AQIM with its affiliated member; MUJWA, possessed regional control of northern Mali. This being the case, it was considered by both western powers that northern Mali may turn into a training centre for al-Qaeda, thereby posing a serious security threat, not only to sub-Saharan African and the Shael, but also to western societies.

Aside from the international panic, Ansar Dine, with the assistance of its ally; MUJWA, implemented Jihâdi shariah rule. A strategy for enlisting the Tuareg into al-Qaeda based groups was through radicalising the youth through the forum of Quranic schools, especially in Gao.[108] The youths were taught on subjects such as "How to wage holy war," and "How to terrorise the enemy in combat."[109] The Islamists imposed the ban on smoking, music and educational services for women as they were forced into seclusion. The imposition of *huddud* punishments (stoning to death) were meted out to simple offences such as couples living together as partners[110] and any opposition to the Islamists style of Jihâdi shariah. Perhaps as a retaliatory strategy towards Ansar Dine, the MNLA in June 2013, called for a cease fire with the Malian military and decided to relinquish its bid for independence. The MNLA also gave up the town of Kidal to the Malian government after Ansar Dine abandoned its grip over the region.

On a broader level, it is suggested that Islam can be deployed as a mechanism for political mobilisation in northern Mali. This is a credible factor for engendering unity amongst Muslims in the region. However, the local communities attempted to protest the strict imposition of sharia, their remonstration had little or no effect. It seems

---

108 Larson, Krista. 2013. 'Mali Islamists claimed to have recruited child soldiers from schools', accessed on the 26th of June 2014 at: http://africajournalismtheworld.com/tag/ansar-dine/
109 Ibid
110 Ahmed, Baba & Callimachi, Rukmini. 2012. 'Mali Couple Stoned To Death, Ansar Dine Spokesman Says', accessed on the 25th of June 2014 at: http://www.huffingtonpost.com/2012/07/30/mali-couple-stoned-to-death_n_1720941.html

that the presence of the Islamists had an overwhelming effect on the people in northern Mali. Over and beyond these observations, the dynamics of human relations in northern Mali, especially when a common identity is shared among people helps us to understand the essence of the strong identity marker provided by Islam. However, in some ways the support of the Islamists and the MNLA was divided amongst the Tuareg. In shedding some light on this perspective, Lecocq, et al. (2013:12) tells us that:

> *The other communities of the north felt strong resentment toward the MNLA and its separatist project, as well as the violence and looting surrounding their 'conquest' of the north. This led in some instances to a benign vision of the Salafi tenets of the Mujahideen, but that vision proved hard to reconcile with the violent huddud punishments and petty harassments they inflicted on ordinary citizens, the overwhelming majority of whom were themselves Muslim.*

After the defeat of the MNLA, a vast number of their fighters defected to Ansar Dine. Another crucial event is that in January 2013, a new group evolved from Ansar Dine; the Islamic Movement of Azawad (MIA) under the leadership of Alghabass Ag Intalla. The group propounded a conservative form of Islam in order to appeal to the vast majority of Muslims in the region. The MIA has taken concerted efforts to negotiate for peace and to have abandoned the salafist ideology of the Islamist groups. This division has exceedingly weakened Ansar Dine as the battle against their Malian military became, to some extent, ineffectual. However, in MUJWA, a vast number of fighters defected due to the discrimination meted to black fighters. It should be noted that the group's main weakness, as would be seen later, lies in their perception of race, i.e. light skinned Arab or dark skinned African.

Huckabey (2013:478) brings us closer to this viewpoint by noting that: "The contradiction of claiming to be a West African group while alienating many black West Africans, in particular, made the group's operations increasingly difficult." One of such fighters—Hicham Bilal, who was an eminent commander of MUJWA, defected from the group and headed back to his homeland in Niger. The depiction here reminds us of the hostility between Arabs and blacks in Sudan which led to the unstitching of South Sudan from Sudan. Perhaps it is now understood that, to the Tuareg, its national identities are subsumed under the banner of a common religion (Islam) in respect of Ansar Dine and under the umbrella of ethnicity/race in respect of MUJWA. This exemplifies that Islam and ethnicity connects to the origins and history of the Tuareg. Therefore, Anderson's (1991) invented tradition helps us to explain the Tuaregs's history of nationhood as a result of a metamorphosis of religious, historical and political trajectories. Most crucial through the channel of a religious identity (Islam) the Tuareg imagine that they are an exclusive nation. In providing a useful analysis of the effects of invented tradition of Mali, Cristiani and Fabiani (2013: 79) note perceptively that:

> *Mali is a typical case of a post-colonial state whose borders were drawn without taking account of the situation on the ground. This has historically represented a major structural weakness.*

Since the defeat of the MNLA, the remaining faction of the nationalist group has endeavoured to seek a peace agreement with the Mali government and has been assisting the French government in fighting the Islamists.[111] The French government has taken the opportunity in liaising with the MNLA since its defeat by MUJWA.

It seems clear that Ansar Dine and MUJWA have different identity markers. While Ansar Dine may have a seeming similar

---

111 'Mali: Fire In The North', assessed on the 25th of June 2014 at: http://www.strategypage.com/qnd/mali/articles/20140529.aspx

identity marker as members of the MNLA, which is oscillating between nationalism and religion, members of MUJWA are based of ethnicity/race. In this confused and chaotic depiction, it seems that the Ansar Dine used religion as a mobilisation mechanism to procure individuals to identify with an Islamist group in order to channel their political grievances. The MUJWA on the other hand do not have a political ambition. Their objective is to generate a jihâd in Mali in line with the ideology of Salafist rhetoric of a globalised jihâd. Perhaps, one may suggest that Salafist ideals are strongly tied to race. This ideology is strongly linked to the perception that the Arabs are the progenitors of Islam. Over and beyond the objective of MUJWA is that they have an imperative to accumulate wealth by abducting individuals and smuggling narcotics from northern Mali. It hardly seems misleading to suggest that the Islamists groups have taken an opportunity to seize the secularist ideology of the MNLA and cementing jihâd in a region that has been practicing Islam for over a thousand years. Thus, Brian J. Peterson (2012) rightly observes that:

> ...local imams and ordinary Muslims have stated that they don't need any foreigners coming to tell them how to conduct their religious lives. Thus, when Malian Muslims hear about the violent efforts of Iyad ag-Ghali and other Salafists linked to Al-Qaeda in the Islamic Maghreb, they see no religious legitimacy or theological rationale for their wars. They are already Muslim, so there is no justification for bringing war to Muslim communities. They see the northern jihadists as warlords aimed at pillaging Malian people and lands for personal gain, while using Islam as an ideological tool to manipulate and dominate vulnerable people.

The targets of Islamist violence in northern Mali are similar to the depiction of Islamism in northern Nigeria. Ansar Dine and Boko Haram are desirous of establishing sharia law in Mali and Nigeria respectively. MUJWA and Ansari are similar in the sense that they both target western civilians for the purpose of abduction. Another unique similarity between the two groups is that both Ansari and MUJWA are linked with AQIM. Beyond the differences of these groups, Dowd & Raleigh (2013:503) precisely observe that:

> *On structural, political, or activity grounds, aggregating distinct violent groups to a single, homogeneous and monolithic entity is misleading, and confounds our understanding of their targeted actions and the differential vulnerability of civilians in their areas of operation.*

## International Intervention in Mali

The international community was quick to react to the deteriorating situation in Mali and ECOWAS announced it was not going to recognise the Sanogo led junta. ECOWAS efforts helped in restoring stability after series of negotiations. Following a series of meetings, Sanogo relinquished authority and handed it over to a unity government led by Boubacar Keita. The transition process was followed up with the mobilisation of an intervention force for the purpose of expelling the Jihâdists from northern Mali. ECOWAS in pursuance of its Protocol on Democracy and good governance sought to intervene in Mali and asked for the needed authorisation from the United Nations Security Council. One of the reasons for the ECOWAS intervention was the growing nature of the jihâdist threat and its potential for destabilising the entire region. It was observed that four ECOWAS states (Nigeria, Mali, and Mauritania) were already finding it difficult to confront the jihâdist threat. It was therefore crucial that the regional body intervene to stem the tide of the growing insurgency. Furthermore, the hijacking of territory by AQIM signified that the group was gaining momentum. Most terrorist groups usually stay hidden for a while to avoid unnecessary attention from security forces, especially at the early stage of their growth. Thus, the seizure of territory and the establishment of an independent Islamic state meant that the group was indeed already stronger than the Malian government and this was evident in the swiftness of the militant insurgency by the group.

However, the French government, the former colonial master of the Mali state had interests in securing resources in the Sahel—particularly oil and uranium, which the French energy company, Areva, had been extracting for decades in neighbouring Niger. In addition, Katrin Sold of the German Council on Foreign Relations (DGAP)[112] noted that: "France fears that Mali could become a retreat and training center for Islamist terrorists if an Islamist state were established there." France's vast political interest in stability of Mali and the entire region co-opted the commencement of Operation Serval. The reason behind the operation was also based on the lack of capacity of the ECOWAS coalition to quickly mobilise. Furthermore, European Union member-states offered inadequate support to France (Cristiani and Fabiani, 2013).

The need for cooperation and collaboration between states in defeating the Jihâdist threat is based on an understanding of the transnational nature of these terrorist groups. For instance in Nigeria, the Chad multinational joint task force was set up and the results have been tremendous, leading to the killing of a large number of Boko Haram members and commanders, and surrender of over 130 members of the Boko Haram sect in September 2014.

The international community and key states, especially France, responded to the situation in Mali in early 2013. Some of the strategic factors considered which precipitated international response include the territorial gains of the terrorist groups, their increasing internationalisation and their increased criminal tendencies within the region. The shift in activities of terrorist/jihâdist groups from operating covertly

---

112  See 'The interests behind France's intervention in Mali', accessed on the 23rd of September 2014 at: http://www.dw.de/the-interests-behind-frances-intervention-in-mali/a-16523792 the interests behind France interest in Mali.

within ungoverned spaces to overt seizure of territory and established control over such territory usually results in a significant boost in recruitment, seriousness of ideology and also strength of the group. For instance, the Islamic State in Iraq and the Levant (ISIS) Caliphate established under Abu Bakr Al Baghdadi was once estimated to have just fewer than 10,000 fighters. However, since the capture of vast territorial areas and strategic resources, it is now estimated to have about 35,000 fighters, with a large number of foreigners within their ranks.[113] Such is the boost in recruitment received by Jihâdist groups. The capture of territory also increases mobility of jihâdists in furtherance of their campaigns through access to supplies and re-enforcements.

The increasing internationalisation of jihâdist groups in the Sahelian region also triggered international intervention. According to U.S. Representative Mike Rodgers,[114] these terrorist groups may attract foreigners who have unrestricted access to return to the Western countries and carry out attacks on their home soil. As mentioned earlier, both MUJWA and Ansar Dine boast of foreign fighters who are nationals of various countries within their ranks. According to Abbott, Rogers, and Sloboda, (2006) multivariate membership of these groups allow them to interact and collaborate with international networks, and feed on a global perception and target a global audience. Increased criminal activities of the terrorist groups if left unchecked will result in more harm to Western interests in the long run. Not only would the war against illegal trafficking in narcotics be made more difficult, the proceeds from the illegal business will help finance these terrorist groups. Abbott, et al (2006) further notes that these groups have adopted an entrepreneurial view of armed activity and violence. This has led to a sort of criminal partnership with both the new traffickers (drugs, arms, humans, etc.) and traditional actors and agents of conflict (bandits, smugglers, Tuaregs) in an obviously dangerous mix. For

---

113   See http://edition.cnn.com/2014/09/11/world/meast/isis-syria-iraq/
114   CNN (2013) Op. Cit.

example, Mokhtar Belmoktar is also known as Mr. Malboro, because of his smuggling activities, especially tobacco. In line with this observation, Vilanova (2013:220) noted that:

> *Based on the underlying and cross-cutting threats and factors, and beyond the current phase of active militarisation, the response to the Sahel's problems requires a comprehensive and multi-dimensional approach, encompassing diplomacy, security and development. Such an approach would include three overlapping types of interventions: intrastate, that is, within a single state in the region (territorial); interstate, that is, between neighbouring countries (regional); and external, meaning, interventions by the EU and the US carried out in parallel with the others (global), which, while respecting each state's independence, would prevent bilateral issues and struggles for regional hegemony from deteriorating the situation further.*[115]

In the light of the above, it was critical that ECOWAS had to play a key role in the political/religious emulation in Mali. Haysom (2014: 4) summarises the ECOWAS response in Mali as follows:

> *The first response of regional bodies and neighbouring states was to try to mediate a resolution to Mali's political crisis. ECOWAS denounced the March coup... On 30 March, 2012 it imposed economic and diplomatic sanctions on Mali, and ECOWAS member-states bordering Mali closed their borders, thereby blocking Mali's access to neighbouring seaports. Thereafter, ECOWAS focused on political negotiations to remove the military junta. President Blaise Compaoré of Burkina Faso was appointed the lead negotiator, and an agreement was reached in April, outlining a transition to civilian government... Meanwhile, in April, the AU imposed sanctions, asset freezes and travel bans against the junta*

---

115  http://www.iemed.org/observatori-es/arees-danalisi/arxius-adjunts/anuari/iemed-2013/Vilanova%20Castro%20Mail%20Sahel%20EN.pdf

*and others deemed to be involved in 'contributing to the "destabilisation" of Mali'*

France launched military operations against insurgent targets in northern Mali in January 2013, following a request from the Malian government for help in repelling insurgent advances toward the south. France's concerns were that French citizens, especially those who had dual citizenship, could be attracted to Mali, joining the ranks of AQIM and allied groups in northern Mali. Furthermore, their fears were magnified by the possibility of French citizens receiving training or financing from the said terrorist groups to perpetrate terrorist attacks in France or against French interests in the region. France also launched rescue missions to free their citizens who were held hostage by AQIM. In April 2013, the UN Security Council approved the creation and deployment of a 12,600-strong peacekeeping force, called the Multidimensional Integrated Stabilisation Mission in Mali (MINUSMA). On 25 June, 2013 UN Security Council approved the July 1 deployment of a Mali peacekeeping force tasked with helping the government regain control of rebel-held areas and organise crucial elections. Elections were held in July and August, and Ibrahim Boubacar Keïta was elected president.

The existence of a legitimate government is a necessary condition for the successful fight against terrorism. An example here can be drawn from the experience of Iraq where the Nouri-al Maliki government secluded segments of the Sunni population which resulted in the ISIS playing on their grievance, thus, a temporary alliance was formed between the Sunni leaders for the purpose of defeating the Iraqi government. However, the Sunni leaders were soon forced to pledge allegiance to the caliphate established by the ISIS. Thus, the steps taken by the international community in restoring stability to the country was to ensure that a legitimate government was installed. The need for legitimacy is characterised by the fact that the quickest way to defeating a terrorist invasion is by building a united front against the jihâdist campaign. This is necessary as postwar reconstruction efforts and sustaining the peace depends on a stable government.

One of the notable things that happened in Mali was the restoration of government and simultaneous restoration of political order in the territories that were captured by the Islamist insurgents. This was achieved through the establishment and mandate of separate intervening forces in Mali. Thus, while the ECOWAS intervention force was focused on ending the Islamist insurgency, there was an International peacekeeping force in Mali focused on restoration of political order and also ensuring that the transition process went smoothly. While this was ongoing, mediation efforts aimed at bringing together various stakeholders (political parties, civil society, and religious groups) to agree on certain crucial issues relating to Mali's political future were carried out by ECOWAS in cooperation with other organisations such as the United Nations Office for West Africa. Furthermore, financial assistance was provided to the Malian government for the purpose of aiding the distressed population and also to facilitate the transition process. According to Arieff A (2013:12):

> *On December 14, the United Nations announced a 2013 consolidated appeal (CAP) of $370 million for Mali, reflecting proposed funding requirements from U.N. agencies, non-governmental organisations, and other relief agencies for activities in the country in 2013. The appeal was aimed at funding assistance for nearly four million people in Mali affected by the food and nutritional crisis, including 1.5 million people in the north.*[116]

Thus, the intervention process was broad-based and focused on the multi-variate dimensions of the Malian crisis. This approach was necessary and seems to reflect the general approach taken by international organisations and concerned parties to ending Islamic radicalism and

---

116   Arieff A. (2013) Crisis in Mali. 'Congressional Research Service', accessed on the 10th of September 2014 at: http://fas.org/sgp/crs/row/R42664.pdf

insurgency in troubled spots. It also shows that, apart from the military approaches to countering radical groups, there is also the socio-economic and political aspect which tries to stem the factors which are responsible for encouraging the growth of radicalism in the territory concerned.

Another important lesson that can be learnt from the Mali intervention is the timing of the intervention. It reflects comprehensive planning by concerned stakeholders involved at various levels in the Mali intervention. The intervention started in January 2013 with the launch of Operation Serval, followed by the intervention of ECOWAS and African-led International Support Mission in Mali (AFISMA) in May/June 2013 and subsequently MINUSMA playing well defined roles. Before and during the gradual restoration of political order was the launch of the intervention funds. Arieff (2013:12) also notes that there were contingency plans in case the intervention created other problems for the population concerned.

## Conclusion

It seems that the confrontation and the crises stages are over in Mali. The concerted efforts of France, ECOWAS and the Malian military have curtailed Mali from slipping into a state of anarchy such as Somalia. While this has restrained long sought for nationalist ideals of the Tuareg and the recently inspired salafist ideologies, it is suggested that the seeds of radical Islam has been sown. Radical Islam has taken a leap with nationalist ambitions which has been struggling for independence for decades. A new struggle being generated in Mali is Salafi jihâd. If this seems to be the case, then it appears that northern Mali will continue to play a pivotal role as a haven and recruitment centre for al-Qaeda-linked groups such as Ansar Dine, al-Qaeda in the Islamic Maghreb and the MUJWA.

However, a strategy that could be used against this factor is that the Malian government should implement a divide and rule policy towards al-Qaeda-linked groups in order to disintegrate them. This is for the reason that elements of racism persists in the MUJAU, whilst Ansar Dine is saddled with a diverse and conflicting attachment towards nationalism, secularism and jihâdist ideals. By communicating acts of discrimination and its division in ideology within these groups, the information would restrict their metamorphosis into an efficient terror group such as Boko Haram. Conversely, there is the foreboding notion that once the French and ECOWAS forces leave Mali, the ugly head of the Islamists would rise again with an imagination to finish what it started.

# References

Abbott, C., Rogers, P., & Sloboda, J., 2006. 'Global Responses to Global Threats. Sustainable Security for the 21st Century', assessed on the 23rd of September at: *http://www.oxfordresearchgroup.org.uk/publications/briefing_papers/pdf/globalthreatspdf*

Adekanye, J. B., 2007. *Linking Conflict Diagnosis, Conflict Prevention, and Conflict Management in Contemporary Africa: Selected Essays.* Ababa Press Ltd.

Al-Ma'ali, M. M. A., & Mahmoud, M., 2012. 'Al Qaeda and its Allies in the Sahel and the Sahara', Al Jazeera Center for Studies'. Assessed on the 119th September 2014 at: http://studies.aljazeera.net/ResourceGallery/media/Documents/2012/4/30/2012430145241774734Al%20Qaeda%20and%20its%20allies%20in%20the%20Sahel%20and%20the%20Sahara.pdf

Arieff A. 2013. 'Crisis in Mali', Congressional Research Service, accessed on the 10th of September 2014 at: http://fas.org/sgp/crs/row/R42664.pdf

Anderson, B., 1991. *Imagined Communities:* Reflections on the Origin and Spread of Nationalism, London: New York: Verso.

Castelli, Laurent de, 2014. Mali: From Sanctuary to Islamic State, The RUSI Journal, 159:3, 62-68.

Cline, Lawrence E., 2013. Nomads, Islamists, and Soldiers: The Struggles for Northern Mali, *Studies in Conflict & Terrorism*, 36:8, 617-634.

Cristiani, Dario & Fabiani, Riccardo, 2013. 'The Malian Crisis and its Actors', *The International Spectator: Italian Journal of International Affairs*, 48:3, 78-97.

Dante, Idrissa, Gautier, Jean-Francosi, Marouani A. Mohamed & Raffinot, Marc. 2003.'Mali', in Booth, David. 2003. *Fighting Poverty in Africa: Are PRSPs Making a Difference?* London: Overseas Development Institute.

Dowd, Caitriona and Raleigh, Clionadh, 2013. 'Briefing the Myth of Global Islamic Terrorism and Local Conflict in Mali and the Sahel', *African Affairs*, 112/448, 498–509.

Haysom Simone, 2014. 'Security and Humanitarian Crisis in Mali. The Role of International Organisations', HPG Working Paper, assessed on the 27th of September, 2014 at: http://www.odi.org.uk/sites/odi.org.uk/files/odi-assets/publications-opinion-files/8829.pdf.

Horowitz, Donald L., 1985. *Ethnic Groups in Conflict*, Berkeley: University of California Press.

Huckabey, M. Jessica, 2013. 'Al Qaeda in Mali: The Defection Connections', *Orbis* 57(3):467–484.

Larson, Krista. 2013. 'Mali Islamists claimed to have recruited child soldiers from schools', accessed on the 26th of June 2014 at: http://africajournalismtheworld.com/tag/ansar-dine/

Lecocq, B., et al., 2013. 'One Hippopotamus and Eight Blind Analysts: A Multivocal Analysis of the 2012 Political Crisis in the Divided Republic of Mali', *Review of African Political Economy*, DOI: 10.1080/03056244.2013.799063

Peterson, J. Brian, 2012. 'Mali 'Islamisation' tackled: The Other Ansar Dine, Popular Islam, and Religious Tolerance', accessed on the 26th of June 2014 at: http://africanarguments.org/2012/04/25/confronting-talibanization-in-mali-the-other-ansar-dine-popular-islam-and-religious-tolerance-brian-j-peterson/

Seely C. Jennifer, 2001. 'A Political Analysis of Decentralisation: Coopting the Tuareg Threat in Mali', *Journal ofModern African Studies* Vol. 39, No. 3, 499-524.

Solomon, Hussein, 2013. 'Mali: West Africa's Afghanistan', *The RUSI Journal,* 158:1, 12-19

Smith, Gregory A., 2009. 'Al-Qaeda in the Lands of the Islamic Maghreb', *Journal of Strategic Security,* 2 (2): 53-72.

Thornberry W & Levy J., 2011. 'Al-Qaeda in the Islamic Mahgreb', Washington DC: CSIS. Assessed on the 3nd of September 2014 at:

http://csis.org/files/publication/110901_Thornberry_AQIM_WEB.pdf

Vilanova, Pere. 2013. 'Mali and the Sahel: From Crisis to Military Intervention', assessed on the 23rd of September at: http://www.iemed.org/observatori-es/arees-danalisi/arxius-adjunts/anuari/iemed-2013/Vilanova%20Castro%20Mail%20Sahel%20EN.pdf

# 8

# Opening the Pandora's Box of Boko Haram[117]

## Introduction

Conflict is inherent in all societies. All societies are prone to violent conflict associated with perverse and irrational behaviour. There is little doubt that, no phenomenon is caused by nothing. Behind any social phenomenon, there is a cause. The aim in studying social phenomenon is to determine its primary cause. What is real in one society is different in another societies. Perhaps then, it may not be surprising that religious militancy tends to be experienced in societies where there is a strong primordial attachment to religion.

While concurring with the imperative of religion occupying a central place in international politics, it must be emphasised that religion preceded political theories as a platform for human identity and consciousness. Particularly, Huntington's (1996) thesis has stirred several scholarly debates by political scientists (Faoud Ajami, 1993; Jacob Heilbrunn, 1997; Pierre Hessner, 1997; Said Tariq & Anwar, 1998), in determining whether religion can lead to a new civilisational conflict after the Cold War.

---

117  Some of the materials in this chapter are culled out from Olomojobi, Yinka, 2013. Islam & Conflict in Northern Nigeria. Lagos: Malthouse Press. They are, however, amended and updated with new insights.

Religious identification is considered as having the potential to create group division, which leads to segregation and violence. It is viewed by most scholars as having conflict potentials. Religion has often been associated with a culture of conflict and not within a paradigm of peace.

This chapter examines how radical Islam facilitates violence in a deeply divided non-Western society (northern Nigeria). It argues that although religion has the potential to generate social bonding between different identity groups, religious primordialism may create a tendency in the individual to place excessive emphasis and loyalty on his religious beliefs and religious identity which tends to generate violent ideologies. Furthermore, due to this strong identity mark, one may argue that political leaders can manipulate the common people to support conflict by using religion to legitimise such violence. Religion has been given different interpretations to suit political purposes, thus implying the possibility of religion to be humanly manipulated, corrupted, misrepresented, and misinterpreted. This explains the foundation of the pervasive religious crisis today in northern Nigeria.

Bearing this in mind, the following theoretical parameters are taken into cognisance: Huntington's (1996) 'clash of civilisations' to highlight the clash between Western civilization and Islam; I chart Gurr's (1970) relative deprivation thesis (Grievance) to highlight that "men who are frustrated have an innate disposition to do violence to its source in proportion to the intensity of their frustration" (Gurr, 1970: 37). In addition to these are: Almond, Appleby & Sivan's (2003) arguments on the perceptions of justifiable homicide in the eyes of religious extremists and underscoring of Juergensmeyer's (1993) arguments that the loss of faith in secular nationalism is as a result of the breakdown of social order in society.

## Ethnic and religious composition of northern Nigeria

An important aspect of northern Nigeria's demographic constitution is that it is dominated by peoples of the Islamic faith. The Muslim faith is largely practiced in the northern region of Nigeria in sixteen states: Adamawa, Bauchi, Bornu, Gombe, Kano, Kaduna, Katsina, Kebbi, Kogi, Kwara, Jigawa, Nassarawa, Niger, Sokoto, Zamfara and Yobe. Three states, Benue, Plateau and Taraba have a Muslim minority. Other non-Muslims are found on the boundaries between the major Islamic emirates of Sokoto and Katsina, Katsina and Kano, Kano and Zaria. Furthermore, Kano, Kastina and Sokoto are historically centres of Islamic education and missionary activities.

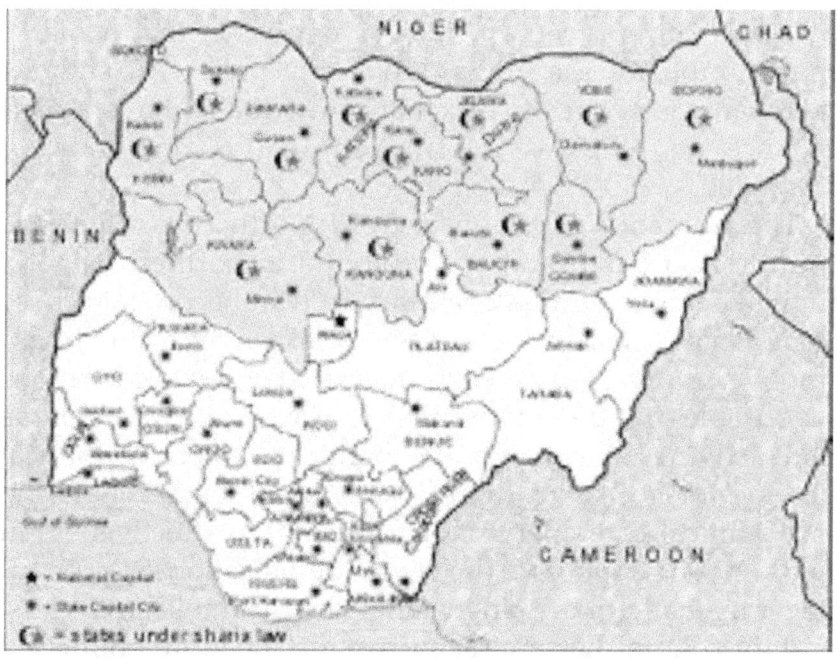

Map showing Nigeria's major ethnic groups and religious affiliation. Courtesy: LES Editions J.A.

## Religious rivalry in northern Nigeria

The causal pattern for conflict in northern Nigeria amongst others is based on religious identities. A common attribute of religion is the fact that it is an identity frame for individual and collective differentiation, especially within the context of the struggle over socially inadequate values. Religion within the aforesaid context, simultaneously serves paradoxical functions of empowerment of ethnic groups, religious entrepreneurs and co-religionists, and the disempowerment of those that do not belong to these identity frames. In many ways, religion in northern Nigeria has been used for dual purposes; as a mechanism of perpetually dividing and ruling people by neo-colonial politicians and as a tool to mesmerise the individual by religious entrepreneurs. An obvious reason that explains the triumph for the 'divide and ruin' policy of religious merchants is given the fact that individual(s) have a high reliance on religious information that is not critically evaluated.

The influence of Islamists from North Africa and the Middle East has been very profound in northern Nigeria in the last three decades. Military rule and economic crises which have both engendered social anomie and mass impoverishment have combined to produce conditions favourable for the maturation of Islamists' orientations and activities. Hence, in the hand of Nigeria's political elite of northern extractions, Islam is not just a religion; it is a political machinery of super-ordinary effectiveness in mass mobilisation and the institutionalisation of political hegemony and in certain instances by the intellectual class, and for counter-hegemonic purposes. The more politicised Islam is, the more the tendency it has to feed into ethno-religious crisis provoked by political elites seeking political capital for personal and group interests.

Clearly, the overwhelming evidence from an assemblage of conflict in northern Nigeria goes on to suggest that they are primarily religious in nature. Religion has been at the forefront of most of these conflicts. Now, it is our task to explore in greater detail the conflict dynamics of Boko Haram.

## The Birth of the Boko Haram Jihâd

An understanding of the causes of this 'jihâd' cannot be separated from the unmasking of the central figure and motivating force of the movement, in the person of Ustaz Mohammed Yusuf, an 'Islamic' preacher, leader of the sect and famously known as the Nigerian Taliban leader. Mohammed Yusuf was born on the 29th of January, 1970, in the rural village of Girgir in Yobe State. Yusuf started his journey as an Islamic scholar as a Tsangaya Quranic teacher. He was formerly a Shiite loyalist and later joined the *Izalatul-Bid'a wa Iqamat al Sunna (Izala)* movement. He later left Izala and joined the *Shababul Islam*. *Shababul Islam* was founded in 1995 in northern Nigerian by Abubakar Lawan. It was also known then as *Ahlulsunna wal'jama'ah hijra* and later acquired its new image 'Boko Haram' (also known as *Jama'atul Alhul Sunnah Lidda'wati wal Jihâd,* which means 'People Committed to the Propagation of the Prophet's Teachings and Jihâd) in 2002, with Mohammed Yusuf becoming its leader. Once, Yusuf was at the helm of affairs, he changed Boko Haram's ideology to Islamist doctrines. His main ideology centred on pervasive ignorance; that Western education is a sin and that the earth was made flat by God, in contrast to Westernised theories of Darwin's evolution. Thus, it's meaning *boko* (book) as *haram* (sinful).

Beyond the meaning of Boko Haram, which has become synonymous with evil, it is strongly suggested that the dearth of economic development and the culture of squander mania imbibed by previous oppressive military regimes and prebendalistic politicians is the root of the problem that gives the sect chance to germinate in the eastern part of northern Nigeria. These grievances have set the pace for radical Islam in northern Nigeria. However, the great paradox of this movement was that Mohammed Yusuf was a college drop-out, but he was able to enlist a former state commissioner into the sect. A greater absurdity is the fact that Mohammed Yusuf, who adumbrated that Western education is a sin, rode in the latest Lexus Jeep and had a personal physician.[118] More crucial, in 2009, Mohammed Yusuf had a stronghold estimated at 280,000 followers.[119] A significant characteristic of his followership was its constitution of mainly the poverty stricken, the wretched of society and lumpen-proletariat elements. These individuals were mainly the unemployed youths otherwise known as the *talakawa* (the grass-root people/peasants) and the *almajirai* (students of Quranic schools). However, a few of his followers comprised of the graduates who were resisting institutionalised poverty in their societies.

Mohammed Yusuf, a charismatic Islamist, was known to his followers as a reformer and to others as an extremist. As noted by Riesebrodt (2000), religious reformers as well as fundamentalists (extremists) nonetheless share common characteristics. Both believe that there exists a profound societal crisis in their community or nation. Thus, both attempt to go back to the traditions of their religious beliefs. He further posited that:

> *Reformers claim to transform social institutions in order to realise the spirit of the ancient community. The fundamentalists, on the other hand, claim to restore social institutions according to the letter and the law of the ancient community with regard to the past,*

---

118  See Boko Haram Planned to Attack Lagos, Abuja Saturday Punch, August 1, 2009, p. 3
119  'Boko Haram', World Almanac of Islamism, American Foreign Policy Council, U.S. State Department's Country Report on Terrorism, accessed on the 7th of July 2015 at: almanac.afpc.org/sites/almanac.afpc.org/files/Boko%20Haram.pdf

> *their approach can be called 'mythical,' referring to a timeless, unchangeable, fixed eternal truth. With regard to the present and (near) future, their view is often eschatological and chiliastic* (Riesebrodt, 2000:272).

Boko Haram's overzealous ideology aims at improving the plight of grassroot people's oppression by implanting sharia law, not only in northern Nigeria, but in the entire Nigerian state. It is perceived that they are desirous of purging northern Nigeria from the culture of *rankadedism (rankadede)*.[120] This ambition is perceived by members of the sect to be in harmony with the Uthman dan Fodio jihâd of 1804 — eliminating lax Muslims and the systemic oppression by the elites. More to the point, they perceive that the root of the cause of extreme poverty and oppression in the region is the institutionalisation of westernisation. This message of the sect reminds one of Huntington's (1996) clash of civilisations theory. Islam conveyed Arabic/Islamic education to the Middle East and Islamic states, whilst Christianity conveyed *boko*; A clear separation of cultural identities.

Clearly, one may suggest that in societies where religion is a strong identity marker, an eloquent speaker may persuade and incite the common people to profane religious doctrines. This is attained by spiritual leaders harnessing grievances and mystifying spiritual texts to support conflict or a holy war (Stern, 2003). Arguing in a similar fashion, Pearlstein (2004:28-30) argues that one of the factors that influence violent ethnic conflicts is religious conflicts that are manipulated by religious radicalism. Presumably, in terms of propensity for conflicts, religious reformism and fundamentalist religious orientations are highly culpable. In line with this suggestion, Gopin (2000) proposes that the rise in religious warfare is due to the rise in religious revivalism.

---

120  This is word used by the common people to greet the rich and opulent elites. It is also a custom where the less priviledged have accepted their life of penury as ordained by the wishes and whims of the elites.

Nelson-Pallmeyer (2003), drawing on the suggestions of Juergensmeyer (1991) and Girard (1977) underscores that religious justified violence is first and foremost a problem of sacred texts and not a problem of misinterpretation of the texts. Thus, he opines that religion sanctions the use of violence. If we assume, but do not concede that religion sanctions the use of violence, then does religion sanction the use of terrorism? This obscures the division between terrorism and religious violence.

At this point, one must emphasise that religious radicalism, has given rise to pervasive, crude and malevolent groups, such as the Hamas suicide bombers. The antecedent of these thoughts may be found in religion. For instance, the Bible and Qur'an base their foundations on victorious warfare. The wandering tribe of Israel had to utterly destroy desert tribes, on their journey to the promised land. This is perhaps one of the reasons why Dawkins (2006:31) in his book titled '*The God Delusion*', views the God of the Old Testament as "arguably the most unpleasant character in all fiction, jealous and proud of it; a petty, unjust, unforgiving control-freak; a vindictive, bloodthirsty ethnic cleanser; a misogynistic, homophobic, racist, infanticidal, genocidal, capriciously malevolent bully." However, Dawkins in his book prevaricated the definition of religion, avoided explaining its complex nature and ignored what it means to the individual.[121] This plausibly informed McGrath (2007: xi) to note that 'religion to Dawkins is like a red rag to a bull — evoking not merely an aggressive response, but one that throws normal scholarly conventions about scrupulous accuracy and fairness to the winds'. This perhaps explains why Dawkins does not understand that religion is considered with awe and at the same time as a source of inspiration, given the usual mysteriousness it is associated with, which is due to its transcendental dimensions and its ontological and ecclesiastical postulation concerning life,

---

121   Dawkins views religion in terms of a naturalist, evolutionist and biological point of view.

death, the hereafter, and its associated karmic consequences. This perhaps, informed Huntington (1996:27), to define religion as 'the central force that motivates and mobilises people'.

The supposed jihâd started from Bauchi on the 25th to the 30th July, 2009, and extended to Borno, Yobe, Gombe and Kano states. Their main targets were the security forces, westernised establishments, non-Muslim places of worship (in Maiduguri, twenty churches were razed whilst three Pastors and one Reverend were killed)[122] and surprisingly, Muslims that did not belong to their sect. They raided police stations and army barracks in an unprecedented fashion unknown in sectarian violence in Nigeria. The Boko Haram was a religious phenomenon of unparallel dimension in Nigerian history, both in terms of style, followings, methodologies, zealotry and military-like execution. A military tactic employed by Yusuf was the use of civil populace as a shield from the reprisal attack by the police and the army.

The Guardian Newspapers[123] reported that in Jalingo, Taraba State, a school was discovered to be the training ground for the Islamists. Moreover, the Red Cross alleged that 780 people (including police and military personnel) were killed in days of violence in Maiduguri alone, which had the most casualties. In addition, there were 3,500 internally displaced persons.[124] While in Kano, the state government demolished a mosque used by the militants as a centre for preaching its perverse ideologies opposed to Western civilisation. In Yobe State, the sect called its training cell 'Afghanistan'. In Bauchi State, in a place known as Fadama Madawas, the sect stockpiled its arms and ammunition. It was reported that Boko Haram planned to raid Lagos, and other states situated in south-west Nigeria.

---

122   Northern Govs Move to Stem Religious Crises: The Guardian, Tuesday, August 4, 2009, p. 1
123   http://www.ngrguardiannews.com/news/article01//indexn2_html?pdate=300709&ptitle=Fighting%20rages,%20death%20toll%20hits%20300%20in%20Borno
124   The Nation, Monday, August 3, 2009, p 2

Thirty-eight members of the sect were arrested on their journey to Lagos.[125] This establishes the fact that the sects were desirous of not only destabilising northern Nigeria, but also the entire polity.

Strictly speaking, the sects' crucial position and contention were in respect of the secularity of the Nigerian state, the desire to Islamise Nigeria and coerce Muslims to affirm their allegiance solely their perverse ideology, rather than the traditional practice of Islam and the Nigerian Constitution. Perhaps in the distorted minds of members of the group, a perceived question they might consider is Albert Einstein's intriguing enquiry, 'Am I or the others crazy.' Clearly, this gave the riot a sort of religious construction. The state inefficiency, even when it pertains to matters bordering on its sanctity and continued existence, like other times, was highly palpable as events before and during this riot clearly showed this to be the case.

Religion, especially Islam in northern Nigeria, is sometimes used as a salient economic tool of control. 'Psychologically, the infusion of faith into the public domain often functions to control thinking and stifle debate' (Spilka et al, 2003: 201). In most non-Western societies, such as northern Nigeria, there is widespread poverty amongst people. Essentially, a vast majority of people in northern Nigeria are generally in need of resources to ease poverty. In particular, Agbiboa (2013: 151) avers that:

> *It is no coincidence that one of the worst forms of political violence in Nigeria today originates in the most socio-economically deprived parts of the country. In the North, for example, where unemployment and chronic poverty are rife, radical Islamist groups have challenged the authority of the state. It is argued that the impact of the state of emergency declared in May 2013 in Borno, Adamawa, and Yobe states will have little or no effect as "leaders should have been more*

---

[125] See Boko Haram Planned to Attack Lagos, Abuja: Saturday Punch, August 1, 2009, p 13

*sensitive to the idea of poverty. Boko Haram has attracted a lot of sympathy from the lower-class and the downtrodden.*[126]

It is not surprising that the National Bureau of Statistics in 2010 accounted that Yobe State, the nerve centre of Boko Haram, has the utmost percentage of unemployed persons of all the states in Nigeria at 33.2% (Osumah, 2013: 543).

In the early history of English peasantry, religion was used as a control mechanism of the people; the papacy used religion to control the Papal States, which at the time were enslaved in poverty. It could therefore be argued that, religion could be used as a tool of control over people. In portraying the life in northern Nigeria, using the words of Sanusi,[127] "the poor peasant farmer in Zaria, condemned to life-long penury by the circumstances of his birth, the inadequacy of his education and the deprived state of his general existence, feels a stronger bond with and affinity for his rich, capitalist Emir than his fellow farmer in Wusasa..." In this sense, religion may be used to manipulate people to the wishes and whims of the elites. This is not unexpected, as noted from Smith's (2000:795) observation:

*Of course, it is not difficult to cite cases where 'nationalism' or 'religion', or a combination of both, have been used to whip up popular passions and foment bitter conflicts. But that is a very different proposition from the claim that religious or nationalist belief-systems are in and of themselves irrational, violent, and destructive. Many religions are pacific in intent, and not a few nationalisms have sought to eschew conflict....religion and nationalism may be used by elites and others both to underpin and to undermine political orders and global relations.*

---

126  In the words of a journalist from Maiduguri in accessing the violence of Boko Haram and the impact of the state of emergency: Parker, Gillian. 2013, May, 28. 'In Boko Haram country, Nigeria's new crackdown brings mixed feelings.' Assessed on the 23rd of May 2014 at: http://www.csmonitor.com/World/Africa/2013/0528/In-Boko-Haram-country-Nigeria-s-new-crackdown-brings-mixed-feelings

127  Religion, the Cabinet and a Political Economy of the 'North', accessed on the 10 of August 2010 at: http://www.nigerdeltacongress.com/rarticles/religion1.htm

This statement clearly defines Yusuf's religious objectives and ideology. It must be reemphasised that Muhammad Yusuf took advantage of the prevailing socio-economic conditions which are prevalent in northern Nigeria. Hence, most of his followers were the unemployed people, who are easily swayed into religious radicalism. One may argue that this indoctrination is possible, for the reason that religious primordialism may create a tendency in the individual to place excessive emphasis on his religious beliefs and religious identity. It is argued that since Islam is primordially the existing essence of all Muslims in northern Nigeria, it is not surprising then that the sect had a large followership in the North.

Religious identity was the channel used to convey socio-economic grievance, through radicalising the perceptions of Islam. One may speculate here that, religion being central to the identity of the grassroot people, had the potential to convey public grievances. It is advisable to primarily draw on Smith's (1991) analysis of religion as a primordial institution. It is important to note that Smith (1991:6) states that religious identity as distinct from national identity, and he suggests that a religious identity originates from 'communication and socialisation' based on values, symbols, myths, and traditions. In this sense, it is acceptable that "religion then, may preserve a sense of common ethnicity as if in chrysalis…" (Smith, 1991:35). It is important to note that the Hausa-Fulani and other ethnic groups professing Islam in northern Nigeria merged under a common religious identity due to 'communication and socialisation' of Islam in the region, which started in 1804 through the Uthman dan Fodio Jihâd. It should be explicated that the identity of an individual in a non-Western society, such as northern Nigeria is primordial in nature, in contrast to secular heterogeneous identity found in Western societies. This then makes religion to have a conflict potential in northern Nigeria.

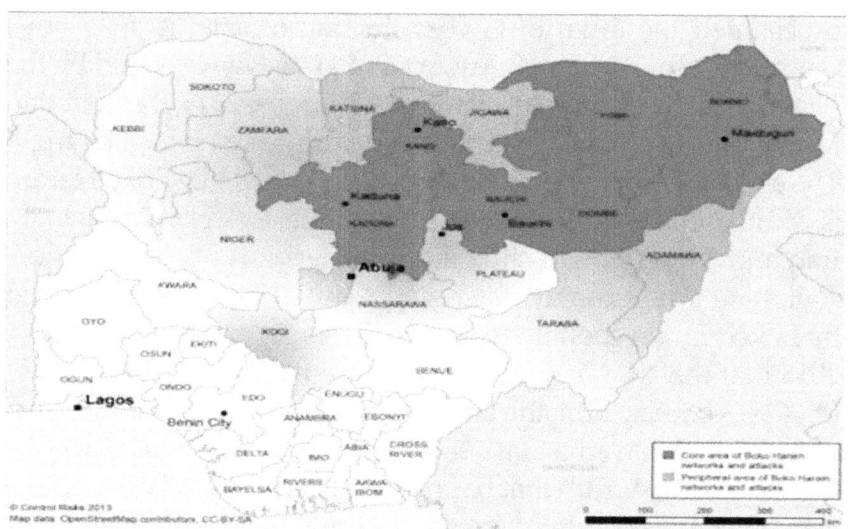

Map showing Boko Haram strongholds & areas of attack. Courtesy: Control Risks 2013

## Political paradox of Boko Haram

Since the death of Yusuf, members of Boko Haram have embarked on a revengeful and sporadic mission of killing, maiming and destruction of public institutions and its agencies (soldiers and police personnel). These killings have been coordinated by new leader of the sect; Abubakar Shekau, a student of Mohammed Yusuf. Shekau is notoriously noted for his often quoted words, "I enjoy killing anyone that God commands me to kill—the way I enjoy killing chickens and rams."[128] In July 2010, Abubakar Muhammad Shekau, assumed the leadership of the group. Shekau was born in Shekau village near the border of Niger Republic. He attended Borno State College of Legal and Islamic Studies. Shekau is also multilingual. He speaks fluent Hausa, Fulani, Kanuri and Arabic. However, he speaks little or no English. On 6 August, 2014, Shekau

---

128 'Profile of Abubakar Muhammad Shekau leader of the Islamist Group Boko Haram', accessed on the 15th day of April, 2014 at: http://news2.onlinenigeria.com/headline/164633-profile-of-abubakar-shekau-leader-of-the-militant-islamist-group-boko-haram.html#ixzz2yxszfiQ5.

proclaimed the town of Gwoza, in Borno State as an Islamic Caliphate. However, on 8 August, 2014 Gwoza was freed by the Nigerian army.[129] Subsequently, on 25 August 2014, the Nigerian Military denied that Gwoza had been captured by Boko Haram.[130] The action of declaring Gwoza as a Caliphate is that Boko Haram is simulating the 'expansionist' attempts of Islamic State in Iraq and Syria (ISIS) of situating Iraq, Syria and Lebanon into a Caliphate. It is strongly suggested that Gwoza was recaptured by Boko Haram soon thereafter as it was reported on 27 March, 2015 that the Nigerian military captured the town of Gwoza.[131] On 4 November, 2014, the terrorist group also captured the town of Mubi in Adawama State and renamed it *Madinatul Islam* (the City of Islam). A truth that has not been generally acknowledged is that Nigeria is undergoing another civil war. The explanation? Boko Haram is desirous of seceding from Nigeria—this is revealed by the attempt to secede from Nigeria. In a disparate analysis from the first Nigerian Civil War, the causal effect was associated with the political self-determination based on ethnicity of the Igbo people. It seems that religion (radical Islam) is the causal explanation for the perceived self-determination of the group to create a caliphate. Over and beyond this comparison is that, this 'religious' self-determination is extremist in the sense that it rationalises murder and is associated with the love and adoration of dying and killing for God—this sentiment explains why the Nigerian military is finding it almost impossible to deal with the Boko Haram menace.

There is a thought that Shekau sidelined Mamman Nur, who was the third in command to Yusuf. What is important to observe

---

129  See 'Nigerian Military To Restore Law & Order In Damboa, Gwoza, Others Taken By Boko Haram', accessed on the 6th of May 2015 at: http://onobello.com/nigerian-military-restore-law-order-damboa-gwoza-others-taken-boko-haram/#sthash.m6lGqAus.dpuf; see also 'Nigerian military destroys Boko Haram headquarters in Gwoza', accessed on the 6th of May 2015 at: http://news2.onlinenigeria.com/headline/406075-nigerian-military-destroys-boko-haram-headquarters-in-gwoza.html#ixzz3ZOIN1OLz

130  accessed on the 6th of May 2015 at: http://news2.onlinenigeria.com/headline/406075-nigerian-military-destroys-boko-haram-headquarters-in-gwoza.html#ixzz3ZOIN1OLz

131  see 'Nigerian troops capture Gwoza, the last stronghold of insurgents', accessed on the 6th of may at: http://www.voiceofnigeria.org/nigeria/nigerian-troops-capture-gwoza-the-last-stronghold-of-insurgents.html

is that Shekau was shot and imprisoned after the death of Yusuf.[132] However, he was later released, or perhaps rescued from prison by unknown persons. Once again, on 21 September, 2014, the Nigerian military, through the Defence Headquarters (DHQ), claimed to have shot and killed Shekau in Konduga, Borno State. Pictures of Shekau (alleged to be Bashir Mohammed) were depicted on the web and in Nigerian newspapers. However, on the 2nd of October, 2014, Abubakar Shekau appeared to have 'resurrected' from the dead. Boko Haram released a video of the 'second coming' of Shekau, where he said: "This is Abubakar Shekau. I'm alive and not dead as your military has claimed. Shekau cannot die like that except Allah takes my soul," the man in the video boasted in his usual unstable posture. [133]

To complicate matters, the Federal Government issued a statement on 16 October, 2014 alleging that they had struck a peace deal with Boko Haram. The story claimed that Nigerian representatives struck the deal in Chad through a Saudi Arabian representative of Boko Haram named, Danladi Ahmadu. The paradox behind this claim is that on 18 October, twenty-five females were kidnapped in the village of Garta, a mountain village near the border with Cameroon. Furthermore, on 2 November, 2014, Abubakar Shekau, in a video denied that there was a ceasefire deal with the Federal Government. Shekau also made it clear that the kidnapped girls of Chibok secondary school had been converted to Islam and married off to members of the sect.[134] Conversely, this provides a causal explanation that where religion is a strong variable in conflict, the essence of dying for one's belief becomes a desire. The point is that the contention of Boko Haram does not directly pertain to achieving economic and political objectives. The big picture and underlying causal explanation is about religion—the desire to establish a caliphate.

---

132 'Borno Shivers over Threats of Boko Haram's Return,' Sunday Trust, July 4, 2013; 'The Boko Haram Terror Chief Who Came Back from the Dead,' France 24, January 13, 2012.
133 'See I'm alive, says Shekau in new video', assessed on the 7th of November 2014 at: http://www.punchng.com/news/im-alive-says-shekau-in-new-video/
134 See 'Boko Haram Leader Shekau Speaks on Ceasefire Talks and Abducted Chibok Girls', accessed on the 2oth of November 2014 at: https://www.youtube.com/watch?v=15Xh-rf2FoU

It would then be certainly unwise for the Nigerian government to assume that a ceasefire can be achieved by mere dialogue. It is also argued that mere dialogue may not resolve persistent onslaught of the radical group as their utopian ideology lies firmly in unstitching an Islamic state out of Nigeria. Radical Islam in North-eastern Nigeria is essentially different from the crisis in the Niger Delta where the objective centres on economics. Thus, it is correct to assert that: "Beyond the basic needs dictated by our biological requirements like air, food, shelter, humans need and seek meaning. Religion is a meaning system" Hood et al. (2005:12). Therefore, it hardly seems surprising that radical Muslims fight to connect with the meaning of life after death. It is beyond the physical senses of man. This explains the reason why it is difficult to purge the group. Even a 'smoke them out'[135] approach may not capitulate to sustainable results. Another underlying lesson is that one must not negotiate with terrorists, especially in an era of exploitation, unemployment and high crime rates, otherwise ragtag street gangs or even other defamed religious and political fanatics would desire to emulate terrorists' activities of inculcating the fear factor to the public in order to acquire monetary gains from the state. The ability and willingness to defeat the enemy is to eliminate the conditions that generate the enemy to exist. In a broader perspective, the tides of violence emanating from radical Islam in northern Nigeria does not lie in mere dialogue, but in destroying political kleptomania and bridging the gap between affluent politicians and people living in destitution.

There is, it must hastily be noted that there are a bundle of ironies in the following observations—On August 2014, a former Minister of the Federal Capital Territory—Nasir El-Rufai and Lt-General Azubuike Ihejirika (a non-Muslim and ex–Chief of Army Staff from 2010-2014) a Southeastern Nigerian and Nigeria's First Igbo Army Chief in forty-four years accused each other of

---

[135] Phrase used by President George Bush jr. See Terror in America / 'We're Going to Smoke Them Out': President Airs His Anger', accessed on the 19th of April 2012 at: http://www.nytimes.com/2001/09/19/news/19iht-t4_30.html

sponsoring Boko Haram.[136] What is critical is that Nasir El-Rufai started the imputation on Facebook which was based on a news item from a TV station which read: "Breaking News: Sheriff and Ihejirika Just Named as Boko Haram Kingpins – Arise TV – August 28, 2014." [137]

In another usual twist, an Australian negotiator—Dr. Stephen Davies, an international negotiator, who was engaged by the Nigerian Federal Government came to Nigeria in August 2014, with a lofty aspiration to negotiate the release of the abducted Chibok secondary school girls. What is even more critical, is that Dr. Davies contacted Boko Haram chieftains where he gathered that the former governor of Borno State, Governor Ali Modu Sheriff[138] and General Ihejirika,[139] were the sponsors of Boko Haram. Furthermore, he said that an anonymous senior official of the Central Bank of Nigeria was also a sponsor of the group. Davies alleged that General Ihejirika sponsored Boko Haram by providing the group with military weapons. It should be noted that the late Alhaji Buji Foi, a Boko Haram leader was appointed as the Commissioner for Religious Affairs by Modu Sheriff in 2009. Furthermore, Davies claimed that both Sheriff and Ihejirika selected targets for elimination and execution. The Northern Elders Forum (NEF) has decided to take General Ihejirika to the International Criminal Court of Justice for these allegations.[140] Over and above these allegations, if they are any way near the truth, the striking and intriguing issue is whether this is the causal explanation of gross incapacitation of the military in the fight against Boko Haram. On closer observation, another

---

136  See 'Boko Haram Sponsor: Ihejirika, El-Rufai Trade Accusations', accessed on the 2nd of December 2014 at: http://www.vanguardngr.com/2014/08/el-rufai-boko-harams-executive-commander-ihejirika/#sthash.7kHq5SNe.dpuf
137  See 'Nigeria News Online' accessed on the 2nd of December 2014 at: http://nigerialatestpolitics.blogspot.com/2014/08/el-rufai-front-line-commander-of-boko.html
138  See 'How Modu Sheriff Sponsored Boko Haram by Femi Falana (SAN)' accessed on the 2nd of December 2014 at: http://saharareporters.com/2014/09/04/how-modu-sheriff-sponsored-boko-haram-femi-falana-san; 'Modu Sheriff: In the Centre of a Storm' accessed on the 2nd of December 2014 at: http://www.thisdaylive.com/articles/modu-sheriff-in-the-centre-of-a-storm/188659/
139  See 'Ihejirika, sponsor Boko Haram?' accessed on the 2nd of December 2014 at: http://www.vanguardngr.com/2014/09/ihejirika-sponsor-boko-haram/
140  See 'Northern Elders Ill-Conceived, Says General Ihejirika', accessed on the 2nd of December 2014 at: http://www.thisdaylive.com/articles/northern-elders-ill-conceived-says-general-ihejirika/169191/

conspicuous issue is why did General Ihejirika keep silent on the question of his knowledge of Nasir El-Rufai as the sponsor of Boko Haram whislt he was the Chief of Army Staff. Why did General Ihejirika counter accuse Rufai after El-Rufai accused him? It should be reiterated that Nasir El-Rufai responded to the allegations presented by Dr. Stephen Davies. One would confess that the deeper one begins to analyse and speculate about Boko Haram, the more flummoxed one becomes.

The Nigerian military is a well trained and disciplined organisation. The Nigerian armed forces have exhibited high levels of professionalism and competence. This is evident in twenty-five peacekeeping missions since 1960. The most outstanding missions were in the Congo (1960-1964), New Guinea (1962-1963) Liberia (1990-98), Sierra Leone (1991-2000) and Cotê d'Ivoire (2000-till date). During these assignments, the Nigerian military was distinguished as an effective force. However, the contradiction in terms is that the Nigerian military is having a challenging task in contending with a ragtag force of Boko Haram fighters. The Nigerian media has reported that Nigerian troops flee from Boko Haram. In May 2014, there was a report of a mutiny of soldiers over dead soldiers at Maimalari Barracks, (the 7th Division the Nigerian Army).[141] In September 2014, twelve of the soldiers involved in the mutiny were sentenced to death.[142] In another case, fifty-four soldiers who participated in mutiny (refusing to comply with a commanding officer's order to take part in an operation to recapture Delwa, Bulabulin and Damboa in Borno State) were sentenced to death by firing

---

[141] See 'Nigerian Troops Flee Gwoza As Boko Haram Captures Tank and Driver, Commander Whereabouts Unknown', assessed on the 5th of November 2014 at: http://saharareporters.com/2014/08/08/nigerian-troops-flee-gwoza-boko-haram-captures-tank-and-driver-commander-whereabouts; 'Soldiers Run from Gwoza: Boko Haram Captures Military Tank, Army Commander Missing' assessed on the 5th of November 2014 at: http://talkloaded.net/2014/08/09/soldiers-run-from-gwoza-boko-haram-captures-military-tank-army-commander-missing/#sthash.fXoHEupV.dpuf; 'Army arrest 5 military commanders for abandoning Mubi to Boko Haram' assessed on the 5th of November 2014 at: http://www.gistplaza.com/army-arrest-5-military-commanders-abandoning-mubi-boko-haram/#sthash.Ctn8ugZe.dpuf; 'Near Mutiny At Army Barracks In Maiduguri Over High Number Of Nigerian Troops Casualty In Gwoza', assessed on the 5th of November 2014 at: http://saharareporters.com/2014/08/07/near-mutiny-army-barracks-maiduguri-over-high-number-nigerian-troops-casualty-gwoza.

[142] See Nigerian soldiers given death penalty for mutiny', accessed on the 24th of December 2014 at: http://www.bbc.com/news/world-africa-30526725

squad.¹⁴³ Another appaling incident is that a Colonel (a Muslim), in conjunction with some junior officers whilst taking part in a military engagement against Boko Haram terrorists in Adamawa State, were arrested for setting three Armored Personnel Carriers (APCs) on fire.¹⁴⁴ It seems that there is ineptitude on part of the Nigerian forces to tackle Boko Haram. It also appears that military decisions are politicised when seeking for solutions in curbing the menace of the sect.

Perhaps, due to the unexplainable failure of the Nigerian military in curbing Boko Haram, the African Union has created a 7,500 man multi-nation military task force, comprising the armed forces of Niger Republic, Chad, Cameroun and the Republic of Benin. These forces have embarked on a regional/cross border military campaign. This regional force is commendable since military intervention in Africa usually connotes the intervention of Western military forces. But what is surprising is that, Nigeria, having one of the largest military forces in Africa, is trying effortlessly in attempting to win the war against Boko Haram. What is the etiological explanation for this phenomenon? A rationalisation of this paradox is that the Nigerian military has in the recent past indulged itself as coup planners/plotters and usurpers of democratic governance under the pretext of reforming society and ridding the state from corruption. Crucially, the Nigerian military has been politicised as it has been entangled with political conspiracies and seizing the mantle of power. Most crucial, is that the Nigerian military has for a long time lost its *esprit de corps*. This loss of camaraderie has withered away the ambience of a disciplined armed force, whilst triggering a demoralised military whose banner seems to be within the paradigm of mutiny and the marshalling of soldiers. It is suggested that a searchlight on these issues is not unconnected

---

143 See Army sentences 54 soldiers to death for mutiny', accessed on the 20th of December 2014 at: http://www.punchng.com/news/army-sentences-54-soldiers-to-death-for-mutiny/

144 SHOCKER: Colonel, 10 officers set armoured tanks ablaze during Boko Haram attack in Adamawa','accessed on the 12th of December 2014 at: http://dailypost.ng/2014/10/11/shocker-colonel-10-officers-set-armoured-tanks-ablaze-boko-haram-attack-adamawa/; see also Mutiny: Army arraigns General, 14 senior officer; to court-martial 100 soldiers", accessed on the 23rd of December 2014 at: http://dailypost.ng/2014/12/24/mutiny-army-arraigns-general-14-senior-officer-court-martial-100-soldiers/

with the political interference with the duties of the armed forces. Are members of the armed forces well equipped to fights the war on terror? Are they paid adequately in the sight of financial corruption of the politicians? It seems that it is becoming extremely difficult to distinguish between the military and rabble-rousing politicians. Thus, it is not surprising that Captain Sagir Koli of the Nigerian military informed the Nigerian Press that politicians of the Peoples' Democratic Party (PDP) used the military to rig the June 21, 2014 governorship election in Ekiti State.[145] The unwillingness of the Nigerian army to risk of losing life or limb reveals the absence of a love for country. It seems what Nigerian soldiers are telling us is why die for a country where politicians are concerned with politics of the belly.

Another crucial but striking and intriguing question is whether there are any elements within the Nigerian Army that are complicit in facilitating terror? When a question is phrased in this way, perhaps an accurate observation is provided by the governor of Borno State — Kashim Shettima who observed that:

*Boko Haram are better armed and are better motivated than our own troops....Given the present state of affairs, it is absolutely impossible for us to defeat Boko Haram.*[146]

However, in a strange act of coincidence, after General Muhammadu Buhari was declared the winner of the March, 28 2015 Presidential Election, Boko Haram seems to be failing in its jihâdi campaign in north-east Nigeria. It seems that a renewed will may have been enkindled within the Nigerian army — thanks to the combined efforts of the Chadian, Cameroonian and Nigerien forces. In addition, the Nigerian military began to hire South African mercenaries to fights its war on terror. In addressing the weakness of the Nigerian military, President Buhari criticized this strategy by stating: "The military has never been so incapacitated like now. It is a shame that the

---

[145] See 'How Fayose, Obanikoro, others used soldiers to rig Ekiti poll — Army Captain', accessed on the 16th of February, 2015 at: http://www.punchng.com/news/how-fayose-obanikoro-others-used-soldiers-to-rig-ekiti-poll-army-captain/

[146] Nigeria Islamists better armed, motivated than army: governor', accessed on the 20th of December 2014 at: http://www.reuters.com/article/2014/02/17/us-nigeria-violence-idUSBREA1G1AO20140217

Military cannot secure 14 out of the 774 local governments in the country.¹⁴⁷ Since the merger of the coalition forces, Boko Haram has lost some its important strongholds in Dikwa (50 miles east of Maiduguri), which was liberated by Chadian forces, Malumfatori, a border town, Gowza, Goniri and Bama. Above and beyond the liberation of these Boko Haram strong holds, it is observed that there is a vicious circle of recapturing Boko Haram strongholds by the coalition forces, whilst other towns in northeast Nigeria are captured by the group.¹⁴⁸ This observation is noted on 17 May 2015, when the jihâdists recaptured the town of Marte, a strategic town linking Nigeria Cameroun and Chad. It is important to note that this town has been subject to being swapped between the radical group and the Nigerian military on several occasions¹⁴⁹—it seems to be a game of 'you win some, you lose some.' However, undeterred by this 'game-plan', the Nigerian army on March 28, 2015 swept the Simbisa forest and rescued 293 persons comprising 200 girls and 93 women. Furthermore, on March 29, 2015, the army rescued 160 persons consisting of 60 women and 100 children. Again on March 30, 2015, another batch of 234 women and children were rescued near Kawuri and Konduga, which is a part of Sambisa forest. However, it was established that these girls were not part of the Chibok girls that were kidnapped on April 15, 2014.

Despite the presence of South African mercenaries and the coalition forces, much remains to be achieved in Northeast Nigeria. This is evident in the 24 hour military curfew imposed on May 14, 2015 in Maiduguri, Borno State following Boko Haram attacks on a military barracks (Giwa Barracks), Bale and Kayamla.¹⁵⁰ Notwithstanding, the partial victory of the coalition forces and foreign mercenaries in recapturing Boko Haram strongholds, it is strongly projected that the group will continue

---

147 See The Vanguard, May 19, 2015 at page 5: 'Buhari Slams military for hiring mercenaries'
148 Note as previously stated that the town of Gwoza was recaptured by Boko Haram and then recaptured by the military
149 See 'Boko Haram recaptures key town in northeast Nigeria', accessed on the 17th of May 2015 at: http://news.yahoo.com/boko-haram-recaptures-key-town-northeast-nigeria-083402136.html
150 See The Guardian, May 15, 2015 at page 3: Military imposes curfew in Maiduguri over attack

to conduct guerrilla warfare against security personnel and use of hit and run attacks on civilian targets.

It is strongly suggested that the tactics employed by the police in the extra-judicial killing of Yusuf may have contributed to the reprisal attacks by Boko Haram. More to the point, on 3 August, 2009, President Yar'Adua ordered a probe into Yusuf's activities and how he died. The truth of the above 'finger pointing' became evident on 9 August, 2010, when it was uncovered that Yusuf was hastily killed by the police whilst in custody. In July 2011, seven police officers were charged with the unlawful killing of Yusuf. The officers were J.B. Abang, Muhammad Ahmadu Bada Buba, Ahmadu Gado and two constables, Anthony Samuel and Linus Luka.

Furthermore, the sect has caused mayhem by targeting non-Muslims in their pursuit of Islamising Nigeria. An important point worthy of mention is that members of the sect do engage in suicide bombing like their al-Qaeda counterparts. On 16 June, 2011, the group launched its first suicide attack (the first suicide attack in the state) in Nigeria by bombing a police station in Abuja. This was followed by another suicide attack on the 26 August, 2011 on the UN building in Abuja. The sect also plants bombs in targeted locations and use motorcycle ambushes. A few of the sect members of the group have died as a result of the bombs going off prematurely. However, there have been many instances where the bomb explosion has been executed as a suicidal act.

On the 24th Sept., 2011, the Punch newspapers reported an interview held with Aliyu Tishau, a co-founder of Boko Haram, with the African Independent Television. Tishau made damaging remarks that he had met with the Inspector-General of Police, Mr. Hafiz Ringim (now retired) and informed him on the sect's activities and places where they were going to implement terrorist attacks. Tishau also affirmed that politicians are the source of Boko Haram's sporadic attacks on security personnel, noting that states in northern Nigeria had militias under their pay roll.¹⁵¹ He mentioned that in Borno State, the governor funds a group of armed youths known as 'ECOMOG'. In addition, he alleged that in Gombe State, the governor funds the *Kalari* and in Bauchi State the government finances the armed group called the *'Tarafuka'*.

These personal militias are used as political thugs and as enforcers in settling political scores. It is clear that if these allegations are indeed true, it illustrates how the elites have manipulated religion for prebendalistic purposes and the fact that the elites are predominantly concerned with 'politics of the belly.' Perhaps, it is then now clear that the root of Boko Haram's notorious activities is based on the connection between the elites and politicians and the Islamists. Another yet intriguing question is why and where-fore was Aliyu Tishau not arrested by the Inspector-General of Police after meeting with him. In the usual tradition of finger-pointing between the police and the army, the police through its public relations officer, Deputy Commissioner of Police, Olusola Amore, claimed that Tishau was handed over to a 'sister security agency' on 7 July, 2011, following a request by this 'agency'. However, the Army and the State Security Service denied having custody of Tishau.¹⁵²

It is then perhaps not surprising that on March, 2012, the deposed Emir of Gwandu, Alhaji Al-Mustapha Jokolo contended that Boko Haram was created by northern politicians in order to recapture political power at the centre in 2015.¹⁵³ Above and beyond this assertion, it is strongly proffered that northern Nigerian leaders would not wilfully create a destructive group to kill and destroy people with whom they share the same faith (Islam). The lurking observation for this predication is that Islam in northern Nigeria promotes social harmony among its adherents (Olomojobi, 2013). There is one must state, perceptions

---

151 See The Punch, 21st September, 2001.
152 See Saturday Punch, September 24, 2011.
153 see 'BOMBSHELL: Northern politicians created Boko Haram – Mustapha Jokolo, former Emir of Gwandu – Says North should forget about the presideny in 2015', accessed on the 1st of May 2015 at: http://transformationwatch.com/2012/03/28/bombshell-northern-politicians-created-boko-haram-mustapha-jokolo-former-emir-of-gwandu-says-north-should-forget-about-the-presideny-in-2015-naijapundit/

that Boko Haram is a creation of northern politicians who are ggrieved about being set aside from leadership in Nigeria. The rational of this suggestion is that in the last 16 years, a northerner has held on to power for only 2 years. This acuity is altogether misleading as Boko Haram became prominent during the reign of President Yar' Adua, a northerner from Katsina State. An intriguing question is that if northern politicians are aggrieved about the existence of non-Muslim leadership, what then is the quintessence for creating a radical group which is causing death and destruction to a majority of northern Muslims.

An unusual political phenomenon of radical Islam in northern Nigeria is that it has the potential of reducing inter-religious conflict. It is observed that there is an absence of inter-religious conflicts since the rise of Boko Haram in northern Nigeria. From 1999-2010, there were over twenty-five major conflicts between Muslims and non-Muslims in northern Nigeria (Olomojobi, 2013). From 2010 till the time of publishing, there has not been any significant inter-religious skirmish. The explanation for this observable fact is that Boko Haram is threatening with absolute impunity both Muslims and non-Muslims. In such an atmosphere, co-religionists of the different Abrahamic faiths are dispossessed of searching for perceived grievances towards the other.

## Funding and Networking of Boko Haram

The immense paradox confronting Boko Haram was that, each member had to contribute a levy of ₦1 daily to Mohammed Yusuf. This amounted to a whooping ₦16 million (about £64,800) a month. Aside from the daily contributions of members, presently at the time of writing this chapter, the sect is widely believed to have a link with al-Qaeda in the Islamic Maghreb (AQIM). Although it is a daunting task for the Nigerian Security Service to trace how Boko Haram receives its funding, it is not difficult to speculate that money laundering and the smuggling of arms and ammunition is coterminous with the flow of ransome demands. This is made easy due to the porous borders. This was made easy due to the fact that Borno State shares a border with Cameroun through Ngoshe in Gwoza local government and easy access to Chad and Niger through Konduga local government. Thus, it is not surprising that most of Boko Haram's strategic posts are located close to border towns and villages. In addition, most of the militants consist of foreign nationals of Chad, Somalia and Sudan. Using porous borders with Chad, Niger and Cameroon in the uninhabited forest which encompasses Lake Chad, has bolstered transnational terrorism. Furthermore, these pervious borders have made the easy access of smuggling of weapons and abduction of citizens of Nigerians and its neighbours. However, an important observation is that Boko Haram is no longer a 'local insurgency', it has transnational affiliation.

Crucial to the above observation is that Nigeria has about 480 irregular border crossings in its 4,500 kilometre borders with Niger and Chad. Another area of funding by the sect was the raiding of banks in northern Nigeria. In 2011, about 30% of bank robberies were thought to be committed by Boko Haram.[154] It has been strongly speculated that Osama Bin Ladin was in contact with Boko Haram and other radical groups.[155] It is then strongly proposed that Boko Haram's source of funding was channelled by al-Qaeda.

## Unholy blemish on Islam in Northern Nigeria

Notwithstanding these conjectures, northern Governors have unanimously condemned the acts of the sect. Specifically, Governor Danjuma Goje of Gombe State ordered the destruction of Yusuf's home in the State, when he came on a visit months before the sectarian clashes took place.[156] Yet again, it is worthy to note that in 2009, the governors of Bauchi and Kano States;

---

154  See 'Nigeria: Boko Haram' Funding Sources Uncovered'. All Africa 12 February, 2012
155  See Burke, Jason, 2012. 'Bin Laden files show al-Qaida and Taliban leaders in close contact, accessed on the 17th of November at: http://www.theguardian.com/world/2012/apr/29/bin-laden-al-qaida-taliban-contact
156  See After Boko Haram, Time to Move on: The Nation, Monday, August 10, 2009 p. 20

Isa Yuguda and Ibrahim Shekarau, took cautionary measures by giving the security forces the direction to avert the insurgence of the sect.

Now it is important, that what needs to be recognised here is that Boko Haram's ideologies are not supported by a great majority of northern Nigerian Muslims. The Jama'atu Nasril Islam (JNI), an umbrella for all Muslims in northern Nigeria seeking to advance political, social and economic interests of co-religionists in northern Nigeria has explicitly condemned the sect and the violence that ensued. The chairman of the Muslim Council of Nigeria (MCN), Alhaji Inuwa Jauro Manu said emphatically that 'sect called itself a religious organisation, its actions and activities does not conform to Islam'.[157] In addition, the northern Governor's Forum (NGF), an umbrella body of the 19 state governors of northern Nigeria agreed to enact legislation that would curb sectarian violence in the region.[158]

Given the above, if one assumes but does not concede that there is a stain on Islam in northern Nigeria, due to the activities of Boko Haram, it is suggested that there is a gap between scriptural Islam, that is, what it preaches and what its followers may practice. Likewise, one may assume that Islam acquired a degree of misconception in western societies through the western media due to the 911 incident. However, what one must clearly concede to is that these perverse activities are not supported by mainstream Muslims. Clearly, there is a great tradition that Islam in northern Nigeria draws a clear boundary between those individuals professing Islam and those professing non-Islamic faiths. On the other hand, Islam facilitates an overarching solidarity among people in northern Nigerian divided by ethnic, linguistic and cultural differences. However, this sometimes is not reflected in intra-religious interaction. It should also be noted that severe intra-religious conflicts is not a reoccurring incident in northern Nigeria unlike

---

[157] http://www.ngrguardiannews.com/news/article01//indexn2_html?pdate=300709&ptitle=Fighting%20rages,%20death%20toll%20hits%20300%20in%20Borno

[158] See 'Northern govs plan laws against sectarian violence': The Punch, Tuesday, August 4, 2009, p.2

inter-religious conflicts. A notable incident similar to Boko Haram was the Maitasine Riots in 1980, which was based on Islamic radicalism. However, when religion (Islam) is practiced in deeply divided societies such as Nigeria, it is not surprising that Islamic radicalism has the tendency to emerge and generate conflict.

At this juncture, it is pertinent to point out that although the Boko Haram crisis is deeply rooted in religious zealotry and Islamism, the sect's doctrines and preaching were in many respects contrary to mainstream and popular Islamic positions and theology. Paradoxically, as earlier noted, Muslims who were not members of the sect were not spared from their venous attacks. It is important to bear in mind that the threat to Islam here pertains to the purification of Islam. This is not surprising, as noted by Ahmadu U. Jalingo (1980:24):

*Muslim radicals have not changed their position till today. Whenever and wherever compromises by Muslims appear to threaten the basic identity of society, they call for a reaffirmation of the unchanging truth of Islam.*

Yet, sometimes this reaffirmation may be characterised by perverse ideologies which may give rise to intra-religious conflicts, on issues pertaining to adulterating the Islamic identity. This ideology may be seen to be consistent with Islamic tradition, for the reason that Uthman dan Fodio called for a Jihâd in 1804, against Muslims he considered to be unorthodox and lukewarm.

## Hoodwinked? A Web of Conspiracy?

Let us begin by noting that Muslim leaders and military personnel had warned the State authorities about Boko Haram. However, these early warning signs were ignored.[159] *The Guardian Newspapers*[160] reported that the Minority Leader of the

---
159    Nigeria accused of ignoring sect warnings before wave of killings". The Guardian, Sunday, 2, 2009.
160    http://www.ngrguardiannews.com/news/article01//indexn2_html?pdate=300709&ptitle=Fighting%20rages,%20death%20toll%20hits%20300%20in%20Borno

House of Representatives, Mohammed Ali Ndume, has blamed the Federal Government for not acting enough to reign in the terrorists, in spite of the earlier security information available to it. Those warnings were reportedly ignored. Incongruously and in harmony with our conspiracy theory, Senator Mohammed Ali Ndume was arrested by the State Security Service (SSS) on the 22nd of November, 2011 on charges of financially supporting the sect. The sect had some degree of popularity. This is evident by the act of the Governor of Bornu State; Modu Ali Sheriff, who provided the sect with 80 kilometres of land.[161] Moreover, all attempts by the State Security Service (SSS) to lure the governor to revoke the expanse of land to Yusuf were futile.[162] Furthermore, Yusuf had previously been arrested in Maiduguri on the 13th of November, 2008, on suspicion of attempting to disrupt the peace and security of the State. However, he was released on bail on the 20th of January 2009.[163] More crucial is the fact that a former commissioner of religious Affairs, in Modu Ali Sheriff's cabinet; Alhaji Buji Foi[164] was the second in command in Boko Haram. Even more crucially, on July 14, 2009, 21 reports were submitted on Mohammed Yusuf's activities and members of his group to the appropriate authorities.[165]

The existence and growing influence of Boko Haram was evident even among the northern governors who reportedly sponsored the group in order to prevent attacks on their territory and maintain their hold on power. According to Byman (2005:221) there are various reasons which make groups 'ignore' the activities of terrorist organisations, such as the lack of a direct threat, or popular support for the movement, or limited costs to the government.

One characteristic of most African states offering safe havens is that they do so in passivity. Passive support can be described as knowingly allowing a terrorist group to raise money, enjoy

---

161 Security Reports on Sect's Leader indicts Governor: The Nation, Wednesday, August 5, 2009, p.1
162 ibid
163 Security Reports on Sect's leader indict Governor: The Nation, Wednesday, August 5, 2009, p. 2
164 He was killed in the uprising and his body later taken to the State House
165 See http://www.thisdayonline.com/nview.php?id=150277

a sanctuary, recruit, or otherwise flourish without interference from a regime that does not directly aid the group itself. According to Byman, passive support can be when the regime in question itself does not provide assistance but knowingly allows other actors in the country to aid the terrorist group; or lack of capacity or lack of political will to deploy such capacity; or when political parties, wealthy merchants, or other actors in society that have no formal affiliation with the government give passive support (Byman 2005:222). 'Passivity in the face of terrorism' according to Byman can 'be deadly.' He cites the deadly attack on the World Trade Centre as an example:

> *In conducting the September 11 attacks, al-Qaeda recruited and raised money in Germany with relatively little interference, enjoyed financial support from many Saudis unobstructed by the government in Riyadh, planned operations in Malaysia, and sent operatives to America. None of these governments are 'sponsors' of al-Qaeda – indeed, several are bitter enemies – but their inaction proved as important as, if not more important, than the haven the group enjoyed in Afghanistan in enabling al-Qaeda to conduct the attacks. As Deputy Secretary of Defense Paul Wolfowitz testified about the attacks, "Even worse than the training camps [in Afghanistan] was the training that took place here in the United States and the planning that took place in Germany (2005:222).*

More crucially, the internet whistle blower, Wikileaks, revealed that the United States government had intelligence and fore-knowledge of the July 2009 Boko Haram 'Jihâd'. In a cable dated 29 June, 2009, which was emitted from the Secretary of State, with reference number 09STATE67105 and classified secret/noforn was titled "Nigeria-Extremists believed to be planning a massive terrorist attack." The cable further referred to the sect as the 'Nigerian Taliban.' However, the report did not disclose whether the Nigerian authorities were aware of the attack. An important dimension of the report is that a certain 'well trained veteran Chadian extremist', Abu-Mahjin, had travelled to northeast Nigeria to mobilise and facilitate the 'Jihâd'.

Perhaps even more crucially, the United States government cable released by Wikileaks exposed a deed that assisted certain terrorist suspects belonging to the Boko Haram sect to escape trial after being arrested. The cable with reference number 08ABUJA538 was sent to Dr. Robbin Rene (US Ambassador to Nigeria) on 20 March, 2008. The cable revealed that the Nigerian State Security Service (SSS) reached an agreement with certain elites of the northern traditional clique for the secret release and non-trial of terrorist suspects. Thus, it is argued with a strong amount of certainty, that there are certain unseen elites behind the facade of Boko Haram.

It is then not surprising that one may begin to speculate about the politicians being aware that religion as a strong identity marker could be used as a potent instrument. Therefore, it may be safe to suggest that the politicians have hijacked religion for political currencies. In furtherance to our suggestion of the unseen powers behind the sect, a broader conspiracy theory may provide some support. Mohammed Yusuf was captured alive and handed over to the Police, but later died in controversial circumstances in their custody. Clearly, there is a fair amount of controversy concerning the circumstances of Mohammed Yusuf's death. Was his death imminent to veil those behind the sect? Who were his sponsors? How did the sect acquire sophisticated arms and ammunition? Why were the early warnings from security reports of the SSS not acted upon? A national newspaper, *The Vanguard*, comments that 'some very powerful sponsors of the Islamist whose mindset was already beginning to work upside down, may not want him to expose them, and, therefore, may have caused the Police to take him out.'[166]

Moreover, accusing fingers between the Commander of the Military Operation, Colonel Ben Ahonotu, claimed that Yusuf was handed over to the Police alive, whilst the former Commissioner

---

166   'Killing of Boko Haram leader: Haram vs Haram', accessed on the 2nd of October 2010 at: http://www.vanguardngr.com/2009/08/08/killing-of-boko-haram-leader-haram-vs-haram/

of Police, Borno State Command, Mr. Christopher Dega, claimed that the leader of the sect died in a shootout with the Police.[167] One may suggest that devious politicians informed the less privileged people, using the instrumentalism of religion that westernised establishments are their enemies, rather than informing them that their state governments are to blame for economic degradation. In explaining how identity and religion interrelate, Kakar (1996) tells us that identity threats are the root cause of religious conflict, and that these threats may arise as a result of economic interests, a perceived discrimination by the state, or a change of a political regime. In using the variable of economic interests, the less privileged were then able to channel their relative deprivation towards western education and whenever grievance reaches its limits, the result is that frustration leads to conflict. It is easy to understand that the tone and substance of this shows that, Islam in northern Nigeria can be politically hijacked and manipulated to generate conflict, when there is a perceived threat to its sacrosanct nature.

Now in the current context, it could be quite useful here to underscore Gurr's theory of grievance, which is used to explain the religious causes of discrimination which are generative mechanisms that lead to violence. The problem of tackling the group is that it is faceless. It is important to note that Boko Haram has widened its scope of terrorist activities by introducing abduction of people for ransome—the kidnapping of a French family in Cameroun in February 2013 and their eventual release upon the payment of $3 million ransom illustrates this. It is strongly speculated that Ansaru, a disintegrated group from Boko Haram may have collaborated in the kidnapping. This shows that the terrorist tactics of the group is shrouded with complexities as it uses insurgency campaigns and criminal operations in its 'Jihâdist' crusades. From what can be gathered so far, is that there are no active leads to determine who is behind Boko Haram.

---

167  Boko Haram Planned to Attack Lagos: Saturday Punch, August 1, 2009, p.13

However, what is true is that the group is connected with a network of heinous activities by government officials in high places in the Nigerian government. What is equally, if not more important, is that former President Goodluck Jonathan at inter-denominational service to mark the 2012 Armed Forces Remembrance Day claimed that the group has infiltrated the three arms of government and the military.[168] Perhaps, this explains the foiled attempts by the military in repressing the group, especially in locating the kidnapped 234 secondary school girls from Chibok, Borno State. In support of this, experts on Boko Haram have proposed that the kidnapping of the schoolgirls could not have been successful without the help of police or military collaboration.[169] Despite the international condemnation of kidnapping the Chibok girls, on the 3rd of January 2015, Boko Haram committed its most outrageous act—an unabated and premeditated cruelty, shrouded with terror and destruction by killing 2,000 people of Baga in Borno State. This act reveals that the group has become increasingly violent and deranged. Furthermore, an unprecedented attack by Boko Haram which occurred on the 10th of January, 2015, was the use of a ten year old in a suicide bombing attack, killing sixteen people.

---

[168] 'President: Boko Haram has infiltrated govt, military'. Assessed on the 20th of May 2014 at: http://www.thenationonlineng.net/2011/index.php/news/32611-president-boko-haram-has-infiltrated-govt-military.html

[169] Nigeria: Was the Nigerian Military Complicit in the Chibok Abductions? Assessed on the 20th of May 2014 at: http://allafrica.com/stories/201405191657.html

## Table showing Significant Incidents of Boko Haram: 1995-04/2014-04

| Date | Event |
|---|---|
| 1995 | Boko Haram sect started as Shabaab Muslim Youth Organisation. |
| 2002 | Boko Haram is reformed by Muhammad Yusuf. |
| July 25-30, 2009 | Jihâd starts in Borno, Yobe, Gombe and Kano States, targeting security forces, westernised establishments, non-Muslim places of worship. In Maiduguri, twenty Churches were razed whilst three pastors and one reverend were killed. In total, 780 people (including police and military personnel) were killed in Maiduguri. In addition, there were 3,500 internally displaced persons. |
| July 26 2009 | Muhammad Yusuf is arrested. |
| July 29, 2009 | Muhammad Yusuf is killed by the police. |
| August 1, 2009 | It is revealed that Boko Haram's leaders were trained in Algeria and Afghanistan in 2006. They are linked to a guerrilla group called *Jamatul Salafia* which is based in the desert in Algeria. |
| August 4, 2009 | President Jonathan orders probe into Muhammad Yusuf's death. |

| | |
|---|---|
| April 16, 2010 | A court in Borno awards N100million as damages to the family of Baba Fugu Muhammad (father-in-law of Muhammad Yusuf), who was killed in custody in July 2009. |
| August 31, 2010 | The ward head of Bulama is killed in Maiduguri suburbs. |
| September, 5, 2010 | A Trader (a retired policeman) killed in Bama Town. |
| September 7, 2010 | The death of 800 people occurred as a result of a jail break attempt in Bauchi prison in which 700 Boko Haram prisoners were released. |
| September 11, 2010 | Bombing of a police station in Gamboru, Old Maiduguri (3 policemen injured). |
| September 21, 2010 | A man killed and another wounded at Railway Terminus quarters, Old Maiduguri. |
| October 19, 2010 | A police officer killed in Maiduguri. |
| October 25, 2010 | A policeman killed whilst on duty on the Bauchi-Kano Road. |
| November 5, 2010 | Policemen were shot at Gwabba Street, Bauchi. |
| November 7, 2010 | An attempt to kill a ward head at Bolori Village. |
| November 13, 2010 | A soldier killed and another injured in Maiduguri. |
| November 17, 2010 | A younger brother of the ward head of Ngarnam is killed by militants who mistook him for his brother. |

| | |
|---|---|
| November 19, 2010 | Three people killed and one injured at Gombari Mosque in Maiduguri. |
| November 21, 2010 | Army settlement attacked in Jajeri, Maiduguri. |
| December 24, 2010 | The Victory Baptist Church at Dala-Alamderi, Maiduguri is burnt to ashes and five people, including the church pastor, Rev. Bulus Marwa and two choir members rehearsing carols are shot and killed. In addition, Church of Christ in Nigeria ((COCIN) in Maiduguri is set ablaze. In a separate incident, six other people are shot and killed by the sect. |
| December 24, 2010 | Bombings in Jos, Plateau State; 80 people killed and 100 injured. |
| January 1, 2011 | A Church attacked in London Cinkiu, Maiduguri. |
| January 3, 2011 | A police killed whilst on duty at Gwande Ward in Maiduguri. |
| January 9, 2011 | A Church ransacked, policeman killed and two injured at Gomari, Maiduguri. |
| January 19, 2011 | Five people, residents of Dala Alemderi ward in Maiduguri are killed by gun men. |
| January 24, 2011 | A soldier killed and two persons injured in Maiduguri. |
| January 28, 2011 | Goni Sheriff (Borno State Governor, Ali Modu Sheriff's brother), Modu Fannami Gubio (the All Nigeria Peoples Party governorship candidate) and six others killed in Maiduguri. |

| | |
|---|---|
| February 8, 2011 | The sect gives conditions for peace on the condition that the Borno State Governor, Ali Modu Sheriff, vacates office with immediate effect. In addition they demand that their confiscated mosque in Maiduguri be granted back to them. |
| February 21, 2011 | Police in Maiduguri arrest a leader of the Boko Haram sect; Muhammad Zakaria Alia Jiddo. |
| February 24, 2011 | A police inspector is shot dead in Maiduguri. |
| February 28, 2011 | Armed members of Boko Haram besiege the residence of a Divisional Police Officer, Mustapha Sandamu, and kill two policemen. |
| March 3, 2011 | Bomb blast at the office of the Independent National Electoral Commission (INEC) in Suleja, Niger State, killing sixteen persons. |
| April 9, 2011 | A polling centre for the elections is bombed in Maiduguri. |
| April 15, 2011 | The Maiduguri office of the INEC is bombed. |
| April 20, 2011 | A Muslim cleric who preached against the atrocities of the sect is ambushed and killed. |
| April 22, 2011 | Members of the sect ambushed and freed fourteen prisoners from a jail in Yola, Adamawa State. |

| | |
|---|---|
| May 6, 2011 | A bomb is set off near a police station in Maiduguri, killing two people and injuring one person. |
| May 9, 2011 | Boko Haram rejects offer for amnesty made by the new elected Governor of Borno State, Kashim Shettima. |
| May 11, 2011 | Alhaji Mukhtar Tijjani, district head of Mairari is killed by the sect. |
| May 12, 2011 | Police Inspector Mai Kadai is shot in the head at a railway intersection near Maiduguri. |
| May 17, 2011 | A police corporal is killed at Dala Alamderi, in Maiduguri. |
| May 27, 2011 | Twelve people are killed in an armed robbery attack by seventy Boko Haram militants at the First Bank in Damboa, Borno State. |
| May 29, 2011 | Series of bombings in northeastern Nigeria as a remonstration of the inauguration of President Jonathan Goodluck. During the mayhem, Anas Ibn Umar Garbai (the younger brother of the Shehu/king of Borno) is killed. In addition, the army barracks in Bauchi was ransacked with bombings, fourteen people are killed. |
| June 13, 2011 | An explosive uncovered at the gates of the Nigerian National Petroleum Corporation staff quarters in Naraji, Kaduna Metropolis. |

| | |
|---|---|
| July 13, 2011 | The governments of Benue, Kano, Kaduna, Kwara and Plateau send buses to evacuate their citizens over Boko Haram menace. |
| June 14, 2011 | Bomb explosive planted by the sect uncovered behind Dambo International School in Barnawa, Kaduna City in Kaduna State. |
| June 15, 2011 | The Inspector-General of Police, Mr. Hafia Ringim vows to end the sporadic attacks of Boko Haram. |
| June 16, 2011 | Suicide bomb explosion at Police Headquarters, Abuja; 8 people are killed and 73 vehicles burnt. Boko Haram spokesman, Usman Alzawahiri affirms responsibility of the attack and vows to attack the entire North and its capital, Abuja. |
| June 26, 2011 | 25 people killed and 12 injured as three bombs are thrown at beer gardens (popular night spots) in Maiduguri. |
| June 27, 2011 | Three people killed in shootings at a Customs office in Maiduguri. |
| July 3, 2011 | An IED explodes at the Wukari Mammy Market in Maiduguri, killing twenty people. |
| July 6, 2011 | A police station is ransacked in Toro, Bauchi State. |
| July 6, 2011 | Four soldiers injured in an explosion at the mini supermarket, Abbagaanaram Ward, Maiduguri. |

| | |
|---|---|
| July 10, 2011 | Bomb explosion at the All Christian Faith Mission Church, Suleja, killing 3 people. |
| July 12, 2011 | 3 dead and 2 soldiers injured as an Improvised Explosive Device was thrown into a military patrol vehicle on Baga Road, Maiduguri. |
| July 20, 2001 | Boko Haram publicly affirms that it has split into two factions: the Yusifiyya Islamic Movement and the Shekau Bukar faction. The Yusifiyya Islamic Movement desires a peaceful alternative whilst the Shekau Bukar faction insists on carrying out the 'Jihâd'. |
| July 24, 2011 | 8 people are killed in a bomb attack near the palace of the Shehu of Borno in Maiduguri. |
| July 26, 2011 | The district head of Bulatulin and his 9 year old daughter shot dead in Maiduguri. |
| August 4, 2011 | 2 people killed and 2 injured by explosions on Baga Road, Maiduguri. |
| August 12, 2011 | Liman Bana, an influential Muslim cleric, is shot whilst walking after conducting prayers at the mosque. He later died as a result of injuries. |
| August 15, 2011 | A suicide bomber who attempted to bomb the Borno State Police Command headquarters is shot dead. |
| August 26, 2011 | A suicide bomb explosion goes off in the UN headquarters in Abuja, killing 19 and injuring over 100 people |

| | |
|---|---|
| September 14, 2011 | Former President Olusegun Obasanjo, on a peace mission visits the home of slain Boko Haram leader, Yusuf Muhammad. He is received by Yusuf's in-law, Babakura Fugu, in Maiduguri. |
| September 17, 2011 | Babakura Fugu is shot dead outside his home by an unknown gunman. |
| October 1, 2011 | An improvised explosion targeted at a patrol unit in Maiduguri kills 2 civilians. |
| October 2, 2011 | Boko Haram spokesman, Abu Qaga, offers a condition for ceasefire; the establishment of Sharia law in all Muslim States in Nigeria and release of all prisoners and detainees of the sect. |
| October 10, 2011 | An improvised explosive devise injures 3 soldiers at Dalla, Maiduguri. |
| October 15, 2011 | The Federal Government refuses the conditions for ceasefire. |
| October 16, 2011 | Boko Haram gunmen shot and killed Modu Bintube of the Borno State House of Assembly at Gomari Airport Ward, Maiduguri, Borno State. |
| October 22, 2011 | Boko Haram gunmen shot and killed a cameraman, Zakariya Isa, working for the Nigerian Television Authority (NTA) in Maiduguri, Borno State. |
| November 2, 2011 | A suspected kingpin of the sect, Sheriff Shettima, notorious for masterminding a series of bombings, is arrested by police. |

| | |
|---|---|
| November 3, 2011 | A suspected kingpin of the sect, Ali Sada Umar Konduga (Al-Zawahiri), the spokesman for the sect is arrested at Gwange area of Borno State. Under interrogation, he alledged that Boko Haram is a political weapon for embittered politicians from northern Nigeria who are behind the sect. He also names Senator Ndume of the Peoples Democratic Party (PDP) and Saidu Pindar (former Nigerian Ambassador to Sao Tome and Principe) as financiers of the sect. Konduga also narrates that Boko Haram is working for the interests of Peoples Democratic Party (PDP) in Borno State. |
| November 4, 2011 | The sect detonated heavy explosives at the headquarters of the Joint Task Force in Maiduguri killing the suicide bombers. In addition, multiple gun and bomb attacks in beer gardens, churches, mosques and police stations kill 67 people in Damaturu, Yobe State. |
| November 6, 2011 | Members of the sect shot and killed a police inspector as he was driving to the mosque. |
| November 7, 2011 | Reports indicate that the sect has relocated its operational base from Maiduguri, Borno State to Damaturu, capital of Yobe State. |
| November 10, 2011 | Members of the sect attack a police post in Minok village on the Maiduguri-Damaturu Road. |

| | |
|---|---|
| November 11, 2011 | Federal Government approves military operations in six North-East states in Nigeria. |
| November 22, 2011 | Senator Ndume arraigned before an Abuja Chief Magistrate Court. He pleads not guilty. |
| November 24, 2011 | Ali Sada Umar Konduga is convicted for felony at an Abuja Chief Magistrate Court.<br>Abu Qaba, spokesman for the sect confirms link with al-Qaeda. |
| December 4, 2011 | A soldier, a policeman and a civilian are killed in a bomb and gun attack at a police station and two banks in Azare, Bauchi State. A groom and a one person are killed at a wedding in Maiduguri, Borno State. |
| December 13, 2011 | 10 dead and 30 injured at a military check point in Maiduguri, Borno State. |
| December 22, 2011 | 4 policemen and a civilian are killed at a police station in Potiskum, Yobe State.<br>A sect member dies in the process of detonating an IED in London Chiki area of Maiduguri, several people were injured by the blast. |
| December 23, 2011 | Members of the Nigerian Army's Joint Task Force engage in a gun battle with Boko Haram in Damaturu, killing 59 members of the sect. |
| December 25, 2011 | The SSS headquarters in Damaturu is attacked by a suicide bomber leaving 3 SSS persons dead. |

| | |
|---|---|
| December 25, 2011 | Bomb blast at St. Theresa's Catholic Church in Madala, Abuja, leaving 43 people dead. |
| December 28, 2011 | Bombing and shooting at a beer parlour in Mubi, Adamawa State. Unknown causalties. |
| December 30, 2011 | 4 people killed in Maiduguri, Borno State after attending Friday prayers at the Mosque. |
| December 31, 2011 | President Goodluck declares State of Emergency in parts of Borno State, Yobe State, Plateau State and Niger State due to its sporadic religious violence |
| January 3, 2012 | A teenage girl and another wounded at a police station in Birniwa, Jigawa State. |
| January 6, 2012 | 8 people killed in a Church in Yola, Adamawa State. |
| January 6, 2012 | The sect shoots and kills twenty-seven persons in Mubi, Adamawa State. |
| January 6, 2012 | The sect shoots and kills 8 persons and injures 19 persons worshipping at BCGA quarters branch of Deeper Life Church in Mubi, Gombe State. |
| January 7, 2012 | 3 poker players are killed and 7 others injured in Biu, Borno State. |
| January 8, 2012 | Members of the sect kills and shoots 16 members (including the pastor and his son) of the Christ Apostolic Church in Yola, Adamawa State. |

| | |
|---|---|
| January 9, 2012 | An undercover police is killed in Biu, Borno. President Jonathan asserts that Boko Haram has infiltrated the Executive, Legislative and Judicial arm of government. |
| January 10, 2012 | 8 people are shot to death at a beer garden at Damaturu, Yobe State. |
| January 11, 2012 | 4 people killed in Potiskum, Yobe State. The victims were fleeing from Maiduguri to the eastern part of Nigeria. |
| January 13, 2012 | 4 people are killed and 2 others injured in 2 separate attacks in beer gardens at Yola (Adamawa State) and Gombe (Gombe State). |
| January 14, 2012 | Kabiru Umar (alias Kabiru Sokoto the mastermind of the St. Theresa's Catholic Church bombing, is caught by the police at Iro Dan Musa Street, Asokoro, Abuja. |
| January 15, 2012 | Kabiru Umar (alias Kabiru Sokoto) a notorious member of the sect escapes while being taken to his home for a search in Abaji, Abuja. |
| January 17, 2012 | 2 soldiers and 4 Boko Haram members are killed in a shootout at a military checkpoint in Maiduguri, Borno State. |
| January 8, 2012 | A suspect in the 2011 Christmas day bombing escapes from police custody. |
| January 20, 2012 | Multiple explosions kill 185 persons in Kano, Kano State. |

| | |
|---|---|
| January 22, 2012 | The police shoot 4 members of the sect in Maiduguri, Borno State. |
| January 23, 2012 | Police in a gun battle kill 4 members of the sect in Kano, Kano State. |
| January 24, 2012 | President Goodluck Jonathan sacks Inspector General of Police, Hafiz Ringim, over his inadequate performance in tackling the sect. |
| January 28, 2012 | 11 members of the sect are shot dead in gun battle with the Joint Task Force (JTF) in Maiduguri, Borno State. |
| February 6, 2012 | Members of the sect kill 2 persons in Ummarari ward in Maiduguri, Borno State. |
| February 6, 2012 | Members of the sect raid a police station in Sharada, Kano State. |
| February 6, 2012 | The JTF killed 8 members of the sect in a gun battle on the outskirts of Kano, Kano State. |
| February 7, 2012 | A suicide bomber attempted to attack the 1st Mechanised Division in Kaduna. The bomber was killed as he forcefully gained entrance into base. In addition, multiple attacks occurred in Kawo, Kaduna State. Elsewhere, 7 members of the sect were killed in Mariri Quarters on Maiduguri Road, Kano State. |
| February 9, 2012 | Kabiru Umar (alias Kabiru Sokoto) is re-captured by the SSS in Taraba State. |

| | |
|---|---|
| February 17, 2012 | Abu Qaqa 1, also known as Abu Dardaa, Mohammed Shuaibu, Mohammed Bello, Abu Tiamiya and Abdulrahman Abdullahi is apprehended and detained by the police in Kaduna State. He discloses that the sect is funded by some politicians. |
| February 17, 2012 | Members of the sect shot and kill 1 policeman in Maje, Niger State, |
| February 17, 2012 | Members of the sect shot and kill 2 policemen in Minna, Niger State. |
| February 19, 2012 | 5 persons were severely injured by bomb blast near Triumphant Ministries International Church and Christ Embassy Church in Suleja, Niger State. |
| February 20, 2012 | Members of the sect set a blaze Kulagumma Primary School, Abbaganaram School, and Budum Primary School (in opposition to secular and western education) in Maiduguri, Borno State. |
| February 25, 2012 | Members of the sect throw IEDs at a police station in Gombe, Gombe State killing 14 persons. |
| February 26, 2012 | A car bomb kills 3 persons and wounding 38 people outside a church in Jos, Plateau State. Christian Youths kill 2 Muslims in retaliation. |
| March 11, 2012 | A car bomb kills 11 persons outside St. Finbarr's Catholic Church in Reyfield, Jos, Plateau State. In a reprisal attack by non-Muslims, 9 persons are killed. The |

|  | militants also attack a police station, killing a policeman in Kano Kano State. |
|---|---|
| March 13, 2012 | Chris McManus and Franco Lamolinara, a Briton and an Italian held hostage in Sokoto State by the sect are killed during an attempted rescue by British Special Forces and the Joint Task Force (JTF). In addition, 8 members of the sect are killed. |
| March 13, 2012 | Members of the sect shoot and kill a police officer, a soldier and four persons in Mubi, Adamawa State. |
| March 24, 2012 | 2 members of the sect are killed by detonating a car bomb in Kano, Kano State. |
| March 26, 2012 | Abu Qaqa 1's father is killed on March 26 in Maiduguri by suspected members of Boko Haram in retaliation for Abu Qaqa 1's disclosures to the police. |
| April 3, 2012 | Members of the sect kill SSS personnel, Ibrahim Stanley Malgwi, in Maiduguri, Borno State, they also kill 2 other members of the sect in order to prevent their hand over to the police by residents of a neighbourhood. Members of the sect shoot and kill Alhaji Muhammed Abdulsalam Abubakar, a Senior Lecturer of Kaduna Polytechnic and a police officer, Salisu Ahmed in the Rigasa area, Kaduna State. |
| April 7, 2012 | Two members of the sect are killed in a gun duel with the Joint Task Force in Maiduguri, Borno State. |

| | |
|---|---|
| April 8, 2012 | The sect kills 40 persons by an explosion in Kaduna. Elsewhere the sect shoots and kills 7 persons in Dikwa, Borno State. Furthermore, the sect shoots and kills 3 persons (including a 7 year old girl) in Potiskum, Yobe State. |
| April 13, 2012 | Members of the sect shooting sporadically kill 5 persons, including a policeman, in Banki, a Nigeria-Cameroun border town in Borno State. |
| April 14, 2012 | The spokesman for the sect; Mohammed Anwal Kontagora Abu Qada II who took over from Abu Qada 1 is reported to be killed on orders of the sect's leader, Abubakar Shekau. He was thought to have tried to deplore the sect.<br>Members of the sect shoot and kill 5 persons in the village of Rim, Plateau State. In addition, 9 persons were injured at northern suburb of Jos, Plateau State by a bomb planted by members of the sect. |
| April 25, 2012 | 2 bomb explosions occur in the 3rd Mechanised Bridge Bukaru Barracks and in Rejiyar Zaki, Kano State. |
| April 26, 2012 | A vehicle laden with explosives crashes into This Day (newspaper) offices, Jabi, Abuja, and Kaduna, Kaduna State, another vehicle laden with explosives crashes in a building where This Day, The Sun and Moment newspapers have there offices in Kano, Kano State. A total of 6 persons are killed. |

| | |
|---|---|
| April 28, 2012 | 5 persons were killed by the sect in Jimeta, Adamawa State. In a separate incident a police inspector is killed in Jimeta. |
| April 29, 2012 | An explosion by a IED in a lecture theatre (used as a Christian worship centre) at the Bayero University kills 16 people (including Professor Leo Ogbonyomi). |
| April 30, 2012 | 11 people are killed in Jalingo, Taraba State, by suicide bombing. |
| June 3, 2012 | Two churches (Living Faith Chuch and Harvest Field Church) destroyed by bombs in Yelwa Tudu, Bauchi State, killing 15 people and injuring 42 people. |
| June 6, 2012 | Bomb explosion outside a night club in Abuja. No casualties. |
| June 7, 2012 | Suicide bomber kills 5 persons at the Command Headquarters in Maiduguri, Borno State. |
| June 10, 2012 | 3 gunmen shoot at a congregation of the Church of the Brethren (killing 14 people) in Biu, northeastern Borno State. Suicide bomber in Jos, Plateau State drives car to the gates of Christ Chosen Church, and detonates bomb killing 10 people and injuring over 50 people. |
| June 17, 2012 | 4 hour curfew imposes in Kaduna due to suicide bombings of three churches (2 in Zaria and 1 in Kaduna) that killed 16 |

|  |  |
|---|---|
|  | people which resulted in reprisal attack by the youth. |
| January 8, 2012 | 6 soldiers and 2 civilians killed in a suicide attack in Damaturu, Yobe State. |
| August 7, 2012 | 17 members of the Deeper Life Church, Okene, Kogi State shot to death. |
| August 15, 2012 | Suicide bomber kills 3 people in Maiduguri. 9 people are killed in a clash between Boko Haram members and imposters of Boko Haram (they were carrying out criminal activities under the guise of Boko Haram). 2 suicide bombers die in Kaduna, Kaduna State when their IED device goes off. No civilian casualties. |
| September 16, 2012 | 9 people shot and killed in Bauchi, Bauchi State. 10 people shot and killed in Gwange Ward, Maiduguri, Borno State. The JTF claimed that they have killed Abu Qaga, in a shoot-out in Kano, Kano State. Qaga is the head of communication of Boko Haram. Boko Haram denies this claim. |
| October 15, 2012 | 15 explosions in Maiduguri, Borno State: a policeman is shot dead. |
| October 28, 2012 | 8 people killed by bomb blast at St. Rita's Catholic, Kaduna, Kaduna State. |
| January 1, 2013 | President Goodluck Jonathan alleged that Boko Haram suspects are arrested. They are behind the bombing of UN building in Abuja; the Police |

|  | Headquarters in Abuja and the St. Theresa's Catholic Church in Madalla, Niger State. |
|---|---|
| January 1, 2013 | The Emir of Kano and his convoy are attacked. 6 people are killed.<br>5 people are killed and 2 others are injured in Dakata, Kano State. |
| January 21, 2013 | 18 people are shot and killed in Damboa, Borno State. |
| January 22, 2013 | 5 people are shot and killed and 2 others are injured in Dakata, Kano State. |
| January 23, 2013 | 5 people are beheaded in Gwange, Borno State. |
| January 27, 2013 | 8 people are shot and killed in Gajiganna village, Borno State. |
| February 8, 2013 | 10 polio immunisation workers are killed and 3 others are injured in Kano, Kano State. |
| February 10, 2013 | 3 North Korean are killed in Potiskum, Yobe State. |
| February 20, 2013 | 2 people are killed by a suicide bomber in Maiduguri, Borno State. |
| March 3, 2013 | Members of Boko Haram attempt to raid the military barrack at Munguno, Borno State. The attempt fails. |
| March 18, 2013 | Bomb explosion at the Kano Central Motor park killing 65 people. |
| March 22, 2013 | 25 people are killed in attacks at the division police station; a prison; a bank and at a beer garden in Ganye, Adamawa State. |

| | |
|---|---|
| March 24, 2013 | 3 secondary schools are burnt down in Biu, Borno State. |
| March 25, 2013 | 1 person shot and killed in Kano State. |
| March 29, 2013 | 37 killed by a bomb explosion at the New Road Motor Park, Kano, Kano State. |
| March 30, 2013 | Attempted jail break by members of the sect at the State Security Service (SSS) headquarters, Abuja. |
| April 21 & 22, 2013 | 185 civilian casualties occur during an engagement between Boko Haram and the JTF, in Baga, Borno State. |
| May 8, 2013 | 42 people (22 policemen, 14 prison officials, 3 children and 2 soldiers) are killed by gunmen in Bama, Borno State. |
| May 14, 2013 | President Goodluck Jonathan declares a state of emergency in Borno, Yobe and Adamawa states. |
| July 6, 2013 | 20 students and a teacher killed at Government Secondary School, Mamudo, Yobe State. |
| July 27, 2013 | Bomb explosion at the Christ Salvation Pentecostal Church, Kano, Kano State, killing 53 people. |
| July 28, 2013 | 16 Christians were handcuffed and burnt to death in a church in Biu, Borno State. |
| July 28, 2013 | 42 members of Boko Haram are arrested in Lagos State by the army. |
| July 29, 2013 | 45 killed by bomb explosions in Sabon-Garri, Kano, Kano State. |

| | |
|---|---|
| August 5, 2013 | 35 people; 2 soldiers and a policeman are killed in clashes between members of Boko Haram and security forces. |
| August 11, 2013 | 44 people are killed in a mosque in Konduga, Borno State. |
| September 8, 2013 | 14 members of the Youth Vigilance Group are shot and killed in Benishiek, Borno State. |
| September 29, 2013 | 40 students are shot and killed at the College of Agriculture, Gujba, Yobe State. |
| December 20, 2013 | Boko Haram insurgents attack the Kuru Mohammed Barracks in Bama, Borno State. Death toll unknown. |
| December 1, 2013 | Boko Haram insurgents destroy 3 aircrafts and 2 air force helicopters in Maiduguri, Borno State. Furthermore, the 33rd Artillery regiment barracks Maiduguri, Borno State is attacked. |
| January 16, 2014 | Car bomb kills 19 people and injuring 40 others in Maiduguri, Borno State. |
| January 16, 2014 | Unknown numbers of people are killed on a shooting spree. In addition, a police station is ransacked whilst a policeman is killed in Banki village, Borno State. |
| January 24, 2014 | 18 people are shot and killed in Njaba and Kaya villages in Borno State. |
| January 27, 2014 | 74 people are killed by gun attacks in Borno and Adamawa States. (22 killed in a Catholic Church in Waga Chakawa village in Adamawa State; 51 civilians |

|  |  |
|---|---|
|  | and 1 policeman in Kawuri, Borno State). |
| February 4 - 5, 2014 | 82 people shot and killed in 3 attacks in Yobe State (20 people); Plateau State (32 people) and Kaduna State (30 people). |
| February 11, 2014 | 51 people are shot and killed, 20 girls are also abducted in Konduga, Borno State. |
| February 15, 2014 | 90 people are shot in Konduga, Borno State. Gunmen kill 106 people in the village of Izghe, Borno State. |
| February 19, 2014 | Suicide attack in Bama, Borno State, casualty figures are unknown |
| February 25, 2014 | 59 students of Federal Government College, Buni Yadi, Yobe State are shot and killed while some are burnt to death. |
| February 26, 2014 | 32 people are shot and killed in the communities of Shuwa, Kirchinga, Kibla and Michika in Adamawa State. |
| March 1, 2014 | Twin bomb blasts occur in Maiduguri, killing 90 people. |
| March 2, 2014 | 32 people are shot and killed in Maja, Borno State. |
| March 3, 2014 | Explosive laden vehicles kill 90 people in Maiduguri, Borno State. |
| March 4, 2014 | 40 people are shot and killed in Jakana, Borno State. |
| March 12, 2014 | 100 people are killed by gunmen in 4 villages in Katsina State. |

| | |
|---|---|
| March 15, 2014 | 100 people killed in Ugwar Sankwai, Ungwar Gata and Chenshyi villages in Southern Kaduna. 60 Boko Haram members attack the Giwa Barracks, Maiduguri; 4 soldiers are wounded with 60 Boko Haram members killed. |
| April 1, 2014 | Explosion kills 21 people during an attempt to bomb the Nigerian National Petroleum Corporation (NNPC) near Maiduguri, Borno State. |
| April 14, 2014 | 75 people killed and over 100 people injured by bomb blast in Nyanya Motor Park, Federal Capital Territory. |
| April 15, 2014 | 234 girls from the Girls Senior Secondary School, Chibok, Borno State are abducted. |

## The Fight against Terror

The National Assembly of the Federal Republic of Nigeria enacted the Terrorism [Prevention] Act, 2011. Nigeria's Terrorism Prevention Act of 2011 The Act was amended in 2013 via Terrorism (Prevention) (Amendment) Act, 2013. Conversely, in November 2013, the U.S. Department of State designated Boko Haram as an official foreign terrorist organisation. This Act provides law enforcers with the authority to detain and prosecute terrorists and also grants judges with judicial procedures for terrorist suspects. The Act grants the law enforcement agents to seal off properties or a vehicle without a search warrant. Crucially, it authorises judges to detain suspects for a period of thirty days, in so far it is in the interest of the public. Furthermore, the Act gives law enforcement agents the authority access to e-mails, phone calls when it is suspected to be contrary to public interests.

The Terrorism (Prevention) Act, 2011 consists of forty-one sections. Section 1 of the Act has the heading "Acts of Terrorism

and Related Offences". Section 1, Subsection 1 defines a terrorist as:
1. A person who knowingly
    (a) Does, attempts or threatens to do an act preparatory to or in furtherance of an act of terrorism;
    (b) Commits and do anything that is reasonably necessary to promote an act of terrorism;
    (c) Assists or facilitates the activities of person engaged in an act of terrorism, commits an offence under this Act.

Specific acts which constitute a terrorist act under the Act include:
(i) An attack upon a person's life which may cause serious bodily harm or death;
(ii) Kidnapping of a person;
(iii) Destruction to a government or public facility, transport system, an infrastructural facility, including an information system, a fixed platform located on the continental shelf, public place or private property likely to endanger human life or result in major economic loss
(iv) The seizure of an aircraft, ship or other means of public or goods transport and diversion or the use of such means of transportation for any of the purposes in paragraph (b) (iv) of this subsection;
(v) The manufacture, possession, acquisition, transport, supply or use of weapons, explosives or of nuclear, biological or chemical weapons, as well as research into, and development of biological and chemical weapons without lawful authority;
(vi) The release of dangerous substance or causing of fire, explosions or floods, the effect of which is to endanger human life;

The signing of this Act, has listed Nigeria as one of the countries that has taken legislative action to confront terrorism. It is necessary to mention that this Act has the propensity to infringe fundamental human rights of terrorist suspects and prisoners. Thus, gross infringements of human rights as experienced by some terrorist suspects/prisoners of USA and the UK are most likely to occur within Nigeria. It may be argued that this Act may be contentious, particularly when dealing with surveillance which in many cases intrudes on the individual's right to privacy, which in turn contravenes Section 37 of the Nigerian Constitution. One is easily reminded that the right to fair hearing and due process of the law was utterly thrown through the window when Muhammad Yusuf was arrested.

## Conclusion

Perhaps, a most discouraging aspect to the psyche of citizenry and of course the common-man is the myriad of security implications of his socio-occupational mobility in the territorial franchise of Nigeria. To be objective and pragmatic, Boko Haram group has succeeded in holding the Nigeria to ransome. To be more emphatic, this pariah group has situated Nigeria as a political parody, not only in Africa, but in the world. It seems that the deeds of death and destruction emanating from radical Islam have put an indelible stain on Nigeria. But the intriguing question remains—why do a vast number of Muslims from North-eastern Nigeria become enslaved to the dark ideology of Boko Haram? Why do some Muslims in this part of Nigeria become engrossed with radical thought and violence? When questions are phrased in this manner, one readily recalls an event—on January 10, 2010, a section of Muslims in Borno State, northeastern Nigeria went on a violent rampage over the sighting of an eclipse of the moon, which is of course a natural occurrence. Moreover, to complicate matters, this marginal number of Muslims blamed the presence of non-Muslims for the sighting the lunar eclipse. For reasons that are observed below, these Muslims imagined that non-Muslims had brought the wrath of God upon their society. At this point and for obvious reasons, non-Muslims became targets of the violence. It should be emphasised that this incident suggests a strong causal explanation and perhaps provides an accurate answer to a great puzzle—that when moderate Muslims are plagued by scurrilous poverty which is blended with mass unenlightenment, wherein if such individuals are religiously influenced and manipulated by religious charlatans, there is a strong tendency that this socio-economic condition would generate radical Islamist thought with its antecedence of violence. One is then reminded of the proverbial caution—'Ignorance breeds fear—fear breeds hate—hate breeds violence,' whilst 'Education breeds confidence—confidence breeds hope—hope breeds peace.' In weighing these opposing perspectives, one is tempted to query a Marxian thought—is religion the opium for the people in northern Nigeria?

# References

## I. Primary sources

Newspapers

The Guardian, (Nigeria)

The Nation Newspaper, (Nigeria)

The Punch Newspaper, (Nigeria)

## II. Secondary Sources

Agbiboa, Daniel, Egiegba. 2013. 'Why Boko Haram Exists: The Relative Deprivation Perspective', *African Conflict & Peacebuilding Review*, Volume 3, Issue 1: 144-157.

Ajami, F., 1993. 'The Summoning', *Foreign Affairs,* Vol. 72, Issue 4, p.2-9.

Anwar, Said T., 1998'Civilisations Versus Civilisations in a New Multipolar World', *Journal of marketing* Vol. 62,No. 2 p. 125-128.

Burke, Jason, 2012. 'Bin Laden files show al-Qaida and Taliban leaders in close contact, accessed on the 17th of November at: http://www.theguardian.com/world/2012/apr/29/bin-laden-al-qaida-taliban-contact

Byman, D., 2005. *Deadly connections. States that Sponsor Terrorism.* New York.

Collier, P and Hoeffler, A., 2004. Greed and Grievance in Civil War (Civil Wars between 1960 and 1999), *Washington DC:* World Bank 78.

Connor, W., 2002.'A Primer for Analyzing Ethnonational Conflict', in Giannakos, S.A. (ed. *Ethnic Conflict: Religion, identity and Politics.* Athens, Ga.: Ohio University Press, pp 21-42.

Connor, W., 1994. *Ethnonationalism: The Quest for Understanding.* Princeton, NJ: Princeton University Press.

Dawkins, R., 2006. *The God Delusion.* London: Bantam Press.

Girard, R., 1977. *Violence and the Sacred,* Translated by Patrick Gregory, John Hopkins University Press.

Gopin, M., 2000. *Between Eden and Armageddon: The Future of World Religions, Violence and Peacemaking.* Oxford: Oxford University Press.

Gurr, Ted R, 1970. *Why Men Rebel.* Princeton, N.J., Published for the Center of International Studies, Princeton: University Princeton University Press.

Hailbrunn, J., 1998. 'The Clash of Samuel Huntingtons', *The American Prospect* Vol. 39 p.22-28.

Hessner, P., 1997. 'Morally Objectionable, Politically Dangerous', *The National Interest,* Issue. 46: 63-69.

Hood, R. W., Hill, P. C., & Williamson, W. P., 2005. *The Psychology of Religious Fundamentalism.* New York: Guilford.

Huntington, Samuel P., 1993. The Clash of Civilizations? *Foreign Affairs* 72 (3): 22–49.

Jalingo, Ahmadu U., 1981. *The Radical Tradition in Northern Nigeria.* Unpublished Ph.D Thesis, University of Edinburgh.

Juergensmeyer, Mark, 1991. 'Sacrifice and Cosmic War', *Terrorism and Political Violence* Vol 3 Issue3, p101 – 117.

Juergensmeyer, Mark, 1993.*The New Cold War? Religious Nationalism Confronts the Secular State.* Berkeley: University of California Press.

Kakar, Sudhir, 1996. *The Colors of Violence.* The University of Chicago Press.

Kaufmann, E. & Zimmer, O., 2004. 'Dominant Ethnicity' and the Ethnic-Civic' Dichotomy in the Work of A.D. Smith', *Nations and Nationalism,* 10 (1/2) 63-78.

Mcgrath, A. & McGrath, Joanna C., 2007.*The Dawkins Delusion? Atheist Fundamentalism and the Denial of the Divine*. London: SPCK.

Misra, A., 2008.*Politics of Civil Wars: Conflict, Intervention and Resolution*. London & New York: Routledge.

Nelson-Pallmeyer, J., 2003, *Is Religion Killing Us? Violence in the Bible and the Quran*.Harrisburg, Pa.: Trinity Press International.

Olomojobi Yinka, 2013: *Islam and Conflict in norther Nigeria*. Lagos: Malthouse Press.

Osumah, Oarhe, 2013. 'Boko Haram insurgency in Northern Nigeria and the vicious cycle of internal insecurity', *Small Wars & Insurgencies,* Vol. 24, Issue 3, 536-560.

Pearlstein, Richard M., 2004. *Fatal Future? Transnational Terrorism and the New Global Disorder*. University of Texas Press.

Riesebrodt, M., 2000. 'Fundamentalism and the Resurgence of Religion', *Numen* Vol 47, No 3, Religion in the Disenchanted World, 266-287.

Sanusi, L. S., 'Religion, the Cabinet and a Political Economy of the 'North'', accessed on the 10th of March 2007 at: http://www.nigerdeltacongress.com/rarticles/religion1.htm.

Smith, Anthony D., 1991. *National Identity*. London: Penguin.

Smith, Anthony D. 2000. 'The Sacred Dimension of Nationalism', *Millennium* 29(3): 791–814.

Stern, Jessica, 2003. *Terror in the Name of God: Why Religious Kilitants Kill*. New York: Ecco.

Spilka, B.; Hood Jr., W. R., Hunsberger, B. & Gorsuch, R., 2003. *The Psychology of Religion: An Empirical Approach*. Third Edition, New York: The Guilford Press.

# 9

# Ansaru: Brother-in-Arms with Boko Haram

## Introduction

Ansaru, otherwise known as J*amaatu Ansarul Muslimina Fi Biladissudan*, (the Vanguard for the Aid of Muslims in Black Africa) is a splinter group of Boko Haram. The group's motto is "Jihâd Fi Sabilillah," meaning; fighting for Allah's cause. It is also a new emerging radical Islamist group emanating from northern Nigeria. The group was formed in 2012. During the commencement of the group, Ansaru informed the public by distributing pamphlets in Kano, Kano State that: "We will have a dispassionate look into everything, to encourage what is good and see to its spread and to discourage evil and try to eliminate it."[170] They also claimed that the activities of Boko Haram were "inhuman to the Muslim *Umma* [nation]."[171] Ansaru, a splinter group from the dreaded Boko Haram sect employs different tactics from the *modus operandi* of the Boko Haram in certain

---
170  Chothia, Farouk 2013, March 11 'Profile: Who are Nigeria's Ansaru Islamists?' assessed on the 22nd of May 2014 at: http://www.bbc.com/news/world-africa-21510767.
171  Ibid. Ansaru claimed that the loss 150 Muslim civilians (reported as 185 deaths in chapter 5) in a Kano bomb attack on 20th January 2012, by Boko Haram was "loss of innocent Muslim lives."

respects. They restrict their attacks to mainly hard targets and adhere to strict rules of engagement concerning non-combatants (Onuoha, 2013). Furthermore, Ansaru, through its leader, al-Barnawi, commented that the essence of the group is to "restore dignity and sanity to the lost dignity of Muslims in black Africa and to bring back the dignity of Islam in Nigeria and the Sokoto Caliphate."[172]

Ansaru is based on the precepts of Salafi jihâdism. This terminology was first used by Gilles Kepel and Kamil al-Tawil.[173] This term has varied conceptual interpretations. However, it is simply based on the conviction that terrorist activities are a useful mechanism to acquire political goals. This doctrine is known as *al-takfir wa-l-hijra (takfiri)*, a term coined to denote rebellious groups in the Middle East. They perceive that Islam is in a state of losing its doctrinal purity and its philosophical and theological interpretation of the Qur'an and the hadith and the teachings of Prophet Muhammad. Most important, is that they perceive that Muslims are being oppressed by Westernised institutions. Hence, to Salafists, there is a serious clarion call for all Muslims to endeavour to seek to change their society to a purist form of Islam, the quest for Sharia law and to seek a global caliphate. Crucially, this prehensile mandate to this movement can only be achieved by jihâd.

## Ansaru's grievance

The major grievance which led to the formation of jihâdist group Ansaru was for the reason that they viewed the activities of Boko Haram as inhuman to the *ummah*. Shekau reportedly favoured ethnic Kanuris of Borno and this drove other groups such as Hausas, non-Nigerians and

---

[172] 'Rift in Boko Haram, 'Ansaru' Splinter Group Emerges, Calls BH 'Inhuman' To Muslims,' accessed on the 23rd of May at:http://saharareporters.tumblr.com/post/16824744293/rift-in-boko-haram-ansaru-splinter-group-emerges.

[173] Kamil al-Tawil, al-Haraka al-islamiyya al-musallaha fi-l-Jaza'ir [The Armed Islamic Movement in Algeria], Beirut: Dar al-Nahar, 1998, p.60 and Gilles Kepel, 'Le GIA à travers ses publications', Pouvoirs vol.86 (1998), pp.70–1.

other non-Kanuris to ally with Mamman Nur, who was also non-Nigerian.[174] Shekau, however, ordered the 'death penalty' for anyone who did not follow his orders and killed defectors.[175] This may have been the origin of the split between Boko Haram and Ansaru in 2012.

Predictably, the leadership of Ansaru perceived that Muslims were being threatened by external forces, such as Western powers and by internal forces such as the perceived threats of non-Muslims in Nigeria and the killing of Muslims by co-religionists. Furthermore, they perceived that Western economic policies are exploiting Islamic societies. Its message appeared to promote the ideology of Islam, which means 'peace.' The irony of this is that the group specialises in kidnappings, abductions and killings of citizens of Western states. The groups' main grievance is the perceived interference of western states in Muslim territories.[176] The group has links with al-Qaeda in the Islamic Maghreb (AQIM),[177] which also specialises in the kidnapping of individuals. The group operates in and around Kano, Kano State in north-central Nigeria, it is active in other parts of northern Nigeria, Niger and Cameroon.

## Leadership

The leader of the group is Khalid al-Barnawi, aka Abu Usamatul al-Ansari. Al-Barnawi hails from Borno State. He is a skilled fighter, having been trained by AQIM in Algeria. He is also included as one of the three terrorists (including Abubakar Adam Kambar[178] and Abubakar Muhammad Shekau) who are labelled as 'global terrorists' by the US State Department. Al-Barnawi is known to have

---

174 Zenn, J. 2014. 'Leadership Analysis of Boko Haram and Ansaru in Nigeria', assessed on the 7th of September 2014 at: https://www.ctc.usma.edu/posts/leadership-analysis-of-boko-haram-and-ansaru-in-nigeria
175 Ibid
176 On November 14, 2013, Ansaru was sectioned as Foreign Terrorist Organizations (FTO) by the United States Department of State.
177 Formerly called the Salafist Group for Preaching and Combat (GSPC) renamed AQIM in 2007.
178 Kambar is speculated to have been killed in a raid by Nigerian forces at his home residence in Kano on August, 2012.

connections with other radical groups around sub-Saharan Africa. Zenn (2014) suggests that al-Barnawi employed the expertise of these radical groups in successfully carrying out the bombing of the Nigerian Police Force headquarters located in Abuja. According to Jacob Zenn (2014:2): [179]

> *The Abuja attack was recorded as the first suicide bombing in Nigeria's history. Credit for the attack was claimed by the Boko Haram in league with other actors. The attack also was similar to the attack on the UN building as the same tactics were employed. Kabiru Sokoto and Habibu Bama were also alleged to have had knowledge of the attacks. A Boko Haram spokesman who forewarned the Nigerian public and security agencies a day before the attack said that 'brothers who arrived from Somalia, possibly referring to Nur, would launch 'fierce' attacks in Abuja.*

Al-Barnawi is a close associate of Mokhtar Belmokhtar (leader of Al-Mourabitoun and a former chieftain within AQIM). Belmokhtar is the Islamist who masterminded the January 2013 Amenas hostage crisis, where over eight hundred people were taken as hostages at the Tigantourine gas facility near Amenas, Algeria, where thirty-nine hostages were executed and twenty-nine members of AQIM were killed by Algerian forces. Mokhtar Belmokhtar is reported to have trained al-Barnawi.[180] Both al-Barnawi and Belmokhtar were criminals who smuggled cigarettes and cocaine together into Algeria.[181] Indeed, to make the case for a fair argument, it is perhaps clear that both al-Barnawi and Belmokhtar are rogues who have turned jihâdist in an attempt to use Islam as a fog for criminal activities. Another lieutenant of the group is Abu Muhammed, who was trained by al-

---

[179] Zenn J. 2014 'Leadership analysis of Boko Haram and Ansaru in Nigeria', accessed on 24 September 2014 at: https://www.ctc.usma.edu/v2/wp-content/uploads/2014/02/CTCSentinel-Vol7Iss2.pdf last accessed 24 September 2014.

[180] Bey, Matthew and Tack, Sim. 2013, February 21 'The Rise of a New Nigerian Militant Group.' Assessed on the 22nd of May 2014 at: http://www.stratfor.com/weekly/rise-new-nigerian-militant-group

[181] Zenn, J. 2014 January 20.' 'Nigerians in Gao: was Boko Haram really active in Northern Mali?' assessed on the 22nd of May 2014 at: http://www.ctc.usma.edu/posts/cooperation-or-competition-boko-haram-and-ansaru-after-the-mali-intervention.

Barnawi at an AQIM camp in Algeria.[182] Abu Muhammed was arrested in Kaduna on January 26, 2012, after the botched attempt to save an abducted German national. U.S. representative, Mike Rodgers, in an interview with the CNN, made the following statement about Belmoktar and Jihâdist groups in Africa:

*When you look at Mokthar Belmokthar, he clearly has the capability to put operatives outside the Algerian, Malian, Libyan area. He travelled and trained in Afghanistan and Pakistan, he has the ability to get operatives from that region and the intelligence community supports that as well and that makes it a threat and something you have to absolutely take seriously...the taking of the gas facility was a huge success. These different groups are working together in ways we haven't seen before, gaining popularity, gaining in capability...victories and capabilities, going beyond these borders...experienced jihadists now have access to Al-Qaeda core technology, IEDs and suicide bombers that they didn't employ in the past, they now have married their technologies with these capabilities and that's so concerning and its happening at a very rapid pace.*[183]

## Jihâdist activities

Ansaru is a well trained and efficient group. This is evident from the methods of attacks, especially within the area of abductions. Perhaps, its efficiency surpasses the once dreaded Niger-Delta militants for the reason that they use a religious ideology as a front to commit terrorist attacks, whilst the Niger-Delta militants were grieved mainly on economic reasons. An infamous abduction in May, 2011 of a British (Chris McManus) and an Italian (Franco Lamolinara) working

---

182 Zenn, J. 2013, March 27.' Cooperation or Competition: Boko Haram and Ansaru After the Mali Intervention', assessed on the 22nd of May 2014 at: http://www.ctc.usma.edu/posts/cooperation-or-competition-boko-haram-and-ansaru-after-the-mali-intervention.

183 CNN (2013) Rep Mike Rogers talking about the coordination between Al Qaeda and AQIM in North Africa CNN. Accessed on the 22nd of September 2014 at: https://www.youtube.com/watch?v=fDNdQlvBBMs 8 February 2013

at a construction company called Stabilini Visinoni Limited in kebbi State brought Ansaru to limelight. However, both abductees were killed on 8 March, 2012, in a botched attempt to rescue them by a joint coordinated response by British and Nigerian forces under the request of the British Prime Minister, David Cameron. In another incident, in December 2012, Ansaru abducted a French engineer, Francis Colump in the town of Rimi, Katsina State. Ansaru claimed responsibility for the kidnapping. However, Colump escaped from captivity in November 2013.

In another event, a forty-two year old French Catholic priest, Georges Vandenbeusch was abducted on November 13, 2013 in northern Cameroon. However, the combined efforts of Cameroonian and Nigerian governments secured the priest's release from captivity. The rationale for this abduction, according to the group, was pertaining to its grievance over France's intervention in Mali against Islamic rebels who attempted to secede in Mali's northern region. In addition, the group had a perceived grievance over France's decision to ban the wearing of the veil/hijab (wearing of face-covering headgear) on the 11th of April, 2011. In January 2013, the group also killed two Nigerian soldiers in Kogi State who were heading to Mali for deployment. It seems probable, that grievance emanates within radical Islamists when there is some form of military interference in Muslim territories. This is evident from the ideological position of al-Qaeda committing the 9/11 atrocities due to grievance over influence of Western states in Saudi Arabia and its support of Israel over an Islamic territory (Palestine). Later, during the year in May 2012, the radical group in Kaduna, Kaduna State had gunmen kill a Lebanese and a Nigerian construction worker, whilst abducting a Lebanese worker. At a different location (Kano, Kano State), members of the group on January 26, 2012 killed a German hostage during a botched rescue mission by German special operations forces. AQIM admitted they kidnapped the German for the reason that Germany should set free a Turkish-born female jihâdist whose German husband was arrested in 2007 for attempting to bomb Ramstein Air Base.[184] In February 2013, the group attacked a police station in Jama'are in Bauchi State. After this incident, members of the group thereafter proceeded to a construction and civil engineering company called Setraco. Ansaru killed a security guard and kidnapped seven foreign workers (one British, one Greek, one Italian and four Lebanese). The group vehemently warned that: "We announced the capture of seven Christian foreigners and warned that should there be any attempt by force to rescue them will render their lives in danger."[185] The hostages were killed on March 2013.

## Between Ansaru and Boko Haram

It would be absurd to claim that there is no connection between Ansaru and Boko Haram. It is important to note that the main difference of ideology between Ansaru and Boko Haram is that Ansaru has a global agenda co-opting an international jihâd. The group is an undifferentiated and homogeneous element from al-Qaeda in its quest for a global jihâd. Ansaru's grievance is centred on the interference of the West in African states that have a majority Muslim population. The ideology of Ansaru falls within the overarching ambition of al-Qaeda. Boko Haram on the other hand is desirous of achieving a political agenda of constructing Nigeria into an Islamic state. This desire is seemingly similar with the aspiration of the Taliban in Afghanistan. The Taliban ruled Afghanistan as an Islamic Emirate from September 1996 until December 2001.

The differences in target setting is easily observed in the abduction of foreigners by Ansaru which is contrasted with Boko Haram with the targeting of nationals, the security

---

184 Zenn, J. 2013, March 27.' Cooperation or Competition: Boko Haram and Ansaru After the Mali Intervention', accessed on the 22nd of May 2014 at: http://www.ctc.usma.edu/posts/cooperation-or-competition-boko-haram-and-ansaru-after-the-mali-intervention

185 'Nigerian Islamists Ansaru 'kill 7 foreign hostages', accessed on the 23rd of May 2014 at: http://www.france24.com/en/20130309-nigeria-islamists-ansaru-kill-foreign-hostages/

offices and government institutions. However, it seems that Boko Haram is now using Ansaru's strategy of abduction. The abductions of over 200 secondary school girls in Chibok, Borno State could be used as a case in point. The point to bear in mind is that it seems that Boko Haram and Ansaru are working in partnership. This is given the fact that kidnapping is not a usual operational technique of Boko Haram. Boko Haram started its kidnapping operations on February 19, 2013, when they kidnapped seven family members (Moulin - Fournier family) near a tourist park in Dabanga, northern Cameroun. These people were later transferred to Borno State. Shekau alluded that his group kidnapped the victims due to the fact that the Nigerian and Cameroonian government took into custody the wives and children of members of the group. Again, on May, 2013, Boko Haram raided a police station in Bama, Borno State and abducted twelve persons (women and children). The victims were later released after undisclosed negotiations. From these events, it is suggested that Boko Haram is in affiliation with Ansaru, due to the formers experience in abduction which was acquired by fraternising with AQIM and the 'Movement for Oneness and Jihâd in West Africa' (MUJAO) a splinter group emanating from AQIM. Another observation is that both radical groups have transnational capacities.

A potential observation from the foregoing is that Boko Haram targets specific locations, such as police stations, churches or army posts, however, Ansaru targets specific individual(s), such as foreigners. Another crucial observation is that Ansaru does not use suicide bombing, unlike Boko Haram. Notwithstanding these differences, it seems that the groups are laden with grievance towards the Nigerian state. It is suggested that poverty is the main driving force of these groups. There is a wide gap between the rich and the poor in the northern region. The attraction for young men to be members of these groups in order to escape the dearth of poverty and hopelessness is a strong force that binds these groups together. Although distinct in their range of objectives, it seems that Ansaru and Boko Haram are helping each other in target setting and in carrying out terrorist activities. This is probably imminent for the reason that, members of each group are likely to criss-cross when there are animosities within the group. The contextual implication of criss-crossing is that strategic ideas and methods would be transferred among the groups. This is illustrated in November 2012, when Ansaru raided the Special Anti-Robbery Squad (SARS) headquarters in Abuja, the capital of Nigeria. During the raid, they killed police officers and freed jailed terrorists. Ansaru claimed they freed thirty-seven members of the group and 286 other prisoners[186] who were members of Boko Haram. Shekau applauded Ansaru Islamists as "Soldiers of God in the Islamic State of Mali… our brothers and sheikhs in the Islamic Maghreb."[187] The raid set free the wife of Kabiru Sokoto (a Boko Haram chieftain), the culprit behind the Christmas Day church bombings outside of Abuja in December 2011 which killed over twenty people. The reader may now intuit that this raid presupposes the connectivity between the two groups. The significance of this argument is found in the speculation that there are strong indications that Ansaru assisted Boko Haram in the kidnapping of over 200 secondary school girls in Chibok, Borno State.[188]

Another element to this is that both groups may not only cooperate and collaborate, but also compete for relevance by promulgating extreme terrorist activities in order to

---

[186] Jamestown Foundation. 2013, January, 10. 'Ansaru: A Profile of Nigeria's Newest Jihâdist Movement', accessed on the 22nd of May 204 at: http://www.refworld.org/docid/50f69aaf2.html

[187] Zenn, J. 2014 January 20.' Nigerians in Gao: was Boko Haram really active in Northern Mali? accessed on the 22nd of May 2014 at: http://www.ctc.usma.edu/posts/cooperation-or-competition-boko-haram-and-ansaru-after-the-mali-intervention

[188] See 'Ansaru Fear Grips Nigeria Military; Chibok Girls Rescue Mission Threatened', accessed on the 29th of May at: http://www.spyghana.com/ansaru-fear-grips-nigeria-military-chibok-girls-rescue-mission-threatened/

gain notoriety. This development would further inclement Islamic terrorism, not only to Nigeria in particular, but broadly speaking, to other African states and the Western world. It is worthy to note that Sekau has warned that Boko Haram would attack Cameroun if the state interferes with its operations.[189] Crucially, it is likely to threaten foreign investment flowing into Nigeria. Perhaps, more crucial is that it may situate Nigeria into an abysmal state.

## Conclusion

Based on the depletion of Ansaru's sahelian network, and a crackdown on Boko Haram forces, it is strongly suggested that both groups are now confederates. This is for the reason that Ansaru has not been actively invoved in terrorist activities since 2013. Be that as it may, one must state that although there is no evidence on where one can hang his hat on, it seems most probable that there has been a union between the two groups, as there has been incessant bombings in Kano State. On 19 May, 2014, a bomb exploded at a bar in the Sabon Gari district of Kano, killing four people. An even more disastrous act occurred on 28 November, 2014, where two-hundred people were killed by sporadic gunfire and a bomb at the Central Mosque (Grand Mosque) in Kano, Kano State. It is observed that Boko Haram's main enclave is in the northeastern part Nigeria. It then seems most probable that Ansaru whose main hub is in Kano has renuited with Boko Haram.

It should be noted that the construction of how Muslims view their society is influenced by their faith. One must reiterate that Islam in northern Nigeria is a strong identity marker. The reoccurring variable of extreme poverty in northern Nigeria and the repentant approach to prebendalism in Nigeria in general has once again succeeded in creating

---

189  Zenn, J. 2013, March 27.' Cooperation or Competition: Boko Haram and Ansaru After the Mali Intervention.' Assessed on the 22nd of May 2014 at: http://www.ctc.usma.edu/posts/cooperation-or-competition-boko-haram-and-ansaru-after-the-mali-intervention

another radical Islamic group. Henrik Persson (2014:15) adequately captures the improvisation in northern Nigeria:

> *In Nigeria, marginalisation is frequently used in the political discourse and it is commonly stated that there is a significant divide regarding socio-economic development between the North and the South. While there are also other major differences within these regions, the underdevelopment of the largely Muslim Northern Nigeria is commonly seen as one of the root causes of militant Islamism in the area.*

It appears that Ansaru will continue to be the brother in arms with Boko Haram as long as northern Nigeria remains in a penury state. On a broader perspective, Nigeria and its sub-Saharan neighbours are most likely to be adversely affected in terms of regional security. Western institutions are prone to be threatened by al-Qaeda ideologies. More significant is the fact that there exists the likelihood of the emergence of al-Qaeda and other Islamist Movements' (AQIM) related groups in northern Nigeria. The logic behind this thought is that Islam is a basis of an overarching solidarity and unity amongst Muslims in northern Nigeria. Moreover, Islamic identity in the region is a credible factor for engendering group formations. Therefore, Islam has the potential to be used as a mechanism for political mobilisation, a fog for conflict and a ruse by Islamists to provoke radical Islam.

# References

Bey, Matthew and Tack, Sim. 2013, February 21 'The Rise of a New Nigerian Militant Group.' Assessed on the 22nd of May 2014 at: http://www.stratfor.com/weekly/rise-new-nigerian-militant-group.

Chothia, Farouk 2013, March 11 'Profile: Who are Nigeria's Ansaru Islamists?' assessed on the 22nd of May 2014 at: http://www.bbc.com/news/world-africa-21510767.

Kamil al-Tawil, 1998. al-Haraka al-islamiyya al-musallaha fi-l-Jaza'ir [The Armed Islamic Movement in Algeria], Beirut: Dar al-Nahar.

Gilles Kepel, 1998. 'Le GIA à travers ses publications', Pouvoirs vol.86:7

Jamestown Foundation. 2013, January, 10. 'Ansaru: A Profile of Nigeria's Newest Jihâdist Movement,' assessed on the 22nd of May 204 at: http://www.refworld.org/docid/50f69aaf2.html.

Onuoha F. 2013. *'Jama'atu Ansarul Musilimina Fi Biladis Sudan:* Nigeria's Evolving Militant Group', assessed on the 5th of August 2014 at: http://studies.aljazeera.net/ResourceGallery/media/Documents/2013/4/4/201344122625659580JAMBS.pdf

Zenn, J. 2014 January 20. 'Nigerians in Gao: was Boko Haram really active in Northern Mali?', assessed on the 22nd of May 2014 at: http://www.ctc.usma.edu/posts/cooperation-or-competition-boko-haram-and-ansaru-after-the-mali-intervention.

Zenn, J. 2013, March 27.' Cooperation or Competition: Boko Haram and Ansaru After the Mali Intervention', assessed on the 22nd of May 2014 at: http://www.ctc.usma.edu/posts/cooperation-or-competition-boko-haram-and-ansaru-after-the-mali-intervention.

# 10

# Radical Islam and e-Terrorism

**Introduction**

The Internet consists of a wide range of activities. The swift changes in technology and the world's shrinking geographical space has ushered a rapid change in terrorist activities. The days of indoctrinating Muslims in the mosques to become radicalised are over. Personalised methods of radicalisation are obsolete as the social media now acts as the recruiting agent (Torok, 2013). In today's world, the Internet has become a critical function in the strategy of Islamists. In many ways, the Internet has become the propagandist tool of Islamists as it has the tendency to mobilise moderate Muslims and non-Muslims to be converted into radicalised elements. Given this activity, radical Muslims are using the Internet as a weapon for commiting acts of carnage.

Globalisation has improved economic interdependence between states, and at the same time it has relegated economic development in some states. The emerging influence of the Internet has also augmented communication among individuals, groups and governments. The uploading and downloading of literarily any kind of information is the modern foundation of the advanced world. In an age of growing inequality, the Internet has not just made the world a smaller place— it has most crucially made the world into an advanced age. Moreover, the Internet has not only put the world into a global village, but into a global family. Aside from making the world a smaller place, the Internet has situated the Muslim community into a 'virtual *umma*' (Roy, 2004: 180). Perhaps, with this in mind, Weimann (2011: 768-769) tells us that:

> *Postmodern terrorists are taking advantage of the fruits of globalisation and modern technology—especially the most advanced communication technologies—to communicate, seduce, plan, and coordinate their deadly campaigns. In 1998, less than half of the organisations designated as Foreign Terrorist Organisations by the U.S. State Department maintained websites; by the end of 1999, nearly all these terrorist groups had established their presence on the Net. By now, all active terrorist groups have established at least one form of presence on the Internet and most of them are using all formats of up-to-date online platforms—e-mail, chatrooms, e-groups, forums, virtual message boards, and resources like YouTube, Facebook, Twitter, and Google Earth.*

This extract reveals to us the explanation on how radical Islamic groups in Africa are able to effectively plan and execute its crusade of terror, death and destruction. This could, in theory explicate 'how' ánd 'why' security personnel find it difficult curtail terrorism.

### E-Terrorism: An asymmetric warfare?

Hezbollah and Hamas are prominent radical groups that have exploited the use of the media, through the Internet. These groups use the Internet to preach their radical ideology and political ideologies to generate support from potential followers. These groups communicate via the Internet for the purposes of obtaining acquaintance with unseen faces, accessing collective communication through virtual classrooms, preparation and implementing terrorists' activities. The Internet is the main strategic network for communication and logistics for terrorist groups and their tangle of jihâdist networks.

E-terrorism is a complex term as it comprises both computer and cyber crimes. Before delving further, the reader may want to understand what the differences between cyber-crime, cyber-warfare and cyber-terrorism are. It seems that holistically, they are all interlinked and mean the same thing. Thus, these labels would be used interchangeably. The complexity surrounding the use of the Internet is that it could be used for varied purposes. It could be used as a form of defence against the enemy during war; in this sense, it is not considered a crime by the users of such technology. It is important to note that websites termed as terrorist may be conceived by the host of such sites as depicting U.S war crimes in Islamic states.[190] Conversely, it is considered as a terrorist plot, when such activity is used to procure or assist terrorist activities. Furthermore, it could be used to network and encourage political support for marginalised groups, such as women (Dartnell, 2003). E-terrorism is considered as a new frontier of terrorist behaviour due to the Internet's function as an information super-highway. However, the use of the computer for warfare is not a new concept. It started during the Second World War, when the British invented a commuter to intercept German communications.

Computer terrorism could be in the form of hacking, disruption of information and attacking computer networks in order to commit a terrorist activity. Cyber terrorism on the other hand is:

> *A criminal act perpetrated by the use of computers and telecommunications capabilities, resulting in*

---

[190] Websites such as http://www.albasrah.net/index.php portray U.S crimes in Iraq

*violence, destruction and/or disruption of services to create fear by causing confusion and uncertainty within a given population, with the goal of influencing a government or population to conform to particular political, social or ideological agenda.*[191]

E-terrorism in the context of Islamist terrorist groups is an inert phenomenon in terms of scholarly research for the reason that it is usually unnoticed in terms of planning and execution of terrorist activities—Internet users are usually unidentified. The Internet is not within the realm of the real world—the social media is an overlooked aspect of terrorism. Through the Internet, extremist messages can act as a stimulant for people to become radicalised (Silber and Bhatt, 2007). Scholarly literature on e-terrorism usually analyses the content of the online propaganda of Islamist groups. There is little evidence that tells us how many individuals are being swayed by the content of the message. In other words—who are the recipients of these messages? Who are the audience for terrorists on the internet? How do we profile individuals who may likely become the end products of Islamist online propaganda? How do individuals become socially glued to jihâdist messages on the Internet? An overlooked area of research is that the Internet can be used as an influence for generating hatred towards Muslims—it can create sentiments of Islamophobia, especially in Western societies. Geert Wilders, a politician from Netherlands has stirred hatred against Muslims through the social media. Wilders has on numerous occasions posted messages of hate towards Islam on YouTube and twitter (Blanquart, and Cook, 2013). Surprisingly, Wilders escaped being convicted on charges of disseminating hate on the defence of freedom of speech. It may be argued that the posting of Islamophobia messages over the Internet can generate a response by moderate Muslims to begin a journey towards becoming radicalised.

---

191   'The U.S. National Infrastructure Protection Center', accessed on the 12th of November 2014 at: http://www.nipc.gov/publications/highlights/2001/highlight-01-06.htm

Amble (2012: 342) reveals that the Internet has greatly enhanced the terrorists' activities in propaganda, conscription, training, operation and logistics. The vast availability of the Internet is that there is a heightened probability that individuals may become recruited and radicalised (Thompson, 2011). E-terrorism is a strong force for achieving self radicalisation and recruitment of Muslims. Terrorism via the Internet welcomes the disenchanted and aggrieved Muslim who wants to be connected with finding hope and purpose in his/her society. The power of the Internet is evident by the use of social media as it could be used to reach out to individuals and create followership (Thompson, 2011). Thus, "no longer are there six degrees of separation between people. Social media provides one degree of separation between people" (Thompson, 2011:170). If these events reveal the influence of the Internet, then e-terrorism has the predilection to cause havoc to state governments in Africa.

The need for reaching out for succour and to have a listening ear to perceived grievances builds an aura of support and friendship for the potential radical Muslim. A crucial aspect of e-terrorism is that radical Islamist groups can use the Internet to propagate propaganda and manipulate individuals by showcasing their grievances and justifying their terrorists' activities. Brown and Korff (2009:121) note that:

*Terrorist websites make strong efforts to increase public sympathy for their cause and sow doubts about the validity of the status quo. The Internet is an ideal propaganda tool and most extremist groups therefore have a Web presence. Sites are cheap to produce while looking professional, adding validity and legitimacy to a cause.*

Aside from building acquaintances, the Internet has the propensity to become highly addictive (Blog, 2010). The obsession of the Internet has the same effect as the fixation to e-terrorism. The infatuation over jihâdi messages can generate moderate Muslims and non-Muslims to fantasise about killing in the name of God. In addition, solidarity Internet sites could be used as a conveyor of 'sympathetic' and 'militant' messages to moderate individuals. The distorting and manipulating of the Qur'an is usually a strategy for publishing propaganda. An important factor in e-terrorism is to gather both domestic and international support. Aside from this, a more crucial aspect is that the Internet can be used as a recruiting agent for terrorists groups. It is then not surprising that:

> *Terrorists have good reasons to use social media. First, these channels are by far the most popular with their intended audience, which allows terrorist organisations to be part of the mainstream. Second, social media channels are user-friendly, reliable, and free. Finally, social networking allows terrorists to reach out to their target audiences and virtually "knock on their doors" — in contrast to older models of websites in which terrorists had to wait for visitors to come to them* (Weimann, 2014: 3).

Recently, there has been a great usage of the Internet by radical Islamist groups. The advantage of the Internet is that it sends information at a fast and inexpensive rate. Benson (2014: 298) notes that terrorism and the Internet are based:

> *On three primary characteristics of the Internet — anonymity, abundance of information, and cheapness of communication — that works through two mechanisms to increase transnational terrorist operational capacity: increased networking and increased capability.*

Before delving further, e-terrorism is not exclusive to Islamists, it embraces violent extremists such as Neo-Nazi groups, right-wing extremism, and criminal gangs. An important aspect of the Internet is that widespread communication can be shared and networked to a vast number of people (Walker, 2009).

Furthermore, the messages can be encrypted and the messages and Islamists websites can be hidden under different Internet providers' addresses. It is common for Islamist groups to communicate and seek donations through the Internet via emails. Some websites state in their forums that 'violence is the way of jihâd', whilst other websites could be understated in the sense that they may begin with Islamic truths, such as restating the five pillars of Islam before introducing their grievances or to 'develop a sense of persecution' (Brown & Korff, 2009:122). Janbek (2011: 12) informs us that:

> *Tawhid and Jihad Forum's call reads: 'To fight tyrants and their supporters, the Jews and the crusaders to free Muslims from their homes and families and under occupation,' and goes on to say it is 'Fighting those who don't believe in God and those who disobeyed God, as needed.*

Thereafter, these forums introduce violent methods for eliminating grievances of the audience. Brown and Korff (2009:121) reveals that new recruits enlisted as Islamist terrorist are 'armchair jihâdis', who at some point are contacted by an ideologue (an 'international dating service') whose role is to radicalise the 'armchair jihâdis'. After this process, they are transferred to an operational leader, who offers strategic training in specific skills (Brown and Korff, 2009:121).

E-terrorism can serve as virtual classrooms offering technical information on training tools in manufacturing bombs and other weapons for urban warfare. A crucial aspect of training provided by Islamists on the Internet is the use of instructional suicide bomber videos. This makes the avenue for recruiters to seek for vulnerable youth on social media. It could even relate to mundane issues such as cutting the power of an organisation, disabling phone connections in order to benefit a terrorist group and hacking computer networks. It also involves the observation of Internet traffic and intrusion of an individual(s) privacy—'big brother is watching you'. Since the Internet revolution procured by Web 2.0 sites, new interactive mediums have allowed jihâdists and their potential recruits to work together as groups in order to share information. Web 2.0 has also engineered social networking sites: Facebook, YouTube, Twitter and mobile technology help to create friends and increase the exchange of communication across the globe. Perhaps a crucial feature is that e-terrorism has the propensity to generate individual(s) to become self-radicalised. Even more crucial is the fact that this phenomenon has the tendency to generate home grown terrorism and lone wolves—On October 23, 2014, Zale Thompson, thirty-two years old, a graduate student at Teachers College, Colombia University, USA, a self radicalised man attempted to murder two New York Police Division (NYPD) officers with an axe. The point? Thompson became radicalised by frequently visiting websites of jihâdists devoted to al-Qaeda and the Islamic State (ISIS).

## E-Terrorism and free speech

It has been argued that the Internet is not a human right (Skepys, 2012). However, the General Assembly of the United Nations report[192] notes that access to the Internet is a human right— "Given that the Internet has become an indispensable tool for realising a range of human rights, combating inequality, and accelerating development and human progress, ensuring universal access to the Internet should be a priority for all states..."[193] Online freedom is the liberation of information as a crucial element in the globalised world. Internet freedom implies freedom of

---
192  A/HRC/17/27
193  See 'United Nations report: Internet access is a human right', accessed on the 4th of January 2015 at: http://techland.time.com/2011/06/07/united-nations-report-declares-internet-access-a-human-right/

opinion and expression (free speech) which is outside the dormain of state jurisdiction. Most crucial, it implies that any speech whatsoever should be protected on the basis of originality. Online freedom is intrinsically connected with the freedom of association and assembly—this entails the freedom to interconnect with individuals through social networking. However, it could be argued that the freedom of association and assembly connotes people in direct contact as opposed to virtual connectivity with each other. With this protection, the Internet has made it easier for individuals to disseminate their ideology of hate, violence and terrorism. Even where a terrorist website is shut down, there is the daunting challenge of prosecuting the posters of such sites as critics argue that such an action infringes on the right of free speech. The inherent problem faced by security personnel in curbing this problem is that individual(s) can claim protection under the freedom of speech. Added to this is the fact that the procurers of e-terrorist activities are usually anonymous.

The United Nations Universal Declaration of Human Rights (UDHR) 1948 sets the international blueprint of free speech by stating that:

*Whereas disregard and contempt for human rights have resulted in barbarous acts which have outraged the conscience of mankind, and the advent of a world in which human beings shall enjoy freedom of speech and belief and freedom from fear and want has been proclaimed as the highest aspiration of the common people.*

In addition, Article 20(1) of the UDHR states, "Everyone has the right to freedom of peaceful assembly and association." In line with the UDHR, Article 19 of the International Covenant on Civil and Political Rights (1966) provides a source for international guidance for the protection of free speech:

1. *Everyone shall have the right to hold opinions without interference.*

2. *Everyone shall have the right to freedom of expression; this right shall include freedom to seek, receive and impart information and ideas of all kinds, regardless of frontiers, either orally, in writing or in print, in the form of art, or through any other media of his choice.*

3. *The exercise of the rights provided for in paragraph 2 of this article carries with it special duties and responsibilities. It may therefore be subject to certain restrictions, but these shall only be such as are provided by law and are necessary:*

    (a) *For respect of the rights or reputations of others;*

    (b) *For the protection of national security or of public order (ordre public), or of public health or morals.*

An expedient source of guidance for understanding Article 19 is the United Nation Human Rights Committee's general comment:[194]

*Paragraph 1 of article 19 requires protection of the right to hold opinions without interference. This is a right to which the Covenant permits no exception or restriction. Freedom of opinion extends to the right to change an opinion whenever and for whatever reason a person so freely chooses. No person may be subject to the impairment of any rights under the Covenant on the basis of his or her actual, perceived or supposed opinions. All forms of opinion are protected, including opinions of a political, scientific, historic, moral or religious nature. It is incompatible with paragraph 1 to criminalise the holding of an opinion. The harassment, intimidation or stigmatisation of a person, including arrest, detention, trial or imprisonment for reasons of the opinions they may hold, constitutes a violation of article 19, paragraph 1.*

---

194   See (UNHRC/GC34)

Furthermore, Article 22 of the ICCPR states that "everyone shall have the right to freedom of association with others," while Article 22 of the ICCPR recognises the right to peaceful assembly. The African Charter on Human and Peoples' Rights states categorically in Article 9:

1. *Every individual shall have the right to receive information.*
2. *Every individual shall have the right to express and disseminate his opinions within the law.*

From the above instruments, it should be noted that the freedom of speech is not an absolute right. It is clear that the protection of national security would restrict terrorist communication via the Internet. Furthermore, the Siracusa Principles on the Limitation and Derogation Provisions in the International Covenant on Civil and Political Rights (1984), Principle 29 provides that:

*National security may be invoked to justify measures limiting certain rights only when they are taken to protect the existence of the nation, its territorial integrity or political independence against force or threat of force.*[195]

Despite the clear language of these instruments, it seems that it is difficult to strike a balance between the boundaries of freedom of expression and terrorist speech on the Internet for the reason that some Internet communication may not directly promote terrorist activity. The freedom of speech does not only affect the behaviour and beliefs held by individuals in direct contact with the publisher, it also affects the attitudes and opinions held by other individuals. Communication may give accounts of detailed but factual grievances that may lead individuals to put on the cloak of hatred and inspire them to become radicalised. For instance, supposing a website communicated atrocities of American

---

195 Note that Article 9 of the African Charter on Human and Peoples' Rights (1981) provides that:
 1. Every individual shall have the right to receive information.
 2. Every individual shall have the right to express and disseminate his opinions within the law.

soldiers in the torture of prisoners of war in Iraq in 2003 (the Abu Ghraib torture scandal) or the detailed exposition of the sexual assault/humiliation of prisoners in Guantanamo Bay. Let us not pretend by ignoring the fact that this communication may enhance sentiments of grievance to moderate Muslims — it may start the cause-effect of radicalisation of the individual and may put evil notions in the minds of men. This may generate the posting of jihâdi content on the Internet. The antithesis of this observation is that derogatory depictions of Islam which is a common occurence by Western media, especially through the Internet could be regarded as a provocateur of terrorism. It should be reiterated that radicalisation is the mental journey towards extremist ideologies.

The Internet as an information superhighway may be argued to accommodate divergent views of groups and individuals. The striking question is: Should there be any limits on what people can put on the Internet? It may be argued that since the Internet is unrestrained in communicating hardcore pornography and other bizarre sexual content which may be offensive to groups and conservative individuals. It could be argued further that pornography infringes on these peoples rights. If pornography is an online freedom and does not violate an individual's right, then it may be argued that terrorist dialogue may seem to be within the realm of free speech. This may be a tenable argument since an individual has the choice to solicit websites of Islamists. In other words, 'you are paying for access — you have to search for the content'. By the same token, it could be argued that people should be free to make their own choices whether they want to access information pertaining to terrorist propaganda. Moreover, if they do access such sites, they have the free rational choice of deciding whether to condemn or approve the fanatical communication. A perplexing feature of this argument is that it seems to disregard the fact that the use of the Internet is a potential source of creating hatred towards individuals or groups.

In order to simplify a prolonged and multifaceted argument, it is readily observed that the viewing of a crime film—*Natural Born Killers* a 1994 film by Quentin Tarantino encouraged and inspired copycat crimes of the film throughout America.[196] Perhaps, an outlandish remark would be to argue that the producers of this film should be arrested and punished as the film has the tendency to promote crime and possibly terrorist activity. The Internet and the freedom of speech are interesting dialogues which this study cannot entertain exhaustively. However, beyond the quest for free speech is the need to regulate the content on the Internet that is geared towards hatred such as racism and xenophobic literature—which is against public interest and therefore has the tendency to become disastrous to world security. It now seems sparingly obvious that the freedom of expression must not incite individual(s) to violence—it then seems clearer that the right to publish by the media must not ridicule the religious sensibilities of individuals. Thus, satirical literature of Prophet Muhammad as propagated by Western media such as the *Charlie Hebdo* should be purged. It then appears absolutely clear that the freedom of speech should not condone or propagate Islamist terrorism.

## Social media and radical Islam

Almost 90 % of terrorism on the internet is organised through social media.[197] Messages can be posted via social media with the purpose of recruiting and grooming individuals to become radicalised. The common social media used by radical Muslims are discussed below:

---

196 Incidents such as the 1997 Heath High School shooting ( three people killed and five wounded) in West Paducah, Kentucky, United States; the 1999 Columbine High School massacre (thirteen people killed) in Colorado. United States and the 2006 Richardson family murders (three family members are killed) in Alberta United States are considered copycat crimes of Natural Born Killers.
197 See 'Terrorist groups recruiting through social media', accessed on the 1st of December 2014 at: http://www.cbc.ca/news/technology/terrorist-groups-recruiting-through-social-media-1.1131053

## Twitter

A form of e-terrorism can be in the form of tweeting. Twitter is a type of micro blogging that has been trendy since 2006 — it was the fastest growing Internet brand in 2010, with about fifty million tweets a day being posted the first six months of the year (Crystal, 2011). Twitter is an easy route for the radical Muslims to connect with their followers for the reason that the two main apparatus of Twitter are the Direct Messages (DMs) and the Retweeted messages (RTs). Therefore, the original message has the capacity to radicalise consumers of the tweet (Romero, et al, 2011). In this sense it could be a useful tool for acquiring recruits and grooming potential Islamists. Another advantage of Twitter is that the site supports thirty-five languages and 80% of Twitter users are on mobile.[198] The power of social media cannot be underestimated as governments in Egypt (2011), Tunisia (2011) and in Libya (2012) were overthrown due to the organisation of protests through the social media. More than 75% of people who used Twitter links during Arab Spring were from outside the Arab world.[199] Above and beyond the use of the Internet to communicate to enormous groups, the Internet can influence the foreign policies of state governments (Denning, n.d.). Tweets are open to the public or limited to individuals who prefer to 'follow' him or her. Twitter is particularly appropriate for real time information. Twitter has been used to glorify radical Islam — a woman named Mujahidah Bint Usama, a British medical student, used twitter to showcase herself holding the decapitated head of an unknown person.[200]

---

198  See https://about.twitter.com/company. Accessed on the 1st of December 2014.
199  See 'Jihadist Use of Social Media—How to Prevent Terrorism and Preserve Innovation', accessed on the 24th of November 2014 at: http://www.gpo.gov/fdsys/
200  See 'Jihadi Doctor Stands with severed head in her hand as kids look on in horror', accessed on the 10th of January 2014 at: http://www.dailystar.co.uk/news/latest-news/398717/Jihadi-doctor-Syria-Islamic-State-executing

## *Facebook*

Facebook is the chief online social network—Facebook has up to 800 million active users all over the world.[201] In January 2014, it had 1.31 billion users. In the Middle East, Facebook has had a 67 percent penetration in 2010, and 23 percent in Asia (Weimann, 2014). The U.S. Department of Homeland Security illustrates through dialogue collected from radical discussion on the benefits of facebook:

> *This Facebook is a great idea, and better than the forums. Instead of waiting for people to [come to you so you can] inform them, you go to them and teach them! God willing, the mujahedeen, their supporters, and proud jihadi journalists will use the site, too. First, it has become clear that the market of social networking websites is developing in an astonishing manner and that it fulfills important needs for Internet users, particularly younger ones.*
>
> *Facebook has become very successful in this field; therefore, it is our duty to use it, as adherents of jihad and members of the blessed jihadi media. I mean, if you have a group of 5,000 people, with the press of a button you can send them a standardised message. That means if you send one message with a link to forum names, a clear path to jihadi media is open.*
>
> *I entreat you, by God, to begin registering for Facebook as soon as you finish reading this post. Familiarise yourselves with it. This post is a seed and a beginning, to be followed by serious efforts to optimise our Facebook usage. Let's start distributing Islamic jihadi publications, posts, articles, and pictures. Let's anticipate a reward from the Lord of the heavens, dedicate our purpose to God, and help our colleagues.* [202]

---

201  See 'Jihadist Use of Social Media—How to Prevent Terrorism and Preserve Innovation', accessed on the 24th of November 2014 at: http://www.gpo.gov/fdsys/

202  See 'Terrorist Use of Social Networking Sites Facebook Case Study', accessed on the 24th of November at: http://publicintelligence.net/ufouoles-dhs-terrorist-use-of-social-networking-facebook-case-study/

The above extract was showcased in November 2014, when a twenty-nine year-old American woman—Heather Coffman, was charged to court for promoting violent jihâd when she posted on her facebook: "I love ISIS" and the phrase "jihâd for Allah's sake."

## *YouTube*

Naim (2007) tells of the power of YouTube:

> *Welcome to the YouTube effect. It is the phenomenon whereby video clips, often produced by individuals acting on their own, are rapidly disseminated throughout the world, thanks to video-sharing Websites ... Every month, YouTube receives 20 million visitors, who watch 100 million video clips a day.*

YouTube is an essential element of terrorist activities. The images of Islamists in balaclava masks standing behind innocent Western hostages for the purpose of decapitation have been a common reflection YouTube. The purpose of this view is to strike fear in the hearts of the perceived enemies of the terrorists. Furthermore, the jihâdist is intent of showing that beheading is for the point of illustrating the jihâdi ritual of killing the Kuffir.

YouTube allows users, radical Islamists to upload and share videos. It is used to send messages to terrorist targets pertaining to death and destruction executed by these groups. It is also used as a medium for sharing messages and videos to potential recruits. The Islamic State of Iraq and Syria (ISIS) use the Internet as its main recruiting agency. ISIS uses the Internet to romanticise jihâdist ideology to youths from Western societies. In August 2014, between 4,000 and 5,000 teenagers with EU passports were in Syria fighting for ISIS.[203] Gabriel Weimann (2014:1) tells us the

---

[203] See 'Is this ISIS' youngest foreign jihadist? Shocking picture emerges of Belgian boy, 13, brandishing a gun thought to have joined 5,000-strong army of European teens in Syria', accessed on the 28th of November 2014 at: http://www.dailymail.co.uk/news/article-2731657/Is-ISIS-youngest-jihadist-Picture-emerges-Belgian-boy-13-thought-joined-army-child-fighters-Syria.html#ixzz3KOtx5Waw

narrative of the power of the Internet to propagate jihâdist thoughts:

> *On the evening of March 1, 2011, Arid Uka, an Albanian Muslim living in Germany, was online looking at YouTube videos. Like many before him, he watched a jihadist video that presented the gruesome rape of a Muslim woman by US soldiers—a clip edited and posted on YouTube for jihadi propaganda purposes. Within hours of watching the video, Arid Uka boarded a bus at Frankfurt Airport, where he killed two US servicemen and wounded two others with a handgun.*

YouTube has the power to generate propaganda and radicalisation through clips and films that can be viewed all over the world. The advantage of YouTube is that it does not require the physical presence of the terrorist and the clip has the potential to be watched by a vast audience.

## *Bluetooth*

The use of banned programmes such as beheadings and hardcore militant messages are networked via Bluetooth. Al-Qaeda has an e-terrorist arm known as the *Fariq Jawwal Al-Ansar* (FJA) which mainly sends its communications with Bluetooth technology (Gold, 2011). These requests are sent to a vast amount of people. The crucial point is that the Internet can publish material that cannot be published by the conventional media, due to censorship and public opinion. The numbers game tells us that the more people read/view or are involved in chat rooms, the more there is the likelihood that an individual(s) may heed to these requests. It should be noted that chat rooms are a viable medium for recruitment and indoctrinating young, vulnerable, the unemployed and individuals seeking adventure.

## Funding of e-Terrorism

One of the negative effects of globalisation is that money can be laundered and used for criminal purposes. E-terrorism attracts the money laundering and/or terrorism financing. The Internet is an effective tool for appealing for funds. Specifically, al-Qaeda has gained immensely through this channel. The group uses the Internet to raise funds/donations through Islamic oriented charities, non-governmental organisations, chat rooms and forums (Ogun, 2012: 206). In most cases, terrorist groups use fronts (that lack direct contact with the group) to seek donations on behalf the radical group (Ogun, 2012: 206). The United Nations Convention on the Suppression of the Financing of Terrorism, entered into force on 10 April, 2002 and has not been able to adequately respond to e-terrorism due to the intricacies surrounding information through the Internet. It is presupposed that the UN did not anticipate that there would be a new technological challenge. It is intriguing to enquire how do radical Islamic groups in Africa access funds to carrying out their jihâdist activities. Groups such as Boko Haram and al-Shabaab have a stockpile of sophisticated weapons which have been used to challenge state security.

The low operational costs of implementing terrorist attacks are relatively low due to the ease of technology in sending funds around the world. It is therefore not surprising that the Bali bombing cost below $35,000, the assault on the USS Cole cost about $50,000, the 9/11 atrocity cost less than $500,000 and the July London bombings cost around £8,000.[204] Perhaps, this explains the ease of bombing escapades of Boko Haram. However, the inherent difficulty of implementing the UN Convention is that terrorism does not require large disbursements of funds for terrorist activities. The reason for this shortfall is due to the complexity in defining the ambits or terrorism. Another obvious problem is that African states that are affected by radical Islam lack the technical potentials to probe online

---

[204] See (2003) Financing Islamist Terrorism, Strategic Comments, Vol.9; 10: at page 1. See also http://security.homeoffice.gov.uk/counter-terrorism-strategy/pursue/666564; accessed 20th of 14 April 2010.

terrorist activity through funding. Moreover, there is a need for an African regional legal instrument on Counter-Financing of Terrorism regulation, in order to ensure co-operation on curbing the funding of terrorism on the continent. Co-operation and collaboration amongst the American states was co-opted by the Inter-American Convention against Terrorism (2002) which has in many ways curbed terrorism amongst the Organisation of American States (OAS). The regional instruments creating anti-terrorism alliance between African states is Organisation of African Unity Convention on the Prevention and Combating of Terrorism (1999) and the Economic Community of West African States directive on fighting cybercrime (2009). However, these instruments have not been effective in preventing terrorism in Africa. The simple reason is that there is an absence of a political and legal will amongst African states to co-operate and collaborate with each other in order to find a lasting solution. For instance, evidential procedures for collating data and detecting cyberterrorists are absent. Furthermore, the diversities in terrain, cultures and economic development hinder the effective collaboration between African states. Beyond the need for proactive regional instruments for preventing terrorism, a UN convention specifically relating to the prevention and suppression of terrorist use of the Internet is crucial to tackle e-terrorism. The UN should be urged to promptly provide an international convention in line to meet emerging growth in technology. There is also the need to generate high levels of commitment between African states in building linkages between states in curbing the financing of terrorism and most crucial in 'following the money'. Perhaps, the greatest challenge in fighting terrorism financers is corruption at the state level with the system of secretive banking practices in African states.

## Radical Groups and e-Terrorism

The early beginnings of jihâd via the Internet started in 1997 with the setting up of *Azzam.com*. This website hosted a list of jihâdists around the globe. In 1998, about fifteen terrorist groups hosted a website, whilst during the period of 2003 and 2005, there was an increase of terrorist websites to 4,300 (Weimann, 2006: 16). Amongst these websites was al- Qaeda. The 9/11 tragedy executed by the group was mainly planned, coordinated and executed by password-protected emails via the Internet. However, since the death of Osama bin Laden, al-Qaeda has become unsystematic in its activities.

Despite the speculation that al-Qaeda (since the death of Osama Bin Laden) and other terror groups in the Middle East are a disorganised group (Sageman, 2008), a renowned Internet Jihâdist was Anwar al-Awlaki, an American born Yemeni Islamic radical (the bin Laden of the Internet), who was killed by a drone attack in Yemeni in September 2011, was known to be a specialist in Internet jihâd for al-Qaeda. He was known to have motivated the 9/11 terrorists. He was known to be the brain behind the Internet newslet—'Inspire', amongst many YouTube videos. Awlaki used the Internet to inspire and preach jihâdist justification, using the titles such as "Targeting the populations of countries that are at war with the Muslims." Nidal Malik Hasan, a former United States Army psychiatrist and Medical Corps officer fatally shot thirteen people on November 5, 2009 after being indoctrinated by emails sent by Anwar al-Awlaki. In another event, on 14 May, 2010, Roshonara Choudhry a British prize winning student of King's College, London, stabbed a British MP, Stephen Timms when she became an al-Qaeda sympathiser due to online sermons of Anwar al-Awlaki. In another event, Said Kouachi, one the two brothers suspected in complicity in the butchery of twelve individuals at Paris on 9 January, 2015, met with Anwar al-Awlaki in 2011. It is suspected that al-Awlaki used the Internet to preach his message of hate to Said Kouachi.

The Internet is a notorious propagandist tool for luring westerners to join ISIS. Aside from propaganda, the Internet can serve as a dating agent to lure women in becoming terrorists. A former singer, Sally Jones (she changed her name to Sakinah Hussain) became engrossed with radical Islam after meeting her computer hacker-turned jihâdi boyfriend; Junaid Hussain, through an online dating site. Sally Jones became an ISIS fighter.

It is important to note that al-Qaeda has moved beyond the use of e-mails. The use of mobile phone technology is a new method of communication by al-Qaeda through Bluetooth technology which does not require an IP address as the Internet. Bluetooth is a Personal Area Network (PAN) with a limit transmission range of 100m (via a Class 1 100mW transmitter). It seems that this technology is being used by al-Qaeda affiliates in Africa.

AQIM has acquainted its members with the use of jihâd through the Internet. Weimann (2011:770) notes that:

> In March 2005, the Salafi Group for Call and Combat (GSPC), today known as Al Qaeda in the Maghreb (AQIM), issued a fatwa for jihad against foreigners in Algeria. The Fatwa calls for the killing of "the Jews and the Christians and all other non-believers" in Algeria. The fatwa, signed by Abu Ibrahim Mustafa, the Emir (prince) of the Salafi Group, is being circulated on jihadist websites. Abu Ibrahim Mustafa took over leadership of the Salafi Group in October 2003 and immediately pledged loyalty to bin Laden and al-Qaeda. According to the fatwa, "the Salafi Group states in these hard circumstances for the Muslim nation in general, and especially the mujahideen, to declare war on every foreigner non-believer—in the Algerian lands.

At the core of the jihâdist activities of AQIM is the propagating of videos and messages for global viewers of supporters in order to rationalise the requirement for a Jihâd in Algeria. From 1998–2009, AQIM used the Internet for 153 communiqués totalling 76.9% of the distribution methods of propagandist literature (Soriano, 2010).

Given the fact that Somalia is in a state of infrastructural failures as regards electricity and the Internet, there is little activity over the Internet. Somalia is not linked with the International Telecommunication Union. Conversely, it should be noted that most attacks emanating from al-Shabaab occur outside the borders of Somalia were sufficient Internet activity is located. Al-Shabaab on its September 2013 attack on Westgate Mall in Nairobi, Kenya, provided a real time discourse on its terrorist activities on Twitter. Furthermore, al-Shabaab's allegiance with al-Qaeda informs us that online technology plays a pivotal role in its group organisation. This is evident in the fact that al-Shabaab recruits Somalian Americans mainly through facebook.

Boko Haram releases video clips when the group has committed grave acts of destruction to lives and property. These video clips are for the purpose of creating fear to the public. They are used solely for the 'fear factor'. They usually portray Abubakar Shekau, telling the world of the group's atrocious exploits. Horrific video clips such as 'Boko Haram Militants Display Control of Captured Towns in northeastern Nigeria';[205] 'How Boko Haram Members Decapitated Nigerian Airforce Officer';[206] 'Boko Haram video claims to show missing Nigerian schoolgirls'[207] are among the horrendous video clips used by the sect. In continuing its terror propaganda, in January 2015, Boko Haram established an online media channel, *The Indissolube Link* (or *Urwah al-Wuthqa*). However, it now seems likely that Boko Haram has changed its technique of communication—on March, 28. 2015, Shekau released its first message via twitter.[208] In the tweet, Shekau in his usual rant, vowed to disrupt the Nigerian elections slated for March 28 and April 11, 2015.

## Conclusion

Soriano (2012) has argued that the Internet has some peculiar disadvantages to the Islamists. He notes that in most of the states where jihâdi Internet originates from, the government politically and socially controls the type of information that is

---

[205] https://www.youtube.com/watch?v=77YwVoM7_JA. Accessed on the 1st December 2014
[206] See https://www.youtube.com/watch?v=IZsCUEHqvLs&oref=https%3A%2F%2Fwww.youtube.com%2Fwatch%3Fv%3DIZsCUEHqvLs&has_verified=1. Accessed on the 1st December 2014.
[207] See https://www.youtube.com/watch?v=A9sJnldKRg8. Accessed on the 1st December 2014
[208] See The Punch Newspaper, February, 19th 2015, p.8: 'B'Haram releases new video, vows to disrupt polls.'

retrieved from the web. In such societies, Soriano argues that e-terrorism is difficult to procure due to state restrictions. He further notes that:

> *Online terrorism addicts are forced to operate in a public environment that harbors a latent threat that their browsing has been monitored by infiltrated police officers or informers or that the security forces may be tipped off by other users, including the owners of the premises. "Cyber Jihâdists" are fatally dependent" on public computers. They need them even though they are aware that every connection entails a dangerous exposure to discovery* (Soriano, 2012: 264-265).

It is imperative to understand the science and technology behind e-terrorism in order to curtail the use for terrorist activities. The advice of Sun Tzu, in the 6th Century B.C. is instructional: "If ignorant, both of your enemy and of yourself, you are certain in every battle to be in peril" (Griffith, 1971:84). This argument indicates that the Internet has its own security mechanisms that can surveil and infiltrate e-terrorism on the Internet network for the reason that they could be discovered by the process of counter-terrorism and other deterrent technologies. This observation is amplified by Benson (2014: 303) who argues that:

> *When considering fully the advantages the Internet confers simultaneously upon the state and terrorists, it becomes apparent that the Internet has not tipped the balance of power toward terrorists. To the extent that online anonymity allows terrorists to avoid surveillance, it also allows counter-terrorists operating online to avoid counter-surveillance. Cheapness of communication allows easier coordination of counter-terrorism. Because the large body of information available online includes information about terrorists, states and their allies are able to exploit that information. These combine to allow mobilised states, which generally possess greater resources than terrorists,*

*to interdict terror attacks that are hatched on the Internet.*

These complexities pointed out by the above scholars reveals that e-terrorism is a double-edged sword. The Internet can be a useful mechanism in combating e-terrorism as groups involved in such activities leave 'tracks in the snow' (Benson, 2014: 303). As a consequence, the US government is now using the social media for de-radicalising young adults in the Muslim world ISIS and al-Qaeda.[209]

A crucial problem attached with e-terrorism is that radical groups spend more time developing e-terrorism than local security personnel in African states. African states that are eroded with Islamist terrorism lack an efficient collaborative mechanism to prevent cyber terrorism. The *raison d'être* behind this Islamist terrorism and e-terrorism are transnational. The Internet exceeds physical and geographic borders. Furthermore, most African states lack an adequate response unit and e-intelligence to combat terrorism and its disastrous results. Aside from this inadequacy, a majority of African states lack legal activism, intelligence sharing mechanisms and the technological ability to situate Internet users under surveillance.

However, what is crucial about Internet surveillance in most African states is that it is difficult to create profiles to target potential suspects for the reason that the majority of the state's population, (where there is a prevalence of radical Islam) is Muslim. This variable is absent in Western societies where Muslims are profiled in order to enquire about their likelihood of being radicalised. However, this surveillance procedure/personal data collection is criticised for discriminating against the rights of individuals. Another crucial point is that African states lack adequate mechanisms for collection, analysis, and dissemination of data on e-terrorism. It is strongly suggested that a reverse process of de-radicalisation may be obtainable by the same

---

[209] See 'US cyber-warriors battling Islamic State on Twitter', accessed on the 1st of December 2014 at: http://phys.org/news/2014-08-cyber-warriors-islamic-state-twitter.html#jCp

process that instigated the individual to become radicalised. Perhaps, African states grossly affected by radical Islam should enquire how Islam can be used as a definitive action to de-radicalise radical Muslims as the proverbial saying goes: 'You cut diamonds with diamonds'—Islam being a religion of harmony and peace could act as a counter-terrorist tool for state governments in Africa. The Internet as a super highway should be capable of facing new changes and novel challenges of Internet security in Africa.

# References

Amble, John, Curtis, 2012. 'Combating Terrorism in the New Media Environment', Studies in Conflict & Terrorism vol. 35:5, 339-353.

Benson, David C., 2014. 'Why the Internet Is Not Increasing Terrorism', Security Studies vol. 23:2, 293-328.

Blanquart, Gabrielle & Cook, David M., 2013. 'Twitter Influence and Cumulative Perceptions of Extremist Support: A Case Study of Geert Wilders', Originally published in the Proceedings of the 4th Australian Counter Terrorism Conference, Edith Cowan University, Perth, Western Australia, 2nd 4th December, 2013. Assessed on the 1st of December 2014 at: http://ro.ecu.edu.au/cgi/viewcontent.cgi?article=1021&context=act

Blog, Andrew-Retrevo, 2010. 'Is Social Media a New Addiction?' assessed on the XXX day of XX at: http://tinyurl.com/ydvkm4g www.retrevo.com/content/blog/2010/03/socialmedia-New-addiction%3F).

Brown, Ian & Korff, Douwe. 2009. 'Terrorism and the Proportionality of Internet Surveillance', European Journal of Criminology 6: 119-134.

Crystal, David. 2011. Internet Linguistics. London: Routledge.

Dartnell, Michael. 2003. 'Information Technology and the Web Activism of the Revolutionary Association of the Women of Afghanistan (RAWA) – Electronic Politics and New Global Conflict', in Robert Latham (ed.), Bombs and Bandwidth: The Emerging Relationship Between Information Technology and Security . New York; London: The New Press: 251–67.

Denning, D. (n.d.). 'Activism, Hacktivism, and Cyberterrorism: The Internet as a tool for influencing foreign policy', accessed on the 2nd of December 2014 at: http://www.rand.org/pubs/monograph_reports/MR1382/MR1382.ch8.pdf

Gold, Steve. 2011. 'Terrorism and Bluetooth', Network Security, 5-7.

Griffith, Samuel, 1971. Sun Tzu: The Art of War. New York: Oxford University Press.

Janbek, Dana. M. 2011. 'Terrorism in the Age of the Internet: The Case of Muslim Arab Foreign Terrorist Organizations', Journal of Religious & Theological Information vol. 10:1-2, 5-15.

Naim, Moises, 2007. 'The YouTube Effect', Foreign Policy (January/February); 103–104 accessed on the 29th of November 2014 at: http://www.foreignpolicy.com/articles/2006/12/27/the_youtube_effect

Ogun, Mehmet, Nesip, 2012. 'Terrorist Use of Internet: Possible Suggestions to Prevent the Usage for Terrorist Purposes', Journal of Applied Security Research vol. 7:2; 203-217.

Romero, D.M., Wojciech, G., Asur, S., and Huberman, B. A., 2011.'Influence and Passivity in Social Media', In Machine Learning and Knowledge Discovery in Databases Vol 6913, Springer Link; 18 - 33.

Roy, Olivier, 2004. Globalised Islam: The Search for a New Umma. London: Hurst & Co.

Silber, M.D., & Bhatt, A., 2007. Radicalisation in the West: The Homegrown Threat. New York, U.S: The New York Police Department.

Sageman, Marc, 2008. Leaderless Jihad: Terror in the Twenty-First Century. Philadelphia: University of Pennsylvania Press,

Skepys, Brian, 2012. 'Is There a Human Right to the Internet?', Journal of Politics and Law; Vol. 5, No. 4; 15-30

Soriano, Manuel R. Torres, 2012. 'The Vulnerabilities of Online Terrorism', Studies in Conflict & Terrorism, Vol.35:4, 263-277.

Soriano, Manuel R. Torres, 2010. 'The Road to Media Jihad: The Propaganda Actions of Al Qaeda in the Islamic Maghreb', Terrorism and Political Violence vol. 23:1, 72-88.

Thompson, Robin L., 2011. 'Radicalisation and the Use of Social Media', Journal of Strategic Security 4: 4: 167-190.

Torok, R., 2013. 'Developing an explanatory model for the process of online radicalisation and terrorism', Security Informatics vol. 2(6), 1 - 10

Walker, M. Karen, .2009. 'New Media's Influence on the Assessment of Publicly Communicated Terrorist Threats', in Forest, James J. F., (ed) 2009. Influence Warfare: How Terrorists and Governments Fight to Shape Perceptions in a War of Ideas. Westport, CT: Praeger Security International; 75-91.

Weimann, Gabriel, 2006.Terror on the Internet: The New Arena, the New Challenges Washington, DC: United States Institute of Peace.

Weimann, Gabriel, 2011. 'Cyber-Fatwas and Terrorism', Studies in Conflict & Terrorism Vol. 34:10, 765-781.

Weimann, Gabriel, 2014. 'New Terrorism and New Media', Washington, DC: Commons Lab of the Woodrow Wilson International Center for Scholars, Research Series vol. 2 accessed on the 24th of November 2014 at: http://www.wilsoncenter.org/sites/default/files/STIP_140501_new_terrorism_F.pdf

# Epilogue

Islamic State in Iraq and the Levant (ISIS) formerly known as al-Qaeda in Iraq is the new generation of radical Muslims. It is important to bear in mind that ISIS transmuted from al-Qaeda in Iraq. Paradoxically, it could be argued that ISIS emerged due to the failure of the Obama administration to take a decisive step in the Syrian crises. Conceivably, one should not be overtly critical of this impasse, as President Obama may be aware of the consequence of intervening in Middle-Eastern and ideological conflicts (Iraq, Afghanistan and Vietnam amongst others). It should perhaps be added that in substantive terms, but fortuitously, ISIS may have emerged as the fallout of America's military interference in Iraq over the mendacity of Iraq's weapons of mass-destruction.

Granting all these, the main contention of ISIS is its desire to establish a caliphate. This idea is analogous to the ambition of al-Qaeda. The crescent of terror emanating from Boko Haram in West Africa over to the Sahel, the Maghreb to Hamas in Gaza to ISIS in Iraq, Syria and Lebanon, and berthing in Somalia shows that the quest for a global caliphate is being provoked and networked to radical Muslims all over the world. Most crucial, is that there are attempts by ISIS to acquire the al-Qaeda franchise in Africa. There are reliable indications to suggest that Boko Haram and ISIS have an understanding or a sense of consensus to create a supranational caliphate. This was illustrated on 6 August, 2014, when Shekau proclaimed the town of Gwoza, in Borno State as an Islamic caliphate and applauded Abu Bakr al-Baghdadi (leader of ISIS). In making sense of this acclamation, on 7 March, 2015, Shekau, pledged allegiance to the Islamic State by affirming that: "We announce our allegiance to the caliph of the Muslims, Ibrahim ibn Awad ibn Ibrahim al-Husseini al-Qurashi."[210] In exhibiting the truth of this new allegiance, five Boko Haram radicals were shot and killed in Dargaza, Mosul in Iraq. The Boko Haram members were in Iraq for a military training exercise.[211] It is important to note that al-Qaeda fighters from Yemen and al-Qaeda in the Maghreb are now regrouping and joining ISIS. This constructs ISIS as the largest Islamist radical group on the planet. This acceleration is also evident by ISIS making gestures to al-Shabaab to join their crusade. Furthermore, ISIS is luring to capture the failed state of Libya and other disgruntled elements in North Africa. If this collaboration becomes feasible, it would enable ISIS to expand its base away from the Middle East into Africa.

ISIS is now the central point of debate for the West. The question then is what happens to the al-Qaeda franchise? Will al-Qaeda still be relevant in Africa? Certainly, there is a paradigm shift from al-Qaeda to ISIS. Al-Qaeda is dwindling in terms of its size and strength. In some ways, ISIS and al-Qaeda are antithetical. However, they share commonalities—they are desirous for dominance and for the establishment of a caliphate—ISIS is focused on a regional agenda, whilst al-Qaeda is focused on a universal agenda. However, an important aspect that should not be ignored is that the two groups complement each other as they seem to have the same objective—terror against the West. Thusly, there is the pre-eminence of ISIS to launch out attacks against the United States and its Western allies in the near future. There is then a remote possibility of the two groups forming an alliance. In simple terms, the ideological war against the West is just starting—it has begun with the Islamisation of the West.

---

210   See 'Boko Haram leader pledges allegiance to Islamic State group', accessed on the 8th of March 2015 at: http://news.yahoo.com/boko-haram-leader-pledges-allegiance-islamic-state-group-210202677.html
211   See The Sun May 15, 2015: 5 'Boko Haram Militants shot dead in Iraq'.

It seems correct to state that the world is now becoming increasingly divided on ideological grounds. It may be accurate to state that Africa has been drawn into this deep division. This expands the borders of the ideological differences. In a broader perspective, the essence of the clash of ideologies is revealed by the accounts of former Senator Bob Graham, the co-chair in the Joint Congressional Inquiry into the 9/11 terrorist attack, noted in March, 2012, that the 800-page report in 2002, which has the last twenty-eight pages classified, indicts Saudi Arabian government diplomats and intelligence officers. Senator Graham alleges that the report states that these government officials provided financial and logistical support to the 9/11 terrorists (fifteen of the nineteen hijackers were Saudi nationals). This allegation was supported by Zacarias Moussaoui, a 9/11 terrorist serving a life sentence for his role in 9/11 attack.[212] This purported cover-up tells us that there are unseen forces behind this apocalyptic confrontation of ideologies. It is speculated that not too far in the future, America's reliance on Saudi oil (oil is the foremost national security agenda for America) will cease, partly because of alternative sources of energy supply. When this event occurs, will America and Saudi Arabia still be 'political/economic friends'? Would this political amity last despite the fact that Saudi Arabia, is a theocratic state (practices Wahhabism)[213] which is not tolerant towards religious freedoms?

A potential observation from this study is that religion is a continous factor in human life. Perhaps, this explains the *raison d'être* of religion emerging as a dividing line in the modern age. This is evident in the quest for the Western world to limit Iran's nuclear capacity, which is perceived as a threat to Israel and the West. Unquestionably, the

---

212 See 'Saudi prince paid for 9/11 pilots to learn to fly': Incredible claims of '20th hijacker' serving life in prison for terrorism as he asks to testify again in court and reveal all', accessed on the 23rd of November 2014 at: http://www.dailymail.co.uk/news/article-2837261/Saudi-prince-paid-9-11-pilots-learn-fly-Incredible-claims-20th-hijacker-serving-life-prison-terrorism-asks-testify-court.html

213 Wahhabi Islam is wholly anti-western and it seeks to situate Islam to its pure and traditional state as it existed during the time of Prophet Muhammad (SAW).

quintessence of Islam has taken a new form after the fall of communism in 1989, as it has ushered a clash with Western ideologies. Both ideologies represent sentiments of fear and the consequent perception of being threatened. Yet, it is important to emphasise that, Fukuyama's (1989) theory of democracy being the final berth of civilisation in the advanced age has been rejected due to the emergence of the clash of ideologies. The clash of ideologies is the final confrontation of ideas in the modern world. History reminds us that the clash of political ideologies produces a political/economic vanquisher. From the lens of a critical realist, the present clash of ideologies would usher in a new era which would be based on a political-religious government in the world—one government—a new world order—the end of the history of the world. A question that remains pivotal is: What will Africa's role be in this ideological war?

# References

Fukuyama, Francis, 1989. *'The End of History*?', National Interest, 16.

# Index

# Index

Abacha, 35
Abane, Ramdane 180
Abang, J.B. 256
Abd al-Qadir al –Jilani, 118
Abducted Chibok Secondary School Girls, 251
Abductions, 299, 304
Abolition of religion, 52
Abrahamic
- faiths, 258
- mythology, 76
- related faith-Christianity, 78

Abu Bakr, 106
Abu Hafs al Masri 165
Abu-Hamza al-Mazri, 102
Abu-Mahjin 264
Abu-Yahya al-Libi, 114
Acts of terrorism, 33, 126
Adebolajo, Micahel 13
Adebowale, Michael 13
Afghan
- jihad, 130
- Soviet war, 130

Afghanistan
- /Soviet war, 184
- war,14, 130, 186

African
- Islam, 118
- led International Support Mission in Mali (AFISMA), 230
- National Congress (ANC), 123
- political system-importance of religion (Islam) on, 39
- Traditional religion, 129
- Union (AU), 122, 218, 253
- African Union Mission to Somalia (AMISOM,) 158-159, 161, 169

Ag Intalla, Alghabass 221
Age of globalization, 67
Ahlu Sunna Waljama'a , 157
Ahlulsunna wal'jama'ah hijra, 239
Ahmad ibn Idris, 118
Ahmad, Ghulam 88
Ahmadu, Danladi 249
Ahmed, Mai 86
Ahmed, Shirwa 170
Ahonotu, Ben 264
Al-Itihaad al Islamiya (AIAI), 156, 161
Aided, Muhammed Farah 150
Al Bafhdadi, Abu Bakr 226
Al-Sadat, Anwar 28
Al-Amin –Al kanem Sheikh Muhammad 87
Al-Baghdadi, Abu Bakr (leader of ISIS), 337
Al-Barnawi, Khalid aka Abu Usamatul al-Ansari, 298-301
Algerian
- Association of Ulama, 180
- nationalism, 180

# Index

- Based Salafist Group for Preaching and Combat (GSPC), 211
Al-Ikhwan al-Mushimeen (the Muslim Brotherhood), 100
Al-Khorasan group, 187
Allah's law, 16
Alliance
- for Restoration of Peace and Counterterrorism, 159
- for the Re-liberation of Somalia (ARS), 157
- of America, 15
- *pour la Democratie en Mali (ADEMA)*, 201
*Almajirai* (students of Quranic school), 240
*Almajiri*, 32
- School Project, 32
Al-Qaeda
- bombings, 159
- ideologies, 307
- In Mali, 136
- in Mauritania,136
- in Morocco,136
- in Sudan,136
- in the Islamic Maghreb (AQIM),28,86,79-80, 86, 118, 136, 187, 189-192, 194, 204-205, 208, 210-211, 216, 218-220, 224, 228, 258, 299-304, 307, 329
    - foundation of, 185-194
- in Tunisia,136
- influence and support of, 165-167
- Islamic terror group), 100, 102
- Islamists, 186

- networking, 203
Al- Qaeda's motto
- 'You love life, we love death', 137
Al-Qaradawi, Sheikh Youssef, 94, 100
Al-Quds, 98
Al-Shabaab, 158, 160-164, 167, 169-170-174, 193, 326, 330,
- fighters, 170
- Leadership and power struggles , 161-165
Al-Sharia'a wa al –Hayah, 94
Al-takfirwa-l-hijra(takfiri), 298
Al-Zawahiri, Ayman 100,105
Amadou, Cheikou 208
Aman, Sethi 205
Americanization of the Middle East, 51
Amir Abd al-Qadir, 29
Amir al –Mu'minin (Commander of the faithful), 106
- in Somalia, 158
Amniyat network, 165
Amore, Olusola 257
Analytical dualism, 11
Anikulapo-Kuti, Fela 31, 60
Ansar al Sharia Tunisia and Okba Ibn Nafaa Brigade
– merger of, 136
Ansar Dine, 130, 200, 203-208, 210-212, 213, 217-223, 226, 230-231
- Movement for unity and Jihad in West Africa (MUJWA a.k.a MUJAO), 192
Ansaru
- (a.k.a. jamaatu Ansarul

Muslimina Fi.Biladissudan, (Vanguard for the Aid of Muslims in Black Africa), 287-307
- Movement for unity and Jihad in West Africa (MUJWA a.k.a MUJAO), 192

Ansaru's grievances, 298-299
Anti
- colonial movement, 179
- Islam, 1
- Islamic warlords, 159
- Semitism, 104
- Terrorism Alliance, 327

Anwar al-Awlaki (internet jihadist), 328
Apocalyptic caliphate, 20
Arab
- ethno nationalism, 51
- Nationality/Nasserism, 14
- Spring Uprising,122, 217
- in Libya, 203
- Tuareg, 215
- world, 21

Arabic/Islamic education, 241
Armchair jihadist, 315
Armed
- conflicts, 133
- Islamic Group (GIA), 183-186
- Islamic Movement (MIA), 183

Asymmetric warfare by Islamists, 137
Aweys, Sheikh Hassan Dahir 161, 163
Ayatollah Khomini of Iran, 128

Ayman az –Zawahiri (leader of al Qaeda), 113
Ayro, Aden Hashi 161
Azzam.com, 327

**B**adr O Maghrib 289
Bahanga, Ibrahim 216
Bakr, Abu 89
Balance of power to the literate scholars (malami, sing, malami), 87
Bali bombing, 326
Barre, Mohammed Said 153
Basques separatist group, 127
Battle of Hunayn, 84
Baudrillard, 126
Belief systems, 127
Belmoktar, Mokhtar 227
- (ak.a Khalid Abu Al-abbas a.k.a Laa'ouar (one –eyed), 186
- (leader of Al-Mourabitoun), 299

Bendjedid, Chadli 182
Benhaj, Ali 182
Berber/Arabic Tuaregs, 215
Bilal, Hicham 222
Birth of the Boko Haram Jihad, 239-246
Black Sub-Saharan Tuaregs, 215
Bluetooth, 325
Boko (book) as haram (sinful), 239
Boko Haram
- (a.k.a Jama'atul Alhul Sunnah Lidda'wati wal Jihad
    – people committed

to the Propagation of
the Prophet's teachings
and Jihad), 239
- crisis, 261
- fighters, 252
- funding and networking of, 258-259
- group, 291-significant incidents of, 267-289
- ideologies, 260
- in northern Nigeria, 32, 97
- jihad
  - birth of, 239-246
- members, 225
- radicals, 338
- sect, 117, 166-167, 225, 264, 297
- terrorists, 253
- video, 330

Boudiaf, Mohammed   183
Boumediene, Houari   181
Brain drain, 62
Brand terrorism, 134
Brotherhoods, 116
Buba, Muhammad Ahmadu Bada   256
Buddhism, 63, 75-76
Buhari, Muhammadu 254
Bush, George 82

Cameroon, David   191, 302
Campaore, Blaise   218
Chechnya Muslims, 189
Causal analysis, 9
Central Government
  - absence of, 169-170

Chadian
- Libyan conflict, 217
Chaieb, Khaled (a.k.a Lokman Abou Sakhr), 136
Chibok girls, 255, 266
Choudhry, Roshonara 328
Christian
- crusades, 76, 80
- extremism, 61
- missionaries, 127
- movements, 56
Christianity, 76, 78, 85, 127, 131, 241
Civilizational conflict, 235
Civilizations theory, 241
Clanism in Somalia, 151
Clans, 151-156
Clash of
- civilization, 236
- ideologies, 127, 339-340
Classical
- liberalism, 67
- theories of religion, 51-56
Clinton, President   83
Coffman, Heather   324
Cold War, 1, 16, 38, 57, 120, 131, 235
Collective
- excommunication of Muslims (a.k.a. takfir al-Mujtama), 184
- grievance, 17
- obligation (fard Kifaya), 78
- violence (aggression), 20
Colonial boundaries, 214
Colonialization, 65
Colump, Francis 302
Commander's Emergency Response Program (CERP), 33
Communal living, 113

Communication and
  Socialization of Islam, 246
Competitive political system, 199
Complexities of Terrorism, 120-128
Complexity of Islamists ideology
  in Africa, 2
Computer terrorism, 311
Conditions of possibility, 10
Conflict
  - behviour, 11
  - prone areas, 38
Consumer cultures, 67
Consumerism behavior, 62
Cook, David  88
Council of Scholars from the
  Arabian Peninsula, 95
Counterfactual thinking, 9
Counter
  - Financing of Terrorism
    regulation, 327
  - terrorism, 331
Critical
  - realism, 1, 5-6, 9-10
  - Realist Approach-
    criticism, of, 5-9
Crusader-Zionist alliance, 81-82
Crusaders of the Islamic faith, 129
Cultural
  - identities, 241
  - theory, 1
  - Theory-the Construction
    of Radical Groups, 25-27
Culture of martyrdom, 98
Cyber
  - crime, 311
  - terrorism, 311, 332
  - terrorists, 327
  - warfare, 311

Dar al Islam by non believers
  (Kuffir), 103
Dar-al Hard, 103-105, 107
Davies, Stephen, 251-252
Defenders of the faith, 200
Defensive jihads, 103
Dega, Christopher  265
Democratic elections, 218
De-radicalization, 332
Diarra, Cheick Modibo  218
Digil-Mirifle  152
Direct Message (DMs), 322
Droukdel, Abdel Malek  188-
  189, 204
Drug
  - trade and narcotic
    smuggling network, 209
  - trafficking, 212
Dynamics of group identity, 13

Early Christian crusades, 57
Economic
  - Community for
    West African States
    (ECOWAS), 218, 224,
    227, 229-231, 327
  - crises, 238
  - deprivation, 20, 30
  - entrapment, 31
  - expansionism, 77
  - grievance, 20, 30, 33, 36, 133,
    172, 182
  - hegemony of Islam, 77
  - incentives, 33
  - marginalization, 140

Egyptian
- Islamic
    - Group (EIG), 136
    - Jihad (EIJ), 114, 136
- terrorists, 28

Electoral system, 37
El-Moudjahid (the Jihad fighter), 180
El-Rufai, Nasir 250-252
Embassy bombings in Nairobi, Kenya 1998, 115
Epistemic fallacy, 3
e-Terrorism, 63, ,307-333
- an asymmetric warfare, 310-316
- and Free speech, 316-321
- funding of, 326-327
- meaning of, 311

Ethiopian
– Somali war (Ogaden war), 149

Ethnic
- and religious composition of Northern Nigeria, 237
- animosities, 20
- conflicts, 241
- diversity, 147
- domination, 199

Ethnic groups, 147, 151, 191, 209, 214, 238, 246
- and cultures, 90

Ethno
- nationalism, 51
- religious crisis, 238

European Union, 225
Evangelical Christianity, 127
Extra-judicial killing of Yusuf 256
Extremism, 57-62

Facebook, 323-324
Fadam Madawa, 243
Failed states Index, 170
Family networks, 135
Fariq Jawwal Al-ansar (FJA), 325
Fatwa, 28
- in Australia, 168

Fazul Abdullah Mohammed, 159
Fidaai (martyrdom), 101
Fight Against Terror, 289-291
Five pillars of Islam (Confession of faith, prayer, fasting, alms-giving and pilgrimage), 78, 315
Foi, Alhaji Buji 251, 262
Foreign fighters, 163, 165
- and Social networking, 167-169

Foreign terrorist organization, 204, 289
Foundation of Islamic Terrorism in Africa, 128-133
Fowler, Robert 186
Free speech, 317
Freedom
- fighter, 123
- of association and assembly, 317
- of expression, 319, 321
- of speech, 317, 319, 321
- of thought and religion, 67

French
- army, 214
- imperialism, 180
- Revolution (1789-1799), 120

Frustration
- Aggression, 22

- mechanism, 20
Fulani jihadists, 87
Functional (definition of religion), 49
Functionalist approach, 51-52
Fundamental human rights, 291
Fundamentalism
    - and Extremism
        – between (them), 57-62
    - definition of, 59
Fundamentalist, 57-58
Funding, 171-172

Gaddafi's private army, 129
Gado, Ahmadu 256
Gamou, Elhaj 216
Generative mechanism, 3, 10
Ghadaffi of Libya, 35
Ghadafi, Muamur 38, 217
Ghaly, Iyad Ag 203-206
Ghana Empire, 129
Ghraib, Abu 320
Global
    - battlefield, 8
    - caliphate, 24, 130, 140, 298, 337
    - economic growth, 62
    - ideology of Jihad, 158
    - Islamic
        - Family, 135
        - identity, 135
    - Jihad, 80, 113, 132, 158, 160, 188, 200, 303
        - group, 208
        - in Africa, 118
            – new terrain of, 115-119
    - jihadisation, 127
    - Jihadist group, al-Qaeda, 118
    - jihadist terrorism, 34
    - Muslim community, 28
    - religious ideology, 74-75
    - religious revitalization, 56
    - terrorists, 299
    - threat of radical Islam, 119
    - war, 130
Globalised
    - caliphate, 23, 135
    - jihad, 223
Globalization, 62, 66-68, 195, 309
    - by products of, 63
    - factoss behind, 63
    - negative effects of, 62, 326
Goje, Danjuma 259
Golden
    - age of Islam (the Ottoman era), 14
    - era of Islam, 77
Graham, Bob 339
Great Satan by Islamists, 15
Grievance
    - relative deprivation), 1
    - theory, 22
    - as Model in understanding why Islamists Rebel, 17-22
Group
    - behavior, 11
    - dynamics, 15, 17
    - for Preaching and Combat (GSPC), 28
        -/al-Qaeda alliance, 185-188, 192-194
    - theory, 1, 16
        - as a Model in

   understanding
   radical Islam, 11-17
Growth of al-Shabaab
- factors responsible for, 165
Guay, Loius 186
Guerilla
- campaigns, 137
- fighters, 133
- groups, 187
- tactics, 124, 159, 186, 192
- warfare, 138, 256
Gurr's theory, 17
- of grievance, 265

Haj Amin el-Husseini 62
Hamas suicide bombers, 242
Hamas, 310, 337
Hammami, Omar 168
Hamoud al Aqla al Shuebi 100
Harakat ansar al-dine (defence of the faith), 204
Hasan ibn Sabah (da'i) 93
Hasan, Nidal Malik 328
Hassan Al-Banna, Sheikh (1906-1949), 99-100
Hassan al-Turabi 114
Hattab, Hassan 185-186, 188, 194
Hezbollah, 310
Hierarchal communities, 65
Hinduism, 63, 75
HIV/AIDs, 62
Hizbul Islam, 157
Holy war, 204
- against Kuffir (non-believers), 103
Home grown terrorism, 316

Hostage taking, 115
Huddud punishment (stoning to death), 220
Human rights abuse, 150, 153, 169
Hussain, Junaid 329

Ibn Taymiyyah (1263-1328), 99
Ibn-Abd-al-Wahab, Muhammad (1703-91), 99
Identity threats, 265
Ideological conflicts, 337
Ideologies of Islam, 24
Ideology of
- democracy, 68
- global jihad, 80
- Nazism in Germany, 61
- radicalization of Islam, 134
Ifogas clan, 212-213
Ihejirika, Azubuike 250-252
Imagined communities, 23
Individual identity, 56, 67, 151
Instructional suicide bomber videos, 315
Instrumentalist approach, 56-57
Inter
- American Convention against Terrorism, 327
- Governmental Action Group against money laundering in West Africa (GIABA), 38
Internalization, 225-226
International
- community, 119, 224-225
- Covenant on Civil and Political Rights, 317, 319

- crimes, 83
- Criminal Court, 83
- guidance, 317
- Intervention in Mali, 224-230
- Jihad, 303
- jihadists organization, 188
- markets, 62
- Organization, 229
- politics, 80, 138, 235
- relations, 1
- Telecommunication Union, 329
- Terrorism, 190

Internet
- freedom, 316
- security, 333

Interpretation of Jihad, 73

Inter-religious
- animosities, 20
- competition, 131
- conflicts, 35, 258
- riots, 13

Intra
- groups conflicts, 150
- religious conflicts, 260-261

Invented Tradition, 22-25
- (imagined identities), 1

Irish Republican Army (IRA), 120, 127

Islamic
- activism, 131
- caliphate, 113, 115, 248, 337
- civilization in Africa, 80, 129
- Courts Union (ICU), 155-157, 159, 162, 173
- Culture, 68, 73, 90, 113, 135
  - and history, 219
- education, 237
- Emirate, 237, 303
- empire, 141
- extremism, 119, 135, 217
- faith, 237
- fighters, 131
  - in Afghanistan, 130
- global war, 130
- hegemony, 77
- identity, 141, 261, 307
  - among Muslim, 14
- ideology, 29, 148
- law, 210, 219
- Legion, 217
- Liberation from western values, 29
- Maghreb, 179, 230, 305
- Movement of Azawad (MIA), 208, 221
- movements, 100
- nationalist, 203
- nationhood, 23
- Organization (al-Itihaad al islamiya AIAI), 156
- Pan-African Legion, 217
- Political Organization, 100
- practices, 87
- radical groups, 190
- radicalism, 128, 155, 229, 261

- radicals, 95, 139
- rebels, 302
- resurgence, 58
- revival and militancy, 16
- revivalism and revolutionary Islam, 99
- revolution in
    - Iran, 58
    - Tehran, 14
- rules, 204
- Salvation Army (AIS), 182
- Salvation Front (FIS), 182-184
- societies, 66, 81, 299
- State in Iraq and Syria (ISIS), 118-119, 187, 190, 228, 248 316, 324, 328, 332, 337-338
    - Caliphate, 226
- style of Jihadi Shariah, 220
- Terrorism, 30, 119, 141, 156, 169, 306
    - in Africa, 134
        - foundations of, 128-133
- Terrorist Networks, 133-138
- terrorists, 225
- tradition, 261

Islamization, 127
Islamism in Africa, 193
Islamist
- based terrorist networks, 134
- Education, 33
- empire, 137
- fighters (Mujahedin), 123
- groups, 13, 33, 60, 100, 119, 135, 131, 137-138, 212-213, 221, 223
    - in Africa, 34, 130, 132, 134
- identity, 23-24, 33
- ideology, 183
- insurgency, 38
- insurgents, 229
- Jihadists group formation, 119
- nationalist group, 190
- nationalism, 22
- radical, 88
- group, 338
- revolt, 86
- Salafists groups in Africa, 136
- terrorism, 119, 190, 137, 332
    - does it work in Africa, 138-140
    - in Mali, 199
- terrorists groups, 127, 141, 312
- violence, 18
- websites, 315

Islamophobia, 104, 312
- in the West
    – foundation of, 130

Ismaili Islam 93
Istishhad (martyrdom) in Islam, 107
Iwellemmeden, 213
Izalatul –Bid'a wa Iqamat al Suna (Izala movement), 239

Jahiliya (paganism), 61
Jahiliyya (state of Ignorance from the guidance of Allah), 99
Jama'atu Nasril Islam (JNI), 260
Jamaat-i-Islami (Islamic Party), 99
Jaysh al-Hisbah (shariah Enforcer), 161
Jaysh Al-Usr (the army of hardship and suffering), 161
Jeremidisation of Christianity, 64, 80
Jesus Christ, 76, 78
Jihad, 99, 103, 107, 129, 261, 264, 298
- against Jews and Crusaders, 100
- as a revolutionary ideology, 88
- as moral improvement, 90
- as self-defence, 90
- as terrorism, 90
- by western media, 89
- campaigns, 118
- defense, 103
- Fi Sabilillah, 297
- (Holy War), 74-75, 77-81, 85-87, 90
- ideology, 4, 80
- Internet, 330
- movement, 105
- of attack, 103
- on Kanem-Borno, 87
- ritual of killing the kuffir, 324
- Salafi, 211
- stages of Islam, 91-93
- the double edged sword, 77-93
- the sword (jihad bin saif), 77
Jihadisation of Islam, 80
Jihadist
- activities, 301-303
- crusades, 265
- groups, 28, 98, 140, 226
- ideology, 3, 7, 82, 324
    - in Africa, 5
- networks in Africa, 134
- threat, 82, 224
Jokolo, Al-Mustapha (deposed Emir of Gwandu), 257
Jonathan, Goodluck 32, 266
Jones, Sally (later Sakinah Hussain), 328-329
Judaism, 76
Judeo-Christian
- culture, 18
- ideologies, 127
- Christianity, 132

Kalari, 257
Kambar, Abubakar Adam 299
Kanem-Bornu Empire, 86, 129
Kano riots, 13
Kantian transcendental argument, 10
Keita, Ibrahim Boubacar, 218, 224, 228
Keita, Modibo 201
Kel Instar 213
Kheirou, Hamada Owd 200
Kidnapping, 210, 265-266, 290, 299, 302, 304-305

- and ransom demands, 208
Kikwete, Jakaya 19
King Muhammad Ture (1493-1528) (Founder OF Askiya Dynasty), 34
Kin-groups, 151
Koli Sagir 254
Konachi, Said 328
Konare, Alpha Oumar 201
Kuffir 118, 173,
- (infidels), 85-86
- (non-Muslims), 104

Lamolinara, Franco 301
La-Shabaab 148
Law of armed conflict (Hague Conventions), 124
Law of life is belief, 50
Lawan, Abubakar 239
Leadership, 299-301
Lesser jihad (al-jihad al-asghar), 77
Lewis, Bernard 84
Liberal democracy, 62, 67
Libyan
- Civil War, 38, 129, 217
- Fighting Group (LIFG), 114
- Islamic Fighting Group (LIFG), 136
London bombing, 326
Luka, Linus 256

M'Hidi, Larbi Ben 180
Madani, Abbassi 182
Madinatul islam (the city of islam), 248
Madrassa, 117
Madrid train bombings, 139

Maitatsine Riots, 1980 261
Major clans in Somalia 152
Malcom X, 102
Mali
- Empire, 113, 129
- Niger Tuareg Alliance (MNTA), 216
- peacekeeping force, 228
Malian crisis, 209
Mandela, Nelson 123
Mansa Musa of Mali 117
Manu, Inuwa Jawo 260
Mao Man in Kenya 123
Mariam Farahat (Umm Nidal) 101
Martin Luther King Jr. 26, 102
Martyrdom and Jihads
- between (them), 93-103
Marxist ideology, 52
Mass
- migration, 62
- mobilization, 238
Massu, Jacques 181
Maximalist
- culture, 65
- goals, 138
McDonaldisation, 67
McManus, Chris 301
Mee'aad, Ibrahim Haji Jama (a.k.a Ibrahim at –Afghanio), 163
Mengistu haile Mariam of Ethiopia, 149
Mhayana Mahaprinirvana Sutra, 76
Militant Islamist Organizations, 182

Military
- rule, 238
- tactic, 243

Minimalist culture, 65
Modern economy, 67
Modernization, 63
Mohammed, Abu 300-301
Mohammed, Fazw Abdullah 166
Mohamud, Hassan Sheikh 158
Money laundering, 38, 258, 326
Mongol Empire, 129
Mongolian Empire, 129
Moral community, 54
Moussaoui, Zacarias 339
Movement
- for Oneness and Jihad in West Africa (MUJAO), 118, 304
- for the Azawad (MPA), 213
- for Unity and Jihad in West Africa (MUJWA), 200, 208-213, 218 224, 226, 230-231
- Islamique alge'rien (MIA), 182
- National de Liberation Touareg-National Tuareg Liberation Movement (MNLA), 203, 208-209, 211-213, 216-217, 219-223

Mubarak of Egypt, 35
Muhammad Ahamad bin Abd Allah 129
Muhammad ibn Abdille Hassan 29
Muhammed, Ali Mahdi 150
Mujahedin, 130
Mukhtar, Gwoni 86
Muslim
- brotherhood, 100
- commoners, 87
- community, 310
- Council of Nigeria (MCN), 260
- faith, 237
- groups, 27
- in Africa, 8
- jurists, 73
- militants, 74
- rashidun army, 113
- scholars, 117
- societies, 65, 67
- Umma (nation), 297

Najem, Mohamed Ag 203
National
- Bureau of Statistics, 245
- Commission for Reconciliation and Property Settlement, 2001 153
- cultures, 22
- identity, 67, 214, 246
- jihadist group, 188
- Liberating groups, 180
- Liberation Front (FLN), 28, 180-182
- reconciliation in Addis Ababa, 153
- Salvation Council, 1997, 153
- security, 319

- Tuareg Liberation
  Movement (MNLA), 39
Nazi Germany, 61
Nazism 62
Ndume, Mohammed Ali 262
Negative effects of
globalization, 62
Neo-colonial politicians, 238
Neo-colonialism of the Muslim
community, 28
Neo-Nazi groups, 314
New
- cold war, 16
- Terrain of Global Jihad
  in Africa, 115-119
Niger –Delta militants, 35, 301
Nigerian
- Civil War, 133, 248
- security Service, 258
Nkrumah, Kwame 82
Non
- Governmental
  Organization, 326
- Islamic laws, 99
- linear relationship between
  conflict and violence, 22
North Central London Mosque,
Fisbury Park, 102
Northern
- Elders Forum (NEF), 251
- Governor's Forum (NGF),
  260
Nur, Mamman 248, 299

Obama, Barak President 75, 337
Observation statements, 56
Ogbunwezeh, Franklyne 36

Okba Ibn Nafa a Brigade 136
Omar al-Bashir, General 83
Omar Hammami (Abu
Mansour al amrik), 163
Online
- freedom, 316-217
- social network, 323
- terrorist activity, 327
Ontological dualism (analytical
dualism), 10
Operation
- Restore Hope, 150
- Serval, 218, 225l, 230
Oppression and inequality, 31
Organization of
- African Unity Convention
  on the Prevention and
  Combating of Terrorism,
  327
- American States (OSA),
  327
Organizational
- networks, 132
- structure of a group, 4
Osama bin Laden 15, 28, 81,
100, 105, 114, 137, 158, 165-166, 195,
259, 328
- riots, 13
Ottoman Empire (1299-1923), 77,
106

Page, Ali Mohamud 160
Pakistan's Inter Services
  Intelligence (ISI), 130
Palestine Liberation
  Organization (PLO), 138
Peaceful transition, 214

Peacekeeping missions, 252
Peer group influences, 26
Penal code, 29
People's Democratic Party (PDP), 254
Personal Area Network (PAN),. 329
Political
- adventurism, 148-149
- agenda, 38, 303
  - of al-Qaeda, 194
- ambition, 223
- amity, 339
- analysis, 16
- capital, 238
- change through violence, 127
- conflicts, 199-200, 214
- construction, 87
- crises in Somali 148-151
- currencies, 264
- demands, 138
- dynamics of Islam, 17
- elites, 238
- goal, 74, 102-103, 298
- group
  - marginalization of, 200
- History of the Tuareg, 201
- ideologies, 149, 310, 340
- idiom, 120
- Imbalance, 201-203
- instability, 38
- interference, 80, 254
- invention, 23
- Kleptomania, 250
- leaders, 236
- life, 35
- love affair, 149
- machinery, 238
- militancy or advocacy, 59
- mobilization, 220, 307
- networks, 100
- objectives, 29
- order, 229
- paradox of Boko Haram, 247-258
- parody, 291
- participation, 199
- parties, 63, 182, 201, 263
- phenomenon, 258
- power, 257
- prebendalism, 65
- purposes, 236
- regime, 265
- relevance, 27
- scientists, 235
- scores, 257
- sectarianism, 20
- sentiments, 26
- societies, 199
- structures, 12
- struggle, 98, 180
- subjugation, 20
- Succor, 114
- support, 311
- system, 38, 199
- theories, 235
- thugs, 257
- tool, 113
- violence, 18
- war, 340
- will, 263

Politics of
- Illiberality, 179
- survival, 141

Positive Christianity, 61
Positivist approach, 54-55
Post-colonial struggles of Islamic groups, 29
Poverty, 29-32, 65, 211, 240, 244, 292, 304-306
Power sharing, 214
- arrangement, 215

Primordial Attachment to clans, 151-156
Prophet Muhammad, 84-85, 89, 99, 104, 106, 136, 298, 321,
- offensive publication by Danish newspaper, 13

Protestant fundamentalism in America, 57-58
Protocol on Democracy, 224
Psychoanalysis of religion and individual, 55
Psychoanalyst approach, 55-56
Psychological orientation of radical Muslims, 13

Qadiriyya brotherhood, 118

Racial discrimination, 21
Radical
- groups, 7, 31, 33, 37, 200, 230, 250, 255, 258-259, 300, 302, 304
  - and e-Terrorism, 327-330
- ideology, 80, 195, 310
- Islam, 1-2, 9, 17-28, 30, 32-33, 36-37, 39, 59, 61-63, 80, 82-83, 99, 100, 113, 115, 131-132, 134-135, 137, 139, 154-155, 166, 179, 182, 200, 211, 230, 236, 250, 291, 307-333
  - in Africa, 10, 12, 131, 114
    – a critical realist approach, 2-4
  - in Northern Nigeria, 240
  - in Somali, 147
- Islamic
  - groups, 23, 35, 59, 117, 124, 132, 138-139, 172, 307, 310
    - in Africa, 5, 25-26, 326
  - ideology, 27
- Islamist, 80, 94-95, 119, 130, 141, 302, 324
  - group, 139, 187, 297, 313-314
  - thought, 78
- Muslim, 11-12, 15, 26, 33-34, 37, 58, 60-61, 74, 95, 102, 130-131, 135, 139, 250, 321-322, 333, 337
  - teachings, 102
  - warfare, 59

Radicalization, 24, 211, 307, 325,
- cause effect of, 320
- of Islamic groups, 34
- process, 135
- of Islam in Africa, 1, 27-39

Rankadedism (rankadede), 241
Rashidun Caliphate (632-661), 106, 113
Reconciliatory efforts, 153
Red Cross, 243

Regional
- Cross border military campaign 253
- security, 307

Reid, Richard 102

Relative deprivation, 17, 20
- definition of, 19
- thesis (Grievance), 148

Religion
- as a political tool, 57

Religious
- and
  - globalization – between (them), 62-68
  - interests, 26
  - political violence, 17
  - poverty, 18
  - violence, 74-77
- as a mechanism for social control, 54
- beliefs, 50-52, 55-56, 58, 90, 236, 240, 246
- conflicts, 241, 265
- construction, 244
- Crisis, 51, 236
  - in Mali, 211-213
- cultures, 65- 66
- definition and meaning of, 49-56
- doctrines, 58, 241
- entrepreneurs, 238
- epistemological origins, 55
- extremism, 58, 60
- extremists, 128, 236
- fantasies, 60
- Fundamentalism, 58
- groups, 104
- identification, 236
- identities, 76, 238
- Identity (Islam ), 12, 15, 24, 131, 222, 236, 246
- ideologies, 28, 301
- indoctrination, 60
- information, 238
- instrumentalism, 56-57
- leaders, 131
- loyalties, 17
- militancy, 235
- mysteries, 65
- objectifications, 56
- obligations, 59
- Organization, 260
- primordalism, 33, 63-64, 236, 246
- radicalism, 241-242, 246
- reformers, 240
- reformism, 241
- revivalism, 241
- rivalry in Northern Nigeria, 238-239
- sanctions, 242
- sensibilities of individuals, 321
- sentiments, 33, 36
- symbols, 54
- traditions, 66
- undertones, 3
- utopianism, 139
- values, 29
- violence, 76, 242
- zealotry, 261

Rene, Robbin, 264

Resource control, 18, 200

Resources distribution, 20

Resurgence of Islamist ideology, 65
Retroductive Reasoning
- use of, 9-11
Retweeted messages (RTs), 322
Revolutionary
- Army for the Liberation of the Azawad (ARLA), 213
- groups, 127
- Islam, 99
- postulation, 52
Rida, Rashi (1866-1935), 99
Rigby, Lee 13
Rights of individual s, 332
Right-wing extremism, 314
Ringim, Hafiz 256
Rise of Al-Shabaab 156-161
Rising poverty/rising conflict model, 31
Rival warlords, 151
Robow, Sheikh Mukhtar, 162
Rodgers, Mike 226, 301


Sahrawi, Abd al –Baqi 184
Said Barre, Muhammed (a.k.a Jaalle Siyaad) 148-151
Saif al – Adel 114
Saifi, amari (a.k.a abderrazzak El Para) 186
Salafi
- Jihadism 298
- jihadist 211
- jihadist group, 195
- jihadist ideology in west Africa, 191
Salafist Group, 211
- for Preaching and Combat (GSPC), 136, 184-185
- ideology, 184
- Jihad ideologies in west Africa, 208
Salafiyah model of islam, 99
Saleh Ali Saleh Nabhan, 159
Salfi Jihad, 230
Salihiyya, Brotherhood, 118
Samaale 152
Samuel, Anthony 256
Sanni Mamluk Empire in Egypt, 129
Sanogo, Amadou 207, 217-218, 224
Sayid Abu'L Ala Maududi (1903-1979) 99
Sayyid Muhammad Abdallah Hassan 118
Sayyid Qutb (906-1966) 99-100
Schneider, David 25
Scientific
- information, 9
- Law, 10
- socialism, 149
- theorems, 56
- world, 8
Second World War, 125-126, 311
Secret society, 93
Secular
- law, 15
Secular nationalism, 56, 236
Secularization, 63-64
Security mechanism, 331
Self
- radicalization 313
- rule, 214

- sacrifice, 93-95
- styled jihadists, 27

Shabaab Muslim Youth Organization, 267

Shababul Islam, 239

Shahada Katibat (Martyr's Battalion), 186

Sharaoni, naibl, 188

Sharia , 29
- based Islamic order, 204
- Law, 64,154, 170-171, 212, 215, 241, 298
  - in Sub-Saharan African, 131

Sheikh Ahmed   157

Sheikh Sharif   157

Shekarau Ibrahim   260

Shekau, Abubakar Mohammad 247-249, 298-299, 304-306, 330, 337

Sheriff, Ali Modu, 251, 262

Shermarke, Abirashid Ali 148

Shettima, Kashim   254

Shi'a's Iranian Islamic Revolution, 1979 Shi'ism, 93

Shi'ites, 93-94,106

Shiite loyalist, 239

Shura majhs, 161

Sicilian Mafia in Italy, 125

Significant Incidents of Boko Haram, 267-289

Sissoko, Django   218

Smuggling of arms ad ammunition, 258

Social
- agents, 5
- analysis,16
- behavior, 3
- being, 26
- bonding, 236
- commonality, 54
- communication, 65
- conflicts, 17
- construction,6,9- 11,126
  - of religion, 57
- customs, 113
- exclusion, 21
- groups,4, 11,13,26, 50
- harmony, 257
- integration, 11
- justice, 155
- media, 37,309, 312, 313, 315
  - and radical Islam, 321-325
  - platforms, 208
- mobilization, 63,68
- networking, 37
- order, 236
- phenomenon, 8-9, 54,235
- predictions, 5
- reality, 9
- relations, 16
- relativity, 26
- tension, 20
- transformation, 65
- unity, 54
- world, 8

Socialization of
- religion, 52
- wealth, 90

Societal crisis, 240

Society
- a pluralist social configuration, 11

Socio-economic
- conditions, 20
- meltdown, 34

Sociological approach, 53-54
Sokoto Caliphate, 113, 129, 298
Sokoto, Kabiru 305
Somali
- Armed Forces, 150-Democratic Front, 150
- Democratic Alliance, 150
- guerrilla group, 170
- Manifesto Group, 150
- National Movment, 150
- patriotic Movement, 150
- Reconciliation Conference, 2002, 153
- Religious Union, 174
- Wahhabis 156
- National Peace Conference, 2000, 153

Songhai Empire, 34, 113, 129, 211
Songhai Ifogha, 209
Soviet/Afghan conflict, 15
Spanish Socialist Workers Party (PSOE), 139
Spellbinding traditions, 65
Spiritual
- ignorance, 60
- incentives, 59

State of anarchy, 169
Substantive (definition of religion), 49
Suffi Muslims, 77
Sufi brotherhood,. 154
Sufi shrines, 207, 219
Sufism, 211-212

Suicidal
- warfare, 95
- missions, 95 102

Suicide
- attacks, 97-98, 102, 139
- bombings, 94, 96-98, 101-102, 159, 256, 304
- killing, 95-97, 103

Sunnah (practices of injunctions of Prophet Muhammad), 99
Sunni
- Brotherhood, 118
- leaders, 228
- Muslims, 154

Supranational caliphate, 337
Suwarian tradition, 85
System integration, 11
Systematization control over society, 57

Taghat Melet, 213
Takfir al-Mujtama, 184
Takfiri, 34
Talakawa (grassroot people/peasants), 240
Taliban in Afghanistan, 119, 303
Tanzania bombings, 115
Tarafuka 257
Tarantino, Quentin 321
Territory outside the pale of Muslim Law, 104
Terrorism
- as a military strategy, 107
- definition and meaning of, 120-128, 130

- Terrorism, financing, 326
- in Africa, 32-in global setting, 31
- via the Internet, 313

Terrorist
- activities, 19, 89, 126, 139, 191-192 194, 250, 265, 298, 305-307, 311-313, 324, 331
- behavior, 311
- attacks, 301, 326
- communication, 319
- group, 102, 224-226, 248, 262-263, 314, 316, 326, 328
  - - jihadists groups, 225
- (Prevention) Act, 2011, 289-290
- organisations, 103, 123, 210, 218, 262
- network, 98
- speech, 319
- targets, 324
- violence, 127

Terrorists attacks, 126
Terrorists groups, 115
Thatcher, Margaret, 123
Theory
- of democracy, 340
- of Islamophobia in Wester societies, 188

Timms, Stephen, 328
Tishau, Aliyu, 256-257
Tiumph of democracy, 16
Toure, Amadou Toumani (solidier of democracy), 201-202

Traditional
- African societies, 113
- beliefs, 116
- knowledge, 63

Trans-ethnic issues, 215
Transitional Federal Government (TFG), 153, 155-156, 162, 165, 170
Transnational
- conflicts, 133
- crime, 62
- grievances, 131
- Islamic groups, 132, 134-135
- Islamist identities in Africa, 23
- networks, 141
- radical Islamists groups, 131
- terrorism, 259
- terrorist, 134

Trans-Saharam Trade, 34, 129
Traore, Dioncounda, 218
Traore, Monssa 201
Tuareg, 38-39, 129, 202-205, 214, 221-222, 230
- Rebellion, 217-218
- fighters, 216
- Nationalism, 214, 216
- Quest for Self-Determination and the National Tuareg Liberation Movement (MNLA), 213-216
- revolts, 213
- in Mali, 212

Tutu, Desmond, 102
Twitter, 322

Umar, El Hadj, 208
Umma (community of Muslims), 28, 76-77, 84, 94, 96, 99, 194
Ummah, 298
Umman, 103, 106
UN Security Council, 228
Unbelievers (kuffir bil Takhlit), 86
Unholy blemish on Islam in Northern Nigeria, 259-261
Unified Task Force (UNITAF), 83
UNITA rebel movement in Angola, 133
United Nations (UN)
- Convention on the Suppression of the Financing of Terrorism, 120, 326
- Office for West Africa, 229
- on Drugs and Crime (UNODC), 209
- Operation in Somalia II (UNOSOM II), 150
- Security Council (UNSC), 204, 224
United Somali Congress, 150
United Task Force (UNITAF), 150
Universal Caliphate, 15
Universal Jihad, 130, 212,
Universal jihad, 210
Universal revolutionary creed, 140
Unvented tradition theory, 23
Usama, Mujahidah Bint, 322
Use of Observation, 4-5

Use of Retroductive Reasoning, 9-11
Usman dan Fodio, 29, 86, 117-118.129, 208, 261
Uthman dan Fodio Jihad, 113, 241, 246
Uthman dan Fodio's Jihadist ideology, 33
Utopian ideology, 250
Utopian- illusions, 60-oideologies, 60

Vampidisation of Africa, 35
Vandenbeusch, Georges 302
Violent conflict, 12, 235
Virtual umma, 310

Wahabism, 211
Wahhabi sect, 34
Wahhabi, 99
Wahhabism, 34
War of ideas, 1clash of civilizations, 1
Warlordism, 148
Warlords, 152
Western
- civilization, 17, 118, 236, 243
- colonization, 27
- culture, 100
- democracies, 57
- Economic policies, 80
- education, 137, 140, 239-240, 265
    - is a sin, 101

- European Christian Crusades, 79
- hostages, 324
- ideals of secularization, 34
- ideologies, 340
- imperialists, 29
- institutions, 307
- intrusions, 80
- media, 320-321
- Military in Afghanistan and Iraq, 81
- powers, 80,299

RECRUITS, 208
- scholars, 89
- societies, 18, 21,30,63-64, 66-68, 127, 135, 166, 168, 220, 246, 260, 312, 324, 332,

Westernised establishments, 243
Westernization, 51,66,127
Westernized institutions 18, 90, 298

Westernophobia, 104
Westoxication of Islam, 99
Widers, Geert 312
World of construction, 6, 8

Yar'Adua, President 256, 258
Youtube, 324-325
Yuguda, Isa 260
Yusuf Mohammad, 240,246-247, 258, 262, 264-265, 291
- religious objectives, 246
Yusuf, ustaz Mohammed, 239

Zapata, Emiliano, 102
Zitouni, Jamal 183-184
Zolberg, Aristide 35
Zone Autonome d'alger (ZAA), 180-181
Zouabri, Antar 183-184
Zubeyr, Sheikh (a.k.a. Muktar Abdirahman Godane), 162

www.ingramcontent.com/pod-product-compliance
Lightning Source LLC
Chambersburg PA
CBHW070806300426
44111CB00014B/2436